T0331982

Respectable Banking

The financial collapse of 2007–8 has questioned our assumptions around the underlying basis for stability in the financial system, and Anthony C. Hotson here offers an important reassessment of the development of London's money and credit markets since the great currency crisis of 1695. He shows how this period has seen a series of intermittent financial crises interspersed with successive attempts to find ways and means of stabilising the system. He emphasises, in particular, the importance of various principles of sound banking practice, developed in the late nineteenth century, that helped to stabilise London's money and credit markets. He shows how these principles informed a range of market practices that limited aggressive forms of funding and discouraged speculative lending. A tendency to downplay the importance of these regulatory practices encouraged a degree of complacency about their removal with consequences right through to the present day.

Anthony C. Hotson is an associate member of the History Faculty, University of Oxford, and a research associate of the Centre for Financial History, Cambridge. He worked at the Bank of England during the 1980s, including a secondment as assistant commissioner at the newly formed Building Societies Commission. He was employed by McKinsey & Company before joining S. G. Warburg, where he worked as a corporate financier and director during the 1990s. Thereafter, he has served as a non-executive director on a number of company boards in the insurance, fund management and banking sectors, as well as pursuing his academic interests. More recently, Dr Hotson has been a research fellow at the Winton Institute for Monetary History, Oxford. He teaches macroeconomics and financial history, and has recently co-edited a book on the economic policies of the Thatcher government, and another on British financial crises since the nineteenth century. He is a non-executive director of Cenkos Securities plc and chairs a charity, the Wadenhoe Trust.

Respectable Banking

The Search for Stability in London's Money and Credit Markets since 1695

ANTHONY C. HOTSON

University of Oxford

CAMBRIDGE
UNIVERSITY PRESS

CAMBRIDGE
UNIVERSITY PRESS

University Printing House, Cambridge CB2 8BS, United Kingdom

One Liberty Plaza, 20th Floor, New York, NY 10006, USA

477 Williamstown Road, Port Melbourne, VIC 3207, Australia

4843/24, 2nd Floor, Ansari Road, Daryaganj, Delhi – 110002, India

79 Anson Road, #06-04/06, Singapore 079906

Cambridge University Press is part of the University of Cambridge.

It furthers the University's mission by disseminating knowledge in the pursuit of education, learning, and research at the highest international levels of excellence.

www.cambridge.org
Information on this title: www.cambridge.org/9781107198586
DOI: 10.1017/9781108182614

First published 2017

Printed in the United Kingdom by TJ International Ltd. Padstow Cornwall

A catalogue record for this publication is available from the British Library.

Library of Congress Cataloging-in-Publication Data
Names: Hotson, Anthony C., author.
Title: Respectable banking: the search for stability in London's money and credit markets since 1695 / Anthony C. Hotson.
Description: New York: Cambridge University Press, 2017. |
Includes bibliographical references and index.
Identifiers: LCCN 2017007732 | ISBN 9781107198586 (hardback)
Subjects: LCSH: Banks and banking – History. | Credit – Management. |
BISAC: BUSINESS & ECONOMICS / Economic History.
Classification: LCC HG2986.H68 2017 | DDC 332/.04150941–dc23
LC record available at https://lccn.loc.gov/2017007732

ISBN 978-1-107-19858-6 Hardback

Contents

Tables

Figures

Acknowledgements

Many people have encouraged me to undertake the research for this book, and helped me to complete it. Nicholas Dimsdale supervised my doctoral thesis at Oxford, and thus began an extended discussion about the London money market that has continued over many years. Nick Mayhew let me join his team at the Winton Institute for Monetary History, based at the Ashmolean Museum, and encouraged me to think about currencies as well as banking. Also at Oxford, I relied on the guidance of Erica Charters, Avner Offer, Kevin O'Rourke, Deborah Oxley and Jens Tholstrup. Jane Humphries and Larry Neal offered invaluable advice on the development of the book as well as being my examiners. The classroom is the ultimate testing ground of ideas, and for this I must thank my co-teachers, Michelle Sikes and Nicholas Dimsdale, and a succession of students who elected to take Economics for Economic Historians over the last seven years, and British Financial History over the last four.

I have benefited greatly from my affiliation with the Centre for Financial History in Cambridge, initially under the direction of D'Maris Coffman and latterly Duncan Needham. I am particularly grateful for Duncan's guidance over many years, and for Susan Howson's uncompromising commentary on my manuscripts. I would also like to thank John Trundle for comments on initial research for this project.

The analysis of gold and silver prices was undertaken with Terence Mills at Loughborough University. I appreciate his work and patience. The data were compiled from archival sources in the Special Collections section of Senate House Library, University of London, and the Bank of England Archive. I am grateful for the help of Tansy Barton, Charles Harrowell and their colleagues at Senate House, and Mike Anson, Ben

White and Lorna Williams at the Bank of England Archive. A special thank you goes to Louisa Hotson, who helped to compile the Castaing data, and to Alexis Wegerich, who provided the coal price data.

More recently a number of people have been kind enough to offer comments: Charles Goodhart and William Allen (both of whom happen to have been bosses of mine in a bygone age at the Bank of England) and Felix Martin, Bridget Rosewell and two anonymous readers. I appreciate the time and effort of these reviewers, and thank them for their excellent comments. I am grateful to Michael Watson at Cambridge University Press for providing advice and guiding the book to publication. Sadly, none of the aforementioned can be blamed for remaining errors and misconceptions on my part.

I would like to thank my family – Louann, Chris and Louisa – for putting up with a distracted researcher at home. I am grateful for Louann's proofreading and dogged pursuit of clarity, particularly regarding Figure 3.1.

SOURCES OF MATERIAL SUBJECT TO COPYRIGHT AND OTHER TERMS OF USE

The author and publisher acknowledge the following sources of material subject to copyright and other terms of use. We are grateful for permissions granted:

- Figure 2.6 in this volume was reproduced from a chapter by Duncan J. Needham, 'The 1981 Budget: "a Dunkirk, not an Alamein"' in D. J. Needham and A. C. Hotson (eds) *Expansionary Fiscal Contraction: The Thatcher Government's 1981 Budget in Perspective* (Cambridge: Cambridge University Press, 2014), table 9.1, p. 150.
- Figures 2.7, 2.8, 5.7 and 5.10 were reproduced from a chapter by Anthony C. Hotson, 'The 1981 budget and its impact on the conduct of economic policy: was it a monetarist revolution?' in D. J. Needham and A. C. Hotson (eds) *Expansionary Fiscal Contraction: The Thatcher Government's 1981 Budget in Perspective* (Cambridge: Cambridge University Press, 2014), pp. 123–47; figures 8.3, 8.4, 8.1 and 8.2, respectively.
- Figures 2.11, 5.5, and 6.1 were reproduced from a chapter co-authored by Nicholas H. Dimsdale and Anthony C. Hotson, 'Financial crises and economic activity in the UK since 1825' in N. H. Dimsdale and A. C. Hotson (eds) *British Financial Crises since 1825* (Oxford: Oxford University Press, 2014), p. 28, figure 3.1; p. 29, figure 3.4; p. 30, figure 3.5, respectively.

- Figures 3.8, 3.9, 3.14 to 3.26 and 3.29 were reproduced from a chapter co-authored by Anthony C. Hotson and Terence C. Mills, 'London's market for bullion and specie in the eighteenth century: The roles of the London Mint and the Bank of England in the stabilisation of prices' in Martin Allen and D'Maris Coffman (eds) *Money, Prices and Wages: Essays in Honour of Professor Nicholas Mayhew* (Basingstoke: Palgrave Macmillan, 2015), pp. 211 to 227, figures 12.1 to 12.10.
- Figure 5.11 was reproduced from a chapter authored by Nicholas H. Dimsdale, 'British Monetary Policy since 1945', in N. F. R. Crafts and N. W. C. Woodward (eds) *The British Economy since 1945* (Oxford: Clarendon Press, 1991), page 130, table 4.7.
- Figures 2.2 and 7.1 were prepared using data compiled by Luke Samy and presented in his paper, 'Indices of house prices and rent prices of residential property in London, 1895–1939', *University of Oxford Discussion Papers in Economic and Social History*, no. 134 (April 2015).
- Figures 3.8, 3.9, 3.13, 3.15, 3.17, 3.18, 3.19 to 3.22, 3.24, 3.26, 3.28 to 3.31 were prepared using data extracted from microfilms of John Castaing's reports, *The Course of the Exchange, and other things*, London, from 1698, held in Special Collections, Goldsmiths' Library of Economic Literature, Senate House Library, University of London.
- Figures 4.9 and 4.10 were prepared using data compiled by Forrest H. Capie and Alan Webber and published in their book, *A Monetary History of the United Kingdom, 1870–1982. Vol. I: Data, Sources, Methods* (London: Allen & Unwin, 1985; London: Routledge, 1995, 2008), table III. (10) c, pp. 502.
- Figure 6.10 was prepared using data compiled by Alexis Wegerich, University of Oxford.
- Tables A.1 to A.7 and Figures 3.2 and 3.5 were prepared using data compiled by Anthony C. Hotson and Nicholas J. Mayhew and presented as time series in their spreadsheet, 'English mint silver and gold prices, 1158–1946', *Winton Institute for Monetary History* (May 2015). Much of the data for the time series were extracted from Christopher E. Challis (ed.) *A New History of the Royal Mint* (Cambridge: Cambridge University Press, 1992).

Other statistical information used in this study includes:

- Data made available by UK public bodies under the terms of the UK Open Government Licence (OGL): www.bankofengland.co.uk/Pages/disclaimer.aspx#, www.nationalarchives.gov.uk/doc/open-government-licence/version/3/
- Data in the public domain provided by US federal agencies

Abbreviations

ABS	asset-backed securities; *see also* RMBS
Ag	silver
AHC	Accepting Houses Committee
aka	also known as
Au	gold
BBs	bankers' balances at the Bank of England
BBA	British Bankers' Association
BCBS	Basel Committee on Banking Supervision
BCCI	Bank of Credit and Commerce International
BEQB	*Bank of England Quarterly Bulletin*
BGS	British government stock
BIS	Bank for International Settlements
bl	bushel, 1 British bl = 8 gallons
bMo	broad monetary base: BBs, notes and coin held by the banks and in circulation with the public; *see also* Mo
BOESA	*Bank of England Statistical Abstract*
BoT	Board of Trade
bp	basis point
BSA	Building Societies Association
BSC	Building Societies Commission
BZW	Barclays de Zoete Wedd
C&G	Cheltenham & Gloucester Building Society
CCC	Competition and Credit Control
CD	certificate of deposit issued by a bank or building society
£CD	sterling certificate of deposit
CDO	collateralised debt obligation
CDS	credit default swap

CEPR	Centre for Economic Policy Research
CGB	City of Glasgow Bank
c.i.f.	cost, insurance and freight; *cf.* f.o.b.
CLCB	Committee of London Clearing Bankers
CLSB	Committee of London and Scottish Bankers
CML	Council of Mortgage Lenders
CP	commercial paper
CPI	UK consumer price index, *see also* RPI, RPIX
CSCB	Committee of Scottish Clearing Bankers
CSO	Central Statistical Office; *see also* ONS
ct	carat
CTDs	certificate of tax deposits, previously company tax reserve certificates until 1973, and tax deposit accounts until 1975
Cu	copper
d	denier, old penny, 240 d = £1
DCE	domestic credit expansion, domestic counterpart of M3
DD	Douglas Diamond and Philip Dybvig, proponents of a theory of banking in which depository institutions undertake maturity transformation
DWL	discount window lending by the Bank
dwt	troy pennyweight, 24 gr = 1 dwt; cf. 22 ½ gr = 1 Tower pennyweight; *see also* lbt, Tower pound
ELA	Equipment Leasing Association; *see also* FHA, HPTA, IBA
ELs	eligible liabilities; *see also* IBELs
EMS	European Monetary System
ERM	European exchange rate mechanism of the EMS
fc	foreign currency
FCA	Financial Conduct Authority
FDIC	US Federal Deposit Insurance Corporation
Fe	iron
FEBA	Foreign Exchange Brokers' Association
FECDBA	Foreign Exchange and Currency Deposit Brokers' Association, successor to FEBA; *see also* SBA
FHA	Finance Houses Association; *see also* ELA, HPTA, IBA
FNFC	First National Finance Corporation
f.o.b.	free on board; *cf.* c.i.f.
FOMC	Federal Open Market Committee
FRB	Federal Reserve Bank
FSA	Financial Services Authority
FSB	Financial Stability Board (founded by G20 in April 2009)

FSCS	Financial Services Compensation Scheme
fx	foreign exchange
GDP	gross domestic product
GEMM	gilt-edged market maker
gr	troy grain, 5,760 gr = 240 dwt = 12 ozt = 1 troy libra/ pound weight; 24 gr = 1 dwt; cf. 22 ½ gr = 1 Tower pennyweight
HBOS	HBOS plc created from the merger of Halifax and Bank of Scotland in 2001
HM	His or Her Majesty's
HMSO	Her Majesty's Stationery Office
HP	hire purchase agreement
HPI	UK house price index
HPTA	Hire Purchase Trade Association; *see also* ELA, FHA, IBA
HSBC	Hongkong and Shanghai Bank, latterly Hongkong and Shanghai Banking Corporation, HSBC Holdings PLC
ib	interest bearing
IBA	Industrial Bankers Association; *see also* ELA, FHA, HPTA
IBELs	Interest-bearing eligible liabilities; *see also* ELs
IDBs	interdealer brokers; *see also* broker–dealers
IHC	Issuing Houses Committee
IOU	'I owe you', description of a debt
JMB	Johnson Matthey Bank
LAPR	life assurance premium relief
lb	avoirdupois pound, 1 lb = 16 oz
lbt	troy pound, 5,760 gr = 240 dwt = 12 ozt = 1 troy libra/ pound weight; Troy units of weight were adopted by the Mint in the sixteenth century in place of the Tower lb
LBCH	London Bankers' Clearing House, otherwise known as Bankers' Clearing House, or London Clearing House
LBG	Lloyds Banking Group plc
LBMA	London Bullion Market Association
LDMA	London Discount Market Association
li, l, £	libra, lira, livre, pound sterling, £ used from eighteenth century; *see also* £ s d
LIBOR	London interbank offered rate
LCB	London clearing bank
LOLR	lender of last resort
LPB	limited purpose bank
LSE	London Stock Exchange
LTSB	Lloyds TSB; *see also* Lloyds, TSB

LTV ratio	loan-to-value ratio; *see also* income multiple
M0	monetary base, monetary liabilities of the central bank; *see also* nM0 and bM0
nM0	narrow monetary base, comprising bankers' balances at the Bank (BBs)
bM0	broad monetary base, comprising:
	(i) bankers' balances at the Bank (BBs), plus
	(ii) notes and coin held by the banks and in circulation with the public, comprising current coin issued by the Royal Mint, and the fiduciary note issue of the Scottish and Northern Irish banks
M1	narrow money, comprising:
	(i) notes and coin in circulation with the public; plus
	(ii) sight deposits with UK-based banks
nibM1	non-interest-bearing M1
M2	retail money, comprising:
	(i) M1, plus
	(ii) UK private sector sterling time deposits with UK deposit banks: clearing banks, Giro, Banking Department of the Bank, and the discount houses
	The series was published in 1970, but discarded. It was revived in 1985, including building society shares and deposits
M3	broad money, comprising:
	(i) notes and coin in circulation with the public; plus
	(ii) UK residents' sterling and foreign currency deposits with UK-based banks
£M3	broad sterling money, comprising:
	(i) notes and coin in circulation with the public; plus
	(ii) UK residents' sterling deposits with UK-based banks
M4	wider liquidity, comprising:
	(i) notes and coin in circulation with the public; plus
	(ii) UK residents' sterling deposits with UK-based banks and building societies
	see also PSL2
MAC	money at call – sight deposits – with the London money market, latterly LDMA members and certain other institutions, including SEMBs
MAM	Mercury Asset Management
MBC	monetary base control; *see also* M0
MBO	management buyout
MIAS	Mortgage Investment (Albert Square) Ltd

MIR	mortgage interest rate
MIRAS	mortgage interest relief at source
MLR	Minimum Lending Rate replaced Bank rate in September 1971 and was superseded by dealing rate bands in August 1981
MPC	Monetary Policy Committee
MTFS	Medium-Term Financial Strategy
NBER	National Bureau of Economic Research
nbps	non-bank private sector
NBR	non-borrowed reserves
NCAs	net current assets: stocks, plus WIP, plus accounts receivable, less accounts payable to trade creditors, less bank financing
ndls	net non-deposit liabilities
nib	non-interest bearing
nibM1	non-interest-bearing M1, *see also* M1
nib SSDs	non-interest-bearing Supplementary Special Deposits required for excessive growth of IBELs under the SSD scheme; *cf.* SD
NIESR	National Institute of Economic and Social Research
NII	net interest income
nM0	narrow monetary base, comprising bankers' balances at the Bank (BBs), *see also* M0
NMB	National Mortgage Bank
nsa	not seasonally adjusted; *cf.* sa
NS&I	National Savings & Investments, successor to National Savings
OECD	Organisation for Economic Co-operation and Development
OEIC	open-ended investment company, unit trust
OFI	other financial institution
OMOs	open market operations by the Bank
ONS	Office for National Statistics, formed in 1996 following the merger of the CSO and the Office of Population Censuses and Surveys
OPEC	Organization of Petroleum Exporting Countries
OTC	over-the-counter trading
ozt	troy ounce, 1 ozt = 31.10348 grams; *see also* lbt
p	decimal penny; *cf.* d
Pb	lead
PBBs	prime bank bills
PE	private equity
POSB	Post Office Savings Bank

£	libra, lira, livre, pound sterling
PRA	Prudential Regulation Authority
PSBR	public sector borrowing requirement
PSL1	Private Sector Liquidity 1, comprising:
	(i) £M3, plus
	(ii) private sector term deposits with an original maturity of up to two years, plus
	(iii) private sector holdings of money market instruments: bank bills, Treasury bills (TBs), local authority deposits, certificates of tax deposit (CTDs)
PSL2	Private Sector Liquidity 2, comprising:
	(i) PSL 1 plus
	(ii) Private sector building society shares and deposits, excluding term shares and SAYE holdings, plus
	(iii) National Savings, excluding longer-term savings, minus
	(iv) building society holdings of bank deposits and money market instruments
	see also M4
QE	quantitative easing
RAR	reserve asset ratio
RBS	Royal Bank of Scotland, chartered in 1727
REIT	real estate investment trust
RFS	Registrar of Friendly Societies
RMBS	residential mortgage-backed security, *see also* ABS
RPI	UK retail price index; *see also* CPI
RPIX	RPI excluding mortgage interest payments
s	soldus, sol, shilling; *see also* £ s d
sa	seasonally adjusted; *cf.* nsa
SAYE	Save As You Earn saving scheme
SBA	Sterling Brokers' Association
SD	Special Deposit paying interest but not qualifying as a reserve asset
SEMBs	Stock Exchange money brokers
SGW	S. G. Warburg & Co Ltd.
SIB	Securities and Investment Board, precursor to the FSA
SIFIs	systemically important financial institutions
SIV	special investment vehicle
SLAs	US savings and loan associations
SMEs	small-and-medium sized enterprises
SSD	Supplementary Special Deposit scheme and deposits

std	standard fineness:
	(i) 22 ct gold (out of 24)
	(ii) equivalent to a millesimal fineness of 916
stg	sterling fineness:
	(i) 11 ozt 2 dwt of fine silver per 1 lbt of metal including alloy
	(ii) equivalent to 5,328 gr per 5,760 gr of metal
	(iii) a millesimal fineness of 925
	see also pound sterling
TB	British government and Northern Ireland government Treasury bill
Tower dwt	Tower pennyweight
Tower lb	Tower pound
TSB	TSB Group plc
UDT	United Dominions Trust
VaR	value at risk; *cf.* VAR
VAR	vector autoregression; *cf.* VaR
VEC, VECM	vector error correction model
WIP	work-in-progress, a component of NCA

Select List of Institutions
by Functional Type

MONETARY AUTHORITIES

Bank of England, abbreviated to Bank	Governor and Company of the Bank of England – a plural noun, but the Bank accepted singular usage of the abbreviated form from 1978 (Capie, 2010, xxi)
Mint	Royal English Mint, London Mint

BIG FIVE LONDON CLEARING BANKS

Barclays	Barclays & Co, now Barclays Plc
Lloyds	Lloyds Bank, subsequently Lloyds TSB (LTSB), and then Lloyds Bank Group (LBG)
London & Westminster	London & Westminster Bank Ltd was formed in 1909 as a result of the merger of London County Bank and Westminster Bank
Midland	Midland Bank
National Provincial	National Provincial Bank. National Westminster Bank (NatWest) was created by the merger of National Provincial and London & Westminster in 1968

INVESTMENT BANKING ARMS OF THE LONDON CLEARERS

Barclays Capital	BZW created by Barclays, restructured as BarCap
County Bank	Re-established in 1965 by NatWest, known as County NatWest
Samuel Montagu	Samuel Montagu & Co, acquired by Midland, restructured as Midland Montagu in 1987

MAIN NEO-CLEARERS – SUCCESSORS TO THE TRADITIONAL CLEARERS AND THE MAJOR BUILDING SOCIETIES

Barclays	Acquired Woolwich Building Society
HSBC	Acquired Midland outright in 1992, renamed HSBC in 1999
LBG	Lloyds acquired TSB in 1995, creating LTSB. Halifax and Bank of Scotland merged in 2001 to form HBOS. LTSB acquired HBOS in 2009 to form Lloyds Banking Group (LBG)
RBS	Royal Bank of Scotland acquired National Westminster in 2000
Santander	Banco Santander acquired Abbey National in 2004, Alliance & Leicester in 2008, and Bradford & Bingley's business in 2008

OTHER BANKS AND INSTITUTIONS

Co-op Bank	Co-operative Wholesale Society Bank
POSB/NS&I	Post Office Saving Bank, founded in 1861, renamed National Savings Bank in 1969 and subsequently National Savings & Investments
TSB	Trustee savings banks amalgamated into TSB Group plc and floated in 1985, acquired by Lloyds in 1995

TOP TEN BUILDING SOCIETIES BEFORE CONVERSIONS

Halifax	Merged with Leeds Permanent Building Society in 1995, and converted and floated in 1997; *see also* HBOS
Abbey National	Converted and floated in 1989, acquired by Santander in 2004
Nationwide	Only large society not to convert
Alliance & Leicester	Converted and floated in 1997, acquired by Santander in October 2008
Bradford & Bingley	Converted and floated in 2000. In September 2008, B&B's branches and saving accounts were sold to Santander, and its lending book was put into run-off under state ownership
Britannia	Business acquired by Co-operative Financial Services in August 2009, trading as Co-operative Bank
Cheltenham & Gloucester	Converted to a bank in 1995 and acquired by Lloyds TSB in 1997

Woolwich	Converted and acquired by Barclays in 2000
Northern Rock	Converted and floated in 1997
Bristol & West	Converted and acquired by Bank of Ireland

ACCEPTING HOUSES – MERCHANT BANKING
MEMBERS OF THE AHC

Baring's	John and Francis Baring Company founded in 1762; from 1803 the new partnership was called Baring Brothers & Co
Brandt's	William Brandt Sons & Co, taken over by National and Grindlays Bank in the early 1970s, then part-owned by Lloyds and Citibank
Brown Shipley	Brown, Shipley & Co, London office established 1810
Hambro's	C. J. Hambro & Son, merchant bank founded by Carl Joachim Hambro in 1839
Huth's	Frederick Huth & Co, merchant bank founded in 1809 and dissolved in 1936
Kleinwort's	Kleinwort, Sons & Co, merged to form Kleinwort Benson in 1961
Lazard's	Lazard Frères & Co founded in New Orleans in 1848
Morgan's	London business of Peabody & Co combined with J. S. Morgan & Co, later becoming Morgan Grenfell in London
Rothschild's	N. M. Rothschild & Sons, established in London in 1811
Schroder's	J. Henry Schröder & Co (no umlaut after 1957) acquired the issuing house, Helbert, Wagg & Co, in 1962
Warburg's	S. G. Warburg & Co (SGW) admitted to the AHC via its acquisition of Seligman Brothers in 1957. S. G. Warburg Group plc, listed holding company of the merchant bank, SGW; the fund manager, Mercury Asset Management (MAM); and Warburg Securities, incorporating the stockbroker Rowe & Pitman and the stock jobber Akroyd & Smithers

PRIVATE BANKS

Child's	Child & Co, Francis Child's goldsmith business established in 1664, acquired by Glyn, Mills and Co in 1923, now part of RBS
Coutts	Coutts & Co, founded in 1692, acquired by National Provincial in 1919
Hoare's	C. Hoare & Co, private bank founded by Sir Richard Hoare in 1672

DISCOUNT HOUSES

Union Discount	Union Discount Company of London Ltd. Union Discount overtook National Discount as the largest house in the late nineteenth century
Gerrard and National	Gerrard's acquired National Discount Company Ltd in 1970. National Discount became the largest discount house following the collapse of Gurney's in 1866
Cater's	Cater, Brightwen and Co Ltd subsequently acquired Ryder's, becoming Cater Ryder & Co which subsequently acquired Allen's, becoming Cater Allen; see also Marshall's in the following section
Alexander's	Alexanders Discount Company Ltd
Allen's	Allen, Harvey and Ross Ltd, acquired by Cater's in 1981
Gillett's	Gillett Brothers Discount Company Ltd
Jessel's	Jessel, Toynbee and Co Ltd
King and Shaxson	King and Shaxson Ltd
Ryder's	Ryders Discount Company Ltd, subsequently acquired by Cater's
Seccombe	Seccombe, Marshall and Campion
Smith St. Aubyn	Smith, St. Aubyn and Co Ltd
Clive	Clive Discount Company Limited formed in 1946
Gurney's	Overend Gurney & Co, originally a bill broker, collapsed in 1866

MONEY AND FOREIGN EXCHANGE BROKERS

Marshall's	Rich, Marshall & Co established in 1866, subsequently Marshall & Sons. Founding family re-established M. W. Marshall & Co in 1951 when fx trading resumed after the Second World War. Marshall's was acquired by Cater's in 1967 and resold by way of an MBO.
Others	See also table of listed money-market name-passing brokers (*BEQB*, May 1990, p. 227)

STOCK JOBBERS

Wedd's	Wedd Durlacher, acquired by Barclays, forming part of BZW
Akroyd's	Akroyd & Smithers. Akroyd's was acquired by S. G. Warburg

STOCKBROKERS

Castaing's	John Castaing and his successors
Greenwell's	W. Greenwell & Co, also Greenwell Associates
de Zoete & Bevan	stockbroker acquired by Barclays, forming part of BZW
Messel's	L. Messel & Co
Sebag's	Joseph Sebag & Co, later Carr, Sebag & Co
Cazenove	Cazenove & Co
Laurie Milbank	Laurie Milbank & Co
Sheppards	Sheppards & Co

INSURANCE MARKET

Lloyd's	Lloyd's of London

FINANCE HOUSES OWNED BY CLEARING BANKS

Bowmaker	Lloyds
Forward Trust	Midland
Lombard Finance	National Westminster
Mercantile Credit	London & Westminster, later part of Barclays
North Central Finance	National Provincial
UDT	Barclays, later part of TSB

OTHER FINANCE HOUSES

Cedar Holdings	Second mortgage company
FNFC	First National Finance Corporation; property finance
London and Counties	Property finance
MIAS	Mortgage Investment (Albert Square) Ltd; property company that advertised for deposits

Introduction

The history of London's money and credit markets is one of intermittent crises interspersed with successive attempts to find ways and means of avoiding them. The currency reforms of the eighteenth century and the banking ones of the nineteenth were followed by a period of remarkable confidence in London's financial institutions, starting in the late nineteenth century and lasting pretty well until the 1970s. During this period, market practitioners took it for granted that 'orderly' markets were key to banking stability, and a major contributor to London's standing as a financial centre.[1] Recent scholarship has lost track of these arguments, or dismissed them as an unwanted exercise in financial repression.[2] Instead, economists and historians have emphasised the importance of the Bank of England's role as lender of last resort (LOLR) and its modern extension, state backed deposit insurance.[3]

The role of LOLR was famously advocated by Walter Bagehot, and appears to have been an elegant – and painless – solution to what had been an intractable problem – recurrent banking crises during the late eighteenth and nineteenth centuries.[4] Less heed has been paid to a raft

---

[1] G. A. Fletcher, *Discount Houses in London: Principles, Operations and Change* (London and Basingstoke: Macmillan, 1976), p. 83.

[2] C. M. Reinhart, J. Kirkegaard and M. B. Sbrancia, 'Financial repression redux', *Peterson Institute for International Economics* (June 2011).

[3] T. M. Humphrey, 'Lender of last resort: the concept in history', *FRB Richmond Economic Review*, 75, no. 2 (March/April 1989), p. 8; D. W. Diamond and P. H. Dybvig, 'Bank runs, deposit insurance, and liquidity', *Journal of Political Economy*, 91, no. 3 (1983), pp. 401–19; reprinted in *FRB of Minneapolis Quarterly Review*, 24, no. 1 (Winter 2000), pp. 14–23.

[4] W. Bagehot, *Lombard Street, a description of the money market* (London: Henry S. King, 3rd edn, London, 1873; 14th edn, 1915; New York: Wiley, reprinted, 1999); M. D. Bordo,

of more mundane market practices that supported London's pride: an orderly money market that withstood international crises and offered uninterrupted liquidity without excessive fluctuations in short-term interest rates. Much of this study is concerned with the idea of orderly markets, and the relative importance of the LOLR facility versus other market practices. There is, however, a wider issue to be addressed before we become embroiled in the minutiae of banking practice, and this concerns the unhelpful separation of currency history from banking history.

Much emphasis has been placed on a supposed disjunction between minted currency and bank money, where the former is characterised as a form of commodity money, and the latter is considered to be fiat money.[5] In fact, any form of money worthy of the name combines a monetary instrument with a prescribed value and a counterpart asset that supports its value. Precious metal coins – and notes convertible into coin – were usually exchanged at prescribed nominal values, but they also enjoyed high visibility collateralisation. They were therefore valued on two bases, and there was a risk – a basis risk – that the two would diverge. To put the point another way, these monetary instruments could become over- or under-collateralised relative to their nominal values, and these divergences could lead to problems. Over-collateralisation threatened the stock of coins in circulation because of hoarding, and the incentive to melt them down. Issuers of convertible notes faced the risk of having to buy bullion at a 'losing price', if the underlying coins became over-collateralised.[6] Conversely, there was an incentive to counterfeit under-collateralised coins, with the possibility of inflation and lost seigniorage.

Properly drawn commercial bills were not collateralised, but they were self-liquidating in the sense that the sale proceeds from goods being financed were meant to provide the means of repaying the debt.[7] Book-entry money had a nominal value – sometimes deferred – which was a liability of a deposit-taking bank, and it was backed by asset counterparts, typically liquid investments and loans of various kinds. These assets could comprise self-liquidating bills, secured loans such as mortgages,

---

'The lender of last resort: alternative views and historical experience', *FRB Richmond Economic Review*, 76, no. 1 (January/February 1990), p. 18.

[5] W. S. Jevons, *Money and the Mechanism of Exchange* (London, 1872; London: Henry S. King, 1875; London: Kegan Paul, Trench, Trübner, 9th edn, 1890), pp. 86–7, 217–20, 340–2.

[6] H. Thornton, *An Enquiry into the Nature and Effects of the Paper Credit of Great Britain*, 1802 edn and Thornton's parliamentary speeches and evidence F. A. von Hayek (ed.) (London: Cass, 1939, reprinted 1962), p. 218.

[7] Bank of England, 'Commercial bills', *BEQB*, 2, no. 4 (December 1961), p. 27.

and sovereign debt supported by prospective tax revenues. Banks might make unsecured loans, but these would usually be supported by some sort of recourse to unencumbered assets. We shall go into these technicalities in more detail, but the general point is that these forms of paper money were likewise valued on two bases – and they were subject to basis risk, albeit with different causes and consequences. A sudden fall in the price of commodities financed with bills could lead to defaults, an impairment of bill values, and illiquidity in the money market. Concerns about the value of a bank's assets relative to the nominal value of its deposits could lead to fears about its solvency, and possibly a run. Conversely, a rise in asset values – and thence collateral values – could lead to an increase of credit, followed – in some cases – by over-expansion, and a credit crunch.[8]

The challenge of all monies – be they precious metal coins, notes convertible into specie, paper credit, or deposits – is the management of their basis risk. The search for monetary stability has been a quest for ways and means of keeping the value of money's asset counterparts reasonably well aligned with its nominal value. One strategy has been to adopt a tiered credit structure with a capital margin providing a buffer to absorb asset impairments, and this has become a cornerstone of modern banking under the auspices of the Basel Accords on capital adequacy. A key point to be addressed in this study is whether tiered credit structures – *aka* capital adequacy – have succeeded in protecting holders of monetary instruments, or whether reliance ends up being placed on a more diverse set of mechanisms. This takes us back to the London market's historical preoccupation with the prerequisites of an orderly market, namely: (i) the Bank's provision of routine market assistance through the discount market, (ii) the role played by a corralled group of elite accepting houses, and (iii) the business practices of the clearing banks and building societies. We shall look at each of these in turn.

Since the 1890s, the Bank has operated the so-called 'classical system' of routine market assistance, and it remains in place today despite brief attempts to modify it in the 1970s and 1980s.[9] The Bank stabilised the cash reserves of the banking system, in particular bankers' balances with the Bank (BBs), while retaining the option to set short-term interest rates

[8] C. P. Kindleberger and R. Z. Aliber, *Manias, Panics and Crashes: A History of Financial Crises* (Basingstoke: Palgrave Macmillan, 2015), pp. 21–32; H. P. Minsky, *Stabilizing an Unstable Economy* (New Haven, CT: Yale University Press, 1986), pp. 68–95.

[9] P. M. W. Tucker, 'Managing the central bank's balance sheet: where monetary policy meets financial stability', *BEQB*, 44, no. 3 (Autumn 2004), pp. 368–70.

at levels of its own choosing. The Bank's routine market assistance took the form of outright purchases and sales of securities, and secured lending to the discount houses, practices that subsequently became known as open-market operations (OMOs) and discount window lending (DWL). OMOs could be used to keep the market short, forcing it to use its DWL facilities to borrow at Bank rate, raising market yields into line with the official one. The discount houses' ability to borrow at Bank rate meant that market rates would not normally exceed Bank rate, protecting the market from dramatic rises in rates – and consequential capital losses. This limitation of rate movements became an integral part of what was meant by an orderly market. That said, these day-to-day operations should not be conflated with the Bank's commitment to act in accordance with Bagehot's strictures as LOLR. The latter was supposed to be an intermittent exercise in crisis management – or crisis deterrence – based on the Bank's willingness to lend against 'all good banking securities'.[10]

Under normal market conditions, the Bank insisted that it would purchase only top-quality – that is to say, undoubted – securities as part of its OMOs, and its DWL had to be secured on undoubted collateral. In practice this meant it would only deal in, or lend against, British government stocks (BGS), Treasury bills (TB), or prime bank bills (PBB). For a bill to be of prime quality, and eligible for rediscounting at the Bank, it had to be properly drawn, accepted by an accepting house, and endorsed by a discount house – making it two-name paper.[11] By the 1870s, the accepting of international bills on London was dominated by its leading merchant banks, and when Baring's was threatened with insolvency in 1890, the Bank protected itself – and the wider money market – by orchestrating a rescue, funded by the clearers and accepting houses.[12] Thereafter, the market was given to understand that the Bank would stand behind the elite accepting houses, and this meant that prime bank bills (PBBs) would remain undoubted – and therefore liquid – in the severest of crises.[13]

---

[10] W. Bagehot, *Lombard Street, a description of the money market* (London, 3rd edn, 1873), p. 188.

[11] Bank of England, 'Commercial bills', *BEQB*, 2, no. 4 (December 1961), p. 27; A. L. Coleby, 'Bills of exchange: current issues in historical context', *BEQB* (December 1982), pp. 515–6.

[12] Leaf, W., *Banking* (ed.) E. Sykes (London and New York: Oxford University Press, 1943), p. 184–5; R. Roberts, *Schroders: Merchants and Bankers* (Basingstoke: Macmillan, 1992), xxii, p. 56; E. N. White, 'How to prevent a banking panic: The Barings crisis of 1890', 175 Years of *The Economist*, Conference on Economics and the Media, London (September 2015).

[13] J. S. Fforde, *The Bank of England and Public Policy 1941–1958* (Cambridge: Cambridge University Press, 1992), pp. 749, 751.

The next building block of orderly markets was the modus operandi of the clearing banks and building societies. From the late nineteenth century until the 1970s, the clearing banks were expected to follow certain precepts with regard to their funding, liquidity and lending. They raised funds by way of customer deposits attracted by the convenience of their branch networks and payment system. No interest was paid on current accounts (i.e. those used to make payments) and the clearers' trade body, the Committee of London Clearing Bankers (CLCB), set a common rate for term deposits. Individual clearers made no attempt to manage their funding by adjusting the rate paid for deposits – what we would now call 'liability management'.[14] Nor did they seek to raise funds by selling their own paper in the market, for example, by rediscounting bills drawn by their customers and accepted by the bank.

Instead, the clearers managed their liquidity by holding a substantial proportion of their assets in highly liquid investments, and the rest in loans – known as advances – that could be run-off relatively quickly. The clearers' liquid investments comprised money market instruments – prime bank bills (PBB), Treasury bills (TB), and money at call (MAC) with the discount houses – and British government stocks (BGS). The money market instruments were mostly of short maturity, and immediately saleable because the Bank was always willing to offer cash against them as part of its routine market assistance. BGS were of longer maturity, but here again the Bank stood ready to buy them, or lend against them. The clearers' advances – overdrafts and term facilities of up to a year – were less liquid because the Bank would not accept them as security for a loan, but they were designed to be repayable in short order.[15]

Clearing bankers saw themselves as lending for legitimate trade, rather than for speculative enterprises, and the mainstay of their business was short-term advances to meet the working capital requirements of established firms and estates.[16] These loans could be rolled over, but they were meant to be self-liquidating – in the tradition of bill finance – being repaid from cash realisations on the sale of goods. In addition, the clearers normally expected to take security over fixed assets, or to have recourse to unencumbered assets available for sale in case of a shortfall.

---

[14] Bank of England, 'The supplementary special deposits scheme', *BEQB*, 22, no. 1 (March 1982), pp. 75–7.

[15] W. Leaf, *Banking* (1943), pp. 97, 165.

[16] E. Sykes, *Banking and Currency* (London: Butterworth, 1st edn, 1905; 2nd edn, 1908; 3rd edn, 1911; 4th edn, 1918; 5th edn, 1923; 6th edn, 1925; 7th edn, 1932, 8th edn, 1937; 9th edn, 1947), pp. 197–8.

Lesser businesses without security – or guarantees from wealthy backers – would normally be regarded as too risky, and would have to look elsewhere for finance.

The availability of good quality security in ample quantities was not, however, sufficient for a loan to be granted. The clearers were adamant that maturity mismatching – borrowing short and lending long – was a 'classic error' exposing themselves to refinancing risk.[17] The same applied to their clients, not least because customer defaults could ricochet back on them. For this reason, they believed that companies should finance fixed assets and land by issuing long-term securities – equities and debentures – rather than resort to loans from banks for this purpose. There was a related reason why the clearers insisted on lending short. Their ability to call loans pre-emptively and realise security at the first sight of trouble gave them an unrivalled ability to protect their own position at the expense of their borrowers' shareholders and trade creditors. This allowed the clearers to manage the basis risk between their monetary liabilities and their riskier assets, whereas the provision of longer-term loans would have exposed them to greater risk.

In the 1930s, the building societies competed on rate for funds, and were willing to pay a premium over the clearing bank deposit rate. Liability management allowed them to grow rapidly, and the resultant housing boom could have led to a bust, but for the onset of the Second World War.[18] Thereafter, the building societies were persuaded to abide by a recommended lending rate set by their trade body, the Building Societies Association (BSA). The setting of a common lending rate helped to limit liability management, and provided a mechanism for managing liquidity in a sector that faced considerable maturity mismatching. The BSA adjusted its rate with a lag in response to changes in market rates, and societies moved their savings rates in tandem with the recommended lending rate. Rising market rates limited the inflow of funds to societies, putting pressure on their liquidity and reducing their ability to lend. The BSA did, however, take care to raise its rate sufficiently if societies faced an undue outflow of funds that threatened their liquidity.[19]

---

[17] C. Gordon, *The Cedar Story: The Night the City Was Saved* (London: Sinclair-Stevenson, 1993), p. 92.

[18] A. Offer, 'Narrow banking, real estate, and financial stability in the UK, c. 1870–2010', in N. H. Dimsdale and A. C. Hotson (eds) *British Financial Crises since 1825* (Oxford: Oxford University Press, 2014), p. 163.

[19] A. C. Hotson, 'The 1981 Budget and its impact on the conduct of economic policy: Was it a monetarist revolution?' in D. J. Needham and A. C. Hotson (eds) *Expansionary*

Orderly money and credit markets therefore depended on an inter-locking set of conventions and market practices:

- The Bank provided routine market assistance in accordance with the classical system.
- Clearing banks and building societies invested a significant proportion of their funds in liquid assets that were always convertible into cash as part of the Bank's routine market assistance.
- The clearers accepted the CLCB's curbs on liability management, and the building societies subsequently accepted similar restrictions imposed by the BSA.
- Clearing bank lending was primarily directed at working capital finance, allowing them to avoid significant maturity mismatching of their balance sheets.
- Prime bank bills (PBB) circulating in the discount market were supported by the undoubted standing of the accepting houses and the discount houses.
- The BSA's recommended lending rate was used to manage the building societies' liquidity and lending.

A tendency to downplay the importance of these market practices has encouraged a degree of complacency about their removal. Wholesale market freedoms, allowing liability management, emerged in the Euromarkets in the late 1950s, and became increasingly prevalent in the New York money market during the 1960s.[20] British reforms, known as Competition and Credit Control (CCC), allowed liability management to take root in London's domestic money market in 1971.[21] More significant levels of maturity mismatching – renamed maturity transformation to make it sound more positive – emerged in the 1980s as banks became more involved in mortgage lending, not just in the United Kingdom but across the developed world.[22] Stability was supposed to be

Fiscal Contraction: The Thatcher Government's 1981 Budget in Perspective (Cambridge: Cambridge University Press, 2014), pp. 138–40.

[20] R. B. Johnston, *The Economics of the Euro-Market: History, Theory and Policy* (London and Basingstoke: Macmillan, 1983), pp. 14–17, 133–4.

[21] Bank of England, 'Competition and credit control: text of a consultative document issued on 28th May 1971', *BEQB*, 11, no. 2 (June 1971), pp. 189–93; C. A. E. Goodhart, *Monetary Theory and Practice: The UK Experience* (London: Macmillan, 1984), pp. 152–4.

[22] Ò. Jordà, M. Schularick and A. M. Taylor, 'The great mortgaging: Housing finance, crises, and business cycles', *FRB of San Francisco Working Paper Series*, no. 2014–23 (September 2014), pp. 2, 14–15.

delivered worldwide by the provision of LOLR facilities, state backed deposit insurance, and the Basel Accords with their emphasis on capital adequacy.[23] Not everything went to plan, and the events of 2007–8 suggest a reappraisal is needed.

This book offers two strands of revisionist interpretation. Firstly, the outbreak of stability in London's money market in the late nineteenth century had more to do with evolving market practices than the silver bullet supposedly delivered by Bagehot's LOLR. Secondly, the idea that the risks associated with maturity transformation – née mismatching – can be managed simply by providing a LOLR facility is based on a misunderstanding. The clearers were fearful of long-term lending not just because of its liquidity risks, but because of its associated credit risks. To understand these ideas, we need to re-examine their principles of sound banking practice – the subject of the next chapter.

---

[23] C. A. E. Goodhart, 'The Bank of England over the Last 35 Years' in *Bankhistorisches Archiv, Zeitschrift zur Bankengeschichte*, Beiheft 43, *Welche Aufgaben muß eine Zentralbank wahrnehmen? Historische Erfahrungen und europäische Perspektiven.* 15. Wissenschaftliches Kolloquium am 7 November 2002 auf Einladung der Stiftung "Geld und Währung" (Stuttgart: Franz Steiner Verlag, 2004), pp. 29–38.

2

Principles and Practice

The idea that good banking practice could be expressed as a set of principles – and that respectable bankers could be persuaded to embrace them – is perhaps a tribute to Victorian optimism. The monthly *Bankers' Magazine*, first published in 1844, was one of a number of journals intended to promulgate principles of sound banking, and practical treatises in the same vein proved to be popular.[1] One of the more prolific authors of this genre, James William Gilbart, published *A Practical Treatise on Banking* in 1827 and this evolved, through multiple editions, into an eight-volume work, *Principles of Banking*, published in 1866.[2] A revised and more manageable edition of two volumes was edited by A. S. Michie in 1882, and further editions were prepared by Ernest Sykes from 1907.[3] The last edition of Gilbart's appeared in 1922 – nearly a century after the first one – and was succeeded by Walter Leaf's *Banking*, first published in 1926.[4] These editions were textbooks, primarily directed at bankers, but copies found their way into the bookshelves of an interested public. They have been reprinted in recent decades, and are cited occasionally by modern scholars, but they are rarely read today.[5]

[1] *The Bankers' Magazine: Journal of the Money Market* (49 vols, London: Richard Groombridge, 1844–89).
[2] J. W. Gilbart, *A Practical Treatise on Banking* (London, 1st edn, 1827, 3rd edn, 1834, 5th edn, 1849, 6th edn, 1856).
[3] *Gilbart on Banking: The History, Principles and Practice of Banking* (ed.) A. S. Michie (2 vols, London: George Bells, 1882); (ed.) E. Sykes (2 vols, London: George Bell, 1907, 1922).
[4] W. Leaf, *Banking* (London: Butterworth, 1st edn, 1926; 2nd edn, 1926; reprinted 1927, 1928, 1929, 1931) (ed.) E. Sykes (3rd edn, 1935; reprinted 1937; 4th edn, London and New York: Oxford University Press, 1943).
[5] M. Collins, *Money and Banking in the UK: A History* (London: Croom Helm, 1988; London: Routledge, 1990), pp. 85–6; F. H. Capie and G. E. Wood (eds) *Banking Theory, 1870–1930*, 1, 3, 7 (7 vols, London: Routledge, 1999).

Gilbart, Michie, Sykes and Leaf were all clearing bankers with an interest in professional education and the promotion of what they saw as good banking practice. Gilbart became a director and general manager of London & Westminster Bank, and Michie served as deputy manager of the London branch of Royal Bank of Scotland (RBS). Sykes was the driving force behind the Institute of Bankers, serving as its secretary from 1905, as well as being secretary of the Committee of London Clearing Bankers (CLCB) and the British Bankers' Association (BBA).[6] Sykes's own textbook, *Banking and Currency*, was first published in 1905, and went through nine editions, becoming a standard text for students of the institute's banking exams.[7] Leaf was chairman of London & Westminster Bank in the 1920s, and the later editions of his book were edited by Sykes in the 1930s and 1940s. The indefatigable Sykes also revised the 1931 edition of *The Country Banker*, first published in 1895, and written by George Rae, chairman of the North and South Wales Bank, subsequently part of Midland Bank.[8] The last edition of Sykes's own textbook was published after the Second World War, but it was already being super-seded by the next generation of banking texts, notably *Modern Banking* by Richard Sayers – a book written by an academic rather than a practis-ing banker.[9]

For their own part, the clearing bank authors went to great pains to describe who should do what in the London market, and how the various parties should conduct themselves when dealing with others. Their books were really about the professionalisation of business dealings between market practitioners, and the presentation of bankers – in particular clearing bankers – as respected figures in society.[10] Their preoccupation with the demarcation of roles in the London market reflected the fact that clearing banks were not the broadly based banking businesses we see today. Banking functions were split among a number of institutional

[6] J. W. Gilbart (1882), 2, p. 17; W. Leaf (1943), p. 23; E. Green, *Debtors to Their Profession: A History of the Institute of Bankers 1879–1979* (Abingdon: Routledge, 1979), p. 132.

[7] E. Sykes, *Banking and Currency* (London: Butterworth, 1st edn, 1905; 2nd edn, 1908; 3rd edn, 1911; 4th edn, 1918; 5th edn, 1923; 6th edn, 1925; 7th edn, 1932, 8th edn, 1937; 9th edn, 1947); R. Morris, 'Banking and currency by Ernest Sykes', *Journal of Political Economy*, 14, no. 2 (February, 1906), p. 124.

[8] G. Rae, *The Country Banker* (London, 1st edn, 1885; 5th edn, 1902; 6th edn, 1918, 1930, 1976).

[9] R. S. Sayers, *Modern Banking* (Oxford: Clarendon Press, 1st edn, 1938; 2nd edn, 1947; 3rd edn, 1951; 4th edn, 1958; 5th edn, 1960; 6th edn, 1964; 7th edn, 1967).

[10] C. Gordon, *The Cedar Story: The Night the City Was Saved* (London: Sinclair-Stevenson, 1993), p. 60.

types, not least the Bank of England, the accepting houses, the discount houses, the clearing banks, and – at one remove – the building societies. The insurance and securities markets developed their own sets of dividing lines: Lloyd's of London requiring that the roles of underwriting agent and broker be separate, and the London Stock Exchange (LSE) doing likewise for stockbrokers and stock jobbers.[11] The origins of these various demarcations – and the factors that sustained them – need to be considered in turn, starting with the clearing banks and their role in the payment system.

Banks took instructions from their customers to make payments to other parties, many of whom held accounts at other banks. A bank with a payment instruction would debit the required sum from the payer's account and send a draft to the receiving bank with details of the sum to be credited to the payee's account. The payer bank would settle the payment by remitting cash to the payee bank. Any properly documented payment instruction could be cleared in this way – including bills of exchange, dividend warrants, and cheques – provided the payers had sufficient funds in their accounts, or a borrowing facility with unused capacity. Bank clerks would walk the remittance paperwork and the settlement cash among the various banks during the day. As daily clearing volumes increased in the second half of the eighteenth century, it became clear to the walk clerks that interbank payments could be netted, reducing the amount of cash required to settle them, not to mention the amount of walking. The banks' directors were initially reluctant to adopt net settlement, but in 1773 they acquiesced, and a room was hired in a public house, off Lombard Street, to facilitate centralised clearing among its member banks. By this stage, payments were settled mainly with Bank of England banknotes, and coins were used for small differences.[12]

It took some time for the governance of the clearing system to be institutionalised, a permanent committee of the London Bankers' Clearing House (LBCH) was appointed in 1821, and a purpose-built facility was erected in 1834. The number of banks affiliated to the LBCH stood at 39 in 1834, falling to 25 in 1853, at which point 6 joint-stock banks were admitted, raising total membership to 31. At the same time, it was agreed that bankers' balances at the Bank of England (BB) should replace

[11] D. Chambers, 'The City and the Corporate Economy since 1870' in R. C. Floud, K. J. Humphries and P. Johnson (eds) *The Cambridge Economic History of Modern Britain*, Vol. II: *1870 to the Present* (Cambridge: Cambridge University Press, 2014), pp. 257–8.

[12] P. W. Matthews, *The Bankers' Clearing House* (London: Pitman, 1921), pp. 1–8; E. Sykes (1947), p. 85.

reams of banknotes as the means of interbank settlement, and the Bank was admitted as a LBCH member in 1864. A country cheque clearing was added in 1858 to head off the threat of a rival clearing house to serve provincial banks.[13] By the late nineteenth century, the clearing volumes of the parvenu joint-stock banks came to dominate the system, and their increasing importance was sometimes resented by longer-standing members of the LBCH. The newcomers were wary of their appellation as joint-stock bankers, and wanted to be recognised as the main clearing bankers of the country.[14] To this end, they established their own trade association – the Committee of London Clearing Bankers (CLCB) – to operate in parallel with the LBCH. At some expense, additional storeys were added to the Clearing House, with oak-panelled rooms providing a suitably decorous setting for the CLCB's meetings, and its secretariat.[15] The other deposit banks were coordinated by the Central Association of Banks, the Country Bankers' Association, the West End banks, the Scottish and Irish banks, and the Overseas' banks. The exigencies of the First World War led to the creation of an umbrella organisation, the British Bankers' Association (BBA), which represented the deposit-taking banks as a whole. The BBA was run by the CLCB's secretariat notwithstanding its separate constitution.[16]

The main clearing banks had cooperated informally on the setting of deposit allowances – the rate paid on customers' seven-day deposits. During the period of monetary ease following the German and US crises of 1873, the main London banks were able to increase the margin between Bank rate and their seven-day deposit allowances from 1 to 1½ per cent, and this was increased to 2 per cent in 1920. Discussions about rate setting were initially undertaken through the LBCH, and subsequently transferred to the CLCB.[17] At this stage, the CLCB did not set agreed rates for different types of loan, but customers' advances were normally no less than one percentage point above Bank rate. Borrowers of lesser standing could be charged a higher margin, and loans were subject to a minimum rate, often 5 per cent. Also, there was an understanding about the lending rate for money at call (MAC) placed with discount

---

[13] J. W. Gilbart (1882), II, pp. 312–28; P. W. Matthews (1921), pp. 9–12.

[14] E. Sykes (1947), p. 95; J. S. Fforde, *The Bank of England and Public Policy, 1941–1958* (Cambridge: Cambridge University Press, 1992), p. 751.

[15] E. Sykes (1947), p. 93.

[16] P. W. Matthews (1921), pp. 13–17; W. Leaf (1943), pp. 240–7; R. S. Sayers, *The Bank of England, 1891–1944* (Cambridge: Cambridge University Press, 1976), 2, pp. 552–60.

[17] T. Balogh, *Studies in Financial Organization* (Cambridge: Cambridge University Press, 1947), pp. 25–6, M. Collins (1990), p. 581.

houses. Generally speaking, the clearers followed similar lending practices, and there was little scope for customers to shop around among them – indeed, it was considered bad form for one clearing bank to solicit customers from another.[18] As a result, the cartel was able to protect its members from competitive pressures on rates, and limits were set on the scope for margin compression.

The CLCB provided a means of formalising ideas about respectable banking, and the need to limit dysfunctional forms of competition that led to bank failures. As George Rae put it in 1885:

> Your fear that the newcomers will offer more than the market rate of interest, and this will drain away thousands of your deposits, may be equally groundless. The Bolchester Bank is a respectable institution, and it is unlikely to give more than the current rate for deposits: but, if otherwise, and its rates are what you are informed and believe them to be, the Bolchester Bank will not trouble Oxborough or any other place for long. The first money panic will bring it to book.[19]

Inhibitions against competing on rate for deposits meant that it was difficult for an ambitious clearing bank to grow organically at a significantly faster rate than its peers. Even if it found ways of lending more aggressively than its rivals, borrowers would spend their advances, and the funds would be recycled around the system, being split among banks depending on their branch coverage. A lending programme that punched above the weight of a bank's normal deposit base could not be funded by what we would now call liability management – bidding aggressively for deposits by offering better rates. Without additional funding, the bank's liquid asset position would be eroded, eventually requiring it to moderate its lending ambitions. Above average growth could be achieved by extending a bank's branch network, and this was most easily done by acquiring independent banks, and their associated customers.[20] For a time, this was the main outlet for ambitious bankers, the amalgamation movement reducing the number of English banks from a peak of around 800 in the early nineteenth century to 115 by the end of the century.[21] By 1917–18,

---

[18] J. W. Gilbart (1882), I, p. 245; W. Leaf (1943), pp. 108–9; L. S. Pressnell, 'Cartels and competition in British banking: a background study', *Banca Nazionale del Lavoro Quarterly Review*, 95 (1970), p. 387.

[19] G. Rae (1885), p. 187.

[20] W. T. C. King, *History of the London Discount Market* (London: Cass, 1936), pp. 290–1; T. Balogh (1947), pp. 24–6; C. W. Calomiris and S. H. Haber, *Fragile by Design: The Political Origins of Banking Crises and Scarce Credit* (Princeton, NJ, and Oxford: Princeton University Press, 2014), pp. 125–8.

[21] F. H. Capie and A. Webber, *A Monetary History of the United Kingdom, 1870–1982*, Vol. I: *Data, Sources, Methods* (London: Allen & Unwin, 1985; London: Routledge, 1995,

the CLCB was dominated by the big five High Street banks: London &
Westminster, Lloyds, Barclays, Midland, and National Provincial.[22] The
big five subsequently became the big four when National Provincial and
London & Westminster merged to form National Westminster (NatWest)
in 1968. (The full names of the leading clearing banks are summarised in
the Select List of Institutions by Functional Type.)

The clearing banks did suffer some disintermediation in the 1920s as
high interest rates encouraged insurance companies and others to buy
money market instruments directly, rather than accept CLCB rates on
their deposits, but the fall in market yields in the 1930s ended this particular leakage.[23] The CLCB cartel was not just tolerated, but endorsed
by the authorities in the 1930s, not least because the banking sector
remained an important source of government funding. Most countries
came to rely on restrictions on competition to control the animal spirits
of their bankers, although cartelisation was not the only means of doing
so.[24] In the United States, Regulation Q of the Glass-Steagall Act 1933
put limits on the payment of interest on deposits, thereby using statute to
restrict competitive bidding for funds.[25] In continental Europe, universal
banks were prevalent, and the strength of their client relationships provided another means of restricting competition.

The discount market (*aka* the money market) played a distinctive role in
London's financial system. As one parliamentary committee member put it
in the mid-nineteenth century:

The bill brokers in London are the ... medium through which the spare capital of
one class of the community is employed usefully by another class of the community
where it is required ... The capital which is not required in particular districts of the
country is sent up to London to the bill brokers, and money which is to spare in the
hands of bankers in London is also placed in their hands for use.[26]

In most countries, mainstream banks were quick to intermediate these
flows directly, but in London rivalries between the Bank and the clearers

2008), p. 226, appendix III, pp. 576–7; M. Collins (1988, 1990), p. 78; G. A. Davies, *Building Societies and Their Branches: A Regional Economic Survey* (London: Franey., 1981), p. 47.
[22] T. Balogh (1947), p. 15.
[23] L. S. Pressnell (1970), p. 376.
[24] L. A. Hahn, *Economic Theory of Bank Credit*, translation of 1920 edn and second part of 1930 edn by Clemens Matt, introduction by Harald Hagemann (Oxford: Oxford University Press, 2015), p. 66; L. S. Pressnell (1968).
[25] R. A. Gilbert, 'Requiem for regulation Q: what it did and why it passed away', *FRB of St. Louis*, 68, no. 2 (February 1986), p. 22.
[26] W. T. C. King (1936), pp. 175–6.

in the 1830s and 1840s created a niche for bill brokers to act as intermediaries between the clearers, and between the clearers and the Bank.[27] These institutions did not normally lend to each other directly, and there was no interbank market in the modern sense of the term. Instead, they squared their books each day by trading bills through bill brokers that started to deal as principals, becoming discount houses. This allowed the Bank to deal with the houses, rather than directly with the banks.[28] The clearers outsourced much of their liquidity management to the houses, placing money at call (MAC) with them, secured on money market instruments, mostly bills. When the clearers withdrew their MAC, the houses sought accommodation from the Bank, and the bills that had been pledged to the clearers were either re-pledged to the Bank, or sold outright. By the first decade of the twentieth century, there were around 20 discount houses, and in 1914 they established their own committee to represent their interests, and this eventually became the London Discount Market Association (LDMA). During the interwar period, the number of discount houses declined, falling to 11 by 1945. The market was led by a trio of houses – Union Discount, National Discount, and Alexander's – followed by two other public companies – Jessel's and Smith St. Aubyn. The rest of the market comprised five private companies – Allen's, Cater's, Gillett's, King and Shaxson, and Ryder's – and one partnership – Seccombe's – which acted as the Bank's agent. (The full names of the discount houses and their evolution are summarised in the Select List of Institutions by Functional Type.)[29]

The rise of the discount houses in the nineteenth century did not mean that bill brokers ceased to have a role. Brokers, such as Castaing's and Marshall's, acted as intermediaries, trading stocks over exchanges, and in less formal markets where securities were traded across counters. Bills, bullion and specie were traded in over-the-counter (OTC) markets, and brokers allowed principals – including discount houses – to deal anonymously without revealing their positions. Bill brokers facilitated cross-border payments because it was usually cheaper for a merchant with a debt in Paris to use a broker to find a bill payable in Paris, rather than remit specie, and vice versa for Paris merchants with debts in London.

---

[27] N. H. Dimsdale and A. C. Hotson, 'Financial Crises and Economic Activity in the UK since 1825' in N. H. Dimsdale and A. C. Hotson (eds) *British Financial Crises since 1825* (Oxford: Oxford University Press, 2014), p. 38.

[28] Bank of England, 'Changes in banking statistics', *BEQB*, 12, no. 1 (March 1972), p. 76.

[29] T. Balogh (1947), p. 144; *BEQB* (June 1967), p. 145, fn. 1; W. M. Scammell, *The London Discount Market* (London: Elek Books, 1968), p. 80; G. A. Fletcher, *Discount Houses*

The use of bills of exchange to settle two-way trade was a netting mechanism that helped to economise on the cost of shipping precious metal. To the extent that there was a trade surplus or deficit between two foreign centres, the balance would have to be financed in some other way, or settled by remitting specie.[30]

The clearers and discount houses came to rely on the Bank to manage day-to-day shortages and surpluses in the domestic money market. Payments between clearing banks could be financed by recycling funds within the money market, but payments outside the banking sector would give rise to an outflow from the market, reducing bankers' balances at the Bank (BBs). For example, a surplus of tax receipts over government disbursements would give rise to an accumulation of Exchequer balances at the Bank, and a corresponding reduction in BBs. An increase in public demand for coins or Bank of England banknotes would have the same effect, draining cash from the market (i.e. reducing BBs).[31] The Bank responded in a piecemeal fashion to the problem of market pressures resulting from routine market flows, but by the end of the nineteenth century it started to provide day-to-day market assistance to offset these 'autonomous factors'.[32] From the 1890s, the Bank operated the so-called 'classical system' whereby it stabilised total BBs while retaining the option to set short-term interest rates at levels of its own choosing.[33] The Bank insisted that it would purchase only top-quality securities as part of its open-market operations (OMOs), and that its discount window lending (DWL) had to be secured on top-quality collateral.[34] In the main, it would only deal in, or lend against, prime bank bills (PBBs), Treasury bills (TBs), and British government stocks (BGS), otherwise known as gilt-edged stocks or gilts.

By the 1870s, the acceptance market in London was already dominated by half a dozen merchant banks, followed by a tail of smaller houses. In terms of acceptance business, Baring's was the largest, followed by

---

in London: Principles, Operations and Change (London and Basingstoke: Macmillan, 1976), pp. 245–8.

[30] J. S. Mill, *Principles of Political Economy* (2 vols, London: J. W. Parker, 1848), 2, chapter 20, paragraph 2, pp. 147–53.

[31] Bank of England, 'The Role Of the Bank of England in the money market', *BEQB*, 22, no. 1 (March 1982), p. 91.

[32] R. S. Sayers, *Bank of England Operations 1890–1914* (London: P. S. King, 1936), pp. 1–18; Bank of England, *BEQB*, 3, no. 1 (March 1963), pp. 15–21; P. M. W. Tucker, 'Managing the Central Bank's balance sheet: where monetary policy meets financial stability', *BEQB*, 44, no. 3 (Autumn 2004), p. 368.

[33] R. S. Sayers (1936), pp. 19–48; C. A. E. Goodhart, *The Business of Banking, 1891–1914* (London: Weidenfeld & Nicolson, 1972), p. 11; P. Tucker (Autumn 2004), p. 368–70.

[34] P. M. W. Tucker (Autumn 2004), p. 363.

Schroder's, Kleinwort's, Hambro's, Rothschild's, and Brandt's. (The main merchant banks are set out in the Select List of Institutions by Functional Type.)[35] Although the Accepting Houses Committee (AHC) had a total of 20 members at the time of its formation in 1914, a number of houses – notably Morgan's, Lazard's, Huth's and Brown Shipley – were included on account of their international standing, rather than as major acceptors of London bills.[36] This meant that the accepting of international bills on London was concentrated in half a dozen hands, and when Baring's was threatened with insolvency in 1890, the Bank protected itself – and the wider money market – by orchestrating a rescue.[37] Thereafter, the market was given to understand that the Bank would stand behind the AHC and its members. The Bank drew most of its governors from the accepting houses, and they would be expected to look after their own.[38] The AHC's protected status also meant that its membership remained largely static until the market reforms of the 1980s, the main exceptions being the demise of Huth's and Brandt's, and the arrival of Warburg's, after the Second World War.[39]

The provision of routine market assistance from the 1890s should not be conflated with earlier arguments suggesting that the Bank should nip crises in the bud by being willing to buy, or lend against, a *wider* range of assets.[40] The Bank remained concerned about the implications of acquiring poor quality assets in a crisis and wanted the discount houses to hold more reserves. After the 1857 crisis, it announced that the houses should be more self-reliant on their own reserves, and not depend on the Bank for accommodation in a crisis.[41] The editor of the *Economist*, Walter Bagehot, mounted a campaign against this policy, arguing that panics could be prevented if the market and wider public believed that the Bank would act as a backstop lender to the banks and houses. As he put it, the

[35] W. Leaf (1943), p. 184–5; R. Roberts, *Schroders: Merchants and Bankers* (Basingstoke: Macmillan, 1992), xxii, p. 56.

[36] R. J. Truptil, *British Banks and the London Money Market* (London: J. Cape, 1936), pp. 137–56; A. Ellis, *Heir of Adventure: The Story of Brown Shipley & Co., Merchant Bankers, 1810–1960* (London: Brown Shipley, 1960); R. Roberts (1992), xxii, p. 43.

[37] E. N. White, 'How to Prevent a Banking Panic: The Barings Crisis of 1890', 175 Years of The Economist, Conference on Economics and the Media, London (September 2015).

[38] J. S. Fforde (1992), pp. 749, 751; C. Gordon (1993), pp. 53–4.

[39] J. Attali, *A Man of Influence: Sir Siegmund Warburg 1902–82* (London: Weidenfeld & Nicolson, 1986), pp. 200–2; J. S. Fforde (1992), pp. 750, 754.

[40] B. Norman, R. Shaw, G. Speight, 'The history of interbank settlement arrangements: exploring central banks' role in the payment system', *Bank of England Working Paper*, no. 412 (June 2011), p. 23.

[41] W. T. C. King (1936), pp. 193–205.

Bank should 'advance freely and vigorously' in times of impending panic, rather than hesitantly – a policy that had exacerbated earlier crises.[42]

The success of Bagehot's advocacy, and the Bank's adoption of a lender of last resort (LOLR) policy after the 1866 crisis were, indeed, followed by a markedly more stable domestic banking environment.[43] The Bank's willingness to buy, or lend against, money market instruments – in bad times as well as good – meant that they retained their liquidity in difficult market conditions. Bankers could rely on an 'orderly' money market – that is to say, a liquid one – in all but the most extreme circumstances.[44] Modern writers have tended to present the Bank's LOLR role as the main game in town for stabilising the London markets since the 1870s, but contemporary practitioners – including our clearing bank authors – suggested that a wider range of factors played a part.[45] Writing in 1905, Sykes pointed out that the London markets had been remarkably stable since the Baring's crisis of 1890 – not so much since the 1870s – and attributed this to benign market conditions, and sounder banking practices. He pointed to subdued fluctuations in commodity prices, limiting the scope for speculation and making it easier to prevent overly exuberant credit cycles (Figure 2.1).[46] Leaf argued that national banking networks tended to be more stable, pointing out that country and district banks could be undermined by attempting to support local interests.[47] Amalgamations, branching, limited deposit competition, and a corralled acceptance market all seemed to be important factors, contributing to a banking system that proved to be resilient in the face of international crises and assorted insolvencies at home.

The maintenance of an orderly money market in the late nineteenth century did not preclude the possibility of sizeable bank failures, not least City of Glasgow Bank (CGB) in 1878. CGB was one of the nation's largest deposit takers, having the third largest branch network in the United Kingdom. It managed to do most of the things that lead to bank

---

[42] W. Bagehot, *Lombard Street, a Description of the Money Market* (London, 3rd edn, 1873), p. 196.

[43] S. Quinn, 'Money, Finance and Capital Markets' in R. C. Floud and P. Johnson (eds) *The Cambridge Economic History of Modern Britain*, Vol. 1: *Industrialisation, 1700–1860* (Cambridge: Cambridge University Press (2004), pp. 149–50, 167; N. H. Dimsdale and A. C. Hotson (2014), pp. 41–3.

[44] G. A. Fletcher (1976), p. 83.

[45] F. H. Capie, 'British financial crises in the nineteenth and twentieth centuries' in N. H. Dimsdale and A. C. Hotson (2014), pp. 15–19.

[46] E. Sykes (1905), pp. 220–2; R. Morris (1906), p. 125.

[47] W. Leaf (1943), p. 171.

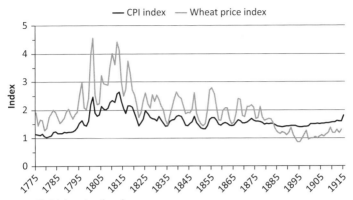

FIGURE 2.1 British price level, 1775–1915.
Sources: S. Hills, R. Thomas, N.H. Dimsdale, *BEQB* (Q4 2010) (CPI); G. Clark and P. Lindert (2006) (wheat price).

failures: 45 per cent of its lending was to three borrowers (large exposures); its directors were heavily indebted to the bank (connected lending); it accepted bills financing international trade without having the requisite foreign agencies and underwriting skills (uncontrolled credit risk); it held long-term speculative investments in US railroads and New Zealand land (maturity mismatch); and the bank's directors and managers falsified its accounts (fraud). Following its collapse, CGB's shareholders faced unlimited liability for losses of £5.2 million, amounting to approximately 4 per cent of Scottish GDP.[48] The resultant calls for capital averaged £12,000 per shareholder, equivalent to more than £1 million in today's money.[49] Shareholders were jointly and severally liable, and therefore unpaid calls on bankrupted shareholders were redistributed to other shareholders until the shortfall was met. The draconian treatment of the bank's shareholders allowed its banknote holders and depositors to be repaid in full without recourse to a rescue scheme. Other Scottish banks were sufficiently confident of their ability to recover funds from the liquidator that they accepted CGB banknotes immediately, as well as transfers of deposits from CGB (other than deposits held by shareholders of CGB).[50]

The contrast between the insolvency of CGB in 1878 and the more recent demise of Northern Rock in 2007 is quite striking. In the former

[48] J. D. Turner, *Banking in Crisis: The Rise and Fall of British Banking Stability, 1800 to the Present* (Cambridge: Cambridge University Press, 2014b), p. 85.

[49] J. D. Turner 'Holding shareholders to account: British banking stability and contingent capital' in (eds) N. H. Dimsdale and A. C. Hotson (2014a), p. 156.

[50] J. D. Turner (2014a), pp. 150–1.

case, there was no need for official intervention, depositors escaped unscathed with limited inconvenience, and the bank was laid to rest by its liquidators. In the case of Northern Rock, the Financial Services Compensation Scheme (FSCS) covered 90 per cent of customer deposits up to £20,000, but there was no mechanism for phased withdrawals.[51] Deposits covered by the FSCS could not be released immediately, followed by phased repayments by the liquidator depending on realisations. Instead, there were queues round the block as customers tried to withdraw all their funds, despite an assurance from the Chancellor of the Exchequer that the government would guarantee retail deposits in full. Having given guarantees that failed to stem the outflow of deposits, the government had to use taxpayer funds to recapitalise the bank, manage the run-off of its impaired loans, and sell its branch business to Virgin Money. By all accounts, the authorities appeared to have forgotten the CGB precedent, possibly because retail banking panics had been few and far between in the intervening 120-year period.[52]

Although depositors and taxpayers did not suffer as a result of the CGB debacle, the calling up of capital to meet losses had impoverished its shareholders, leaving many of them bankrupt. In banking circles, it was felt that too much pain had been borne by shareholders, and that noteholders and depositors should have suffered a modest penalty. Michie's edition of Gilbart suggested, 'It was but fair that the depositing public of banks should take some of the risk'.[53] It was accepted that losses suffered by directors with shareholdings provided a useful discipline, but should outside shareholders face unlimited liability, combined with joint and several liability? Leading bankers, supported by Bagehot, argued that increasing numbers of shareholders were of modest means; that had the effect of placing more risk on a smaller number of rich shareholders.[54] If rich investors were deterred, and bank stocks became income shares for widows and orphans of limited means, depositors could be left worse off.[55] These arguments were accepted by officialdom, and over time the banks were allowed to change from unlimited liability, to a somewhat

[51] M. I. Reid, *The Secondary Banking Crisis, 1973–75: Its Causes and Course* (London: Macmillan, 1982), p. 197; P. Jackson 'Deposit protection and bank failures in the United Kingdom', *Bank of England Financial Stability Review* (Autumn 1996), p. 38.

[52] J. D. Turner (2014b), pp. 84–8.

[53] J. W. Gilbart (1882), I, p. 433.

[54] W. Leaf (1943), pp. 225–6; J. D. Turner (2014a), pp. 151, 154.

[55] M. A. King, *The End of Alchemy: Money, Banking and the Future of the Global Economy* (London: Little, Brown, 2016), p. 108–9.

more restricted form of liability – known as reserve liability – and finally to limited liability.[56]

Wealthy families had acted as stewards of banks, but this model seemed less applicable over time. It was accepted that the big High Street banks were too large to be supported by banking families with dynastic shareholdings. The great and the good were appointed to the clearers' over-large boards, but their directors were not necessarily significant shareholders.[57] A new breed of general manager was increasingly promoted from within, and these career bankers did not have independent means to purchase shares for themselves. Clearing bankers were salarymen with company pensions, more akin to civil servants than the dwindling number of banking dynasts that ran the remaining private banks, notably Coutts, Hoare's and Child's.[58] For the major banks, the owner–manager model had had its day.

Following the Baring's crisis of 1890, banking reformers focused on the need for banks to bolster their cash reserves – both BBs and smaller banks' balances with the clearing banks. In addition, the clearers made moves to accumulate gold reserves, supplementing those of the Bank.[59] Then-Chancellor of the Exchequer George Goschen, made a widely reported speech to the Leeds Chamber of Commerce in 1891, suggesting that banks should publish more frequent statements of their financial position and, in the same year, sixteen of the main joint-stock banks started to issue monthly returns.[60] It was hoped that publicity, mainly in the *Times* and the *Economist*, would cajole more banks to report monthly, and encourage higher cash ratios.[61] In the event, the number of monthly reporting banks did not increase, but amalgamations with non-reporting banks significantly increased the coverage of the reported sector. It was recognised that reporting banks managed their balance sheets so that their cash balances were higher than normal on reporting days – a practice known as window dressing – but the norm for reported cash

[56] W. Leaf (1943), p. 112–13; E. Sykes (1947), pp. 77, 194; J. D. Turner (2014a), pp. 144–5; J. D. Turner (2014b), pp. 126–7.

[57] W. Leaf (1943), p. 227.

[58] J. W. Gilbart (1882), I, p. 441–3; W. Leaf (1943), p. 234; M. Collins and M. Baker (2003), pp. 150–8.

[59] L. S. Pressnell, 'Gold Reserves, Banking Reserves, and the Barings Crisis of 1890' in C. R. Whittlesey and J. S. G. Wilson (eds) *Essays in Honour of R. S. Sayers* (Oxford: Clarendon Press, 1968), pp. 167–228.

[60] G. J. Goschen, *Essays and Addresses on Economic Questions* (London: Edward Arnold, 1905), pp. 116–7; C. A. E. Goodhart (1972), pp. 4–5, 26, 39.

[61] C. A. E. Goodhart (1972), pp. 42–4.

ratios rose from around 10 per cent to 15 per cent in the years prior to 1914.[62] Balance sheet ratios provided a point of departure in the search for stability, but no magic wand.

The last functional demarcation to be considered was the division between the clearers and the building societies. This was codified in later years by an agreement between the CLCB and the Bank to the effect that the clearers would not provide first mortgages for home purchase. The Bank's opposition to mortgage lending by banks had longstanding antecedents, eighteenth-century experience giving it a 'dislike of real property or mortgages as a banker's security.'[63] Mortgage lending was not typically intermediated by bankers, but by brokers – conveyancers and other legal practitioners with access to family funds and trust monies which could be invested in loans secured on land.[64] Their borrowers tended to be owners of landed estates and commercial property with established rental incomes. During the Napoleonic wars, some country banks did try their hand at lower quality mortgage lending, notably to farmers acquiring marginal land with a view to increasing acreages under cultivation. The fall in grain prices and the value of marginal land after the war led to mortgage defaults, and this contributed to the failure of some banks. This salutary experience encouraged the view that banks should avoid mortgage lending, Rae commenting that: 'House or shop property, even of a superior class, is not a desirable security ... on the ground of its uncertainty of sale.'[65] This advice was generally followed, and vindicated, firstly, when agricultural land values declined in the late nineteenth century and, secondly, when residential house prices in the London area slumped by more than one-third during the first decade of the twentieth century (Figure 2.2).[66]

The banks' disinterest in mortgage lending and conveyancing brokers' focus on landed estates meant that home buyers found it difficult to secure loans. Some prospective owner–occupiers formed clubs – building

---

[62] C. A. E. Goodhart (1972), p. 114.

[63] J. Clapham, *The Bank of England: A History*, I (Cambridge: Cambridge University Press, 1944) p. 249, also see p. 250.

[64] W. Leaf (1943), p. 166–7; F. T. Melton, *Sir Robert Clayton and the Origins of English Deposit Banking, 1658–1685* (Cambridge: Cambridge University Press, 1986), pp. 10–15, 52–7; Temin and Voth, 2013, pp. 41, 55.

[65] G. Rae (1885), p. 105; J. W. Gilbart (1849), p. 37–51.

[66] J. P. Lewis, *Building Cycles and Britain's Growth* (London: Macmillan, 1965), pp. 151–63, 316–7; A. Offer, 'Narrow Banking, Real Estate, and Financial Stability in the UK, c. 1870–2010', in N. H. Dimsdale and A. C. Hotson (eds) *British Financial Crises since 1825* (Oxford: Oxford University Press, 2014), pp. 158–73 2014, p. 162; L. Samy, 'Indices of house prices and rent prices of residential property in London, 1895–1939', *University of Oxford Discussion Papers in Economic and Social History*, no. 134 (April 2015).

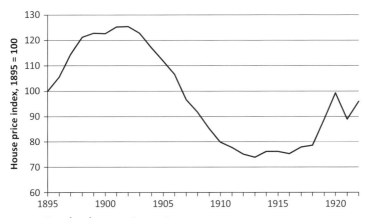

FIGURE 2.2 London house prices, 1895–1922.
Source: L. Samy, 'Indices of house prices and rent prices of residential property in London, 1895–1939', *University of Oxford Discussion Papers in Economic and Social History*, no. 134 (April 2015).

societies – constituted as friendly societies for pooling their savings, allowing members to take turns borrowing for house purchases.[67] The number of building societies grew to a peak of 2,795 in 1890, before amalgamations reduced their number to 1,026 by 1930. The sector nevertheless remained more fragmented than High Street banking with local societies competing with regional and national societies on the same High Streets (details of the larger building societies are set out in the Select List of Institutions by Functional Type).[68] The residential building boom of the late 1930s was supported by increased lending by societies, offering longer repayment periods and higher loan-to-value (LTV) ratios.[69] Societies found they could attract ample funds by offering a modest margin over the CLCB's cartelised deposit rate, when the Bank adopted a low interest rate policy after sterling's exit from the gold standard in 1931. This was another example of the clearers' being disintermediated, and it is a moot point whether the housing boom of the 1930s would have led to a bust, but the Second World War intervened.[70] Attempts were made to

[67] G. Speight, 'Building society behaviour and the mortgage-lending market in the interwar period: Risk-taking by mutual institutions and the interwar housebuilding boom', DPhil thesis, University of Oxford (2000), pp. 11–15.

[68] R. J. Truptil (1936), pp. 59–61; G. A. Davies (1981), p. 48–9.

[69] M. H. Best and K. J. Humphries, 'The City and Industrial Decline', in B. Elbaum and W. Lazonick (eds) *The Decline of the British Economy* (Oxford: Clarendon, 1986), pp. 234–5.

[70] G. Speight (2000), pp. 8–10, 248–50; W. A. Allen, 'Asset choice in British central banking history, the myth of the safe asset, and bank regulation', *Journal of Banking and Financial Economics*, 2, no. 4 (2 June 2015), pp. 9–10.

moderate 'excessively aggressive competition', and the Building Societies Association (BSA) was able to establish cartelised pricing and market discipline from 1939.[71]

Whereas the CLCB's main area of margin control was that between seven-day deposit rates and Bank rate, the BSA set a recommended lending rate for its members' mortgage loans.[72] This mirror-image set of margin controls meant the clearers could offer loans at differential rates, but they had to be content with a standard deposit account that was not particularly competitive. This meant their emphasis was on lending rather than saving. In contrast, building societies were free to compete for deposits, offering savers a proliferation of special offers, but they had to be content with a standard mortgage offering and abide by the BSA's recommended lending rate.[73] This gave smaller societies the option to offer slightly better savings rates and accept some margin compression. Standardised lending meant that societies catered for middle-income owner–occupiers and eschewed mortgages for high-end borrowers, subprime ones, and buy-to-let. As we shall see, rate setting by these two trade bodies – the CLCB and the BSA – had important implications for the controllability of money and credit – and thence the stability of the financial sector.

The final part of the City of London jigsaw was the London Stock Exchange (LSE), which operated its own set of restrictive practices, including the separation of stockbroking and stock jobbing, and since 1912 the imposition of minimum broking commissions.[74] Its member firms – both stockbrokers and stock jobbers – had to be partnerships, precluding corporate ownership and bank proprietors. Stockbrokers acted as agents for their clients in the buying and selling of shares, and they were precluded from taking proprietary positions. Stock jobbers acted as market makers and could deal only with stockbrokers, not end investors. They were allowed to take positions in securities and funded their books with secured loans from the clearers, intermediated through Stock Exchange money brokers (SEMBs) – money broking desks operating within stockbroking firms.[75]

---

[71] G. A. Davies (1981), p. 47.

[72] Wilson, J. Harold, baron Wilson of Rievaulx, *Committee to Review the Functioning of Financial Institutions*, Cmnd. 7937 (2 vols, London: HMSO, 28th June 1980), p. 107.

[73] M. Boddy, *The Building Societies* (London and Basingstoke: Macmillan, 1980), pp. 86–8.

[74] R. C. Michie, *The London Stock Exchange: A History* (Oxford: Oxford University Press, 1999), pp. 113–15; L. D. Neal and L. E. Davis, 'The evolution and the structure and performance of the London Stock Exchange in the first global financial market, 1812–1914', *European Review of Economic History*, 10, no. 3 (December 2016), pp. 279–300.

[75] W. Leaf (1943), pp. 90–1, 128–9; R. S. Sayers, *Lloyds Bank in the History of English Banking* (Oxford: Clarendon Press, 1957), p. 180.

In the 1950s, three of these firms – Cazenove, Laurie Milbank and Sheppards – had the largest SEMB businesses.[76]

New issues of securities were underwritten by issuing houses of various shapes and sizes. When the Issuing Houses Association (IHA) was formed after the Second World War, it had around 60 members, but most of them were small firms.[77] By the 1950s, merchant banks rather than stockbrokers dominated the new issues market, combining securities underwriting with a form of bill finance known as acceptance credits.[78] The major players were therefore members of both the elite AHC and the not so rarefied IHA.[79]

It is important to note that traditional regulation in the Square Mile of the City of London demanded separate ownership of the various types of firm, but not a compartmentalisation of exposures. There was no firewall around the clearing banks, protecting them from exposures to merchant banks, discount houses and stock jobbers. On the contrary, their strength as institutions depended on the reliability of the leading merchant banks, the discount houses, SEMBs and, ultimately, the Bank as both tacit guarantor of AHC paper and provider of a LOLR facility. The clearers were protected, not because they were ring-fenced, but because they could rely on the undoubted standing of the specialist houses.

From the 1890s until 1971 the main High Street banks did not liability manage in their home market: 'There was virtually no competition between [clearing] banks for [domestic] deposits via interest rates.'[80] Liability management staged a revival in the Euromarkets in the late 1950s when international banks, based in London, began to create US dollar denominated credit, free from US and UK domestic regulations.[81] Euromarket banks were able to syndicate loans and to operate as pure liability managers, tapping the international wholesale markets to 'match fund' loans, without holding traditional liquid assets.[82] In the United

---

[76] R. C. Michie (1999), p. 406.

[77] R. Roberts (1992), xxii.

[78] S. Hurn, *Syndicated Loans: A Handbook for Banker and Borrower* (New York and London: Woodhead-Faulkner, 1990), p. 9; R. C. Michie (1999), p. 412.

[79] D. Kynaston, *The City of London* (4 vols, London: Chatto & Windus, 2001), III, pp. 74–5, 227.

[80] G. W. Taylor, 'New techniques in British banking: An examination of the sterling money markets and the principles of term lending', Gilbart Lecture on Banking (London: King's College London, 1973), p. 23.

[81] C. R. Schenk, *The Decline of Sterling: Managing the Retreat of an International Currency, 1945–1992* (Cambridge and New York: Cambridge University Press, 2010), pp. 225–7.

[82] Bank of England, *BEQB*, 10, no. 1 (March 1970), p. 37; G. W. Taylor (1973), pp. 28–9; S. Hurn (1990), pp. ix, 1–3, 11–12.

States, Regulation Q was progressively circumvented from the late 1960s, allowing US money-center banks to use New York's wholesale money market to manage their domestic liabilities.[83] Their treasury departments started to make decisions about the rates at which they would bid for time deposits, and they issued negotiable own-name paper, known as certificates of deposit (CDs), which could be traded in the money market.[84] Major companies were also able to tap the market with commercial paper (CP): own-name corporate paper which was issued without being accepted – or otherwise guaranteed by a bank – and without the paraphernalia required of bills.

There were some stirrings of liability management in Britain's domestic markets in the 1950s, notwithstanding the BSA's success at limiting it in the home finance sector. The accepting houses started to bid more aggressively for deposits and expanded their balance sheets. This led to complaints from the clearers, but the Bank declined to curb this business.[85] At the other end of the banking spectrum, finance houses grew, providing various forms of consumer credit including hire purchase (HP). At the behest of customers, finance houses would purchase cars and consumer goods and rent them to their customers. The user of the goods would pay a weekly or monthly hire charge, covering interest and repayments of principal. When the HP contract ended, ownership of the goods would be transferred to the user, if all contracted payments had been made.[86] In the mid-1950s, some finance houses started to advertise in the press for deposits, offering better rates than the clearers and disintermediating them. A number of questionable parties also started to advertise for deposits, not least a property company which traded under the name of MIAS, and went bust to the detriment of its depositors.[87] (Details of the main finance houses are set out in the Select List of Institutions by Functional Type.)

The demarcation between clearing banks, on the one hand, and finance houses, on the other, reflected the British class system. The middle classes earned salaries which were paid into current accounts at clearing banks, and they used overdrafts for short-term borrowing. The working classes

[83] R. A. Gilbert (1986), p. 26, 36.
[84] C. A. E. Goodhart, *Monetary Theory and Practice: The UK's Experience* (London and Basingstoke: Macmillan, 1984), pp. 150–2.
[85] J. S. Fforde (1992), p. 751.
[86] Lord Crowther, *Report of the Committee on Consumer Credit* (2 vols, London: HMSO, March 1971), pp. 42–6.
[87] Mortgage Investment (Albert Square) Ltd, J. S. Fforde (1992), pp. 761–71.

were paid weekly in cash and borrowed on HP. The Bank's instinct was to maintain a demarcation between the clearers and the finance houses, much preferring the term 'finance house' to that of 'secondary bank', or 'fringe bank'. Consumer finance was nevertheless a growing sector, and the clearing banks were well placed to provide funds for the finance houses, and even own them.[88] One regulatory option would have been to establish a statutory registrar of finance houses modelled on the Registrar of Friendly Societies (RFS), which covered industrial benevolent insurance societies and building societies. This might have encouraged the various trade associations in the finance sector – FHA, ELA, HPTA and IBA – to merge into a single trade association, equivalent to the BSA.[89] This was considered, but did not happen and the domestic credit markets moved in a different direction.[90]

Credit controls became more intrusive in the 1960s with the imposition of quantitative and qualitative controls on credit provided by the clearers and finance houses. The CLCB started to set agreed rates for different types of lending, partly to protect its members from undue margin compression on loans to nationalised industries and local authorities.[91] The quantitative control of credit went beyond traditional forms of self-regulation and was motivated by a desire to regulate credit flows in support of Keynesian macroeconomic policies. The Radcliffe Committee took the view that fiscal policy should be the primary tool for managing aggregate demand, and monetary policy – which in practice took the form of credit controls – should play a supporting role.[92] Whatever their merit as a tool of economic management, credit controls placed the domestic operations of the clearing banks in a straitjacket.[93] Critics of their repression became more vocal in the late 1960s, comparing London's ossified domestic banking market with the freewheeling Euromarkets and New York's growing interbank market (Figures 2.3 and 2.4).[94]

The Bank became increasingly uncomfortable about the effects of direct controls and developed proposals for deregulation known as

---

[88] Lord Crowther (March 1971), pp. 40, 71.

[89] Lord Crowther (March 1971), pp. 105–6; Lord Wilson (28th June 1980), pp. 470–1.

[90] J. S. Fforde (1992), pp. 768–74.

[91] E. T. Nevin and E. W. Davis, *The London Clearing Banks* (London: Elek, 1970), p. 175; F. H. Capie (2010), pp. 443–4; D. J. Needham, *UK Monetary Policy from Devaluation to Thatcher, 1967–82* (Basingstoke: Palgrave Macmillan, 2014), Table 1.2, p. 15.

[92] Radcliffe Committee, *Committee on the Working of the Monetary System*, Cmnd 827 (London: HMSO, August 1959), paragraphs 978–85; E. T. Nevin and E. W. Davis (1970), pp. 265–7.

[93] C. W. Calomiris and S. H. Haber (2014), pp. 139–41.

[94] Kynaston (2001), IV, pp. 348–9; M. Collins (1988, 1990), pp. 365–79, 416–21, 439–47.

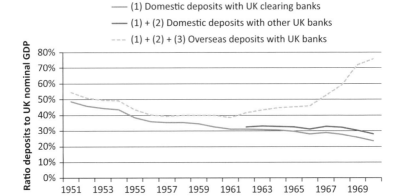

FIGURE 2.3 Euromarket deposit growth, 1951–1970.
Sources: Bank of England Statistical Abstract (BOESA), no. 1 (1970), Table 10 (1);
BOESA, no. 2 (1975), Table 8 (1).

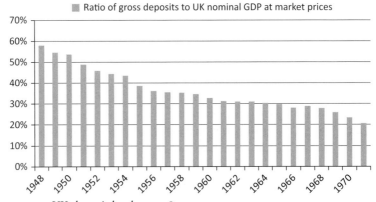

FIGURE 2.4 UK deposit banks, 1948–1971.
Sources: BOESA, no. 1 (1970), Table 9; *Economic Trends Annual Supplement,*
32 (2006).

Competition and Credit Control. CCC was launched in 1971 and included proposals for the ending of the CLCB's cartel, and the abolition of quantitative credit controls.[95] Greater reliance was to be placed on interest rates as a policy instrument, and there was some optimism within the Bank that monetary growth could be used as an indicator for setting rates.[96] In the event, everything went wrong: the forecasting equations

---

[95] N. H. Dimsdale, 'British Monetary Policy since 1945', in N. F. R. Crafts and N. W. C. Woodward (eds) *The British Economy since 1945* (Oxford: Clarendon Press, 1991), pp. 117–9.

[96] C. A. E. Goodhart and A. D. Crockett, 'The importance of money', *BEQB,* 10, no. 2 (June 1970), p. 180.

used for setting interest rates broke down; the Heath government cavilled at the need for higher interest rates; and there followed an explosion of credit, a boom and bust in the property market, and a secondary banking crisis.[97] Although the clearing banks had not lent significant sums directly to property developers, they had lent to secondary banks and these funds had been on-lent for commercial property schemes. A 'lifeboat' operation was launched to save a number of failing secondary banks, setting a precedent for subsequent bail outs.[98] Direct controls on banks' balance sheet growth were re-imposed, in the form of the Supplementary Special Deposits (SSD) scheme, colloquially known as the corset.[99] Credit growth was brought back under control, but some of the changes introduced by CCC remained. In particular, the clearing banks were allowed to operate on lower levels of liquidity than had hitherto been the case, and they came to rely more heavily on the interbank market for their funding.[100] In other words, the clearers started to liability manage in domestic markets, as well as in international ones.[101]

A number of factors conspired to make money and foreign exchange (fx) broking a growth sector in the 1970s. Bills of exchange had been the main means of intermediating foreign exchange, although banks did start to offer direct rates of exchange between currencies in the nineteenth century. A London bank's letter of credit could be used in other countries, against which foreign currencies could be drawn, at a rate of exchange set by a correspondent bank. Foreign currency transactions through banks – without bill intermediation – grew in the interwar period and resumed in London in 1951, when the foreign exchange market reopened. Eight broking firms were admitted to the newly formed Foreign Exchange Brokers' Association (FEBA), including M. W. Marshall & Co – a firm incorporated by the descendants of the nineteenth-century broker of the same name. In 1968, the Bank authorised the members of the FEBA to act as brokers of currency deposits as well, and in 1972 the FEBA was

---

[97] G. Hacche, 'The demand for money in the United Kingdom: Experience since 1971', *BEQB*, 14, no. 3 (September 1974); F. H. Capie (2010), pp. 524–86; M. I. Reid (1982), pp. 102–12.

[98] M. Ackrill and L. Hannah, *Barclays: the Business of Banking, 1690–1996* (Cambridge: Cambridge University Press, 2001), pp. 206–8; F. H. Capie (2014), pp. 21–2.

[99] Bank of England, *BEQB*, March 1982, p. 78.

[100] Bank of England, 'The role of the Bank of England in the money market', *BEQB*, 22, no. 1 (March 1982), p. 75.

[101] G. W. Taylor (1973), pp. 30–1; C. A. E. Goodhart (1984), p. 148; W. A. Allen, 'Liquidity regulation and its consequences', *Central Banking*, XXI, no. 4 (2010), pp. 33–4; C. R. Schenk (2010), p. 214; C. A. E. Goodhart, *The Regulatory Response to the Financial Crisis* (Cheltenham and Northampton, MA: Edward Elgar, 2010), p. 5.

reconstituted as the Foreign Exchange and Currency Deposit Brokers' Association (FECDBA).[102]

Greater volatility of exchange rates, following the breakdown of Bretton Woods, led to increased bank trading of foreign exchange, much of which was facilitated by FECDBA members. The growing domestic interbank market and a parallel market in local authority deposits were likewise facilitated by domestic money brokers, represented by the Sterling Brokers' Association (SBA). There was an opportunity for the discount houses to diversify into these broking markets, and Cater's acquired Marshall's in 1967. It supported Marshall's international expansion and established a domestic broker covering the sterling interbank and local authority markets. (The full names of Cater's and Marshall's, and their evolution are summarised in the Select List of Institutions by Functional Type.) The idea of an international money and fx broking business subsequently proved to be successful, but Cater's lacked the means – and the Bank's acquiescence – to bring it to fruition. In 1972, Cater's sold out to the managers of the broking business in what was then a relatively novel transaction – a management buyout (MBO) funded with relatively high levels of debt. Cater's experience led other houses to shun the possibility of developing full-scale international broking businesses even though the two leading ones – Union Discount and Gerrard and National – had the resources to do so. Union took the view that its strength lay in trading, and it sought to grow by establishing a New York base – an initiative that did not succeed. The houses' collective inability to evolve meant that they – and indeed the indigenous merchant banks – withered on the vine when the Bank no longer had a use for them. All this took some time and was a consequence of a wider deregulatory process to which we should now turn.

The election of the Thatcher government in 1979 offered the prospect of renewed attempts at deregulation. The strength of sterling – reflective of North Sea oil – encouraged the government to move quickly to abolish exchange controls. This meant that the SSD scheme could be circumvented by offshore disintermediation, and it was abolished in short order.[103] The mortgage and securities markets were both candidates for deregulation, allowing new entrants, including banks, to become involved. The clearers were wary of the mainstream mortgage market because they expected

---

[102] Bank of England, 'The role of brokers in the London money markets', *BEQB*, 37, no. 2 (May 1990), pp. 222.

[103] F. H. Capie (2010), pp. 700–1.

the building societies to defend their market share, taking advantage of their lower cost ratios. Their mutual status also allowed them to accept lower returns on capital. Interest margins were already pretty competitive, societies relying on fee income, notably commissions received from insurance companies for the sale of endowment policies alongside mortgage loans.[104] Endowment mortgages allowed borrowers to maximise tax relief on both interest payments (MIRAS) and life assurance premiums (LAPR), by repaying the mortgage at the end of its term out of their endowment policy. This type of loan also happened to maximise the interest income and fees arising for lenders and insurers, but these happy days looked numbered when the government ended MIRAS and LAPR in the mid-1980s. At this juncture, it was not obvious that the clearers should launch themselves into the mortgage market and, for many, the securities market seemed a more propitious move.[105]

The securitisation of traditional banking products was a problem that needed to be addressed, and London's Big Bang reforms of 1986 allowed banks to coalesce with stockbrokers, and jobbers, potentially allowing the clearers to offer a wider range of services under one roof. Barclays acquired the largest stock jobber, Wedd Durlacher, and the stockbroker, de Zoete & Bevan, forming the broker–dealer Barclays de Zoete Wedd (BZW).[106] Midland already had an interest in the merchant bank Samuel Montagu and acquired two stockbrokers, Greenwell's and Simon & Coates. NatWest assembled a new firm, County Bank, and the recently floated TSB Group acquired the merchant bank Hill Samuel. Of course, the clearers were not the only folk allowed to operate in London as integrated houses. Major investment banks from the United States and elsewhere set up shop in London as broker–dealers, and as underwriters of securities. London's home-grown investment bank, Warburg's, acquired the second largest stock jobber, Akroyd's, and the stockbroker Rowe & Pitman. HSBC acquired James Capel, and UBS acquired Phillips & Drew. The new gilt-edged market makers (GEMMs) needed to deal anonymously with each other, and this created an opportunity for London's money and fx brokers to become interdealer brokers (IDBs) in London, with the prospect of acting as IDBs across international financial centres.

[104] R. Taylor, *Going for Broke: How Banking Mismanagement in the Eighties Lost Billions* (New York: Simon & Schuster, 1993), p. 280.
[105] A. C. Hotson, 'The 1981 Budget and Its Impact on the Conduct of Economic Policy: Was It a Monetarist Revolution?' in D. J. Needham and A. C. Hotson (eds) *Expansionary Fiscal Contraction: The Thatcher Government's 1981 Budget in Perspective* (Cambridge: Cambridge University Press, 2014), p. 137–41.
[106] M. Ackrill and L. Hannah (2001), pp. 241–8.

Under the leadership of Sir Brian Pitman, Lloyds followed a different strategy from the other clearers. It withdrew from the Big Bang fracas, having briefly tested the waters, and directed its attention at retail customers, focusing on savings, mortgage loans and related insurance products. Pitman became an advocate of the bancassurance model, acquiring the life assurer Abbey Life in 1988 and the savings bank TSB, in 1995, forming Lloyds TSB (LTSB).[107] Contrary to many people's expectations, home finance proved to be an attractive market for LTSB, and the rest of the clearers. Mortgage margins remained intact mainly because the endowment mortgage remained a staple of the sector through the 1990s, notwithstanding the abolition of MIRAS and LAPR. Also, the Building Societies Act 1986 had the effect of stimulating consolidation within the building societies sector and opened the door to mergers between societies and banks, including foreign banks.[108] Cheltenham & Gloucester Building Society (C&G) grew to be the sixth largest society by acquiring a raft of smaller societies, before being acquired by LTSB in 1997. The life assurer Scottish Widows was acquired by LTSB in 1999.[109]

The second largest society, Abbey National, was the first to use the new powers granted by the 1986 Act to demutualise and convert to banking status. Abbey floated in 1989 and was acquired by Santander in 2004. The largest society, Halifax, announced a merger with the Leeds Permanent Building Society in 1995, indicating that it would subsequently convert and float, and it did so in 1997. Northern Rock and Alliance & Leicester were demutualised and floated in 1997, and likewise Bradford & Bingley in 2000. Like C&G, Woolwich and Bristol & West converted with a view to becoming part of larger banking groups. The only large society to resist the lure of conversion was Nationwide, ranked number three before the other conversions. Mortgage lenders of all kinds grew through consolidation, and none of the major players sought to replace the endowment mortgage. Societies no longer required a savings record before granting a mortgage, and an increased proportion of loan applications were sourced through broking introductions. Brokers assisted borrowers with the burgeoning forms required of mortgage applicants, and were remunerated through commissions on endowment sales. Lenders

---

[107] I. Fallon, *Black Horse Ride: The Inside Story of Lloyds and the Banking Crisis* (London: Robson Press, 2015), pp. 7–26.

[108] M. Boleat, *National Housing Finance Systems: A Comparative Study* (London: Croom Helm, 1985), pp. 54–6.

[109] D. Rogers, *The Big Four British Banks: Organisation, Strategy and Future* (Basingstoke: Macmillan, 1999), pp. 45–66.

did not want to bite the hand that fed them new business, and throughout the 1990s no major lender challenged the fees enjoyed on endowment mortgages.[110]

Barclays was modestly successful in the securities markets, building a debt capital presence in the form of Barclays Capital (BarCap), with a structured products business that proved to be remarkably profitable for a time, and a successful investment in a tracker fund business. The latter is now part of BlackRock. The Big Bang acquisitions of the other clearers mostly failed. Midland rationalised its broker–dealer business, but retained an ambitious treasury function called Midland Montagu. The group had been weakened by its disastrous purchase of Crocker Bank in California – acquired in 1981 and sold to Wells Fargo in 1986 – resulting in sizeable losses. The bad news flow continued as losses on Latin American debt crystallised, and Midland Montagu suffered a serious loss on its treasury operations in 1990 as a result of an interest rate play that went wrong. HSBC had been allowed to take a 15 per cent stake in Midland in 1987 and secured full ownership in 1992.[111]

NatWest's County Bank suffered the ignominy of a failed equity raising, and attempts to cover it up led to the Blue Arrow scandal. Thereafter, its securities operations were progressively dismantled.[112] Its branches continued to dominate middle England banking, but its exposure to small and medium-sized enterprises (SMEs) led to significant losses in the cyclical downturn of the early 1990s. At the time, NatWest suggested that it was over-exposed to SMEs – an incongruous statement from the heirs of Gilbart – and it was eventually acquired by RBS in 2000. In the following year, Bank of Scotland merged with Halifax, creating HBOS. Both RBS and HBOS had to be rescued in 2008, and their recapitalisation resulted in the government holding majority stakes in both banks.

Pitman's emphasis on shareholder value at Lloyds had become the orthodoxy for all the High Street banks, but the big four no longer constituted a distinct group with control over their own market.[113] The CLCB merged with the Committee of Scottish Clearing Bankers in 1985

[110] A. C. Hotson in D. J. Needham and A. C. Hotson (eds) (2014), p. 140.

[111] D. Rogers (1999), pp. 177, 185–6; R. Roberts and D. Kynaston, *The Lion Wakes: A Modern History of HSBC* (London: Profile Books, 2015), p. 262; R. Taylor (1993), p. 273.

[112] D. Rogers (1999), pp. 131–3, 137–46; R. Taylor (1993), pp. 264–6.

[113] M. Ackrill and L. Hannah (2001), p. 211; W. A. Allen, 'International banking as it happened: A review of "The Lion Wakes – a Modern History of HSBC" by Richard Roberts and David Kynaston' (9th September 2015).

to form the Committee of London and Scottish Bankers, and the CLSB was subsumed into the BBA in 1991. The line-up of High Street banks became HBOS, HSBC/Midland, Barclays, LTSB, RBS/NatWest, and Santander/Abbey National, followed by Alliance & Leicester, and Bradford & Bingley. The remaining 60 or so building societies continued to be represented by the BSA, and the Council of Mortgage Lenders (CML) was formed to represent providers of home finance, be they a bank, a society, or a specialist lender. The CML collected statistics and developed codes of practice, but power gravitated away from the trade associations towards the major institutions. For the most part, self-regulation was superseded by government-sponsored regulators with statutory powers. A succession of statutory bodies with a plethora of acronyms oversaw the markets: the Securities and Investment Board (SIB), followed by the Financial Services Authority (FSA), and then the Financial Conduct Authority (FCA), together with the Prudential Regulation Authority (PRA).

The demise of self-regulation did not lead to a free-for-all. Oversight of 'market conduct' became an industry in its own right, employing tens of thousands of people in the supervising agencies, advisory firms, and the compliance departments of market practitioners. In addition, prudential standards had been developed from the late 1980s by the Basel Committee on Banking Supervision (BCBS), in which capital requirements were related to risk exposures.[114] The promulgation of capital standards had been motivated, in part, by the mushrooming growth of cross-border lending, resulting from petro-dollar recycling following the OPEC oil price hikes. The bulk of these flows were intermediated in the Euromarkets in which the British clearers were significant participants, alongside the US money-center banks, the major Swiss banks and a number of others, including some undercapitalised Japanese banks (Figure 2.5).[115]

The setting of prudential requirements was viewed as a separate exercise from traditional monetary policy, and the two were run in parallel. The organisational disjunction between them was perhaps one reason why those responsible for monetary policy were wrong-footed by the ferocity of the credit upswing following the post-1979 deregulation, notwithstanding the experience of CCC in the early 1970s. Although the Thatcher government made much of its monetarist credentials, monetary targeting in various

---

[114] C. A. E. Goodhart (2011), pp. 1–8, 167–96, 211.
[115] R. B. Johnston, *The Economics of the Euro-Market: History, Theory and Policy* (London and Basingstoke: Macmillan, 1983), pp. 1–34; S. Hurn (1990), pp. 11–12, 189–95.

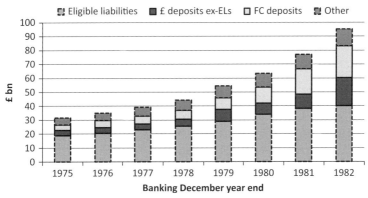

FIGURE 2.5 London clearing banks – £ and fc liabilities.
Source: BOESA (1995).

Period		Objective	Outturn	Source
1968	M3	Below £1.2 billion	£986 million	1967 Letter of Intent
1969/70	DCE	Below £400 million	minus £541 million	1969 Letter of Intent
1970/71	DCE	Below £900 million	£1.4 billion	1970 Budget speech
1971/72	M3	3% per quarter	15% in 1971/72	1971 Budget speech
1972/73	M3	20%	27%	Unpublished
1973/74	M3	'not more than 15%'	25%	Unpublished
1974/75	M3	Below nominal GDP	10% (vs. 13% GDP)	Nov. 1974 Budget
1975/76	M3	Below nominal GDP	9% (vs. 26% GDP)	1975 Budget speech
1976/77	M3	Below nominal GDP	10% (vs. 18% GDP)	1976 Budget speech
1976/77	M3	12%	10%	22 July 1976 statement
1976/77	£M3	9-13%	8%	Dec. 1976 mini-Budget
1976/77	DCE	£9 billion	£3.8 billion	1976 Letter of Intent
1977/78	£M3	9-13%	16%	1977 Budget speech
1977/78	DCE	£7.7 billion	£4.1 billion	1976 Letter of Intent
1978/79	£M3	8-12%	11%	1978 Budget speech
1978/79	DCE	£6 billion	£6.8 billion	1976 Letter of Intent

FIGURE 2.6 British targets for money and credit, 1968–1979.
Source: D. J. Needham in D. J. Needham and A. C. Hotson (eds) (2014), Table 9.1,
p. 150 (Table reproduced with kind permission of Duncan Needham and Cambridge
University Press, see page xii).

forms had been part of the British macroeconomic policy scene since the
late 1960s.[116] Official policy emphasised broad money – M3 or £M3 – and
its credit counterpart – domestic credit expansion, DCE (Figure 2.6). £M3
encompassed most of the UK banking sector's sterling liabilities, other than
overseas sterling deposits and net non-deposit liabilities (nndls – mostly

[116] D. J. Needham, 'The 1981 Budget: "a Dunkirk, not an Alamein"', in D. J Needham and
A. C. Hotson (eds) *Expansionary Fiscal Contraction: The Thatcher Government's 1981
Budget in Perspective* (Cambridge: Cambridge University Press, 2014), pp. 151–80.

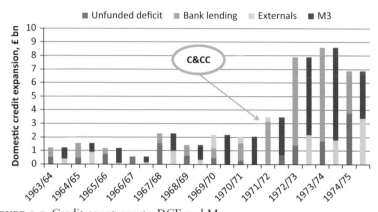

FIGURE 2.7 Credit counterparts, DCE and M3.
Source: BOESA, no. 2 (1975), Table 12/3 (Figure reproduced with kind permission of Cambridge University Press, see page xii).

share capital and latterly hybrid debt). M3 included UK residents' foreign currency deposits with UK based banks as well as the sterling denominated components in £M3, but UK residents' foreign currency deposits were relatively small on account of exchange controls (Figure 2.7).

The other side of the banking sector's balance sheet comprised lending to the public and private sectors, plus certain net external claims. This balance sheet identity could be restated in differences so changes in £M3 were expressed in terms of changes in bank lending to the public and private sectors – otherwise known as DCE – less various external and other influences. Bank lending to the public sector was the residual of the public sector borrowing requirement (PSBR), less public sector debt sales to non-banks. This meant that changes in £M3 could be expressed in terms of the PSBR, less public sector debt sales outside the banking sector, plus bank lending to the private sector, plus external influences – the so-called 'credit counterparts' of money. The upswing in the credit cycle following deregulation in the early 1980s meant that bank lending to the private sector remained persistently strong, and this was reflected in persistently rapid £M3 growth (Figure 2.8).[117]

Before their deregulation in the 1980s, building societies' lending had been interest rate sensitive, not so much because a rise in rates tempered borrowers' demand, but because societies were slow to compete for more expensive funds. The BSA cartel sought to protect existing borrowers from rate rises, rather than raise rates and maintain funding for new

[117] C. A. E. Goodhart (1984), pp. 131–2.

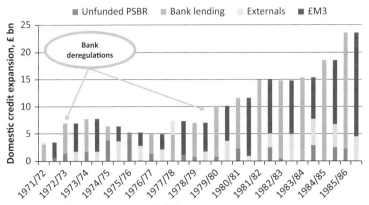

FIGURE 2.8 Credit counterparts of £M3.
Source: Bank of England Quarterly Bulletin (BEQB), Table 11.3 (Figure reproduced with kind permission of Cambridge University Press, see page xii).

borrowers (and offer savers competitive rates). The authorities' use of the interest rate weapon was therefore made effective by the slow response of the rates paid on societies' share accounts and deposits. An official rate hike led to a reduced inflow of funds to societies, and thence to an attenuated supply of mortgage credit. Deregulation allowed rates to be set more flexibly, and banks and building societies competed in the same market.[118] More competition meant that interest rate policy became a less effective tool for regulating the credit cycle.[119]

At the time, Milton Friedman argued that a fixed rule for monetary growth could still be enforced irrespective of regulatory changes, but there seemed little prospect of moderating the credit cycle – and £M3 growth – without reverting to a less competitive banking structure.[120] This did not fit with the neoliberal agenda of the time, and it was effectively decided that attention should be focused on stabilising the exchange rate – and latterly consumer price inflation – leaving the credit cycle and £M3 to their own devices. Monetary targets were deemphasised in the mid-1980s, and an attempt was made to shadow the deutschemark in 1987–8. This was followed by entry into the European exchange rate mechanism (ERM) in

[118] J. C. R. Dow and I. D. Saville, *A Critique of Monetary Policy: Theory and British Experience* (Oxford: Clarendon Press, 1st edn, 1988; 2nd edn with new preface, 1990) pp. 62–3.

[119] C. A. E. Goodhart and A. C. Hotson, 1979, 'The Forecasting and Control of Bank Lending' (1979) in C. A. E. Goodhart, *Monetary Theory and Practice: The UK Experience* (London: Macmillan, 1984), pp. 139–45.

[120] Friedman, Treasury and Civil Service Committee, 17 July 1980, pp. 55–61; N. H. Dimsdale in Baranzini, 1982, p. 190.

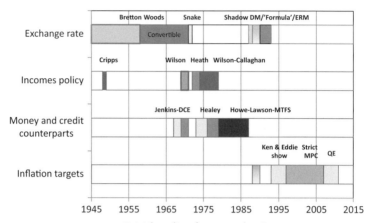

FIGURE 2.9 British policy frameworks since 1945.
Source: Author's diagram.

1989, which came to an abrupt end when sterling was forced out three years later. It seemed that exchange rate targeting would have to be put in the too-difficult box, alongside monetary targeting (Figure 2.9).[121]

Sterling's ignominious exit from the ERM in 1992 left the Conservative government, by then led by John Major, without a policy, and his chancellor, Norman Lamont, was replaced by Kenneth Clarke. Faced with a situation where the government's credibility in the markets had hit rock bottom, Major and Clarke were willing to consider a more independent role for the Bank and its governor, Eddie George. It was agreed that the government would set an inflation target, the Bank would publish an inflation forecast, and minutes of periodic meetings on interest rates between the chancellor and the governor would be published (Figure 2.10).[122] The process became known as the 'Ken and Eddie show' and proved to be a considerable success. The chancellor retained final control over Bank rate, but greater transparency encouraged prompt policy responses to deviations of prospective inflation from target. This radical change in British procedures was influenced by New Zealand's pioneering use, since 1989, of an inflation target and rate setting by

[121] N. Lawson, *The View from No. 11: Memoirs of a Tory Radical* (London: Bantam Press, 1992), pp. 783–803.
[122] C. A. E. Goodhart, 'The Bank of England over the Last 35 Years', Bankhistorisches Archiv, Zeitschrift zur Bankengeschichte, Beiheft 43, Welche Aufgaben muß eine Zentralbank wahrnehmen? Historische Erfahrungen und europäische Perspektiven. 15. Wissenschaftliches Kolloquium am 7 November 2002 auf Einladung "Geld und Währung" (Stuttgart: Franz Steiner Verlag, 2004), pp. 42–3.

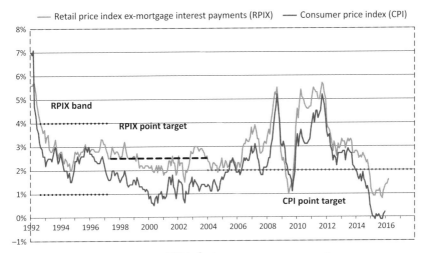

FIGURE 2.10 UK inflation targets, 1992–2016.
Source: Office of National Statistics (ONS), RP07, CPI12.

an independent central bank.[123] Other countries were to follow this example, Canada being an early adopter in 1991.[124] In 1997, the incoming Blair–Brown government retained the inflation targeting regime and developed the process further by appointing an independent Monetary Policy Committee (MPC) within the Bank, charged with making monthly interest rate decisions. In its first term, the New Labour government sought to distance itself from tax-and-spend policies and emphasised financial prudence, adopting a golden rule for public sector deficits over the cycle. Not everyone had become a monetarist, but counter-inflation policy was given pride of place.[125]

Michael Woodford characterised the use of interest rate policy to meet an inflation target as neo-Wicksellian – Knut Wicksell having argued, in the

---

[123] C. A. E. Goodhart (2004), p. 44; S. K. Howson, 'Money and Monetary Policy since 1945' in R. C. Floud and P. Johnson (eds) *The Cambridge Economic History of Modern Britain, Volume 3* (Cambridge: Cambridge University Press, 2004), p. 166.

[124] B. S. Bernanke, T. Laubach, F. S. Mishkin and A. Posen, *Inflation Targeting: Lessons from the International Experience* (Princeton, NJ: Princeton University Press, 1999), pp. 41–171.

[125] M. D. Woodford, *Interest and Prices: Foundations of a Theory of Monetary Policy* (Princeton, NJ: Princeton University Press, 2003), pp. 610–23; A. C. Hotson, 'The 1981 Budget and Its Impact on the Conduct of Economic Policy: Was It a Monetarist Revolution?' in D. J. Needham and A. C. Hotson (eds) *Expansionary Fiscal Contraction: The Thatcher Government's 1981 Budget in Perspective* (Cambridge: Cambridge University Press, 2014), p. 144.

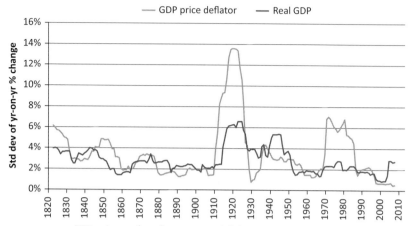

FIGURE 2.11 UK price and real output variability, 1822–2007.
Sources: S. N. Broadberry et al. (2011); S. Hills et al. (2010); ONS (2013)
(Reproduced with kind permission of Oxford University Press, see page xii).

late nineteenth century, that such a policy should be adopted as an alternative to the gold standard:

> The regulation of prices would constitute the prime purpose of bank rate, which would no longer be subject to the caprices of the production and consumption of gold or the demand for the circulation of coins.[126]

The neo-Wicksellian label did not stick, and instead the rationale for inflation targeting attracted the confusing label of New Keynesian, at least among saltwater academics – US Keynesians congregating in coastal universities.[127] Whatever its doctrinal provenance, inflation targeting proved to be strikingly successful at generating expectations about the future path of interest rates and exchange rates that helped to stabilise CPI-inflation and real output – a state of grace that became known as the Great Moderation (Figure 2.11).[128] Wicksell and his contemporary, Gustav Cassel, had envisaged that price stability would be achieved by stabilising the credit cycle, as Cassel put it:

> The problem of securing stability to the money scale [i.e. the price level] is essentially a question of the regulation of credit.[129]

[126] K. Wicksell, *Interest and Prices: A Study of the Causes Regulating Money*, English translation by R. F. Kahn (Jena: Gustav Fischer, 1898; London: Macmillan, 1936), p. 194.
[127] M. D. Woodford (2003), pp. 74–5; P. R. Krugman, *New York Times* (5 March 2012).
[128] J. B. Taylor, 'Discretion versus policy rules in practice', *Carnegie-Rochester Conference Series on Public Policy*, 39 (1993), pp. 195–214, 198–9, 209–10; M. A. King, 'Monetary policy: Practice ahead of theory', Mais Lecture, *BEQB*, 45, 2 (Summer 2005), pp. 226–36.
[129] K. G. Cassel, *The Nature and Necessity of Interest* (London: Macmillan, 1903), p. 162.

The problem for the neo-Wicksellians – *aka* the New Keynesians – was that this did not happen in the first decade of the twenty-first century. In a very different banking environment to that of Wicksell and Cassel, low CPI-inflation masked an unprecedented upturn in credit, continuing after the dotcom crash of 2000, and accelerating after 2004. Asset price inflation created higher collateral values against which to borrow, and the deregulated banks and building societies relied heavily on the wholesale market to fund their rapidly expanding mortgage books. Hedge funds and other investors were also able to leverage their balance sheets using sale-and-repurchase agreements (repos): selling assets spot, subject to a margin requirement, and agreeing to repurchase them at a fixed price in the future. The repo market allowed a much wider range of financial institutions to raise unprecedented amounts of collateralised credit, leveraging their balance sheets to such a degree that they became known as shadow banks.[130]

The wildly ambitious Northern Rock was the first to encounter wholesale funding problems, and this turned into a retail-account-holders' panic in the autumn of 2007 – the first of any significance since the First World War. The market started looking for the next weakest links in the chain, and wholesale lending lines to other mortgage lenders were shut down, forcing Alliance & Leicester, Bradford & Bingley and Britannia to go cap in hand to the Bank for emergency funding.[131] It would have been instructive to see how this crisis played itself out without a further shock, but it was overshadowed by the collapse of Lehman Brothers in September 2008. Paralysis followed in the interbank and repo markets, and an even more dramatic credit crunch ensued. Santander acquired Alliance & Leicester in 2008, and the business of Bradford & Bingley in 2010. LTSB merged with HBOS, forming the Lloyds Banking Group (LBG).[132] Bailouts for RBS and LBG, among others, left the government heavily indebted, and the downturn in the credit cycle was followed by a sustained downturn in the trade cycle. The Great Moderation was replaced by the age of austerity with very little warning.[133]

---

[130] J. Greenwood, 'US corporate and household balance sheet update based on flow of funds data for 2010 Q2' (Invesco, 5 October 2010); J. Greenwood, 'UK: Can shadow banking help explain booms & busts?' (Invesco, 19 July, 2013); Financial Stability Board, 'Global Shadow Banking Monitoring Report 2015' (12 November 2015).

[131] Bank of England, *Annual Report* (2010), p. 17; *BEQB* (Q2 2010), p. 100.

[132] I. Fallon (2015), pp. 257–76.

[133] O. J. Blanchard, D. H. Romer, A. M. Spence and J. E. Stiglitz, *In the Wake of the Crisis* (Cambridge, MA, and London: MIT Press with the International Monetary Fund, 2012), pp. 7–13, 31–42; N. H. Dimsdale and A. C. Hotson (2014), pp. 45–6.

The credit crunch of 2008 did reignite a debate about the role of banks as risk takers, and the effectiveness of prudential regulation. Immediately after the panic, there was a flurry of interest in de-risked banks that did not rely on fine judgements about levels of capital required to absorb losses on risky assets. Super-safe banks could simply take people's deposits, and hold them in short-dated government paper – TBs and short dated BGS – a modern-day version of the trustee savings banks and Gladstone's Post Office Savings Bank (POSB). A US version of safe banking was suggested by Laurence Kotlikoff, among others, who argued that traditional bank deposits should be replaced with limited purpose banks (LPBs), akin to money market mutual funds invested in low-risk, short-term assets. This might include short-term paper issued – or guaranteed by – the federal government, states, and municipalities, as well as commercial paper (CP) issued by well-rated major companies. The unit prices of these money funds would be adjusted to reflect their underlying net asset values, and would not therefore be capital-certain, but their volatility would normally be low. Money funds would usually be realisable at short notice, but restrictions could be imposed to limit exceptional outflows, allowing time to sell assets in an orderly manner. A range of money funds could offer a graded scale of return, capital security and liquidity.[134]

In the end, the proposal for de-risking the banks did not gain much traction because politicians and policymakers became as concerned about reviving bank lending as they were about the safety of deposits. Fiscally constrained governments had to place greater reliance on bank credit to stimulate the economy, and there were fears that the banks' continued unwillingness to lend would prolong the downturn.[135] The need to revive credit led policymakers to conclude that deposit funding should be sustained – rather than diminished – and, to do this, depositors had to be reassured that their money was safe. This meant that state-sponsored deposit insurance – the FSCS in the United Kingdom and the Federal Deposit Insurance Corporation (FDIC) in the United States – should

---

[134] L. J. Kotlikoff, *Jimmy Stewart Is Dead: Ending the World's Ongoing Financial Plague with Limited Purpose Banking* (Hoboken, NJ: John Wiley & Sons, 2010), pp. 123–54; J. Kay, 'Narrow Banking: The Reform of Banking Regulation' (2009), p. 4; B. Granville, *Remembering Inflation* (Princeton, NJ, and Oxford: Princeton University Press, 2013), pp. 179–82.

[135] C. A. E. Goodhart, *The Regulatory Response to the Financial Crisis* (Cheltenham and Northampton, MA: Edward Elgar, 2010), pp. 26–9, 102–7; M. Wolf, *The Shifts and the Shocks: What We've Learned – and Have Still to Learn – from the Financial Crisis* (London: Allen Lane, 2014), pp. 200–2.

remain in place, and in some cases coverage should be extended.[136] It was accepted that deposit insurance would allow banks to enjoy lower funding costs, and the quid pro quo for this state subsidy should be prudential regulation, notably capital requirements, to protect the taxpayer as far as possible from bank losses.[137]

A plethora of commissions and review bodies developed these pragmatic lines of argument into a plan, notwithstanding some haziness about the underlying model of money and credit creation.[138] The emergent transnational consensus can be summarised as follows:

1 Banks should accept risk, and the idea of promoting ultra-low-risk savings banks was rejected.[139]

2 It was taken for granted that the neoliberal model for banks' funding and lending should be retained, and that competition in banking would promote wider economic growth.[140]

3 At the same time, it was accepted that retail deposits should be virtually risk free, requiring insurance by nation states. It was recognised that uninsured deposits were destabilising in a crisis, and penalising ordinary depositors was politically difficult.[141]

4 Nation states therefore had to bear some residual risk for the banking system, but to protect state finances, banks should be required to hold sufficient capital to absorb likely losses. In this regard, the BCBS's risk-capital approach should be retained and developed, including value-at-risk (VaR) methodologies.[142]

5 The case for more capital and less leverage led to measures going beyond standards set out in Basel III, including a leverage ratio (without risk weights), more exacting stress tests, and enhanced capital requirements for systemically important financial institutions (SIFIs).[143]

---

[136] P. Jackson (1996), p. 39.

[137] Financial Services Authority, *The Turner Review: a Regulatory Response to the Global Banking Crisis* (March 2009), pp. 53–4; X. Freixas and J-C. Rochet, *Microeconomics of Banking* (Cambridge, MA: MIT Press, 2nd edn, 2008), pp. 306–28.

[138] F. Martin, *Money: The Unauthorised Biography* (London: Bodley Head, Random House, 2013), pp. 248–9.

[139] Sir John Vickers, *Interim Report: Consultation on Reform Options*, Independent Commission on Banking (12 April 2011), pp. 97–9; M. Wolf (2014), pp. 209–13.

[140] Vickers interim report (April 2011), pp. 119–31.

[141] Vickers interim report (April 2011), p. 177.

[142] Vickers interim report (April 2011), pp. 52, 55.

[143] D. Miles, J. Yang and G. Marcheggiano, 'Optimal Bank Capital', External MPC Unit, Discussion Paper, 31 (January 2011); J. Vickers, *Financial Times* (8 Sept 2013); Sir

6 Various proposals were advanced for the compartmentalisation of large financial groups. Multi-local operations and different types of business were to be held in standalone subsidiaries, each with its own dedicated capital. This was expected to mitigate the too-big-to-fail problem.

7 In the United States, the Volcker rule was intended to separate proprietary trading from deposit-taking banks.[144]

8 In the United Kingdom, the Vickers proposals for the ring-fencing of retail banks were accepted with a view to protecting them from the risks of investment banking.[145] Similar proposals were developed in the Liikanen report for the EU as a whole.[146]

9 Living wills and resolution protocols were prepared to assist crisis management and allow banks to be run-off without threatening the system as a whole.[147]

10 Macro-prudential toolkits were developed in the hope that regulators would be able to moderate credit fluctuations. The measures to do this included the possibility of setting limits on LTV ratios, or varying them over the cycle.[148]

11 Reform of banks' governance and remuneration structures were meant to limit operational risks and dysfunctional risk taking.[149]

12 Other issues were reviewed in the light of experience, including triggers for hybrid bonds to absorb losses, and collateral required for official market assistance. For the most part, these were regarded as technicalities.[150]

Despite the long list, the post-2008 prudential consensus did not amount to a counter-revolution ushering in a reversion to the well-tried model that gave London's international banking market its century of stability from the 1870s until 1971. Despite superficial similarities, the

John Vickers, *Final Report of the Independent Commission on Banking* (12 September 2011), pp. 98–100.

[144] Volcker, Dodd-Frank Act, 2010; Vickers (April 2011), pp. 92–3.

[145] Vickers interim report (April 2011), pp. 80–1; Vickers final report (September 2011), pp. 35–77.

[146] E. A. Liikanen, *High-level Expert Group on Reforming the Structure of the EU Banking Sector*, Final Report, Brussels (2 October 2012), pp. 83–7, 94–103.

[147] Vickers interim report (April 2011), p. 53–4.

[148] Vickers interim report (April 2011), p. 51; Financial Services Authority, *Turner Review* (March 2009), p. 111.

[149] Sir David A. Walker *A Review of Corporate Governance in UK Banks and Other Financial Industry Entities: Final Recommendations* (26 November 2009), pp. 106–26.

[150] Vickers interim report (April 2011), pp. 73–4; J. Bulow, J. Goldfield and P. Klemperer, Vox EU (29 August 2013).

Vickers proposals were not about recreating pre-1971 banking structures. No consideration was given to the possibility of curbing liability management, and the report sidestepped any assessment of money market issues.[151] Although the ring-fenced banks are called retail banks, they provide money transmission and plain vanilla lending facilities to major corporates, as well as personal customers and small businesses. As an amalgam of a clearing bank and a building society, they have a reassuringly familiar feel to them, but they lack the traditional protections that formed part of the pre-1971 regime.[152]

It is surprising that greater consideration was not given to the historical role of restrictions on liability management, given the trail of destruction that followed their removal. In Britain, CCC was followed by the secondary banking crisis in the first half of the 1970s. Petrodollar recycling through the Euromarkets was followed by the Latin American debt crisis, starting with the Mexican debt moratorium in 1982. This left at least one London clearer technically insolvent, alongside a number of New York money-center banks.[153] Liability management in the domestic US market allowed a number of ambitious domestic banks to grow rapidly, in an attempt to overhaul the troubled New York money-center banks. Some of the newcomers went bust spectacularly in the face of an unexpectedly weak oil price: Penn Square in 1982, Continental Illinois in 1984, and First City Bancorp of Houston in 1989.[154]

Following the secondary banking crisis of the early 1970s, the UK authorities started down the rocky road of bailing out a motley assortment of failing institutions: Johnson Matthey Bank (JMB) in 1984, and various mortgage lenders, including National Mortgage Bank (NMB), in the early 1990s. JMB relied on wholesale funding and Bank officials were preoccupied with the effect of bankruptcy on the wider market. In the midst of the Latin American debt crisis, they were concerned about its effect on a fragile interbank market, and the risk of contagion affecting the clearers. NMB gave rise to similar worries for the wholesale market, although the saving of lost souls was becoming a bit of a habit

---

[151] Vickers interim report (April 2011), p. 56, para 3.20.
[152] Vickers interim report (April 2011), p. 191.
[153] D. Rogers (1999), p. 44; I. Fallon (2015), p. 12.
[154] T. Ogden, 'An Analysis of Bank of England Discount and Advance Behaviour, 1870–1914', in J. Foreman-Peck (ed.) *New Perspectives in the Late-Victorian Economy: Essays in Quantitative Economic History 1860–1914* (Cambridge: Cambridge University Press, 1991), p. 306; Federal Deposit Insurance Corporation, *History of the 80s*, Vol. I: *An Examination of the Banking Crises of the 1980s and Early 1990s* (FDIC, 1997), chapter 7.

at the Bank. The Bank of Credit and Commerce International (BCCI) was allowed to fail in 1991, but it was not headquartered in the United Kingdom, and the UK authorities were not meant to be the primary decision makers regarding its fate. Ironically, the much more venerable institution Baring's was allowed to fail. As an accepting house, it had been saved first time round in 1890, but by 1995 market assistance was provided by gilt repos, rather than by eligible bills, and latter-day accepting houses were no longer sacrosanct.[155]

A key casualty of the mortgage market revolution was Gilbart's ruling against long-term loans: 'It is contrary to all sound principles of banking for a banker to advance money in the form of permanent loans'.[156] The Victorian principle – sustained by the traditional clearing banks – was that short-term deposits should be matched by reasonably short-term assets.[157] This meant the clearers had the flexibility to contract their balance sheets, if they faced an outflow of short-term deposits, or 'in case of any sudden contraction of banking capital.'[158] As Walter Leaf, put it:

> The banker deals in 'short money' on both sides. He is essentially a broker whose business is to link up money needing temporary investment with borrowers needing temporary loans.[159]

It was taken for granted that clearing banks should not tolerate significant maturity mismatching in their balance sheets. Wilfred King, author of the main interwar book on London's discount market, declaimed the 'cardinal principle that to lend "long" one must also borrow "long."'[160] In the absence of longer-term funding, he suggested that it was the banker's duty to hold 'virtually all his assets in liquid form, and part of them in highly liquid form.'[161] In his textbook, Sykes made the same point in various contexts, noting, 'The province of the banker is to tide over temporary lack of ready money, not to provide capital on which the customer carries on his business.'[162] These views were still common currency among practitioners in the 1960s and 1970s, borrowing short and lending long being regarded as a 'classic error'.[163]

---

[155] P. Jackson (1996), p. 40–1; F. H. Capie (2014), pp. 15–19.
[156] J. W. Gilbart (1907), p. 149.
[157] M. Collins (1988, 1990), p. 583.
[158] J. W. Gilbart (1907), p. 149.
[159] W. Leaf (1943), p. 97; cited in A. Offer (2014), p. 160.
[160] W. T. C. King (1936), p. 237.
[161] W. T. C. King (1936), pp. 183–4.
[162] E. Sykes (1947), p. 150.
[163] C. Gordon (1993), p. 92.

This approach to balance sheet structure was phased out with the reduction of the reserve ratio in 1971, and its abolition in 1981, followed by the advent of mortgage lending by banks from the early 1980s.[164] In contrast with their predecessors, the deregulated clearing banks became property-related lenders, requiring a heroic degree of mismatch between short-term deposits and long-term loans.[165] Money in the form of bank deposits was predominantly backed by multi-year loans secured on real property, and shadow banks funded investment assets with relatively short-term repos, relying on their ability to roll them over. A few voices crying in the wilderness suggested that banks should follow the nineteenth-century principle of holding short-maturity assets to match their quick liabilities – but this was generally regarded as a backward step.[166] The populist appeal of easy home finance helped to fashion an argument that banks' long-term property lending could be funded short term – with heroic levels of mismatch – if sufficient capital were held to cover the risks. As a penance, macro-prudential measures were supposed to be kept at the ready should property prices get out of hand.[167]

The sea change in thinking about maturity mismatching was remarkable. It was given a more positive sounding name – maturity transformation – and it was now said to be a key component of socially useful banking. As the final report of the Vickers commission put it:

Banks are able to fund illiquid assets with short-term, liquid liabilities ... The production of liquidity in this fashion is socially valuable because it allows savers to withdraw funds when they want, rather than when the investments they ultimately fund pay off (Diamond and Dybvig (1983)).[168]

The case for maturity transformation had been developed in the 1980s by Douglas Diamond, a Chicago economist, and Philip Dybvig, among others. The Vickers commission endorsed the Diamond–Dybvig (DD) view of banking, and cited its *locus classicus* – an article published by

[164] F. H. Capie (2010), p. 507.

[165] A. C. Hotson, 'The 1981 Budget and Its Impact on the Conduct of Economic Policy: Was It a Monetarist Revolution?' in D. J. Needham and A. C. Hotson (eds) *Expansionary Fiscal Contraction: The Thatcher Government's 1981 Budget in Perspective* (Cambridge: Cambridge University Press, 2014), pp. 140–1.

[166] Notably, A. Offer (2014), p. 159; F. Martin, *Money: The Unauthorised Biography* (London: Bodley Head, Random House, 2013), p. 256 (argued that 'liquidity transformation is ... a euphemism').

[167] C. W. Calomiris and S. H. Haber (2014), pp. 203–55; M. Wolf (2014), pp. 252–6.

[168] Vickers final report (September 2011), A3.26, p. 276; see also Financial Services Authority, *Turner Review* (March 2009), p. 21.

the two economists in 1983.[169] DD suggested that callable deposits provided bank customers with liquidity in a world where it was not practical to write (Arrow–Debreu-style) insurance policies offering payoffs covering a wide range of spending contingencies.[170] To use Keynes's terminology, we hold precautionary balances to cover uncertain spending requirements that are not covered by insurance.[171] In contrast, production benefits from illiquid investment, giving rise to a mismatch between the needs of households and those of firms. If banks seek to intermediate between the two – accepting short-term deposits and using them to lend long term – the liquidity risk will be borne by the banks.

DD suggested that the problem of maturity mismatching could be overcome, if depositors' need for cash were asynchronous, allowing banks to pool withdrawal risk. This would allow the economy to achieve a superior asset allocation in which liquid deposits funded the acquisition of illiquid assets. DD noted that callable deposits were, nevertheless, a fragile form of funding and bank runs could occur, if depositors became fearful of others making pre-emptive withdrawals. They suggested that this risk could be mitigated by the provision of deposit insurance, which might be best provided by the state. Routine market assistance and LOLR facilities could be viewed as additional forms of liquidity insurance provided by central banks. DD accepted that the availability of liquidity insurance could encourage banks to accept more risk, giving rise to moral hazard problems. This might provide a rationale for bank regulation, for example, minimum standards of capital adequacy.[172]

The early DD literature characterised bank lending as a form of relationship-based funding for SMEs, making it sound more like private equity (PE) investment than commercial bank lending.[173] Loan originators were said to have private knowledge about the businesses of their borrowers and were best placed to recover their loans, making it difficult

---

[169] D. W. Diamond and P. H. Dybvig, 'Bank runs, deposit insurance, and liquidity', *Journal of Political Economy*, 91 (3) (1983), pp. 401–19; reprinted in *FRB of Minneapolis Quarterly Review*, 24, no. 1 (Winter 2000), pp. 14–23.

[170] D. W. Diamond, 'Banks and liquidity creation: A simple exposition of the Diamond–Dybvig model', *FRB of Richmond Economic Quarterly*, 93, no. 2 (Spring, 2007), p. 193.

[171] J. M. Keynes, *The General Theory of Employment Interest and Money*, 1st edn, 1936, reprinted in *The Collected Writings of John Maynard Keynes* (London and Basingstoke: Macmillan and Cambridge University Press, Royal Economic Society edn, 1973), VII, p. 170.

[172] D. W. Diamond and P. H. Dybvig (Winter 2000), p. 22; Tucker (Autumn 2004), p. 360.

[173] D. W. Diamond and P. H. Dybvig (Winter 2000), p. 16.

to sell them in a secondary market.[174] This description of bank lending did not reflect what was happening in Anglophone banking markets at the time. In London, the clearers' traditional company lending – via bills and advances – was rapidly being eclipsed by home finance and consumer credit. Larger companies were rejecting the practice of relying on one banking relationship, and moving to one in which they used multiple banks – a horses-for-courses approach. Personalised lending with decisions made in branches was being replaced by centralised lending using automated underwriting techniques, such as credit scoring. Most significantly, the emergence of securitisation meant that loan originators did not necessarily have to have direct access to funding provided by a large balance sheet. Newly originated mortgage loans – or securitised proxies of them – could be sold to better funded institutions, and non-bank investors. Lowell Bryan went so far as to suggest that this would allow the break-up of vertically integrated banks into their constituent parts: brokers for originating loans, factory-like operations for underwriting and administering loans, credit enhancement provided by insurers, and financing by fund managers.[175]

Bryan's model with its functional specialists was presented as a radical departure, but it had parallels with London's traditional clearing bank model with its demarcations among accepting houses providing bill underwriting and credit enhancement, discount houses providing liquidity, and clearers providing funding from customer deposits. The Bryan and clearing bank models were not the same, but they shared a common approach in which specialist firms operated as intermediaries in the money and credit markets. The glue that had kept the clearing bank model together was an orderly money market that maintained flows among its constituent parts, even in a crisis. The same could not be said of the securitised credit market of the post-1980s era which quickly fell apart during the 2007–8 crisis. One response to this problem would have been to recreate an orderly money market using an updated version of prime bank bills (PBBs), and/or a modern equivalent – perhaps prime asset-backed securities (ABS) and prime collateralised debt obligations (CDOs). Other possible policies, drawn from nineteenth-century experience, would have

174 D. W. Diamond, 'Financial intermediation and delegated monitoring', *Review of Economic Studies*, 51 (July 1984), pp. 393–414; D. W. Diamond and R. Rajan, 'Liquidity risk, liquidity creation and financial fragility: A theory of banking', *Journal of Political Economy*, 109, no. 2 (April 2001), pp. 290–1; 322–3.

175 L. L. Bryan, *Breaking Up the Bank: Rethinking an Industry under Siege* (Homewood, IL: Irwin, 1988), pp. 177–87.

been to restrict bank holdings to relatively short-term assets, or to restrict liability management, but none of these options caught the eye of the reformers.

Instead, the DD theory of banking – the original model and its variants and successors – enjoyed a revival, offering a reassuring rationalisation of the deregulated banking model. Significant maturity mismatching was accepted as part of modern banking life, and its management was seen to depend on reassuring depositors with deposit insurance and adequate capital.[176] It was argued that Bagehot's LOLR policy had been the main factor contributing to London's century of stability, and that deposit insurance – in its widest sense – was the modern equivalent of Bagehot's successful policy.[177] Chapter 4 of this study will seek to demonstrate that there was more to London's century of stability than Bagehot's LOLR policy. Victorian bankers addressed the risk of maturity mismatching by the simple expedient of excluding long-maturity assets (except undated BGS in the form of Consols) from prudently run banks' balance sheets. In addition, they restricted banks' ability to liability manage, and encouraged them to hold money market instruments that retained their liquidity at times of stress.

Chapter 5 examines the dismantling of London's stability regime, starting in 1971 with the discarding of restrictions on liability management. This watered down the resilience of the money market in a crisis, and neutered the effectiveness of the interest rate weapon as a means of regulating the credit cycle. Since the 1980s, the banks have been allowed to hold longer-term assets with collateral values that have free rein – a matter for the neoliberal market. The received wisdom is that state deposit insurance will reassure the public, and capital requirements will protect the state – and thence, the taxpayer.[178] Another possibility would be to stabilise the collateral values that threaten our monetary order. Any form of money worthy of the name combines a monetary instrument with a prescribed value and counterpart assets that support its value. Precious metal coins enjoy high visibility collateralisation, and bank monies have

[176] D. W. Diamond and R. Rajan, 'Liquidity Risk, Liquidity Creation and Financial Fragility: A Theory of Banking', *Journal of Political Economy*, 109, no. 2 (April 2001), pp. 317–20; D. W. Diamond (Spring 2007), p. 195–9; M. Schularick and A. M. Taylor 'Credit booms gone bust: Monetary policy, leverage cycles, and financial crises, 1870–2008', *American Economic Review*, 102, no. 2 (2012), p. 1041.

[177] P. M. W. Tucker (Autumn 2004), p. 360; Vickers final report (September 2014), A3.26, p. 276.

[178] M. Wolf (2014), pp. 223–34, 241–52, 349.

various forms of asset backing. Historically, the key – for both coins and paper credit – has been to find ways and means of keeping the value of the asset counterparts of money aligned with its prescribed value. We did this for guineas in the eighteenth century, and this is the subject of Chapter 3. The application of analogous approaches in more modern contexts is considered in Chapters 6 and 7.

The general public sense that we are currently being offered a thin reed with which to protect ourselves from financial oblivion, and the experts cannot quite broaden their horizons beyond the narrow confines of balance sheet ratios. There is a reason for the experts' tunnel vision, and it is not hard to find. Modern prudential thinking treats banks as being no different from other portfolio managers, and the fact that their debt is used as currency is incidental. There appears to be no reason for treating banks differently from other sectors and, if we are deregulating energy, telecoms, and transport, why not banking? Interestingly, Bagehot struggled with the same problem. Why should classical liberals believe in free trade and not free banking? Bagehot accepted the intellectual case for competitive banking, but he and everyone else in positions of responsibility agreed that a return to the freewheeling banks of the mid-nineteenth century was just not on.[179] The policy choice was so obvious that nobody bothered to examine the intellectual case for treating banks differently.[180] Unfortunately, this has left us with a neoliberal presumption that banking is indistinguishable from other sectors. This issue needs to be confronted, and this is what we shall aim to do in subsequent chapters.

[179] L. S. Pressnell, *Country Banking in the Industrial Revolution* (Oxford: Oxford University Press, 1956), pp. 501–10; R. S. Sayers, *Central Banking after Bagehot* (Oxford: Clarendon Press, 1957), p. 2.

[180] W. Bagehot (3rd edn, 1873), pp. 67–74, 101–9, 329–30; R. S. Sayers, *Central Banking after Bagehot* (1957), p. 3, fn. 1.

3

Minted Currency and the Bullion Market

The problem of wayward collateral values destabilising credit – and thence money – is not a new one. Bullion was used to collateralise minted coins, and it served as a reserve asset supporting the Bank's monetary liabilities. Variations in gold and silver prices could destabilise these monies, just as real estate prices can destabilise modern ones. The problem of bullion price volatility became particularly severe during the great currency crisis of 1695, and a series of measures was subsequently developed in response to the crisis.[1] Mechanisms for anchoring the price of gold were devised, initially by Sir Isaac Newton in his capacity as master of the Mint, and later by a group of currency reformers led by Sir Charles Jenkinson, first earl of Liverpool.[2] The noble lord drew a range of experts into his circle, including Sir Joseph Banks, and his *Treatise on the Coins of the Realm* became a recognised work in the field.[3] His son, the second earl, became prime minister after the Napoleonic wars and presided over the completion of the reforms.[4]

One of the more troublesome aspects of minted currencies was the need to organise a recoinage at least once a generation. Circulating coins suffered from wear and tear leaving them more and more underweight,

---

[1] Sir John H. M. Craig, *The Mint: A History of the London Mint from AD 287 to 1948* (Cambridge: Cambridge University Press, 1953), pp. 184–8.
[2] M-T. Boyer-Xambeu, G. Deleplace and L. Gillard, 'Régimes monétaires, points d'or et "serpent bimétallique" de 1770 à 1870', *Revue Économique*, 45, no. 5 (1994), pp. 1140–1, 1150 fn. 1.
[3] Sir Charles Jenkinson, first earl of Liverpool, *A Treatise on the Coins of the Realm: In a Letter to the King* (Oxford: Oxford University Press for Cadell & Davies, 1805; Bank of England edn, 1880).
[4] G. P. Dyer and P. P Gaspar, 'Reform, the New Technology and Tower Hill, 1700–1966', chapter 4 in C. E. Challis (ed.) *A New History of the Royal Mint* (Cambridge: Cambridge University Press, 1992), pp. 451–3.

		Nominal value per coin					Weight	Fineness			
Stylized recoinage: Assume 100 silver coins/pieces have been in circulation for some decades and are 25 per cent under-weight. Before the exchange terms of the recoinage are announced, each coin has a nominal value of 1 d, see column (A).	before the recoinage is announced	presented for recoinage	received from recoinage	Number of coins received from recoinage	Total nominal value of coins received	Weight per new piece	Per cent weight of silver to total weight per new piece	Exchequer purchase of additional silver per new piece	Total weight of silver in new pieces received	Mint price†
	(A)	(B)	(C)	(D)	(E) =(C)*(D)	(F)	(G)	(H)	(I) =(D)*(F) *(G)	(J) =(E)/(I)
	d/piece	d/piece	d/piece	no.	d	wt/piece	%	wt/piece	Total wt	d/wt
Exchange options:										
1. Call down underweight old coins	1.00	0.75	1.00	75	75	1.00	100%	0.00	75	1.00
2. Devalue new coins	1.00	1.00	1.00	100	100	0.75	100%	0.00	75	1.33
3. Debase new coins	1.00	1.00	1.00	100	100	1.00	75%	0.00	75	1.33
4. Raise denomination of new coins	1.00	1.00	1.33	75	100	1.00	100%	0.00	75	1.33
5. Exchequer subsidy of shortfall	1.00	1.00	1.00	100	100	1.00	100%	0.25§	100	1.00

FIGURE 3.1 Recoinage options – illustrative example.
Source: Author's table.
† nominal value of new coins offered by the Mint per unit weight of silver bullion delivered.
§ the price of bullion is assumed to remain constant at 1 d per unit weight of silver.

even without the problem of clipping. The exchange of old coins for new ones (in mint condition) had to allow for a shortfall of metal, and there were five ways of doing this (Figure 3.1):

- New coins could be minted with the same specification as the old ones, but the nominal value of the old coins could be *called down* to reflect their lower weight *(option 1)*. In effect, a stash of old coins could be exchanged for new ones on a weight-for-weight basis. As a result, the nominal value of the new coins received would be lower than the nominal value of the old coins delivered before they were called down.
- Old coins of given nominal value could be exchanged for new coins at par, but the shortfall of metal could be accommodated by:
  - reducing the weight of the new coins *(devaluation – option 2)*, or
  - reducing their fineness *(debasement – option 3)*, or
  - raising their denomination *(raising, or crying up the coin – option 4)*.
  - exchange at par, and the shortfall made up with an *Exchequer subsidy* to purchase additional metal *(option 5)*.[5]

The history of the English Mint since the twelfth century can be summarised fairly succinctly with reference to these five options. In the early Plantagenet period, silver coins with a nominal value of one penny (1 d) weighed roughly one pennyweight (1 dwt) in mint condition. Recoinages

5 A. Redish, 'The evolution of the gold standard in England', *Journal of Economic History*, 50, no. 4 (December 1990), p. 795.

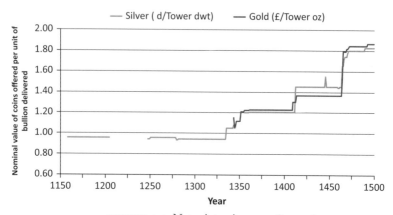

FIGURE 3.2 Net mint prices, 1158–1526.
Source: Compiled mint price data set out in Tables 1 to 7.

were undertaken using *option (1)*, keeping the weight, fineness and denomination of silver coins broadly the same. The problem of under-weight coins was solved by exchanging them for fewer pieces, giving a smaller total nominal value of full-weight coins. The early Plantagenet penny remained of fixed weight and fineness for two centuries, and pro-vided the classic numéraire beloved of microeconomists – roughly 1 dwt of sterling silver was worth 1 d of value, and all other goods could be priced with reference to that unit of account.

One might ask why anyone would wish to move away from such a straightforward standard of value, but the Privy Council adopted *option (2)* during the late Plantagenet period – the fineness and denomination of coins were maintained, but the coinage was periodically devalued, i.e. reduced in weight. At recoinages, old coins were exchanged for new ones on a one-for-one basis (in nominal terms), but the new coins weighed less than their mint-condition forebears. Gold coins were introduced in the fourteenth century and were devalued by similar amounts (Figure 3.2). This meant the mint price of gold and silver – the nominal value of coins offered per unit weight of bullion delivered – was periodically raised, doubling in the two centuries between 1300 and 1500 (Tables A.1, A.5 and A.7).[6] A pending devaluation could give rise to problematic incentives, for example, the hoarding of full-weight coins, but these coins would cease to be current after an exchange period, and would have to be exported to foreign mints, or illicitly melted

---

[6] Sir A. E. Feavearyear (ed.) E. Victor Morgan, *The Pound Sterling: A History of English Money* (Oxford: Oxford University Press, 2nd edn, 1963), pp. 16–20; N. J. Mayhew, *Sterling: The History of a Currency* (New York: Wiley, 2000), pp. 28–33.

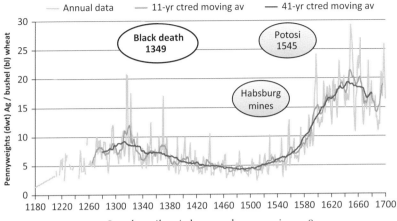

FIGURE 3.3 London silver/wheat exchange ratio, 1180–1700.
Sources: G. Clark (2004); G. Clark and P. Lindert (2006).

down to realise their value. These difficulties could be contained if recoinages took place in a timely manner, before the coin stock became overly worn, in which case only a modest devaluation would be required.[7]

The need for periodic devaluations – their timing and size – could be judged partly by the deterioration of coins in circulation, but also by the reduced throughput of coins at the Mint. In the late Plantagenet period, the price of silver tended to rise as a result of increased demand – consequent upon economic growth – and limited supply, there being insufficient discoveries of new reserves for mining (Figure 3.3). If the market price of silver exceeded its mint price, there was no incentive to deliver bars and specie to the Mint, in which case production could fall, eventually leading to a scarcity of coin.[8] In these circumstances, devaluation – and its corollary, an increase in the mint price – needed to be sufficient to close the gap between the mint price and market prices, but not so great as to elicit price rises of staple commodities, notably grains. As it happens, the measured devaluations of the late Plantagenet period did not disturb the long-run stability of grain prices in the fourteenth and fifteenth centuries, notwithstanding sharp year-to-year fluctuations depending on the abundance of the harvest.[9] This is not to suggest that mint price policy was set with

[7] A. E. Feavearyear (1963), pp. 146–7.
[8] A. Redish, *Bimetallism: An Economic and Historical Analysis* (Cambridge: Cambridge University Press, 2000), p. 9.
[9] M. Casson and C. Casson, 'Modelling the Medieval Economy: Money, Prices and Income in England, 1263–1520' in M. Allen and D'M. Coffman (eds) *Money, Prices and Wages: Essays in Honour of Professor Nicholas Mayhew* (Basingstoke: Palgrave Macmillan, 2015), p. 57–8.

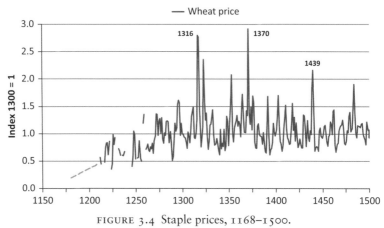

FIGURE 3.4 Staple prices, 1168–1500.
Sources: P. D. A. Harvey (1973); G. Clark and P. Lindert (2006).

reference to long-term prices: indeed, policy was asymmetric in the sense that a chronic paucity of minting did eventually elicit higher mint prices, but mint prices were not lowered in response to plentiful minting and rising staple prices – as experienced in the thirteenth and sixteenth centuries (Figures 3.2 to 3.4). The currency system therefore avoided severe deflation, but bullion discoveries could give rise to inflationary shocks.

The step devaluations of the late Plantagenet era were brought to a close by the notorious Tudor debasement (and devaluation) of 1542–52, when the royal authorities initiated a dramatic rise in the mint price – motivated by a desire to raise seigniorage – dramatically reducing the weight and fineness of the currency.[10] Sound money was restored in England during the reign of Elizabeth I, with coins of traditional fineness and of much greater weight than those issued at the height of the debasement (Tables A.2, A.3 and A.7). Even so, mint prices at the start of the seventeenth century were still three times higher than their base level in the mid-fourteenth century (Figure 3.5). Thereafter, the mint price of silver was kept broadly constant at 5 s 2 d per troy ounce (ozt), and the mint price of gold was raised periodically, keeping it in line with market prices (Tables A.4 and A.6). The upward trend in gold prices was reflected in the House of Stuart's gold piece, the unite: first issued in 1604, its denomination was raised in 1612; it was devalued in 1623, and its

---

[10] P. Spufford, 'Debasement of the Coinage and Its Effects on Exchange Rates and the Economy: In England in the 1540s, and in the Burgundian–Habsburg Netherlands in the 1480s' in J. H. A. Munro (ed.) *Money in the Pre-Industrial World: Bullion, Debasements and Coin Substitutes* (London: Pickering & Chatto, 2012), 2012, pp. 63–8.

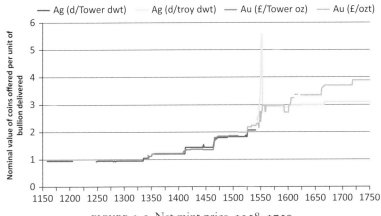

FIGURE 3.5 Net mint price, 1158–1750.
Source: Compiled mint price data set out in Tables 1 to 7.

denomination was raised again in 1661. The guinea supplanted the unite in 1663, raising the mint price because the new coin's lower weight more than offset its lower denomination. The abolition of mint charges in 1666 had the effect of raising mint prices marginally. More significantly, it was decided that the tender value of the guinea should be allowed to vary above its nominal value of £1, effectively allowing the market to raise the exchange value of the guinea still further (Tables A.6 and A.7).[11]

The Privy Council's willingness to accommodate the rising price of gold, but not that of silver (since Elizabeth's restoration of sound English money), leads us to the Locke–Lowndes debate over the correct policy response to the currency crisis of 1695. William Lowndes, secretary to His Majesty's Treasury commissioners, argued that it was appropriate to respond to a chronic scarcity of silver coins by raising their mint prices in line with market prices. He drew a distinction between the late Plantagenet devaluations, which helped to stabilise the currency without giving rise to price rises of ordinary commodities, and the Tudor debasement, which proved to be inflationary and destructive of trade.[12] Whereas the late Plantagenet devaluations had been modest and publicly announced, the scale of the Tudor debasement was unprecedented and involved covert reductions in the fineness of the currency.[13]

---

[11] C. E. Challis (ed.) *A New History of the Royal Mint* (Cambridge: Cambridge University Press, 1992), pp. 338, 343–51, 745; A. E. Feavearyear (1963), p. 97.

[12] W. Lowndes, *A Report Containing an Essay for the Amendment of the Silver Coins* (London: Charles Bill, 1695), pp. 3, 56; A. E. Feavearyear, 1963, pp. 43–5; N. J. Mayhew (2000), p. 98.

[13] M-H. Li, *The Great Recoinage of 1696 to 1699* (London: Weidenfeld & Nicolson, 1963), p. 95.

John Locke disputed Lowndes's advice and noted that the mint price of
silver had remained broadly fixed since Elizabeth's reign (Figure 3.5). Locke
argued that all mint price rises – be they implemented by way of a devaluation, a debasement, or a raising of the coin – were a form of royal expro-
priation, the Tudor one being an extreme example of despotic government.
He pointed out that the revolution of 1688 had put the rights of property
beyond royal prerogative, and that the silver standard should remain inviolate. Locke combined these Whiggish political objectives with the notion
that the value of minted coins should reflect their intrinsic value. He suggested that a silver devaluation (or equivalent forms of recoinage) would
inevitably lead to inflation, and the unwinding of any initial benefit resulting from devaluation – although this did not happen in the late Plantagenet
period.[14] In any event, Locke's stand against silver devaluation won the day
on political grounds, supported by a priori reasoning. His metallist view of
money was sustained by monetary theorists, including Sir James Steuart in
the eighteenth century and Stanley Jevons in the nineteenth century.[15]

The metallist model of minted money continues to be influential, and
modern economists tend to treat minted currencies as a form of commodity money.[16] According to this view, a mint's stamp provides assurance about the weight and fineness of coins' metallic content, and their
exchange ratios with other goods depend on their intrinsic value – that
is to say, their collateral value.[17] The tender (or exchange) value of the
English guinea varied in the run-up to the currency crisis of 1695, providing a good example of a metallist coin – circulating at a price equal
to, or above, its nominal value of 20 shillings (s), reflective of its intrinsic
value. Its price was reported regularly in gazettes, alongside a range of
other commodities, so the public could be informed about their respective exchange values (Figure 3.6).[18]

---

[14] N. J. Mayhew (2000), pp. 98–102.

[15] J. Steuart (1767), vol. II, book III, part I, chapter vi (eds) A. S. Skinner et al. (1998), Vol.
2, pp. 241–3; W. S. Jevons, *Money and the Mechanism of Exchange* (London, 9th edn,
1890), p. 13; see also W. Bagehot, *Lombard Street, a Description of the Money Market*
(London, 3rd edn, 1873), p. 113.

[16] J. E. Stiglitz and J. Driffill, *Economics* (New York: W. W. Norton, 2000), p. 521; T.
J. Sargent and F. R. Velde, *The Big Problem of Small Change* (Princeton, NJ, and
Oxford: Princeton University Press, 2002), pp. 4–14; A. Redish and W. E. Weber, 'A
Model of Commodity Money with Minting and Melting', *FRB of Minneapolis Research
Department Staff Report 460* (July 2011); G. B. Gorton, 'The history and economics of
safe assets', *NBER Working Paper*, no. 22210 (April 2016), p. 4.

[17] W. S. Jevons (1890), p. 57.

[18] J. Houghton, *A Collection, for Improvement of Husbandry and Trade*, nos. 1–582,
1692–1703 (Farnborough, reprint, 1969); J. Steuart (1767), vol. II, book III, part I, chapter vii (eds) A. S. Skinner et al. (1998), vol. 2, pp. 247; Lord Liverpool (1880), p. 79.

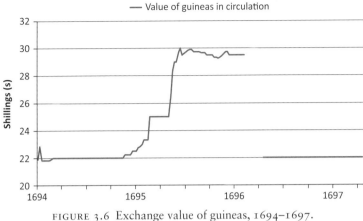

FIGURE 3.6 Exchange value of guineas, 1694–1697.
Source: J. Houghton (1692–1703).

Pre-1695 guineas were, however, the exception rather than the rule for English coins. Silver coinage issued by the English Mint tended to be of a nominalist type – royal proclamations would specify fixed values at which coins were to be exchanged and, in many cases, the amounts were inscribed on their face.[19] Creditors within the realm were obliged to accept these coins at their proclaimed value in settlement of sterling debts – including taxes. As a result, they circulated domestically at their face value, even if their underlying metal (or collateral) value was not the same.[20] Proclaimed and collateral values could diverge, either because underlying bullion prices changed, or because wear and tear of coins could leave them underweight. In the event that collateral values fell below face values, there would be an incentive to put counterfeits into circulation, potentially damaging confidence in the currency, not to mention the loss of seigniorage. If collateral values exceeded face values, there would be an incentive to hoard and export coin, and the stock of circulating coins could be depleted. This was the problem facing the silver coinage in the run-up to the currency crisis of 1695 (Figure 3.7).[21]

In principle, the Mint stood ready to convert any quantity of bullion into coins at its posted price. The (net) mint price was the nominal value of coins offered – after deductions – against delivery of bullion to the

---

[19] W. A. Shaw, *The History of the Currency, 1252–1894* (London: Clement Wilson, 2nd edn, 1896), viii–ix.
[20] D. Fox, 'The case of mixt monies', *Cambridge Law Journal*, 70, no. 1 (March 2011), pp. 144–7; D. Fox, 'The structures of monetary nominalism in the pre-modern common law', *Journal of Legal History*, 34, no. 2 (2013), pp. 139–43.
[21] A. E. Feavearyear (1963), p. 11.

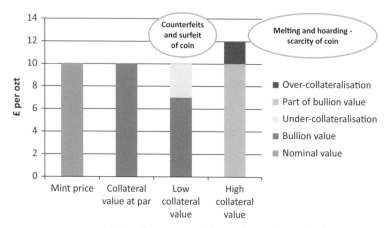

FIGURE 3.7 Minted currency with varying collateral values.
Source: Author's diagram.

Mint. If the coins produced by the Mint could be exchanged for other goods at their nominal value, holders of bullion would be assured that they could sell at the (net) mint price.

$$\text{Net mint price} = p_{nm} = [(n_g - m - s) / w] = n_n / w$$

Where:

n_g = (gross) nominal value of coins minted from bullion delivered
m = nominal value of coins deducted for brassage (mint masters' fees)
s = nominal value of coins deducted for seigniorage
w = weight of bullion delivered of standard fineness
n_n = (net) nominal value of coins returned after deduction of mintage
  (i.e. brassage and seigniorage)

Free coinage was introduced in England from 1666, after which the cost of minting – brassage – was born by the Exchequer, and no seigniorage was deducted, $m = s = 0$. As a result, the gross and net nominal value of coins minted against bullion delivered became the same, $n_g = n_n$, and there was no need to distinguish between gross and net mint prices, $p_m = p_{nm}$.[22]

However, there remained an elapsing of time between the delivery of bullion to the Mint and its return as coin. The floor (or collar) for spot sales of bullion was therefore the mint price less a small margin, reflecting the time cost of delayed delivery of minted coins, $p_{nm} - \alpha$. By the 1770s,

[22] W. A. Shaw, *History* (1896), p. 220.

and possibly before, bullion that had previously been delivered directly to the Mint was sold to the Bank for immediate value. The Bank set its own buying price for gold and took a dealing margin, α.[23]

$$\text{Collar or floor price} = p_l = p_{nm} - \alpha$$

Where:

α = dealing margin reflecting difference between the value of coins supplied immediately and minted coins delivered after some weeks' delay

It is important to note that the effectiveness of the floor on bullion prices depended, not just on the posting of a fixed mint price, but also on the coins offered circulating at their proclaimed/nominal/face value. In other words, the coins had to circulate in a nominalist manner. If the coins did not have a proclaimed value, and behaved in a metallist manner – with exchange values changing in line with bullion prices – the floor would not operate.

The next feature of the mint system to be considered is the possibility of placing a cap on bullion prices. Precious metal could be sourced by acquiring either coins or bars, and if the two were substitutable, a plentiful source of coins at a proclaimed price would place a cap on the cost of bars. Why pay more for bars, if you could buy the same thing in specie? Foundry costs and prohibitions on the melting of regal coins suggest the two were not always fully substitutable, but – even in medieval times – the illicit melting and exporting of coins were common when there was an incentive to do so.[24] By the eighteenth century, coins and bars were largely interchangeable, but the ability to source current coins at their nominal value was not the same as being able to secure mint-condition coins at their nominal value. Current coins could be underweight and offer less metal for the same nominal cost.[25] The unit cost of their metal would therefore exceed the mint price, the premium over the mint price rising as the coinage became more underweight, or foundry costs rose ($p_{nm} / 1 - \beta - \gamma$). In this context, the trading range for silver prices would be at a maximum when the silver coin stock was in poor condition, just before a recoinage.

[23] M-T. Boyer-Xambeu, G. Deleplace and L. Gillard (1994), pp. 1141–2.
[24] A. E. Feaveryear (1963), p. 11.
[25] J. Viner, *Studies in the Theory of International Trade* (New York and London: Harper, 1937), p. 129.

$$\text{Cap or upper price bound} = p_u = p_{nm} / (1 - \beta - \gamma)$$

Where:

> β = underweight circulating coins as a proportion of their weight in mint condition
>
> γ = foundry and other costs as a proportion of mint-condition value

So far, we have considered a situation in which causality has run from the quality of the domestic coin stock to the size of the trading range for bullion prices. There were circumstances, however, when causality could run the other way. An external factor could raise the market price of silver, leading to a deterioration in domestic coin quality, if the mint price were not raised to accommodate it. A raised market price of silver would lead to fuller weight coins being over-collateralised, and their removal from circulation. An equilibrium would be reached when the rump of silver coins left in circulation was sufficiently underweight to offset the uplift from market prices. This relationship can be shown by rearranging the cap price equation, allowing us to express the underweight factor (β) in terms of the mint price/market price relativity.

$$\text{Underweight coin factor} = \beta = 1 - (p_m / p_u)$$

Where:

> p_m = mint price where the gross and net mint prices are the same

At the height of the currency crisis of 1695 the price of silver bars peaked at around a 20 per cent premium to the mint price, and during the eighteenth century the premium rarely exceeded 10 per cent. The implied cap on the silver price during these periods tended to be even higher because of the dire state of the coinage, suggesting that the cap was rarely, if ever, a constraint at these times. Thus, the law attributed to Sir Thomas Gresham that poor-quality coins drive out good ones is in need of some qualification.[26] A deteriorated coin stock raises the price cap, opening the door to a rise in market prices, but they will not necessarily appreciate to the extent allowed by the cap. Bad coins do not, of themselves, drive out good ones. It is price rises – and the resultant over-collateralisation – that drives hoarding and melting, leaving a rump of bad coins.

The final feature of the currency model developed in the 1770s was the mechanism recounted by Lord Liverpool and David Ricardo

---

[26] E. Sykes, *Banking and Currency* (London: Butterworth, 9th edn, 1947) pp. 15, 25.

for maintaining guineas in circulation at close to their full weight. An order-in-council issued in 1774 required creditors to accept guineas at their face value, provided the tendered coins were within certain tolerance limits of their prescribed weight. Guineas outside these limits could be exchanged by weight at the mint price. A further order-in-council issued on 12th April 1776 set a uniform weight limit of plus or minus 1½ grains. Coins outside these limits were no longer legal tender, and this created an incentive for them to be returned to the Mint for melting and repressing in mint condition. The Bank scrupulously followed the order separating its guineas into passable and unpassable ones, returning the latter to the Mint. Lord Liverpool observed that some private bankers were less assiduous at following the rules, but even they would have baulked at significantly underweight pieces for fear of not being able to tender them at par.[27]

In principle, the currency reforms of 1773–6 ensured that anyone could acquire 22 carat gold in the form of passable guineas weighing of 129.4 grains, plus or minus 1½ grains (i.e. +/- 1.16 per cent) at a posted price of 21 s per piece. Gold weighing 129.4 grains was equivalent to 0.26958 ozt, implying a mint price of £3 17 s 10½ d (£3.89375) per standard troy ounce (std ozt) ($\beta = 0$).[28] Passable guineas were close substitutes for gold bars, prohibitions against the melting of coins having effectively been discarded ($\gamma = 0$). There was a plentiful stock of passable guineas in circulation, and therefore little reason for the prices of gold bars and guineas to diverge more than fractionally. As a result, London's gold price was stabilised close to the mint price from 1773 ($p_u = p_m > p_l = p_m - \alpha$). The Bank found that it could offer a price for gold bars of up to 4½ d (£0.0187) per ozt less than the mint price. This discount reflected the convenience of selling spot to the Bank, rather than suffer the time cost of minting and, in some cases, demurrage associated with the storage of bullion.[29] The narrow cap and collar on the price of gold bars persisted, beyond the suspension of note convertibility in 1797 and the onset of the Napoleonic wars, until September 1799 – the minting of guineas having ended in March 1799 (Figure 3.8).[30]

[27] Lord Liverpool (1880), pp. 170–81 (chapter XIX), pp. 240 and 241 especially the footnote; D. Ricardo 'Bullion Essays' in P. Sraffa and M. H. Dobb (eds) *The Works and Correspondence of David Ricardo, Pamphlets and Papers 1809–11* (11 vols., Cambridge: Cambridge University Press, 1951–73), III, p. 225.

[28] J. Steuart (1767), vol. II, book III, part I, chapter vii (eds) A. S. Skinner et al. (1998), vol. 2, pp. 246–7.

[29] D. Ricardo (1951–73), III, p. 179.

[30] M-T. Boyer-Xambeu, G. Deleplace and L. Gillard (1994), pp. 1150.

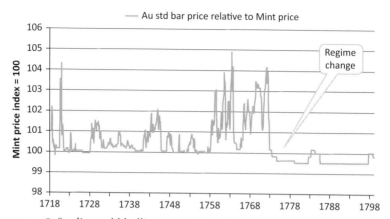

FIGURE 3.8 Sterling gold bullion price in London, 1718–1799.
Source: J. Castaing (from 1698) (Figure reproduced with kind permission of Palgrave Macmillan, see page xiii).

Readers familiar with traditional currency histories might reasonably ask how these metallist and nominalist mint models were affected by bimetallic arbitrage. Posting mint prices for both silver and gold has the effect of setting an official mint ratio between the two metals. If divergences arise between the mint ratios of different kingdoms, there is scope for arbitrage, leading to potentially destabilising flows of silver and gold to find the best price. This is not a problem for our starting model, the metallist or Locke–Jevons mint, which is blissfully free from bimetallic (or poly-metallic) arbitrage, because no attempt is made to prescribe the tender value of its coins, only their weight and fineness. The Locke–Jevons mint does not therefore set an official mint ratio against which arbitrage can take place, if market values diverge.

The English Mint became a bimetallic issuer of coins in the fourteenth century and its indentures did specify a nominal value for both silver and gold coins. These nominal values have been used to calculate an English mint ratio, which did indeed differ from continental mint ratios.[31] However, the scope for arbitrage depended on both gold and silver coins being exchanged at their nominal values. This was normally the case for coins circulating within the realm, but not for the guinea. What mattered for bimetallic arbitrage were differences between the exchange values of coins circulating in the country relative to their *actual* collateral values, after allowing for the fact that many of them could be underweight. Deviations

[31] P. Woodhead, *Herbert Schneider Collection*, Part II: *English Gold Coins 1603 to the 20th Century in Sylloge of Coins of the British Isles*, 57 (London: Spink, 2002), pp. 3–5.

of market prices of bullion from official prices of mint-condition coins was not necessarily a good indicator of real arbitrage opportunities when full-weight coins were not in circulation. Coins used largely for international trade were routinely exchanged by weight rather than by tale, and this was often the case for gold coins, prior to the creation of the guinea in the seventeenth century.[32] In many cases, gold coins – possibly underweight ones – would be exchanged at values reflecting their bullion value, thereby making two-way arbitrage between gold and silver coins less likely.

The currency crisis of 1695 is an example of how matters could go awry. Remittances to support the Nine Year's War against France (1689–98) and poor harvests in the mid-1690s led to an outflow of funds, particularly silver that was undervalued at the Mint.[33] The market price of silver in London went to a premium over the mint price, and there was no incentive to deliver silver to the Mint; instead, over-collateralised silver coins were melted down and exported, contributing to the currency crisis.[34] The problem was contained by allowing the silver coinage to waste away, but the remaining silver pieces became easier to clip and counterfeit, thereby exacerbating the incentive to do so.[35] Because the recoinage had been delayed for far too long, the silver coins in circulation were estimated to be some 50 per cent underweight, requiring exchange terms that allowed for a severe shortfall of metal.[36]

In the face of the 1695 crisis, Lowndes favoured *option (4)*, raising the denomination of most silver coins, leaving some coins to be devalued – *option (2)*. Redenomination was not necessarily practical for all coins because it disrupted their aliquot proportions (i.e. larger denomination coins being integer multiples of smaller denomination coins). To this end, Lowndes argued that the crown piece with a face value of 5 s should be cried up to 6 s 3 d with proportionate adjustments for other silver pieces.[37] This proposal was nevertheless overruled by adherents of Locke's doctrine, which debarred devaluation *(option (2))*, debasement *(option (3))*, or raising the coin *(option (4))*. The existing mint price of silver had to remain sacrosanct at 5 s 2 d (£0.25833R) per sterling troy ounce (stg ozt) of silver, notwithstanding the late Plantagenet devaluations. English

[32] A. E. Feavearyear (1963), pp. 21–5.
[33] W. A. Shaw, *History* (1896), p. 224; S. Quinn, 'Gold, silver and the Glorious Revolution: arbitrage between bills of exchange and bullion', *Economic History Review*, XLIX, 3 (August 1996), pp. 474–9.
[34] S. Quinn (August 1996), pp. 480.
[35] M-H. Li (1963), p. 177.
[36] Lord Liverpool (1880), p. 79; S. Quinn (August 1996), pp. 481.
[37] W. Lowndes (1695), p. 123; J. H. M. Craig (1953), p. 184.

sterling silver had been a constant for centuries at 11 ozt 2 dwt of fine silver per 1 troy pound (lbt) of metal including alloy, equivalent to 5,328 grains of fine silver per 5,760 grains of metal, a millesimal fineness of 925.[38]

This left the Treasury commissioners with limited room for manoeuvre, and, quite remarkably, they opted for *option (5)* for most coins – an Exchequer subsidy which ended up being close to £2.7 million. For a transitional period, old coins were accepted for the payment of taxes at their nominal value (without being called down) and returned to the Mint for recoining. Coins in very poor condition and held by those with no taxes to pay were called down and exchanged on a weight-for-weight basis *(option (1))*. This was estimated to have imposed a loss of £1 million, mainly borne by poorer people.[39] It is noteworthy that the Treasury commissioners resorted to a substantial Exchequer subsidy, rather than the wholesale application of weight-for-weight exchanges as practiced in the early Plantagenet period *(option (1))*, but the state of the silver coinage was so poor in 1695 that a weight-for-weight exchange would have resulted in a halving of the nominal stock of silver coins.

Such a dramatic reduction in the stock of nominal money should not have mattered, if – as Locke argued – the purchasing power of new and old coins reflected their metallic content. In a Lockean world the sterling prices of ordinary commodities should have risen as the coins became more underweight, and fallen – in this case halved – after a weight-for-weight recoinage *(option 1)*. In practice, causality could have run either way in the period before the 1695 crisis: either the degradation of the coinage could have led to bullion price inflation, or an inflationary shock – due to war and bad harvests – could have led to the hoarding of over-collateralised coins, leaving a rump of the most worn coins in circulation.[40] It is possible that causality ran in both directions, and that other factors played a role. What we do know is that the exchange of severely underweight coins for mint-condition ones of the same nominal value was not associated with fully offsetting reductions in the prices of ordinary commodities.[41]

The possibility of a Lockean recoinage – involving elements of *option (1)* – appears to have stoked fears that the purchasing power of the

[38] J. Steuart (1767), vol. II, book III, part I, chapter vii (eds) A. S. Skinner et al. (1998), vol. 2, pp. 246–7.
[39] A. E. Feavearyear, 1963, p. 142; Lord Liverpool (1880), p. 85.
[40] J. Steuart (1767), vol. II, book III, part I, chapter vi (eds) A. S. Skinner et al. (1998), vol. 2, p. 241.
[41] M-H. Li (1963), pp. 85, 105–7.

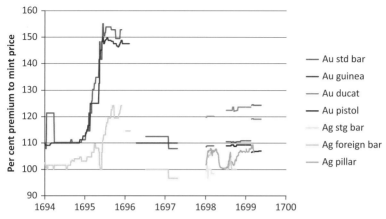

FIGURE 3.9 Bullion and specie prices in the sterling currency crisis of 1695. *Sources:* J. Houghton (1692–1702), J. Castaing (from 1698) (Figure reproduced with kind permission of Palgrave Macmillan, see page xiii).

silver coinage would be reduced.[42] This encouraged people to minimise their holdings of silver coin in favour of guineas and ordinary commodities. Hitherto the prices of guineas and gold bars had moved in tandem in a relatively narrow range, guineas trading between 20 s and 22 s, but between April and July 1695 loss of public confidence in the silver coinage became manifest, and there was a flight to gold and other commodities. Gold bars and guineas moved to a 50 per cent premium to their mint price, guineas reaching 30 s per piece (Figures 3.6 and 3.9).

Silver bars and other commodity prices followed in the wake of the gold price movement: silver and lead prices rising 20 per cent, copper and iron rising around 10 per cent (Figure 3.10). Wheat prices rose by 80 per cent in the second half of 1695, albeit from a low base (Figure 3.11).[43] Ironically, the prospect of a Lockean recoinage, and the resulting flight from silver coins, is one of the better pieces of evidence against Locke's metallist view of the silver coinage during this period (Figures 3.10, 3.11 and 3.12).

The Lockean stance against devaluation applied to silver – not to gold – and the rise in the price of guineas during the currency crisis meant that gold was effectively being devalued by the market, even though its official mint price was not raised. The Treasury commissioners sought to contain the gold price rise by stipulating that guineas were worth 25 s for the payment of taxes. The price of gold bars nevertheless continued to rise and the Treasury relented, accepting that guineas were worth 29 s for the purposes of paying

[42] A. E. Feavearyear (1963), pp. 131.
[43] A. E. Feavearyear (1963), pp. 119–25, 130–31.

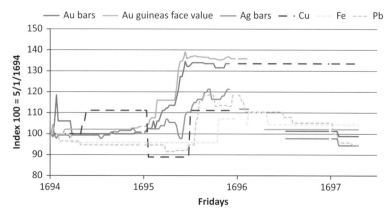

FIGURE 3.10 London metal prices, late seventeenth century.
Source: J. Houghton (1692–1703).

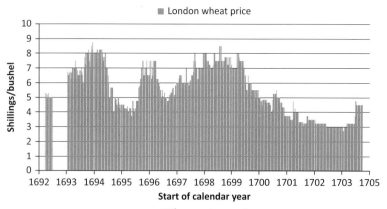

FIGURE 3.11 Wheat prices, 1692–1705.
Source: J. Houghton (1692–1703).

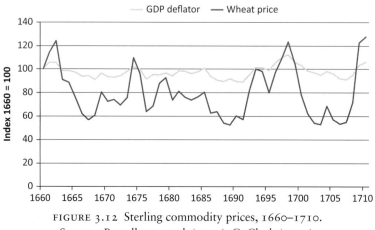

FIGURE 3.12 Sterling commodity prices, 1660–1710.
Sources: Broadberry et al. (2011); G. Clark (2004).

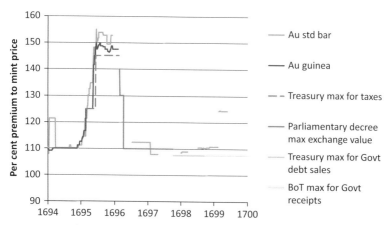

FIGURE 3.13 Policy response to sterling currency crisis of 1695.
Sources: J. Houghton (1692–1703); J. Castaing (from 1698); A. E. Feavearyear (1963), p. 153.

taxes. The market price of guineas broke through the 29 s barrier, reaching 30 s, and the price of gold bars reached a slightly higher equivalent price, but a plateau of around 30 s was established. During 1696, a Parliamentary decree was issued setting a maximum tender value for the guinea of 28 s, and this was progressively reduced to 26 s, and then 22 s. The Parliamentary decree was superseded in 1698 by a Treasury maximum of 21 s 6 d for purchasers of government debt, which subsequently became a Board of Trade requirement for all payments to the government. These stipulations proved effective, and guineas circulated at their prescribed exchange value of 21 s 6 d from 1698. The circulating pieces were modestly underweight, allowing the price of gold bullion to fluctuate around a 10 per cent premium to the mint price, reaching a 20 per cent premium in 1699 (Figure 3.13).[44]

The Treasury commissioners had hoped that a reduction in sterling gold prices would lead to a fall in sterling silver prices, the ratio of gold to silver prices remaining broadly constant. The prices of silver bars and specie nevertheless remained at a premium to the mint price, leaving the newly minted coins over-collateralised. Few of them circulated normally and most were hoarded, or exported. There was no incentive to deliver silver to the Mint, and the lack of small change continued to be a problem despite the costly recoinage (Figure 3.14).[45] From 1718, the Mint's posted prices for gold and silver implied a mint price ratio (of gold to silver) of slightly more than 15 times, and the market price ratio fluctuated between 13 and 15

[44] J. H. M. Craig (1953), pp. 184–8.
[45] A. E. Feavearyear (1963), p. 158; M-H. Li, 1963, p. 162.

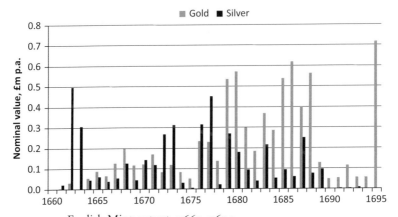

FIGURE 3.14 English Mint output, 1661–1695.
Source: C. E. Challis (1992) pp. 689–698 (Figure reproduced with kind permission of Palgrave Macmillan, see page xiii).

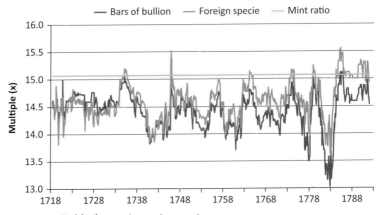

FIGURE 3.15 Gold/silver price ratio, 1718–1792.
Source: J. Castaing (from 1698) (Figure reproduced with kind permission of Palgrave Macmillan, see page xiii).

times.[46] The mint price of silver tended to be below its market price, resulting in a persistently high mint price ratio relative to the market (Figure 3.15).

Gold flows tended to be the mirror opposite of silver flows. There had been inflows of gold from abroad during the currency crisis, attracted by price rises in London, and deliveries for minting reached a peak in 1695. Foreigners had found it attractive to pay for British exports with gold specie in the form of French pistoles (a form of Louis d'Or) and Portuguese

[46] J. Steuart (1767), vol. II, book III, part I, chapter vii (eds) A. S. Skinner et al. (1998), vol. 2, pp. 245, 247–8.

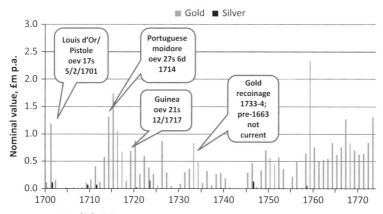

FIGURE 3.16 English Mint output, 1700–1773.
Sources: C. E. Challis (1992) pp. 689–698; J. H. M. Craig (1953) pp. 214–5
(Figure reproduced with kind permission of Palgrave Macmillan, see page xiii).

moidores. Once imported, these foreign coins circulated privately, rather than being delivered to London for minting into guineas. Newton analysed these coins and computed their intrinsic value, reflecting the price of gold in London.[47] By setting proclaimed values for these coins a few pence below their intrinsic value, an incentive was created for delivering them for minting into guineas. On the basis of Newton's advice, a proclaimed value of 17 s was set for French pistoles early in 1701 and, as a consequence, many of them were delivered for minting, a peak level of gold being delivered during the year. A proclaimed value of 27 s 6 d was set for Portuguese moidores in 1714, creating further deliveries of foreign coin to the Mint. The conversion of pistoles and moidores into guineas was a real coup, but Mint deliveries of gold bars and other forms of specie, arising from ordinary trade, were disappointing (Figure 3.16). It was usually more profitable to sell bullion to the East India Company for export to Asia.[48]

Newton sought to address the problem of scarce silver coinage in his report to the Treasury commissioners of 21st September 1717.[49] He had favoured Lowndes's proposal to raise the mint price of silver but was obliged to consider other remedies because Lockean objections to silver devaluation continued to hold sway. Having coaxed the price of guineas down to 21 s 6 d by setting an official exchange price, Newton proposed that the official price of guineas should be reduced by a further 6 d. This

---

[47] W. A. Shaw, *History* (1896), p. 227.
[48] J. H. M. Craig (1953), pp. 214–5; C. E. Challis (1992), appendix 1, Mint Output, pp. 689–98.
[49] W. A. Shaw (ed.), *Select Tracts and Documents Illustrative of English Monetary History 1626–1730* (London, 1896, London: G. Hardy, 1935; reprinted 2009).

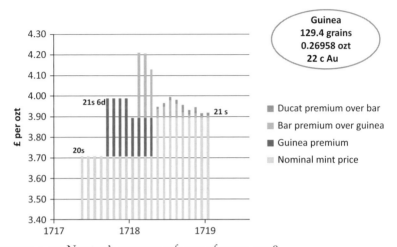

FIGURE 3.17 Newton's currency reforms of 1717–1718.
Source: J. Castaing (from 1698) (Figure reproduced with kind permission of Palgrave Macmillan, see page xiii).

was agreed by the newly formed government, and a proclamation was issued on 22nd December 1717, fixing the exchange value of the guinea at 21 s. It was hoped that a reduced price of gold would help to reduce the price of silver towards its mint price.[50]

The nominal value of guineas – as distinct from their proclaimed value – had been specified in the Mint's initial indenture for the coin, and it had been left unchanged since 1666. Newton advised that it should be raised from 20 s to 21 s to align it with the newly established proclaimed value of 21 s. A new indenture to this effect became effective on 6th May 1718, prescribing a nominal value of 21 s with an unchanged weight and fineness. The raising of the coin from a nominal value of 20 s to 21 s gave official recognition to the 5 per cent devaluation that had already occurred in the market. The new mint price for gold of £3 17 s 10½ d (£3.89375) per std ozt would in time become the totem of the international gold standard of the nineteenth century.[51]

Newton's currency reforms of 1717–18 were effective in the sense that the market price of gold bars fell, and converged on the raised mint price (Figure 3.17). The alignment of the market and mint prices of gold resulted in a surge of guinea issuance, but the reforms did not depress the silver price sufficiently for a resurgence of silver coin production. English silver

[50] J. Steuart (1767), vol. II, book III, part I, chapter vii (eds) A. S. Skinner et al. (1998), vol. 2, p. 247; Lord Liverpool (1880), p. 24.
[51] C. E. Challis (1992), pp. 431, 750; K. Clancy, 'The recoinage and exchange of 1816–17', University of Leeds PhD thesis, 1999.

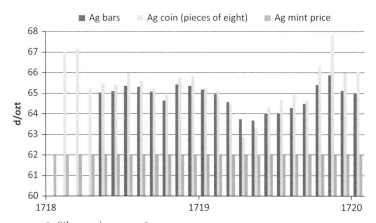

FIGURE 3.18 Silver prices, 1718–1720.
Source: J. Castaing (from 1698) (Figure reproduced with kind permission of Palgrave Macmillan, see page xiii).

coins continued to be legal tender, alongside guineas, and the Mint's posted price for silver was kept at a nominal value of 5 s 2 d (62 d, £0.25833R) per stg ozt (Figure 3.18). It is not immediately obvious why contemporaries thought that reducing the sterling price of gold would necessarily lead to lower silver prices. Contemporaries were well aware that the mint ratio had varied significantly over the centuries, but the dominant continental powers of the seventeenth and eighteenth centuries sought to maintain a broadly fixed mint ratio to support the circulation of both silver and gold coins. Newton recognised that he never quite managed to bring the British mint ratio into line with continental ones, but his reforms did help to restart London's market in bullion and foreign specie.[52]

London had been an entrepôt for precious metals since medieval times, but trading tended to be done off-market by way of private transactions between merchants and the trading houses. A public market with regularly published prices had emerged in the 1690s when John Houghton published prices of a range of commodities, including those of precious metals and guineas, and John Freke did likewise during the 1700s. After the War of the Spanish Succession (1701-14), the public market was revived, assisted by Newton's reforms and the Bank's willingness to act as an intermediary between the market and the Mint. *The Course of the Exchange*, published by John Castaing and his successors, provides a remarkable record of bullion and specie prices in this public market.[53] For the purposes of this study,

---

[52] Lord Liverpool (1880), pp. 267–95.
[53] J. Castaing, E. Jackson, G. Shergold, P. Smithson, *The Course of the Exchange, and Other Things* (London, January 1698 to October 1786).

Castaing's data have been compiled from microfilms of published sheets held in Senate House Library, University of London. There are references to Castaing's prices in a Bank of England bullion ledger, and these have been used to clarify our understanding of the data.[54] Although the microfilm record starts in January 1698, there is a gap in gold and silver prices between 1700 and 1718, when these markets were disrupted by the War of the Spanish Succession and its aftermath. Castaing's record of these prices resumes in May 1718, when Newton's raising of the mint price took effect. There is a two-month gap in early 1721 and thereafter regular reports of gold and silver prices of both bars and foreign specie for the rest of the century. The twice-weekly series recorded prices on post days when foreign bills were negotiated, usually Tuesdays and Fridays, unless displaced by a high day.[55] The series is nearly continuous until January 1792; thereafter it suffers from more 'nil trades', reflecting disruptions to the market in the run-up to the French revolutionary wars. It is nevertheless possible to construct monthly series for four key prices from May 1718 to January 1792, each with 885 observations covering gold and silver in the form of bars and foreign specie, a total of 3,540 observations (Figure 3.19).[56]

The Castaing price data confirm that foreign specie was traded in the London market by weight, rather than by tale.[57] It is noteworthy that the Bank held its foreign specie in sacks of 1,000 ozt, whereas guineas were held in sacks of £1,000. Holding specie by weight reflected the way it was traded, and it is perhaps not surprising that the value of the Bank's sacks of foreign specie and its stacked bars of gold and silver were often aggregated together and reported as bullion.[58]

Specie of the same weight could differ in price because assorted foreign coins could vary in fineness, and market factors could favour certain types of coin.[59] In view of this, the Bank's sacks of specie were sorted by type of

---

[54] Bank of England Archive, 2A 109/1.

[55] *Gilbart on Banking: The History, Principles and Practice of Banking* (ed.) A. S. Michie (2 vols, London: George Bells, 1882), I, p. 290.

[56] J. J. McCusker, *Money and Exchange in Europe and America, 1600–1775: A Handbook* (Chapel Hill, NC: University of North Carolina Press NC, 1978; London: Macmillan, 1978), pp. 29–30; L. D. Neal 'The rise of a financial press: London and Amsterdam, 1681–1810', *Business History*, 30, no. 2 (April 1988), pp. 165–70; L. D. Neal, *The Rise of Financial Capitalism: International Capital Markets in the Age of Reason* (Cambridge: Cambridge University Press, 1990), pp. 20–43.

[57] J. J. McCusker (1978), p. 8.

[58] Bank of England Archive, Bullion ledger, M2/52 & 53.

[59] A. K. Craig, *Spanish Colonial Silver Coins in the Florida Collection* (Gainesville: University of Florida, 2000), pp. 48–62; S. Menzel, *Cobs, Pieces of Eight and Treasure Coins: The Early Spanish-American Mints and Their Coinages, 1536–1773* (New York: American Numismatic Society, 2004), pp. 11–13; X. Calicó, *Numismática Espănola: catálogo*

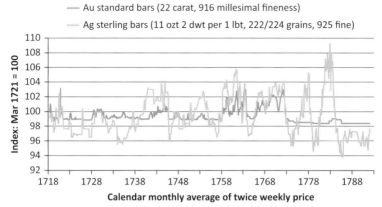

FIGURE 3.19 Sterling bullion prices in London, 1718–1792.
Source: J. Castaing (from 1698) (Figure reproduced with kind permission of Palgrave Macmillan, see page xiii).

foreign coin, and labelled as such. In the second half of the eighteenth century, Castaing reported prices of four types of silver specie, but the leading one remained the pillar piece of eight. Also known as a Spanish silver dollar, it could be recognised by twin pillars depicted on its face.[60] Castaing reported only one price for gold specie from 1718, initially specified as ducats and, later, simply as gold coin. Between 1810 and 1813, a separate price was reported for Spanish new doubloons. It is fair to say that, for most of the eighteenth century, there were four reference prices in the markets for bullion and foreign specie: (i) silver specie represented by Spanish dollars/pillar pieces of eight, (ii) gold specie by Dutch ducats, (iii) gold bullion in bars of English standard fineness, and (iv) silver bullion in bars of sterling fineness.

Specie would be expected to trade at a small premium to bullion, reflecting its greater convenience as a circulating medium of exchange.[61] If specie prices were not at a premium, there would be little incentive to deliver bullion for minting. As it happens, pillar pieces of eight usually traded at a discount to silver bars, mainly because – by the late-eighteenth century – they were of lower fineness. Lord Liverpool observed that purchases of silver dollars at 61¼ d per ozt equated to an adjusted price of 63¼ d per ozt for purchases of silver bars of sterling fineness.[62] In other

general con precious de las monedas espaãnolas acuñadas desde los Reyes Católicos hasta Juan Carlos I: 1474–2001 (Barcelona: Aureo & Calicó, 2008), pp. 441–515.

[60] E. M. Kelly, *Spanish Dollars and Silver Tokens: An Account of the Issues of the Bank of England 1797–1816* (London: Spink & Son, 1976), pp. 18–19.

[61] J. Steuart (1767), vol. II, book III, part I, chapter v (eds) A. S. Skinner et al. (1998) vol. 2, p. 239; N. J. Mayhew (2000), pp. 97–8.

[62] Lord Liverpool (1880), p. 160.

FIGURE 3.20 Silver coin premium, 1718–1792.
Sources: J. Castaing (from 1698); adjustment factor from Lord Liverpool (1880), p. 160; E. M. Kelly, p. 21 (Figure reproduced with kind permission of Palgrave Macmillan, see page xiii).

words, it cost 61¼ d to buy one troy ounce of silver dollar pieces, but it cost an extra 2 d to buy additional pieces so that the pure silver content of the silver dollars equalled the pure silver content of one troy ounce of sterling silver.[63] The adjusted price of silver dollars stood at a premium to the price of sterling silver bars – as one would expect – but the premium was eroded after the currency reforms of 1773–6 (Figures 3.20 and 3.21).

Castaing's data show that gold and silver prices continued to fluctuate in London's public market after Newton's currency reforms took effect in 1718, but gold prices were more closely anchored to their mint price than those of silver. Prior to the currency reforms of 1773–6, the upside limits on the sterling price of bullion were less evident than the collar, but they were still a factor in the market. If bullion prices rose above the mint price, full-weight coins would become over-collateralised and there would be an incentive to melt them down. A plentiful stock of good quality coins in circulation could therefore act as a deterrent against bullion prices rising significantly above the mint price. If current coins in circulation became worn, the bullion cap would be expected to stand at a premium to the mint price, depending on the degree to which they were underweight. In this case, the bullion cap equalled the mint price/$(1 - \beta)$, where β was the weight of current coin as a proportion of their full weight. Underweight coins of 20 per cent would therefore imply a cap at a 30 per cent premium to the mint price.

Both Adam Smith and David Ricardo referred to the state of the coinage affecting bullion prices, and in the 1760s gold bullion prices fluctuated

[63] E. M. Kelly (1976), pp. 22–3.

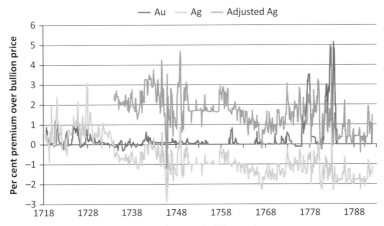

FIGURE 3.21 Foreign specie spreads over bullion price, 1718–1792.
Source: J. Castaing (from 1698) (Figure reproduced with kind permission of Palgrave Macmillan, see page xiii).

within a wider band of up to 5 per cent when the quality of English gold coins deteriorated.[64] For most of the period, however, gold coins were kept in good condition – with recoinages in 1733–4 and 1773–6 – and the gold bullion price fluctuated within a much narrower band than silver. Before the currency reforms of 1773–6, silver traded at a 5 per cent premium to its mint price and its market price was more variable than that of gold. Silver prices normally peaked at a 10 per cent premium to their mint price, although there was a peak of 15 per cent in 1782–3 (Figure 3.22). High silver prices created an incentive for good condition coins to be hoarded, exported or otherwise melted down, leaving underweight coins in circulation.[65] Thus, a low official price for silver (relative to market prices) could have contributed to the deterioration in the silver coin stock, causality running from price to coin quality, rather than the other way round. The process whereby a high price led to deteriorating coin quality could continue until the collateral value of underweight coins in circulation equalled their face value.

The silver price peaks of 10 or 15 per cent over mint price do not fully explain the woefully poor condition of English silver coins, which were at least 25 per cent underweight. The extra degradation arose because coins could be clipped and recirculated at face value, profits being taken from

[64] A. Smith (1776) book I, chapter V, section 32 (eds) R. H. Campbell et al. (1976), 1, 59; D. Ricardo, *Morning Chronicle* (29th August 1809) in P. Sraffa and M. H. Dobb (eds) (1951–73), III, p. 32.

[65] J. Steuart (1767), vol. II, book III, part I, chapter vii (eds) A. S. Skinner et al. (1998) vol. 2, p. 247–8.

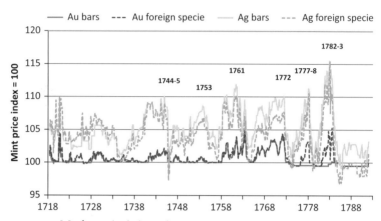

FIGURE 3.22 Market price/mint price, 1718–1792.
Source: J. Castaing (from 1698) (Figure reproduced with kind permission of Palgrave Macmillan, see page xiii).

melting down clipped silver. Coins with milled edges were introduced in the reign of Charles II, making clipping easier to detect, and milled silver coins had been exchanged for the old hammered ones in the recoinage of 1696. The new silver coins were still over-collateralised, and as a result they were hoarded, or exported. The rump of silver coins in circulation was at least 25 per cent underweight suggesting a theoretical silver bullion price cap of 33 per cent, far above the silver price peaks of 10 or 15 per cent. The theoretical silver price cap does not therefore appear to have been binding during this period.

The derisory flow of silver through the Mint during the eighteenth century suggests that the mint price for silver was rarely a lower bound on its market price. Gold coin output was more substantial, particularly after the 1773–6 currency reforms, suggesting that the gold price was more closely anchored to its mint price (Figure 3.23). The quality of circulating gold coins, particularly after 1773–6, suggests that gold prices were constrained within a narrow trading range by a cap and collar, whereas silver prices were rarely bound by their collar (the mint price for silver), or their theoretical cap (the collateral value of underweight coins in circulation).

The relationship between bullion and specie prices did change. The bullion and specie prices of gold were closely aligned between 1718 and 1776, but gold specie became decoupled from gold bullion thereafter. After 1776, there were two episodes in which gold specie prices moved with silver prices (Figure 3.24). Silver specie stood at a premium to silver bullion prices in the 1720s, but the two became more closely aligned later in the eighteenth century.

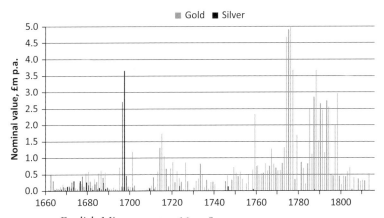

FIGURE 3.23 English Mint output, 1661–1815.
Source: C. E. Challis (1992) pp. 689–698 (Figure reproduced with kind permission of Palgrave Macmillan, see page xiii).

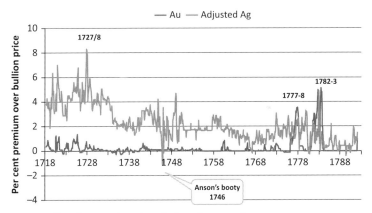

FIGURE 3.24 Foreign specie prices in London, 1718–1792.
Source: J. Castaing (from 1698) (Figure reproduced with kind permission of Palgrave Macmillan, see page xiii).

The availability of high frequency price data for much of the eighteenth century means that time series analysis can be used to study interactions among our four reference variables. Price movements in the period from Newton's reforms in 1718 to those of Lord Liverpool in the 1770s suggest two striking results. Short-run movements in silver prices led those of gold, and bullion prices led those of specie (Figure 3.25).[66] English silver coins

---

[66] A. C. Hotson and T. C. Mills, 'London's Market for Bullion and Specie in the Eighteenth Century: The Roles of the London Mint and the Bank of England in the Stabilization of Prices' in M. Allen and D. Coffman (eds) *Money, Prices and Wages: Essays in Honour of Professor Nicholas Mayhew* (Basingstoke: Palgrave Macmillan, 2015), p. 227.

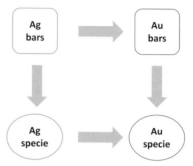

FIGURE 3.25 Price interactions – VEC model – 1721 to 1773.
Source: A. C. Hotson and T. C. Mills in (eds) M. Allen and D'M. Coffman (2015), p. 227 (Schematic reproduced with kind permission of Terence Mills and Palgrave Macmillan, see page xiii).

may have become a moribund means of circulation during this period, but silver bars and foreign specie remained an actively traded commodity in London's public market. Silver was Europe's primary currency, even though Britain was moving towards a gold standard, and events such as the collapse of the South Sea Company and the Seven Years' War appear to have had a greater proportionate effect on silver prices than those of gold.[67] Factors affecting prices in the short term, including the return of Commodore George Anson with his booty from Spanish ships in 1746, had a markedly greater effect on silver prices (Figure 3.26). While the gold price was not anchored in the manner achieved after Lord Liverpool's reforms of 1773–6, the gold price movements were dampened more effectively than those of silver during the 1718–73 period. Shocks would affect silver and gold bullion prices, and these would feed through to specie prices, but the effect on gold prices would be dampened.

The currency reforms of 1773–6 ensured that guineas circulated at close to their full weight, making it easy to buy gold in the form of guineas. To be passable at 21 s a guinea was supposed to be no more or less than 1½ grains of its prescribed weight; otherwise it had to be exchanged by weight.[68] The easy availability of passable guineas meant that it was possible to acquire 129.4 grains of standard gold in the form of a guinea for 21 s, equivalent to £3 17 s 10½ d per ozt. Normally, there would be no reason to pay more for gold in the bullion market and its price did,

[67] H. Thornton, *An Enquiry into the Nature and Effects of the Paper Credit of Great Britain*, 1802 edn and Thornton's parliamentary speeches and evidence (ed.) F. A. von Hayek (London: Cass, 1939, reprinted 1962), pp. 148, 192.

[68] Lord Liverpool (1880), pp. 240 and 241, especially fn.; G. P. Dyer and P. P. Gaspar in C. E. Challis (ed.) (1992), pp. 439–440.

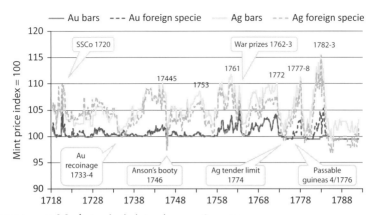

FIGURE 3.26 Market price/mint price, 1718–1792.
Source: J. Castaing (from 1698) (Figure reproduced with kind permission of Palgrave Macmillan, see page xiii).

indeed, remain within a narrow trading range close to the mint price.[69] Gold bullion price stability ensued from 1773 to 1792 and with somewhat less assurance to 1799. Writing in 1809, Ricardo described the successful stabilisation of the gold price as follows:

When our Gold Coin was defective previous to the recoinage in 1774, gold bullion advanced considerably above its mint value, but immediately on it being brought to its present state of perfection, gold bullion fell to something under the mint price, and has continued so for twenty years previous to 1797.[70]

The close alignment of gold bar prices with the Mint price depended on a cap provided by the availability of full-weight guineas, and a floor provided by the Mint price (intermediated by the Bank) and nominalist guineas.[71] There were therefore four key building blocks supporting sterling's eighteenth-century gold standard (Figure 3.27):

1 The Mint's posted price for bullion, which had been in operation for centuries;

2 The Bank's intermediating role with the London bullion market starting in the 1770s and possibly before;

3 Newton's reforms culminating in the fixing of the guinea's proclaimed value at 21 s from 1717/18. This meant that the guinea

---

[69] J. Steuart (1767), vol. II, book III, part I, chapter vii (eds) A. S. Skinner et al. (1998) vol. 2, p. 248 and xvi, pp. 325–37.

[70] D. Ricardo, *Morning Chronicle* (29 August 1809) in P. Sraffa and M. H. Dobb (eds) (1951–73), III, p. 32.

[71] W. A. Shaw, *History* (1896), p. 234–5.

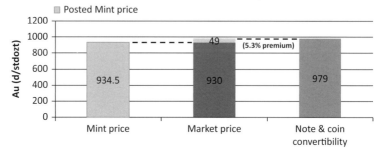

FIGURE 3.27 Gold bullion trading range, 1718–1772.
Source: Author's diagram.

was transformed from being a metallist coin, behaving like foreign specie, to a nominalist coin; and

4 The measures recorded by Lord Liverpool to ensure that guineas circulated at their fullweight from 1773.

The narrow cap and collar for gold survived until 1799, when the right to deliver gold for minting was withdrawn. The gold price quickly went to a premium, exceeding £4 in 1800, and traded between £5 and £6 in 1813 and 1814. Wartime conditions no doubt led to greater volatility, but the loss of the cap and collar was clear. Gold prices reverted to their pre-war parity – close to £3 17 s 10½ d – in 1819, following the introduction of the sovereign in 1817, and in anticipation of the restoration of note convertibility, which finally happened in 1821 (Figure 3.28).[72]

The position of silver coins as legal tender was altered in 1774. Transactions of up to £25 could continue to be settled with silver coin at face value, even if these coins were severely underweight. However, larger sterling debts could be settled by weight at the mint price for silver of 5s 2d per ozt. In principle, this measure should not have undermined the floor price for silver bullion, but creditors in large transactions may have been able to insist that silver coins be valued at their market value, like foreign specie. In any event, the silver price dropped towards the mint price and fell marginally below it in 1774, 1785 and 1788 (Figure 3.29). In 1798, the right to deliver silver to the Mint for coining was withdrawn, and the mint price for silver was effectively suspended for the duration

[72] P. Antipa, 'How fiscal policy affects the price level: Britain's first experience with paper money', *Banque de France Working Paper*, no. 525 (November 2014), pp. 11–16.

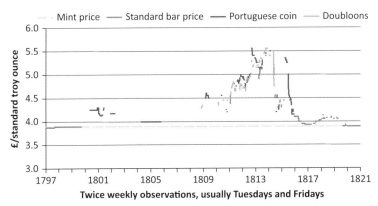

FIGURE 3.28 Gold price during suspension, 1797–1821.
Sources: Bank of England Archive, 2A 109/1; J. Castaing (from 1698).

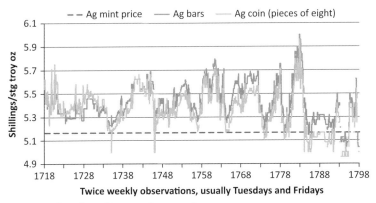

FIGURE 3.29 London silver market, 1718–1797.
Sources: J. Castaing (from 1698); Bank of England Archive, 2A 109/1 (Figure reproduced with kind permission of Palgrave Macmillan, see page xiii).

of the war.[73] This meant that the cap and collar for silver prices were definitely not operative after 1798, and the price of sterling silver bars peaked at 6 s (£0.30) in November 1782 (Figure 3.30). When the minting of silver was resumed in 1815, it was on a different basis – as we shall see later – but before doing so, we should touch on another consequence of the eighteenth-century currency reforms.

The closer alignment of the mint and market prices of gold during the eighteenth century meant that minted guineas were available for circulation. Previously, a rise in bullion prices could lead to a sudden scarcity of

[73] M-H. Li (1963), p. 165; G. P. Dyer and P. P. Gaspar in C. E. Challis (ed.) (1992), pp. 449–50.

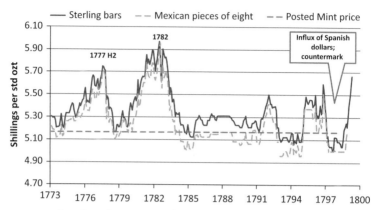

FIGURE 3.30 London silver price, July 1773 to September 1799.
Sources: J. Castaing (from 1698); C. E. Challis (1992), p. 449; K. Clancy (1999), pp. 12, 41.

coin because there was an incentive to hoard coins of fuller weight.[74] By the eighteenth century, the incentive to hoard coins was largely removed because the gold price was kept close to its mint price – so that guineas were not over-collateralised – and the remaining silver coins were so underweight they could not become over-collateralised. Minted coins could be expected to stay in circulation, offering the prospect of the money stock providing a more straightforward proxy for liquidity. As David Hume noted in the mid-eighteenth century, an influx of money, in the form of circulating coins, could be expected to lead to a transient increase in output, followed by higher staple prices and wages:

In my opinion, it is only in the interval or intermediate situation, between the acquisition of money and the rise in prices, that the increasing quantity of gold or silver is favourable to industry … The farmer or gardener, finding that their commodities are taken off, apply themselves with alacrity to the raising of more … It is easy to trace the money in its progress through the whole commonwealth; where we shall find that it must first quicken the diligence of every individual, before it increases the price of labour.[75]

The stabilisation of bullion prices in a range close to the mint price meant that coins issued by the Mint would be expected to remain in circulation, rather than being hoarded. The scope for passing off counterfeited

---

[74] M. Casson and C. Casson (2015), pp. 57–8.

[75] D. Hume, 'Of Money' (1752) in *Essays: Moral, Political, and Literary* (Edinburgh: Cadell, Donaldson and Creech, 1777) (ed.) E. F. Miller (Indianapolis, IN: Liberty Fund, 1987), pt. II, essay III, I.

coins was likewise limited. The stock of coins in circulation – that is to say, the money supply – now reflected Mint output, rather than being dominated by movements in bullion prices relative to mint prices. The quantity of money had become an operational concept with possible implications for the prices of ordinary commodities, rather than a (non-interest-bearing) asset class that could be hoarded or circulated.[76]

Bullion price stabilisation also had important implications for the development of the Bank as an issuer of notes convertible into current coin. The variable price of gold and silver had exposed the Bank to the risk of having to acquire guineas and bullion for minting at a 'losing price'.[77] The Bank could seek to mitigate this risk by holding more bullion and specie, but this asset class was non-interest-bearing and would result in capital losses if precious metal prices fell. The close alignment of bullion prices with the mint price protected the Bank from basis risk between its precious metal assets, and its sterling liabilities. This is an issue to which we shall return in Chapter 5.

Residual bimetallic problems facing Britain's coinage were eventually put to rest in the early nineteenth century by a technological innovation. Steam power was harnessed to press token coins made of copper and silver. These coins were designed to be under-collateralised and, at the same time, uneconomic to counterfeit. Copper coins issued in the 1790s did suffer from a sharp rise in the price of copper, leaving them over-collateralised, but this was an exceptional consequence of the wartime embargo. Silver coins issued from 1815 were under-collateralised and, in general, it was not economic to pass counterfeits. Holders of regal copper and silver coins were able to exchange them for sovereigns at par, that is to say, exchange them for gold coins at their nominal values as legal tender. The market price of silver did fall relative to that of gold in the late nineteenth century, reducing the collateralisation of silver coins yet further, but convertibility at par meant this did not matter for the purposes of domestic exchange. The perennial problem of small change had been solved by minting fully collateralised gold coins – sovereigns and half sovereigns – and a subsidiary coinage made of silver and copper.[78]

After 1815, holders of silver had no right to deliver bullion to the Mint and receive silver coins at a posted price. There was no effective mint price for silver, and no cap and collar on the market price of silver bullion. The

---

[76] T. J. Sargent and F. R. Velde (2002), p. 11.

[77] H. Thornton, 1802 edn (ed.) F. A von Hayek (1962), p. 218.

[78] A. E. Feavearyear (1963), pp. 189–90; A. Redish (December 1990), pp. 799–806; T. J. Sargent and F. R. Velde (2002), pp. 13–14, 302–5.

FIGURE 3.31 Silver prices after 1816.
Sources: J. Castaing (from 1698); C. E. Challis (1992), p. 480.

Mint met the public's demand for silver coins, using silver purchased at
the prevailing market price, allowing the Exchequer to make a profit on
the minting of under-collateralised coins. The bar price of silver stabilised
slightly below the historic mint price during the mid-nineteenth century
but declined to a 50 per cent discount in the late nineteenth century, as
most countries moved on to the gold standard (Figure 3.31). The fall in
the silver price had no monetary repercussions in Britain, but proved to
be a source of angst for silver based currencies elsewhere in the world,
not to mention the mine owners of Nevada and Colorado, and their
advocate, William Jennings Bryan.[79]

Sterling's move from a silver standard to a gold one proved to be a considerable success, but it was not without risk. At the time of the currency
reforms of the 1770s, most countries were wedded to silver standards,
and some attempted to maintain bimetallic standards. The adoption of an
international gold standard in the nineteenth century was by no means a
foregone conclusion, and Britain's adoption of a gold standard in the
eighteenth century was largely a matter of happenstance. Lockean doctrine aside, a less adventurous policy for sterling in the eighteenth century
might have been to devalue against silver by around 20 per cent and retain
silver coinage for middle denomination coins: shillings (1 s), crowns (5 s),
and possibly double crowns (10 s). The guinea could have been allowed to

[79] W. F. Hixson, *Triumph of the Bankers: Money and Banking in the Eighteenth and
Nineteenth Centuries* (Westport, CT, and London: Praeger, 1993), pp. 162–70; M. A.
King, *The End of Alchemy: Money, Banking and the Future of the Global Economy*
(London: Little, Brown, 2016), pp. 76, 86.

revert to a floating exchange value – around 21 s, but not constrained to that level – thereby limiting scope for bimetallic arbitrage. Token copper coinage, convertible at par into silver coinage, could have provided a low denomination medium of circulation. In this Lowndesian scenario, the international gold standard of the nineteenth century might never have happened, although gold bullion and specie – trading at variable prices – would probably have played a more significant role in financial flows.

Whether a Lowndesian silver standard could have survived is a matter of conjecture. Sterling's success in the eighteenth century depended on the management of its collateral value, irrespective of whether it took the form of gold, silver, or possibly some other commodity. The Newton–Liverpool reforms did the trick on the currency front, but they were not sufficient to secure stability in London's equally important credit markets. Crises in the markets for paper credit became endemic in the second half of the eighteenth century, and it is to these markets that we shall turn in Chapter 4. The problem of destabilising collateral values resumed in the latter decades of the twentieth century, and this is considered in subsequent chapters.

4

Credit Markets and Clearing Banks

The successful taming of London's bullion market during the eighteenth century did not extend to its market for paper credit. Writing in the 1790s, the banker and parliamentarian Henry Thornton, described the disruption caused by crises of confidence in country bank notes and the scope for mitigating the problem.[1] To understand Thornton's arguments, it is best to clarify the longstanding role of circulating paper in the form of bills of exchange, accommodation paper and promissory notes. There was a view, popularised in some Victorian histories of money, that credit remained relatively underdeveloped in pre-modern economies. Barter in primitive societies was supposed to have given way to commodity monies and minted currencies, and thence to banknotes convertible into specie and, finally, inconvertible paper and book-entry forms of money.[2] This stadial approach to monetary history presented circulating paper credit as a predominantly modern phenomenon associated with fractional reserve banking – a view that has been trotted out uncritically in textbooks of macroeconomics and money, at least until recently.[3] It has been labelled

---

[1] H. Thornton, *An Enquiry into the Nature and Effects of the Paper Credit of Great Britain* (Philadelphia: James Humphreys, 1807, reprinted, Kessinger, 2008), pp. 154–5.

[2] Sir James Steuart, *An Inquiry into the Principles of Political Oeconomy* (1st edn, 1767; 2nd edn, 1805), vol. II, book III (eds) A. S. Skinner, N. Kobayashi and H. Mizuta (4 vols, London: Pickering & Chatto, 1998), vol. 2, pp. 196–201; W. S. Jevons, *Money and the Mechanism of Exchange*, 1875 (London, 9th edn, 1890), pp. 4–13; W. T. Newlyn and R. P. Bootle, *Theory of Money* (Oxford: Clarendon Press, 3rd edn, 1978), pp. 5–11; C. P. Kindleberger, *A Financial History of Western Europe* (London: Allen & Unwin, 1984; 2nd edn, New York and Oxford, Oxford University Press, 1993), p. 19.

[3] J. E. Stiglitz and J. Driffill, *Economics* (New York: W. W. Norton, 2000), p. 521; references cited in D. Greaber, *Debt: The First 5,000 Years* (New York: Melville House, 2011), pp. 21–8, 40–1.

the 'economists' myth' as scholarship of medieval and early modern credit networks has gained interdisciplinary acceptance.[4]

Deferred settlement did play a part in pre-modern economies, but the extent to which debt obligations were on-sold to third parties is less clear. Merchants routinely provided credit to buyers of their goods, recording amounts receivable in their shop ledgers, with some sort of understanding between the parties about the time allowed for settlement.[5] Collateralised credit was also available: pawnbrokers provided loans against chattels, conveyancing scriveners found investors to purchase mortgaged property, and goldsmiths provided loans against the security of gold and silver bars, plate and foreign specie.[6]

Mortgaging properties meant selling them to a lender with the option to repurchase them at a pre-agreed price in the future. In the interim, the lender would receive rents paid by tenants on the estate, providing a running yield on the loan. If the market price of the property fell below its option price, the borrower could walk away, and the lender would not have recourse to the borrower – in contrast to the position of parties associated with bills. Mortgagees (i.e. lenders) would typically protect themselves against possible falls in property prices by purchasing mortgaged property at no more than two-thirds of its market value, and granting an option for the mortgagor (i.e. borrower) to repurchase it at a similar (in the money) price. Mortgage loans would therefore be over-collateralised, protecting the lender – up to a point – from falls in property values, leaving the borrower with an equity of redemption, and any upside in the property's capital value.[7] Pawnbrokers and goldsmiths likewise relied on pledged assets, and usually had limited recourse to the

---

[4] D. Graeber (2011), p. 52; W. S. Jevons (1890), pp. 1–7.

[5] A. P. Usher, 'The origin of the bill of exchange', *Journal of Political Economy*, 22, no. 6 (June 1914), pp. 575–6; Lord Crowther, *Report of the Committee on Consumer Credit* (2 vols, London: HMSO, March 1971), pp. 31–40; P. Nightingale, 'Monetary contraction and mercantile credit in later medieval England', *Economic History Review*, 43, no. 4 (November 1990), pp. 562, 564–74.

[6] S. Quinn, 'Money, Finance and Capital Markets' in R. C. Floud and P. Johnson (eds) *The Cambridge Economic History of Modern Britain*, Vol. 1: *Industrialisation, 1700–1860* (Cambridge: Cambridge University Press (2004), pp. 158–9.

[7] E. H. Blake, 'Mortgages: Some Notes on Law and Practice', *The Auctioneers' Institute of the United Kingdom* (London, 11th November 1908), p. 15; A. Offer, *Property and Politics 1870–1914: Landownership, Law, Ideology and Urban Development in England* (Cambridge: Cambridge University Press, 1981), p. 137; L. D. Neal, 'The Finance of Business during the Industrial Revolution' in R. C. Floud and D. McCloskey (eds) *The Cambridge Economic History of Modern Britain*, Vol. I: *1700–1860* (Cambridge: Cambridge University Press, 2nd edn, 1994), pp. 163–4.

borrower if the value of their security fell below the amount of the outstanding loan. These lenders also took a margin of security, leaving their borrowers with an equity interest in their pledged assets.

The development of bills of exchange in the Middle Ages opened the door to extended credit networks, and the trading of negotiable instruments. The conventions governing bill market practice differed across countries and between trades, and evolved over time, but the general principles of their governance can be summarised as follows. A seller of a consignment of goods would address an unconditional order in writing to the purchaser specifying:

• an amount in money to be paid for a specified shipment of goods;
• the timing of the payment, which could be on sight, or at a fixed or determinable date in the future;
• the party to whom payment should be made – a specified payee, or to the order of a payee.[8]

The sender of the instruction became the drawer of the bill by signing it. The person to whom the bill was addressed was the drawee, and that person became the acceptor of the bill by signing it. The payee could retain the bill to maturity, and receive the acceptor's payment on the due date, or endorse the back of the bill, and sell it to an endorsee. Bills did not pay interest and would therefore be sold at a discount – reflecting the time cost of money and their credit risks – and the selling of bills became known as bill discounting. The endorsee could retain the bill to maturity, or become the second endorser on the back of the bill, and discount it again. The discounting of a bill could be repeated any number of times, resulting in multiple endorsements, until payment was received from the acceptor.[9] In the event of non-payment on the due date, the bill could be protested, and its owner – the last endorsee – had recourse to the last endorser, and the chain of previous endorsers back to the acceptor, and finally the drawer. All parties to the bill would normally be jointly and severally liable to pay the holder of the bill, although bills could be held temporarily without endorsement; for example, a bill broker, acting as agent, could ask a seller to endorse a bill in blank, leaving the broker free to find a buyer, who would then become the endorsee.[10]

---

[8] W. M. Scammell, *The London Discount Market* (London: Elek Books, 1968), pp. 21–4.
[9] Gillett Brothers, *The Bill on London* (London: Chapman Hall, 1964), pp. 12, 13, 94.
[10] G. Rae, *The Country Banker: His Clients, Cares, and Work* (London: John Murray, 1885), p. 100; W. T. C. King, *History of the London Discount Market* (London: Cass, 1936), xv–xvi; Gillett Brothers (1964), pp. 21–2.

A supplier of goods might be able to distrain the property of a defaulting debtor on grounds of breach of contract, but a discounted bill was not, of itself, secured on the goods being delivered. Third party holders of bills had no legal rights to seize the underlying consignment of goods in the event of non-payment, but the tenor of bills was normally set to give acceptors sufficient time to take delivery of the goods and sell them. This meant that there was a reasonable chance that the debt could be repaid using receipts from the sale. The bill was self-liquidating, even though its holder did not have a lien on the underlying goods. The beauty of the bill was that it did not impede supply chains by encumbering goods with potential claims from third parties, but third-party bill holders took comfort from 'clausing' on the face of the bill, specifying the goods being financed.[11] The self-liquidating nature of bills meant that they did not necessarily economise on the need for currency, but they could help to economise on the cost of transporting coins.[12] Two-way international trade between Amsterdam and London, for example, could be settled by an acceptor in Amsterdam paying an endorsee in Amsterdam, and likewise in London, eliminating the need to transport specie and bullion between the two centres (Figure 4.1).[13]

Clausing could be viewed as a form of quasi-collateralisation, even if bills were not legally secured on consignments of goods. That said, there was no margin of over-collateralisation, and if the price of the underlying commodities fell, the amount due would not be covered by the sale proceeds. The parties involved were expected to be adequately capitalised to cover the solvency risk of capital losses on the underlying goods being traded, but this was not always the case, and bankruptcies could occur. The absence of a collateral margin meant the bill could be abused by speculators, taking leveraged positions on commodity prices. Instead of a natural buyer of grain, such as a miller, agreeing to take a delivery three months hence, and accepting a bill requiring payment of a fixed sum on delivery, a

[11] Gillett Brothers (1964), pp. 22, 92; L. D. Neal, *The Rise of Financial Capitalism: International Capital Markets in the Age of Reason* (Cambridge: Cambridge University Press, 1990), pp. 5–9; P. M. W. Tucker, 'Managing the central bank's balance sheet: where monetary policy meets financial stability', *BEQB*, 44, no. 3 (Autumn 2004), p. 377.

[12] P. Nightingale, 'Monetary contraction and mercantile credit in later medieval England', *Economic History Review*, 43, no. 4 (November 1990), p. 574.

[13] L. D. Neal, *The Rise of Financial Capitalism: International Capital Markets in the Age of Reason* (Cambridge: Cambridge University Press, 1990), pp. 5–9 and Figure 1.1; L. D. Neal and S. Quinn, 'Networks of information, markets, and institutions in the rise of London as a financial centre, 1660–1720', *Financial History Review*, 8, no. 1 (April 2001), pp. 11–12.

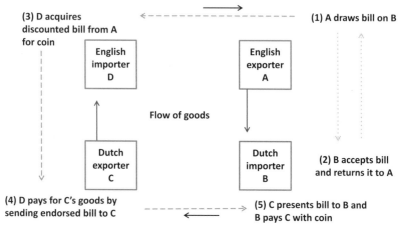

FIGURE 4.1 Mechanics of a bill of exchange.
Source: Author's diagram.

speculator might purchase grain on paper credit, in the hope that it could be resold at a higher price. From time to time, the market could be disrupted by defaults resulting from speculative losses. For this reason, the parties named on a bill, their roles, and their personal wealth were important determinants of bill quality. It mattered whether the acceptor of the bill was a natural buyer of the underlying commodity, or a speculator placing a bet – although the distinction between the two was not always clear-cut.[14]

Sellers could legitimately arrange credit on terms that did not qualify as properly drawn bills, and the resulting paper credits came to be known as accommodation paper, or finance paper. Some accommodation paper could be loosely associated with an underlying consignment of goods, for example, stock finance, but not qualify because it was not a self-liquidating transaction. Other accommodation paper might bear scant relation to an underlying transaction, and be used to fund longer-term fixed investment, but still be expressed as an order to pay with recourse to a drawer, acceptor and endorsers. The underlying problem of all accommodation paper was that it was not self-liquidating. It had to be repaid before sufficient cash flows arose from underlying investments, leaving borrowers reliant on the issuance of new paper to refinance maturing debts, and exposing themselves to refinancing risk.[15]

---

[14] W. Leaf, *Banking* (ed.) E. Sykes (3rd edn, 1935; reprinted 1937; 4th edn, London and New York: Oxford University Press, 1943), p. 172.

[15] E. Sykes, *Banking and Currency* (London: Butterworth, 9th edn, 1947), p. 143.

A disturbance in the market could lead regular buyers of paper credits to hold back, at least temporarily, even if they were offered paper at ever-steeper discounts (and therefore higher yields). Borrowers with a maturity mismatch between their cash flows and their debt obligations might then find themselves unable to meet their liabilities when they became due, and some of them could face bankruptcy. The plight of these distressed borrowers could remain a localised problem, if there were a clear distinction between quality names using properly drawn bills, and lesser ones using accommodation paper. In practice, firms could use a combination of bills and accommodation paper, and quality names could be owed money by lesser ones, making it difficult to discern the market-wide implications of insolvencies, or other disturbances. Faced with these sorts of uncertainty, it was often easier for regular buyers of bills and paper to sit on their hands – hoarding coin and bullion – until the fog had cleared, exposing all and sundry to a contraction of credit.

Needless to say, market abuses could aggravate the problems of solvency risk and maturity mismatching. An unwary purchaser of bills could be presented with accommodation paper, purporting to be a bill: clausing could refer to fictitious goods, or the same consignment of goods might be claused on multiple bills.[16] Paper purporting to be a bill could be cross-fired: that is, a bill drawn by A on B could be matched by a bill drawn by B on A.[17] By all accounts, it was difficult to verify the clausing of bills, unless you were active in the same market, and this was a good reason for bills to circulate within the same or connected trades, and where there was likely to be an ongoing business relationship. In well-ordered mercantile markets, where the parties knew each other, there was an incentive for drawers to follow the rules, and for acceptors to meet their obligations in a timely manner. Those who did not do so were quickly identified, suffering a loss of reputation, and a reduced prospect of raising finance in future.[18] However, it was all too easy for doubtful paper to be bought by ill-informed and insufficiently discriminating buyers, encouraging the further supply of dodgy paper, until the music stopped, and calamity followed.[19]

Promissory notes and IOUs provided a further complication. Instead of a seller preparing a bill to be accepted by a buyer, the record of

---

[16] W. T. C. King (1936), pp. 123–6.
[17] J. W. Gilbart (ed.) A. S. Michie, *Gilbart on Banking: The History, Principles and Practice of Banking* (2 vols, London: George Bell, 1882), I, p. 255.
[18] L. D. Neal and S. Quinn (2001), pp. 12–14; S. Quinn (2004), p. 154.
[19] E. Sykes (1947), p. 142–3.

indebtedness could be prepared by an obligator, expressed as a promise to pay a sum of money, for value received. Negotiable promissory notes, specifying the amount and timing of a payment, could circulate alongside bills and accommodation paper. To be negotiable, promissory notes needed to be sufficiently clear about the terms of payment, whereas simple descriptions of indebtedness were more likely to be non-negotiable IOUs. Promissory notes would be expected to circulate as bearer instruments – ownership passing by delivery and without endorsement – but they could be traded like accommodation paper, if they were endorsed: the maker of the note becoming the acceptor, and the payee becoming the drawer, with a chain of endorsers, and the final endorsee.[20]

At the time of its foundation in 1694, the Bank of England garnered the right to be the sole corporation allowed to issue promissory notes in England. In practice, the Bank's notes circulated mainly in London, and note-issuing country banks proliferated outside the metropolitan area during the second half of the eighteenth century. The country banks did not infringe the Bank's note issuing monopoly because they were partnerships, rather than chartered, or joint-stock banks. The Bank's notes and those of the country banks circulated as bearer instruments, passing from hand to hand without endorsement, with the promise that their issuer would redeem them with real money – current coins of the realm. There was no recourse to the, usually anonymous, chain of past noteholders.[21] During the currency crisis of 1695, the Bank issued specie notes that paid 6 per cent interest, and were repayable 'in the same specie' as those originally tendered, for example, full-weight guineas.[22] After the crisis, the Bank reverted to ordinary banknotes that paid no interest, and were redeemable in current coins, without a commitment to repayment in coins of a specified type and weight.[23] These banknotes usurped coins as the main means for settling wholesale transactions in London: endorsees of maturing bills, for example, would normally accept payment in

---

[20] H. D. MacLeod, *The Theory and Practice of Banking* (2 vols, London: Longman, 3rd edn, 1875), I, p. 31; J. Hutchison, *The Practice of Banking: Embracing the Cases at Law and in Equity Bearing upon All Branches of the Subject* (4 vols, London: Effingham Wilson, 1881), I, pp. 150–7.

[21] J. Hutchison (1881), I, pp. 158.

[22] W. M. Acres, *The Bank of England from Within, 1694–1900* (2 vols, London: Oxford University Press, 1931), I, pp. 72, 77, 92–4; R. D. Richards, *The Early History of Banking in England* (London: P. S. King & Son, 1929), pp. 155–75; Sir John Clapham, *The Bank of England: A History, I: 1694–1797; II: 1797–1914* (Cambridge: Cambridge University Press, 1944), I, 1944, pp. 37, 41–2, 145, 291.

[23] J. Clapham (1944), I, pp. 5–24, 30–3.

Bank of England banknotes, or payment by bank draft credited to their account with a London bank.

London's private banks held the Bank's banknotes as their main liquidity reserve, relying on their ability to convert them into coin at the Bank, if required. By the 1770s, they were settling payments among themselves on a net basis, using a centralised clearing system. Net settlement offered the possibility of much higher payment volumes without the need for matching flows of banknotes. Country banks held their liquidity reserves mainly in the form of deposit balances with their correspondent banks in London, and settled their customers' payments by making transfers among these accounts. Country banks held coins in their tills to meet customer requirements, but the logistics of replenishing their tills with coins from London was relatively straightforward, albeit with some harassment from highwaymen. This pyramidal reserve system meant that the country's bullion reserves were concentrated at the Bank, and the Bank's banknotes were predominantly held by London's banks, and the country banks' liquidity was predominantly held in the form of deposits with London banks.[24]

All three types of bank were operating with fractional reserves, rather than being fully reserved depository institutions (Figure 4.2). In other words, their short-term customer liabilities – banknotes and deposits – were not 100 per cent backed with reserves.[25] In the event of an outflow of funds, reserves provided no more than a breathing space, giving banks time to rebuild their liquidity, by running off soon-to-mature bills and bonds, and curbing their advances and discounts. In practice, overall bank credit provision need not be disturbed, if an outflow of reserves from one bank led to inflows to others, but there were two important instances when the sector could suffer a net outflow of reserves with potentially more dramatic effects.[26]

The Bank's reserves could be depleted by flows of bullion and specie abroad – an external drain. This is what happened in 1695 when bad harvests led to increased imports of grain, and wartime remittances led to outflows on capital account. The financing of these flows led to reduced bullion reserves, and the Bank sought to mitigate the loss by

---

[24] Sir A. E. Feavearyear (ed.) E. Victor Morgan, *The Pound Sterling: A History of English Money* (Oxford: Oxford University Press, 2nd edn, 1963), p. 166.

[25] B. Granville, *Remembering Inflation* (Princeton, NJ, and Oxford: Princeton University Press, 2013), pp. 165–74.

[26] L. S. Pressnell, *Country Banking in the Industrial Revolution* (Oxford: Oxford University Press, 1956), pp. 434–40; W. T. King (1936), p. 7–14.

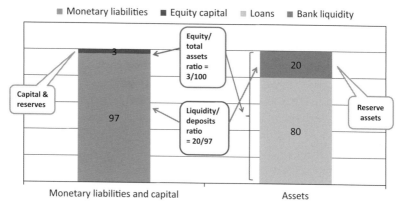

FIGURE 4.2 Fractional reserve banking.
Source: Author's diagram.

restricting its advances and discounts, which had the effect of suppressing its note issuance. The Bank's shortage of reserves was not offset elsewhere in the banking sector by an influx of reserves. As a result, there was no countervailing expansion of credit; indeed, the Bank's suppression of its note issuance limited the reserve position of the London banks, encouraging them to restrict their credit, with a knock-on effect on the country banks.

The other troublesome possibility was for the Bank's reserves to suffer an internal drain as a result of increased public demand for coins. The country banks would accommodate the public's demand for coins by ordering more from the Bank, via their correspondent banks in London. Their purchases of coins would deplete their balances with the London banks, and – when the coins were paid over to their customers – there would be a matching reduction in the country banks' note issuance. The London banks' acquisition of coins, on behalf of the country banks, would deplete their stock of Bank of England banknotes and, when the coins were conveyed to the country banks, there would be a matching reduction in country bank balances with the London banks. The Bank's reduced reserves of coin – and bullion sent for minting – would be matched by a reduction of its banknote issuance. Both internal and external drains would therefore lead to a contraction of the banking sector as a whole.[27]

The Achilles heel of the English banking system in the late eighteenth century was the propensity of country bank customers to take fright

[27] H. Thornton, 1807 edn (2008), pp. 194–5.

en masse and demand that their notes be redeemed in coins. This is an example of Anna Schwartz's description of a crisis:

Fears that the means of payment will be unobtainable at any price … in a fractional reserve banking system leads to a scramble for high-powered money [i.e. bank reserves and publicly held cash]. It is precipitated by the actions of the public that suddenly squeeze the reserves of the banking system … it is short-lived, ending with a slackening of the public's demand for additional currency.[28]

Thornton suggested that up to one-third of country bank notes were returned for cash in 1797, and outflows on such a scale required a broader balance sheet adjustment.[29] Although there was no loss of confidence in the Bank's banknotes, the internal drain from the banking system meant that the Bank lost bullion reserves, and felt compelled to contract its balance sheet, alongside other banks. The banks could sell bills and bonds only at deep discounts (and therefore high yields) to secure Bank of England banknotes and guineas. In his Parliamentary evidence, Thornton pointed out that during the 1797 crisis, the yield on 'Exchequer bills, India bonds and other such securities soon convertible into Bank notes' reached 18 per cent, compared to 8 to 10 per cent on slightly longer maturities.[30] 'The interest paid by the sale and re-purchase of the Stock' for a few weeks was likewise around 18 per cent.[31] The sharp inversion of the term yield curve highlighted a strategic weakness in the English banking system.

Speaking after the suspension of note convertibility in 1797 – but before the problems of devaluation and inflation became evident – Thornton argued that the Bank should seek to reintermediate an internal drain by acquiring good quality bills, funded with its own banknotes. In other words, the Bank should buy assets the banks could not sell to the public, provided they were of good quality. To this end, Thornton and the Banking School argued that the Bank should be free to acquire 'real bills', by which they meant properly drawn bills, rather than accommodation paper. Provided the London banks remained willing to accept Bank of England banknotes as consideration for their bills and bonds, the

---

[28] A. Schwartz (1986), cited in F. H. Capie, 'British Financial Crises in the Nineteenth and Twentieth Centuries' in N. H. Dimsdale and A. C. Hotson (eds) *British Financial Crises since 1825* (Oxford: Oxford University Press, 2014), p. 9.

[29] H. Thornton (ed.) F. A. von Hayek, *An Enquiry into the Nature and Effects of the Paper Credit of Great Britain*, 1802 edn and Thornton's parliamentary speeches and evidence (London: Cass, 1939, reprinted 1962), pp. 283–5.

[30] H. Thornton, 1802 edn (ed.) F. A. von Hayek (1962), pp. 296–7.

[31] H. Thornton, 1802 edn (ed.) F. A. von Hayek (1962), pp. 290–1.

liquidity impasse could be resolved.[32] A similar remedy could be applied in the case of external drains. Thornton suggested the Bank should acquire bills and bonds, if it were to maintain its note issuance in the face of bullion outflows. Thus, it was not always wrong for the Bank to bid more aggressively for bills, and this might be the result of an efflux of bullion, rather than the cause.[33]

The threat to the Bank's reserves during the Napoleonic wars was avoided by the simple expedient of suspending the convertibility of the Bank's notes. The subsequent experience of inflation and devaluation stiffened official resolve to return to convertibility after the war, and this was finally achieved in 1821. The paper currency of the French revolutionaries provided an even more salutary lesson: the assignat was meant to be backed by expropriated church lands, but over-issuance led to a loss of confidence in the notes, and hyperinflation had ensued between 1792 and 1796.[34] The prospect of convertibility after the end of hostilities was sufficient to quell inflation in Britain, but there were recurrent credit crises, the banking collapse of 1825 being particularly severe. The country banks were viewed as villains of the piece, and their right to issue notes was restricted from 1826, leaving the Bank as the main issuer of banknotes.[35]

The Bank was also open to criticism for excessive note issuance, notwithstanding Thornton's earlier arguments. The Currency School gained the upper hand over the Banking School, and official attention was directed towards setting rules for the Bank's note issuance – the basic idea being that a change in the Bank's bullion reserves should be reflected in its banknote issuance. Sir Robert Peel's Bank Charter Act of 1844 split the Bank into Issue and Banking Departments, the former issuing banknotes backed by bullion save for a limited fiduciary issue. A drain of bullion, reducing the Bank's bullion reserves, would be funded by a return of banknotes to the Bank, and a matching contraction of the assets and liabilities of the Issue Department. A reduction in circulating banknotes was intended to reduce domestic prices, improve the trade balance, and ameliorate the external drain. The 1844 Act's preoccupation with banknote issuance was

---

[32] H. Thornton, 1802 edn (ed.) F. A. von Hayek (1962), pp. 84–5, 253, 303–6; B. Norman, R. Shaw, G. Speight, 'The history of interbank settlement arrangements: exploring central banks' role in the payment system', *Bank of England Working Paper*, no. 412 (June 2011), p. 23.

[33] H. Thornton, 1807 edn (2008), p. 90–1.

[34] H. Thornton, 1807 edn (2008), pp. 212–3.

[35] N. H. Dimsdale and A. C. Hotson (2014), pp. 33–4.

understandable in view of Thornton's concerns about under-issuance in the 1790s, and the Currency School's preoccupation with over-issuance during the Napoleonic wars, but changes in the nature of banks' reserves meant that banknotes moved from centre stage.[36]

Nine years after the passage of the 1844 act, the London Bankers' Clearing House (LBCH) started to use bankers' balances at the Bank (BB) to settle payments among its member banks, rather than exchanging reams of banknotes.[37] Customer payments resulted in payee banks gaining bankers' balances (BBs) at the expense of payer banks, a zero-sum game between clearing banks because BBs were not held outside the banking system, and the Bank did not allow overdrafts on its BB accounts. An increase in total BBs depended on the Bank's assets increasing by more than the increase in its non-BB liabilities, and the proceeds arising from the excess growth of its assets being credited to BBs:

Change in bankers' balances at the Bank
$$= \Delta \, \text{BB} = \Delta \, \text{Bank's assets} = [\Delta \, \text{loans} + \Delta \, \text{securities} + \Delta \, \text{bullion}]$$

Less

$$\Delta \, \text{Bank's liabilities ex-BBs} = [\Delta \, \text{banknotes} + \Delta \, \text{Exchequer balances}$$
$$+ \Delta \, \text{other customer balances} + \Delta \, \text{capital and reserves}]$$

Two factors had a notable influence on the Bank's balance sheet and BBs: net payments to the Exchequer would tend to reduce BBs, as would an increase in public demand for notes and coin. A net payment to the Exchequer could arise from a surplus of tax receipts and government borrowing receipts over government disbursements on goods and services and interest payments on the national debt. For these purposes, public take up of notes and coin was a form of government borrowing. These counterparts to BBs are set out in Figure 4.3. BBs had a marked seasonal pattern in the early nineteenth century, reflecting the quarterly shuttings, when interest was paid on Consols. Payment of quarterly interest unleashed a flood of liquidity into the money market, and BBs would rise sharply. For the rest of the quarter, BBs would tend to decline, reflecting net flows to the Exchequer (Figure 4.4). Easter could have a contractionary effect on BBs because of strong seasonal demand for notes and coin. The clearing banks would replenish their stock of banknotes, following customer withdrawals, and there would be a matching reduction in their BBs.

[36] N. H. Dimsdale and A. C. Hotson (2014), pp. 36–7.
[37] J. W. Gilbart (1882), I, p. 293, fn.; W. T. C. King (1936), p. 127, fn. 2.

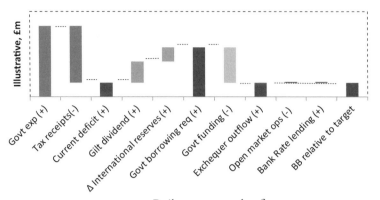

FIGURE 4.3 Daily money market flows.
Source: Author's diagram.

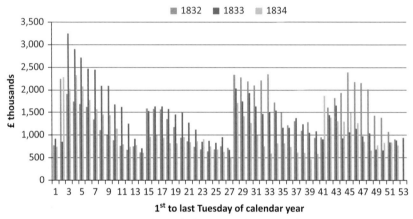

FIGURE 4.4 Bankers' balances at the Bank of England.
Source: BEQB (June 1967), Appendix, Table B.

The Bank was reluctant to alleviate seasonal shortages in the money market, even though BBs could fall to perilously low levels in the weeks before the next payment on Consols, and some banks were in danger of being forced into involuntary overdraft – negative BBs. It was suggested that the problem could be solved by moving some government accounts to private banks, and this helped to persuade the Bank that it was in its commercial interest to alleviate routine market shortages.[38] The Bank found it could use excess Exchequer balances to redeem government debt, saving the government interest, and this helped to stabilise BBs. Another short-term

[38] J. Clapham (1944), II, p. 137.

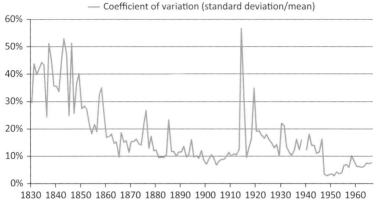

FIGURE 4.5 Intra-year variability of bankers' balances.
Sources: BEQB (June 1967), Appendix.

tactic to alleviate a cash imbalance in the market was for the Bank to lend or borrow on Consols – effectively buying (or selling) Consols for cash, and selling (or buying) them back at the next fortnightly settlement.[39] Lending on Consols is what we would now call a repo, and it has the effect of alleviating a cash shortage in the market. Borrowing on Consols – a reverse repo – drains surplus cash from the market. In time, these practices were regularised in the form of open-market operations (OMO) – outright trades in bills, or other assets, with the banks and discount houses – and secured lending via the houses, namely, discount window lending (DWL).[40] Between the 1830s and the 1890s, seasonal fluctuations in BBs declined markedly, and the Bank started to provide routine market assistance ensuring that total BBs followed a steady path (Figure 4.5).[41]

The use of routine market assistance to stabilise BBs was an updated version of Thornton's plan for the Bank to maintain its note issuance by offsetting internal and external drains of bullion with bill purchases. For BBs to remain on target, Δ BB = 0, the Bank's routine market assistance had to offset autonomous influences on BBs, notably Exchequer flows, bullion drains, and changing public demand for banknotes.[42]

[39] W. Leaf (1943), pp. 208–9.
[40] R. J. Truptil, *British Banks and the London Money Market* (London: J. Cape, 1936), pp. 181–90; A. E. Feavearyear (1963), p. 175.
[41] W. T. C. King (1936), pp. 126–8.
[42] Bank of England, 'Management of money day-by-day', *BEQB*, 3, no. 1 (March 1963), pp. 15–21.

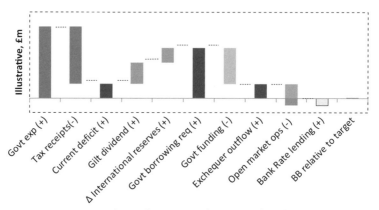

FIGURE 4.6 Classical system and OMO induced shortage.
Source: Author's diagram.

Routine market assistance = OMO + DWL
= Exchequer receipts + Exchequer borrowing
− Exchequer disbursements + Δ banknotes
+ Δ bullion reserves + Δ other Bank liabilities
− Δ other Bank assets

(The preceding counterparts to BBs are set out graphically in Figure 4.6.)

The Bank's practice of stabilising BBs did not mean it disregarded the level of bullion reserves backing its quick liabilities – banknotes and deposits. During the second half of the nineteenth century the ratio of the Bank's reserves to its quick liabilities was maintained at close to 40 per cent, in marked contrast to the variability of its quick ratio in the eighteenth century (Figures 4.7 and 4.8).[43]

The 40 per cent ratio was stabilised by using interest rate policy to keep the Bank's bullion reserves in appropriate alignment with its quick liabilities. Bank rate would be raised in a crisis to stem an efflux of bullion, and, in more demanding circumstances, bullion loans would be extended by the international market, or by foreign governments (Figure 4.9 and 4.10). A rise in Bank rate would not normally be matched by similarly timed rises in the rates of other currencies and, as a result, bullion would be drawn to London in payment for higher yielding sterling bills. This would normally be sufficient to replenish the Bank's reserves.[44] The willingness of other countries to play the gold-standard game in accordance with these informal rules

[43] R. J. Truptil (1936), pp. 42–58.
[44] Cunliffe Report, *First Interim Report of the Committee on Currency and the Foreign Exchanges after the War*, Cmnd 9182 (1918), paragraph 4.

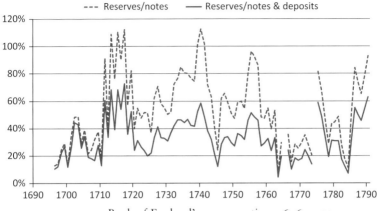

FIGURE 4.7 Bank of England's reserve ratios, 1696–1790.
Source: BEQB (June 1967), Appendix cited on p. 159, Table A.

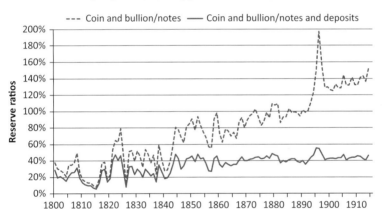

FIGURE 4.8 Bank's bullion-reserve ratios in the nineteenth century.
Source: BEQB (June 1967), Appendix cited on p. 159, Table A.

allowed the Bank to assign the interest rate weapon to regulate its quick ratio, and the availability of BBs was fine-tuned using OMOs and DWL.[45]

At this point, it would be reasonable to ask how the Bank was able to bring short-term market interest rates into line with official rates, rather than the other way round. Bill yields normally traded below Bank rate, but under what became known as the 'classical' system, Bank rate could be 'made effective' from time to time by using OMOs to put the 'market into the Bank'.[46] OMOs could be used to keep the market short,

[45] B. Eichengreen, *Golden Fetters: The Gold Standard and the Great Depression, 1919–39* (New York and Oxford: Oxford University Press, 2003), p. 8, 35–6.

[46] A. L. Coleby, 'The Bank's operational procedures for meeting monetary objectives', *BEQB* (June 1983), pp. 213; P. Tucker (Autumn 2004), p. 368.

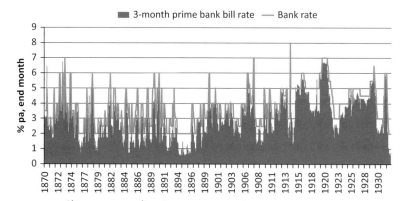

FIGURE 4.9 Short-term sterling interest rates, 1870–1932.
Source: F. H. Capie and A. Webber (1985), Table III. (10) c, pp. 502 (Data for figure used with kind permission of Routledge, see page xiii).

forcing it to use its DWL facilities to borrow at Bank rate, raising market yields into line with the official one.[47] If Bank rate were raised to defend the Bank's reserves and keep sterling within its gold points, market rates could be dragged up to the official rate, drawing in reserves. The discount houses' ability to borrow at Bank rate meant that market rates would not normally exceed Bank rate, and this stopped the extreme yield curve inversion described by Thornton a century earlier. The market was protected from dramatic rises in interest rates – and consequential capital losses – and the limitation of rate movements became an integral part of what was meant by an orderly market.

The classical system remained in situ, and was explained to the Macmillan Committee in 1931 by Sir Ernest Harvey – then deputy governor and previously chief cashier – as follows:

> We regard the Bank Rate as our principal weapon for carrying policy into effect ... Open market operations ... are merely part of the machinery by which the weapon of the Bank Rate is made efficient.[48]

After sterling left the gold standard in 1931, the interest rate weapon was kept in abeyance, Bank rate remaining mostly at 2 per cent, and market rates at even lower levels.[49] A more active interest rate policy was

[47] W. Bagehot, *Lombard Street, a Description of the Money Market* (London, 3rd edn, 1873), pp. 113–6; R. S. Sayers, *Bank of England Operations 1890–1914* (London: P. S. King, 1936), pp. 19–48; R. S Sayers, *The Bank of England 1891–1944* (2 vols and appendix, Cambridge: Cambridge University Press, 1976), I, p. 33.

[48] Macmillan Committee, *Committee on Finance and Industry*, Cmd 3897 (London: HMSO, 1931), 2, Minutes of evidence, p. 173.

[49] W. Leaf (1943), pp. 217–8; S. K. Howson, *Domestic Monetary Management in Britain, 1919–38* (Cambridge: Cambridge University Press, 1975), p. 144–5.

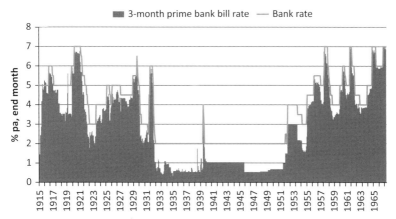

FIGURE 4.10 Interwar and post-war interest rates to 1966.
Source: F. H. Capie and A. Webber (1985), Table III. (10) c, pp. 502 (Data for figure used with kind permission of Routledge, see page xiii).

revived in the late 1950s to help defend sterling's parity against the US dollar under the Bretton Woods system (Figure 4.10). In the late 1950s, Leslie O'Brien, then chief cashier and subsequently governor, explained the classical system to the Radcliffe Committee and advised that there was no need to change the Bank's operating procedures.[50] In 2004, Paul Tucker, then director for markets and subsequently deputy governor, confirmed their longevity, explaining that recent reforms to the Bank's operating procedures were intended to sustain the classical system.[51]

The classical system developed without fanfare in the second half of the nineteenth century, and without openly challenging the intentions of the Currency School, and the framers of the 1844 Act. The suspension of the fiduciary limit for banknotes had proved necessary in the 1847 crisis, when banknotes were still the settlement asset of the banks. It was suspended again in the 1857 and 1866 crises, helping to reassure the public, even though banknotes were no longer used as a settlement asset for bank clearing. Without offsetting action by the Bank, increased banknote issuance would have reduced BBs, exacerbating reserve pressures on the banks, but the announcement of suspension was sufficient to calm the markets, and there was no surge in public demand for banknotes.

This takes us to the problem of shocks in the bill market in the mid-nineteenth century, and their impact on the credit cycle. Prior to the corralling of the acceptance houses that started in the 1860s, a motley assortment

[50] P. M. W. Tucker (Autumn 2004), pp. 369, 379.
[51] P. M. W. Tucker (Autumn 2004), pp. 359–82.

of provincial banks and financiers could endorse inland bills, and seek to rediscount them in the London money market.[52] The credit cycle followed the classic pattern of an upswing in credit, leading to an easing of financial pressures, reduced underwriting standards by endorsers, and a further expansion of credit. This would continue until a disturbance of one kind or another led to a loss of confidence, a tightening of underwriting standards, a contraction of credit, increased financial pressures, and the emergence of distressed borrowers, leading to a further contraction of credit.[53] Banks holding bills bought in the London market relied on the names endorsing the bills, rather than the bona fides of the drawer and drawee, both of whom would probably be unknown to the market.[54] Disturbances, leading to doubts about endorsing names, could lead to a suspension of market trading, and bank depositors might consider the possibility of pre-emptive withdrawals. In these circumstances, prudent bankers would be inclined to limit new advances, allow paper to run off, and hoard the resulting funds in banknotes, BBs, British government stocks (BGS), and the safest of short-term bills. As Thornton had already observed decades earlier, a flight to high-quality assets could exacerbate problems already extant in the market, leading to a downward spiral of credit.

As often seems to be the case, moves to reform the market were triggered by a calamity – in this case the collapse of Overend Gurney & Co (Gurney's), and the consequential crisis of 1866. Gurney's origins lay in bill broking, and – in line with market trends of the time – it started to act as a principal, endorsing and rediscounting bills. It rapidly evolved into a more broadly based investment house overshadowing the Bank of England and the joint-stock banks. Gurney's avoided the expense of a branch network, preferring to meet its funding needs by offering sufficiently attractive rates to both attract deposits and rediscount bills – in other words, it was a liability manager. In its later years, Gurney's started to diversify into longer-term investments, funded with short-term money – a maturity mismatch which left it exposed to refinancing risk. Its aggressive market practices, and rapid growth, presented a challenge to the Bank and the clearing banks, but Gurney's came unstuck. Rumours

---

[52] J. W. Gilbart (1882), I, p. 249; S. Nishimura, *The Decline of Inland Bills of Exchange in the London Money Market, 1865–1913* (London: Cambridge University Press, 1971), pp. 44–55.

[53] C. P. Kindleberger and R. Z. Aliber, *Manias, Panics and Crashes: A History of Financial Crises* (Basingstoke: Palgrave Macmillan, 2011), pp. 21–32; H. P. Minsky, *Stabilizing an Unstable Economy* (New Haven, CT: Yale University Press, 1986), pp. 68–95.

[54] S. Quinn (2004), p. 157.

about an unrelated namesake led to doubts about the company itself, and the Bank let it fail, notwithstanding the resulting market turmoil and consequential insolvencies. The interplay of rumours, rediscounting, and refinancing risk was not lost on the market.[55]

The paralysis of the bill market following Gurney's collapse highlighted the fragility of London's bill market. Bills were endorsed by a fragmented array of names, and held across the banking sector. When a disturbance arose – not least the collapse of Gurney's – nobody could tell how it would affect the solvency of endorsers and therefore the viability of endorsees. The market froze, and normally tradable bills would become untradable, damaging the liquidity position of the banks holding them – and exposing them to the possibility of deposit runs. With hindsight, we know the series of reforms that created the orderly money market of the late nineteenth century, but there was no grand design implemented by a higher authority. The Bank's routine market assistance – the classical system – played a part, but changes in market practice also helped. Clearing bankers with stronger deposit bases argued that respectable banks should not rediscount bills into the market, but should hold their clients' bills to maturity, with the opportunity to roll them over, if appropriate. The rediscounting of accommodation paper into the mainstream market was regarded as unacceptable on the grounds that low quality paper would disrupt the market at times of stress.[56] This was essentially a campaign against weaker banks circumventing the inhibition against rate competition for deposits by aggressively rediscounting paper instead – a form of off-balance sheet finance.[57] (Rediscounting endorsed bills avoided the need to attract deposit funding, but end investors in the bills had recourse in the bank in the event of default by other parties to the bill.)

The other key factor in the acceptance market was the rise of the international merchant bankers – Baring's, Schroder's, Rothschild's, Morgan's, Hambro's, Kleinwort's, Brandt's.[58] Originally based in continental Europe and North America, these firms started as consignment financiers, buying commodities from producers, and shipping them to consumer countries for resale to local merchants. Improvements in transport and

---

[55] W. T. C. King (1936), pp. 242–56.

[56] H. D. MacLeod (1875), I, vi.

[57] G. Rae (1885), p. 204–6; C. A. E. Goodhart, *The Business of Banking, 1891–1914* (London: Weidenfeld & Nicolson, 1972), p. 132.

[58] K. Burk, *Morgan Grenfell 1838–1988: The Biography of a Merchant Bank* (Oxford: Oxford University Press, 1989), pp. 18, 26–7, 33–4; R. Roberts, *Schroders: Merchants and Bankers* (Basingstoke: Macmillan, 1992), pp. 73, 99; W. T. C. King (1936), pp. 197–9; N. H. Dimsdale and A. C. Hotson (2014), pp. 7, 49.

communications opened up oceanic trade to a wider group of merchants, encouraging the merchant bankers to concentrate on financing consignments of goods, without necessarily owning them whilst in transit.[59] The merchant bankers were also well placed to underwrite securities issued by governments and promoters of large-scale infrastructure projects, combining the roles of issuing house and acceptance house.[60] In time, the new-style acceptance houses became known as accepting houses, an elite peer group defined by membership of the Accepting Houses Committee (AHC).[61]

The accepting houses offered a variant of bill finance, the acceptance credit. The houses agreed to accept drawers' bills, and advanced funds against accepted bills up to a facility limit.[62] An accepting house would be the acceptor of the bill, and the buyer of the goods would be its endorser – reversing the traditional practice of inland bills. The accepting house could insist that its agent in the receiving port retain the consignment's bill of lading until the endorser settled the bill, and the funds were used to repay the drawer's advance.[63] These arrangements meant the accepting house had security over the goods being financed, and the bill of lading could be sold if the buyer/endorser failed to repay the bill. Acceptance credits became an established feature of international trade, and demonstrated the adaptability of the bill on London.[64] The clearing banks offered acceptance credits as an alternative financing option for drawers of inland bills, but for the most part these acceptances were retained on their balance sheets. In contrast, the accepting houses lacked the funding base to retain their acceptances, and rediscounted their bills into the market.

As a consequence, most of the paper flowing through the mainstream money market had been accepted by an accepting house, although other fine bills, accepted by a clearing bank, and trade paper did circulate in

---

[59] R. Roberts (1992), pp. 26–7.

[60] L. E. Davis and R. E. Gallman, *Evolving Financial Markets and International Capital Flows: Britain, the Americas, and Australia, 1865–1914* (Cambridge and New York: Cambridge University Press, 2001), p. 177.

[61] P. Ziegler, *The Sixth Great Power: Barings, 1762–1929* (London: Collins, 1988); N. Ferguson, *The World's Banker: The History of the House of Rothschild* (London: Weidenfeld & Nicolson, 1998).

[62] S. Hurn, *Syndicated Loans: A Handbook for Banker and Borrower* (New York and London: Woodhead-Faulkner, 1990), p. 9; O. Accominotti, 'London merchant banks, the Central European Panic and the Sterling Crisis of 1931', *Journal of Economic History*, 72, no. 1 (March 2012), pp. 6–7.

[63] Gillett Brothers (1964), p. 20.

[64] W. Leaf (1943), pp. 186–94.

peripheral segments of the market.[65] The mainstream London market was expected to remain orderly in the face of shocks and disturbances, providing the accepting houses remained undoubted. The houses operated on leverage ratios of three to four times capital, which was markedly more conservative than modern practice.[66] Even so, Baring's was threatened by insolvency in 1890 as a result of Latin American defaults, and a rescue was orchestrated by the Bank with financial support from the London market.[67] The speed with which this was done built confidence that accepting houses would not be allowed to fail. They had to be supported again when belligerents' credits were frozen in 1914, and when continental banking credits became subject to moratoria in 1931, but decisive action maintained confidence in the market.[68] It is notable that the key to managing all three crises – 1890, 1914 and 1931 – was the protection of the accepting houses' credit standing, whereas the Bank's role as lender of last resort (LOLR) – as articulated by Bagehot – was of subsidiary importance.

The Bank's provision of routine market assistance from the 1890s helped to reinforce the role of prime bank bills (PBBs) in the money market. The Bank would buy only certain eligible assets as part of its routine OMOs, and its routine DWL would be secured on eligible collateral. Eligible assets included BGS, TBs, and PBBs – the latter being properly drawn bills, accepted by an accepting house and endorsed by a discount house.[69] PBBs could either be retained by the discount market, and used as collateral for money at call (MAC) from the clearers, or re-pledged for DWL from the Bank, or sold to the clearers, or the Bank, and held by them to maturity. The discount houses remained willing to deal in fine bank bills and trade bills, but they needed to hold PBBs to meet collateral requirements for MAC and DWL. It should be noted that the liquidity of these instruments did not depend on their innate qualities, but on market conventions, for example, the Bank's eligibility criteria, and market norms about rediscounting.[70] PBBs were liquid because they were eligible

---

[65] W. T. C. King (1936), pp. 197–9; Gillett Brothers (1964), p. 18.

[66] R. Roberts (1992), p. 48.

[67] L. S. Pressnell, 'Gold reserves, banking reserves, and the Barings crisis of 1890' in C. R. Whittlesey and J. S. G. Wilson (eds) *Essays in Honour of R. S. Sayers* (Oxford: Clarendon Press, 1968), pp. 192–200.

[68] R. Roberts, '"How We Saved the City": The Management of the Financial Crisis of 1914' in N. H. Dimsdale and A. C. Hotson (eds) *British Financial Crises since 1825* (Oxford: Oxford University Press, 2014), pp. 108–10; R. J. Truptil (1936), p. 290.

[69] J. Hutchison (1881), I, p. 88.

[70] W. A. Allen, *International Liquidity and the Financial Crisis* (Cambridge and New York: Cambridge University Press, 2013), pp. 214–5.

for rediscounting at the Bank, but if prime bills with a tenor of more than one month were deemed ineligible, longer-dated bills would be expected to become less liquid. Bills in the hands of the clearers could be less liquid than the same bills circulating in the discount market because of inhibitions against bill rediscounting by deposit banks.[71] Endorsements on bills were there for all to see and, as Rae noted, unusual rediscounting by a deposit bank could lead to rumours in the discount market. In the late nineteenth century, Consols and MAC (rather than fine bank bills) were the mainstay of clearing bank liquidity, both being convertible into BBs anonymously.[72]

The disclosure provided by bill endorsements also provided a means for the Bank to monitor the accepting houses and discount houses. The Bank's Discount Office kept records of names on its portfolio of bills, and retained the right to decline bills, if its exposure to particular names became excessive. The Bank's tacit application of counterparty limits constrained the ability of individual houses to expand more rapidly than the rest of the market without an explanation, and enabled the Bank to spot Baring's difficulties at an early stage.[73] Since the Bank was privy to the accepting houses' balance sheet figures, it could caution over-trading houses with the ultimate sanction of declining their acceptances.[74] The Bank also bought parcels of bills in the market through its agent, Seccombe's, allowing it to monitor names on bills flowing through the market, checking for improperly drawn bills, as well as excessive rediscounting by houses relative to their resources. The doctrine of nurturing the quality of bills circulating in the market remained at centre stage of the Bank's approach to market conduct well into the 1960s when it could still rightfully claim that

the Bank of England's general policy regarding commercial bills [is]... to maintain the standards of quality long associated with the London prime bank bill and hence its reputation as a liquid asset of undoubted security.[75]

The other practical necessity of the money market was same-day settlement, allowing the clearers and discount houses to square their books

[71] W. Leaf (1943), pp. 211–2.
[72] J. W. Gilbert (1882), I, p. 295; G. Rae (1885), p. 206–15; C. A. E. Goodhart (1972), p. 127.
[73] M. Flandreau and S. Ugolini, 'The Crisis of 1866', in N. H. Dimsdale and A. C. Hotson (eds) *British Financial Crises since 1825* (Oxford: Oxford University Press, 2014), pp. 87–8, fn. 8; E. N. White, 'How to Prevent a Banking Panic: The Barings Crisis of 1890', 175 Years of The Economist, Conference on Economics and the Media, London (September 2015), p. 3.
[74] J. S. Fforde, *The Bank of England and Public Policy 1941–1958* (Cambridge: Cambridge University Press, 1992), pp. 750–1.
[75] Bank of England, 'Commercial bills', *BEQB*, 2, *no.* 4 (December 1961), p. 28.

by close of business each working day.[76] The houses traded over the counter (OTC) for daily settlement, rather than through the London Stock Exchange (LSE) with its fortnightly settlement period. Bills of exchange could be assigned by endorsement, and delivered within minutes by walk clerks to the various houses on Lombard Street. TBs were bearer instruments and change of ownership could be affected by delivery down the street. Consols were registered securities and not same-day settlement, but ways and means were found to use them as collateral for loans – for example, holding them in escrow accounts with signed, but unexecuted, transfer forms (transferred in blank), ready for assignment to the lender if their loan were not repaid. This author has not been able to establish the extent to which loans secured on bills (or other assets) were transferred in blank, or legally assigned to the lender for the term of the loan, and then reassigned back to the borrower.[77] Historical practice seems to have varied, and modern collateral management is more punctilious, but it still has to be said that the resilience of the late-nineteenth-century market was demonstrably better than that of the modern one.[78]

Debates about the stability of the banking system in the late nineteenth century focused on liquidity reserves, not capital adequacy. Rae pointed out that troubled deposit banks could suffer withdrawals of up to one-quarter, the main precedents for this being the Agricultural and Commercial Bank of Ireland in 1836, the Northern and Central Bank of England in 1837, both Western Bank of Scotland and Borough Bank of Liverpool in 1857 and, of course, the City of Glasgow Bank (CGB) in 1878.[79] In all these cases, calls on shareholders had been sufficient to cover depositors in full, but Rae argued that banks should hold one-third of their quick liabilities in high-quality liquid assets.[80] Liquid balance sheets provided reassurance for depositors under normal trading conditions, and provided a buffer of assets acceptable to other banks in the event of a run. The ability to settle a substantial outflow of deposits through the clearing system delayed the need for a pre-emptive stop on payments,

---

[76] *BEQB* (March 1982), p. 86, in particular footnote 3.

[77] C. Gordon, *The Cedar Story: The Night the City Was Saved* (London: Sinclair-Stevenson, 1993), p. 60.

[78] FRB of New York, *Tri-Party Repo Infrastructure Reform, a White Paper Prepared by the FRB of New York* (17th May 2010).

[79] J. D. Turner, 'Holding shareholders to account: British banking stability and contingent capital' in N. H. Dimsdale and A. C. Hotson (eds) (2014a), pp. 148–51; J. D. Turner, *Banking in Crisis: The Rise and Fall of British Banking Stability, 1800 to the Present* (Cambridge: Cambridge University Press, 2014b), p. 119.

[80] G. Rae (1885), p. 204; L. S. Pressnell (1968), p. 182.

providing time for less liquid assets, such as customer advances, to be refinanced with other banks. The aim was not to save banking names that had lost public confidence, but to facilitate an orderly transfer of deposits and advances to undoubted institutions.

Fulsome liquidity reserves were therefore the primary means of maintaining confidence, and efficiently resolving runs on bank deposits. Banking journals were replete with discussions about appropriate cash ratios, and practitioners were concerned that no bank should gain an advantage over its rivals by operating on subnormal ratios.[81] Before the First World War, monthly reporting banks had taken advantage of unsynchronised reporting dates to window dress their balance sheets on make-up days, in particular their cash ratios.[82] The clearing banks agreed to adopt common reporting dates to make it more difficult to window dress reported balance sheets, but cash ratios were still massaged for reporting purposes by drawing on MAC.[83] Although common reserve ratios were not imposed on the clearing banks until after the Second World War, none of them would report a cash ratio in single figures, and they were normally well in excess of 10 per cent.[84]

The clearers adopted a minimum 8 per cent cash–deposit ratio after the Second World War, comprising till money and bankers' balances.[85] The accepting houses and discount houses were not subject to a cash ratio on the grounds that their assets could be rediscounted at the Bank, and converted into cash (in the form of BBs). The same argument could have been applied to the clearers, and this view was formalised in 1951 when the cash–deposit ratio was replaced by the 30 per cent liquidity ratio, subsequently reduced to 28 per cent in 1963. Liquid assets comprised MAC, eligible paper, and cash (BB and till money) and were expressed as a proportion of deposits.[86] There was a private understanding that the accepting houses would hold liquid assets amounting to one-third of their deposits, and one-fifth of their acceptances.[87] In 1971, the 28 per cent liquidity requirement was effectively replaced with a 12½ per cent ratio

[81] C. A. E. Goodhart (1972), pp. 47–9.

[82] W. Leaf (1943), p. 122; C. A. E. Goodhart (1972), pp. 48–9.

[83] W. Leaf (1943), pp. 121–2.

[84] J. W. Gilbart (1882), I, p. 294; W. Leaf (1943), pp. 120–2; R. J. Truptil (1936), p. 93; L. S. Pressnell (1968), pp. 219–20.

[85] F. H. Capie, *The Bank of England from the 1950s to 1979* (Cambridge, 2010), p. 28.

[86] J. C. R. Dow (1964), pp. 230 fn. 3, 304; E. T. Nevin and E. W. Davis, *The London Clearing Banks* (London: Elek, 1970), pp. 136–55; Bank of England, *The Development and Operation of Monetary Policy 1960–1983* (Oxford: Clarendon Press,1984), p. 34.

[87] J. S. Fforde (1992), p. 752.

of reserve assets to eligible liabilities (ELs). Reserve assets were similar to liquid assets, but excluded till money. The 12½ per cent requirement was applied to all banks – rather than just the clearers – with a 10 per cent requirement for finance houses. The reserve asset ratio (RAR) lasted until 1981, when it was abolished, and the banks agreed to maintain an average of 1½ per cent of their ELs in BBs, in what was confusingly known as the cash ratio. The 1½ per cent requirement was simply an informal tax on the banks, allowing the Bank to earn a profit on the placed funds, and cover its expenses.[88]

The role of minimum reserve requirements has been a source of endless confusion. In the context of the late eighteenth century, Thornton argued that there was no fixed reserve ratio that would be suitable for all conditions; prudent private bankers should keep an eye out for signs of trouble, and seek to raise their cash reserves in the face of increased uncertainty, allowing them to fall in benign conditions.[89] The whole point of cash reserves was that they did vary, and they should be available for use in the event of an outflow. This approach did not persist under the classical system, cash reserves being reported as stable, initially because of window dressing. Latterly, cash reserves were genuinely stabilised, and other liquid assets took the strain. Even after the move from the cash ratio to the liquidity ratio, the classical system still allowed the clearers to fine-tune their liquidity by borrowing against BGS, or repoing them, rather than curbing their advances.[90]

The imposition of minimum ratios meant that the banks' usable reserves were now the excess over the minimum, since no bank would wish to report a breach of the ratio for fear of causing disquiet in the market. The liquidity ratio included a mechanism for the Bank to call Special Deposits (SDs) – which did not count as liquid assets – thereby providing an additional mechanism for limiting bank liquidity.[91] The SD scheme was retained, following the introduction of CCC, raising the possibility of official action to restrict reserve assets with a view to discouraging credit expansion. The Bank's commentary on the use of SDs was cautious; the governor, Leslie O'Brien, arguing that the reserve system

---

[88] G. W. Taylor, 'New techniques in British banking: an examination of the sterling money markets and the principles of term lending', Gilbart Lecture on Banking (London: King's College London, 1973), pp. 4–11; Bank of England (1984), p. 147.

[89] H. Thornton, 1802 edn (ed.) F. A. von Hayek (1962), p. 286.

[90] C. A. E. Goodhart and D. J. Needham, 'Why did Britain have broad money supply targets' (forthcoming), pp 5–6.

[91] F. H. Capie (2010), pp. 263–4.

was intended to be used as a fulcrum to fine-tune the term structure of interest rates, rather than provide a substitute for Bank rate policy.[92] A restrictive policy did lead to a rise in the price of reserve assets – and a fall in their yields – but the banks responded by bidding more aggressively for wholesale funds, rather than tempering their supply of credit.[93] This response was unexpected at the time, and leads us to the basis on which the clearing bank sector created credit, starting with the lending practices that developed in the late nineteenth century.

In principle, clearing banks' advances were meant to be self-liquidating, and in this respect their approach to lending was modelled on bill finance.[94] As one writer in the *BEQB* put it:

Although the relative importance of commercial bills in the London market has diminished during this century, the canons of financial practice associated with the bill on London underlie the attitudes of many who are closely concerned with the provision of finance.[95]

The clearers were able to take over much of the inland bill business, either by providing acceptance credits, or by offering advances in place of bills. For customers, a loan facility was often more convenient than the bother of drawing bills and honouring them. Also, the clearers were willing to consider financing the generality of firms' working capital requirements, rather than just accounts receivable on goods in transit – the traditional remit of bill finance. Accounting and banking practice increasingly distinguished between assets and liabilities that were current – that is to say, realisable within a year – and longer-term ones.[96] Investments in fixed assets, including land, buildings and equipment, were expected to be financed with permanent capital, otherwise known as fixed capital, comprising share capital, accumulated reserves, debenture stocks and the like. Current assets were partly funded by bank borrowing, a firm's net current assets (NCA) being its current assets (including stocks, work-in-progress (WIP), bank balances and accounts receivable) less current liabilities (including accounts payable and bank finance). The archetypal clearing bank customer might report positive NCAs, implying that permanent capital was used to finance underlying NCAs, but seasonal

---

[92] Governor's Munich Speech reprinted in *BEQB*, 11, no. 2 (June 1971), p. 197.

[93] Bank of England (1984), pp. 34, 44.

[94] W. Leaf (1943), p. 156–7.

[95] *BEQB* (December 1961), p. 26; see also R. S. Sayers, *Modern Banking* (Oxford: Clarendon Press, 7th edn, 1967), p. 183.

[96] E. Jones, *Accountancy and the British Economy, 1840–1980: The Evolution of Ernst & Whinney* (London: Batsford, 1981), p. 52.

fluctuations in its components – stocks, WIP, receivables, and trade payables – would be funded by a bank facility.[97]

Businesses requiring an external provider of working capital finance could be found across the country in manufacturing, distribution, and agriculture, including landed estates. Managers in the clearers' branches would seek to agree facilities that covered cyclical peaks in borrowing that might be quarterly, monthly, or even weekly. These advances were meant to be repayable by running down the firm's working capital over a relatively short period. Facilities may well have been renewed (i.e. rolled over) for many years, but this did not make repayment reliant on cash flows arising a long way in the future. If doubts arose about the firm's prospects, the bank would be able to terminate the facility at short notice, and be repaid from the run-off of its working capital. If a firm's stocks and WIP had to be sold at a discount, leaving a shortfall, the loan would normally be supported by security over bankable assets – freehold land, machinery, brewery debenture stocks, railway shares etc. – that would be relatively easy to sell at predictable prices in the event of a default. This meant the clearers would not normally provide working capital for borrowers of lesser standing, particularly when they were unable to offer sufficient security in a suitable form. Instead, these borrowers would have sought finance from factors or invoice discounters, operating independently or as part of finance houses.[98] The clearers were not direct participants in these lower quality loans, but they could become indirectly involved by lending to finance houses.[99]

It is important to note that the clearing banks' focus on working capital finance was not sufficient to ensure that their lending was low risk. Firms that borrowed to finance their trading assets faced a basis risk between the market value of their current assets, and their current liabilities. A fall in commodity prices could impair the value of their current assets with the possibility of negative NCAs and insufficient cash realisations to repay bank loans. It is for this reason that bankers' textbooks put so much emphasis on the need for security, the forms it could take, and the pitfalls to be avoided.[100] Various rules of thumb were suggested for valuation margins required on different types of security, and the need to be conservative about resale values in the event of a default.[101]

---

[97] W. Leaf (1943), pp. 164–5.
[98] Lord Crowther, *Report of the Committee on Consumer Credit* (2 vols, London: HMSO, March 1971), pp. 66–74.
[99] C. Gordon (1993), pp. 41–2.
[100] E. Sykes (1947), pp. 151–8.
[101] E. Sykes (1947), pp. 159–60.

A recurring theme was the role of security as a second line of defence, supporting a self-liquidating loan. The loans secured against factories or mines, without identifiable cash flows to repay the loan, were ill advised because the lender often had to fund their continued operation to protect their security.[102] Security over easily saleable assets meant the bank would have priority over unsecured creditors in the event of difficulties.

British branch managers were generalists, rather than sector specialists. They represented their bank in a locality and were expected to make judgements about the reliability of their customers – their character and competence. They would seek to assess firms' working capital requirements without attempting to second guess their directors' judgements about long-term investments.[103] There was a ring of truth in the old joke that the clearers wanted to lend only to people who did not need to borrow.[104] To put the point more fairly, they financed trading assets; they did not seek to offer private equity or venture capital finance. They were not industrial financiers providing long-term capital in the manner attributed to the German banks of the nineteenth century, or long-term credit institutions such as Société Générale du Crédit Mobilier in France.[105]

Businesses would deal with one clearing bank – there were no multi-bank relationships – and their branch manager had a bird's-eye view of cash flowing in and out of the business via accounts held at the bank. Businesses that were over-utilising their borrowing facility – and becoming permanent borrowers – would be called into the branch to discuss the risks of overtrading. They would be asked to consider growing more slowly, recapitalising the business, and providing more security, but persistently high utilisation of borrowing facilities would not be tolerated, even if it could be demonstrated that the business had positive net assets (and positive net worth). Sykes was quite clear that 'it is not a banker's function to lend money permanently' and went on to comment that 'loans which have gradually acquired a permanent character ... ended by becoming bad debts.'[106]

[102] J. W. Gilbart (1882), pp. 424–6.
[103] M. H. Best and K. J. Humphries, 'The City and Industrial Decline' in B. Elbaum and W. Lazonick (eds) *The Decline of the British Economy* (Oxford: Clarendon, 1986), pp. 224–9.
[104] M. A. King, *The End of Alchemy: Money, Banking and the Future of the Global Economy* (London: Little, Brown, 2016), p. 101.
[105] W. Leaf (1943), pp. 159–61; C. Gordon (1993), p. 57; J. Edwards and S. Ogilvie, 'Universal banks and German industrialization: a reappraisal', *Economic History Review*, 49, no. 3 (August, 1996), pp. 428–9, 433–4, 440–4.
[106] E. Sykes (1947), p. 150.

Experience suggested that persistent borrowing was a precursor of default, and branch managers had little reason to offer forbearance, even when there was an outside possibility that a firm might trade itself out of a storm.[107]

The clearers' antipathy towards permanent borrowing meant that most of their surviving customers were not fully borrowed, most of the time. A corollary of this was that customers' working capital requirements determined money and credit, at least in the short term, rather than being regulated by the clearers.[108] That said, the evolution of working capital requirements did not have easily predictable effects on money and credit aggregates, notwithstanding the direction of causality. This uncertainty can be examined by considering the effects of a single payment made by one customer to another, where the latter has an account at a different bank.[109] The payer and payee might start with funds in their accounts, or they might be overdrawn. For the purpose of this exercise, we shall assume that the payer funds the payment from her deposit balance, if funds are available, and borrows, if not. In the interest of simplicity, we are ruling out the possibility of funding the payment partly from a deposit balance, and partly from borrowing. (One can think of the payment as being for the minimum unit of account used in the banks' ledgers.) The payment received by the payee is credited to his account, reducing his borrowing if he is overdrawn, or added to his deposit balance if not. Here again, we are excluding the possibility of the payee partly reducing his borrowing, and partly increasing his deposit balance. For the moment, we are assuming that the two bank accounts are the only form of money available to the payer and payee, and therefore the funds leaving the payer's account must equal the funds received by the payee. There is no scope to exchange customer deposits for coins or other currencies – there are no internal or external drains.

On the basis of these simplifying assumptions, a single payment from one bank customer to another can have differing effects on aggregate deposits (bank money) and aggregate lending (domestic credit), depending on the circumstances of the payer and payee.[110] The effect in each case

---

[107] E. Sykes (1947), p. 150.
[108] C. A. E. Goodhart, 'Competition and credit control: some personal reflections', *Financial History Review*, 22, no. 2 (August 2015), p. 236.
[109] M. McLeay, A. Radia and R. Thomas, 'Money creation in the modern economy', *BEQB* (2014 Q1), pp. 15–17.
[110] W. Leaf (1943), pp. 143–5.

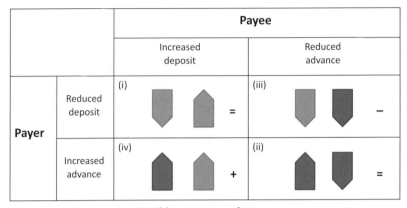

FIGURE 4.11 Possible outcomes of a customer payment.
Source: Author's diagram.

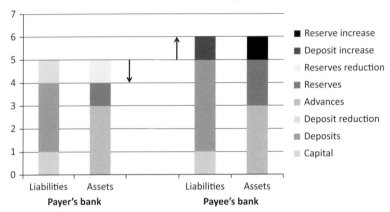

FIGURE 4.12 Customer payment – classic case (i) neutral.
Source: Author's diagram.

is illustrated in Figure 4.11 and described as follows (the four cells in the figure are marked with corresponding lower case roman numerals):

i Neutral: offsetting changes in customer deposits – and therefore no change in bank money, or domestic credit (Figure 4.12);

ii Neutral: offsetting changes in customer lending and therefore no change in bank money or domestic credit (Figure 4.13);

iii Contraction: a reduction in customer lending, and an equal reduction in customer deposits – and therefore an equal reduction in both bank money and domestic credit (Figure 4.14);

iv Expansion: an increase in customer lending and an equal increase in customer deposits – and therefore an equal increase in bank money and domestic credit (Figure 4.15).

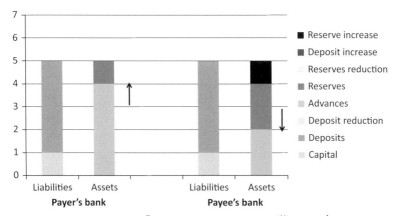

FIGURE 4.13 Customer payment – case (ii) neutral.
Source: Author's diagram

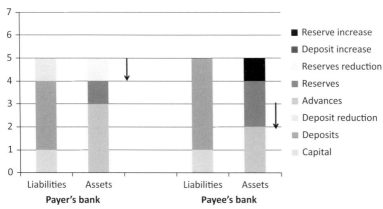

FIGURE 4.14 Customer payment – case (iii) contraction.
Source: Author's diagram.

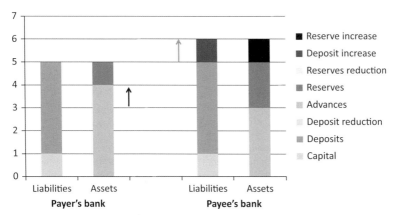

FIGURE 4.15 Customer payment – case (iv) expansion.
Source: Author's diagram.

Suffice it to say, there is no simple link between a payment flowing from a payer to a payee, and the resulting stocks of bank money and domestic credit: they can go up, go down, or stay the same, depending on the circumstances of the transacting parties. The overall effect of a payment would be neutral, if there were an offsetting change in deposits (option i), or an offsetting change in borrowing (option ii). It would be contractionary, if the payer's deposit falls and the payee's borrowing falls (option iii), and expansionary, if the payer borrows more and the payee's deposit rises (option iv) (Figure 4.11). In this simplified example, the change in bank money would always be the same as the change in domestic credit, because we are operating in a closed economy, without Exchequer flows, and there is no change in the banks' capital.

The clearers' role as providers of flexible working capital finance meant that the economy affected their balance sheets in the short run, rather than the other way round. As Leaf put it:

The banks have to follow the currents of trade and production; they have no means of controlling them. They are the servants, not the tyrants of industry.[111]

In the longer term, the clearers could have adopted more or less restrictive credit policies, but the liquidity of clearing bank customers depended as much on their unused borrowing facilities as their deposit balances, leaving the Bank sceptical of the predictive role of monetary aggregates:

The concept of net [consolidated] deposits is certainly not a banking or an accounting concept, and it would not be unfair to say that practical bankers' views of it range from tolerance to frank cynicism.[112]

The clearers could decide to tighten credit provision, leading to an unobserved reduction in unused facilities, and customers' doubts about their facility limits could encourage them to hold more deposit balances. In this circumstance, deposit growth could become a perverse indicator of monetary conditions.[113]

The clearing bank sector could nevertheless facilitate an expansion of money and credit when one customer drew down a facility to finance a payment, and the receiving party increased their deposit balance.[114]

[111] W. Leaf (1943), p. 98.
[112] *BEQB*, 3, no. 4 (1963), p. 289.
[113] R. S. Sayers, *Modern Banking* (Oxford: Clarendon Press, 7th edn, 1967), pp. 1–14; M. Collins, *Money and Banking in the UK: A History* (London: Croom Helm, 1988; London: Routledge, reprinted 1990), p. 582.
[114] L. A. Hahn, *Economic Theory of Bank Credit*, translation of 1920 edn and second part of 1930 edn by Clemens Matt, introduction by Harald Hagemann (Oxford: Oxford University Press, 2015), pp. 23–30.

Credit created by one clearer would be redistributed around the sector, depending on customer payments, rather than allowing one clearer to grow at the expense of another. The ability of the sector to create money from its own credits allowed it to operate differently from other institutions that were deposit-led.[115] Savings banks – such as the trustee savings banks and the Post Office Savings Bank (POSB) – acted as conduits, receiving funds from small savers, which they placed on deposit with the clearers and discount houses and invested in money market instruments and BGS.[116] Savings banks' balance sheets depended on deposit inflows, rather than on customers' use of credit facilities. The building societies provided mortgage loans, and finance houses provided consumer and equipment loans, but, here again, their lending was constrained by the inflow of funds. Their payments and receipts were settled through clearing bank accounts, and they could not rely on their lending being recycled back to their respective sectors.[117]

This is not to suggest that the clearers could ignore competition from other financial institutions, and the possibility of being disintermediated by them. In the 1920s, some insurance companies found they could secure better rates by holding bills directly, and placing fewer funds with the clearers. In the 1930s, the building societies were able to grow by competing on rate for depositors' funds and, during the 1950s, the finance houses started to become more aggressive competitors for deposits, as did the accepting houses.[118] There was usually someone willing to offer a better rate, and the clearers took the view that they should not compete aggressively for saving deposits. As a result, the clearers and their rivals operated in reasonably distinct market segments, but the boundary between them was not set in stone.[119]

The bank lending cycle was notoriously difficult to interpret, reflecting the vagaries of the working capital cycle. An anticipated upturn in the economy might lead to a build-up of orders and stocks, and increased demand for credit, but an unexpected strengthening of demand could lead to inadvertent destocking, and a temporary fall in corporate borrowing. Speculative stock building could lead to stronger credit demand,

[115] J. A. Schumpeter, *History of Economic Analysis* (London: Allen & Unwin, 1954; New York: Oxford University Press, 1954), pp. 1111–17.

[116] L. S. Pressnell (1968), pp. 170–9; L. E. Davis and R. E. Gallman (2001), pp. 132–3.

[117] L. A. Hahn (2015), pp. 45–7.

[118] J. S. Fforde (1992), pp. 751, 761.

[119] Committee of London Clearing Bankers, *The London Clearing Banks, Evidence by the CLCB to the Committee to Review the Functioning of Financial Institutions* (London: Longman, 1978), p. 105.

but so too could involuntary stock building at the onset of a downturn.[120] In general, credit was viewed as being pro-cyclical, reaching a high point near the top of the trade cycle, but it was rarely a consistent indicator of the wider economic cycle. The clearers helped businesses to manage this uncertainty by offering flexible lending to good-quality private sector borrowers. They did this in an era when public sector indebtedness had been on a declining trend, and it had proved necessary to invent the prime bank bill (PBB) regime to provide an alternative safe asset when TBs and BGS were in limited supply.[121]

All this changed in the interwar period when TBs and local authority bills usurped PBBs as the dominant money market instrument.[122] The banking sector effectively underwrote the residual part of government borrowing that was not funded by the non-bank private and external sectors. The government's dependence on borrowing from the banks (including the Bank) was regarded as unavoidable until the 1950s, but increasingly questioned during the 1960s. In 1966, the Treasury published 'Table 48 – Factors Determining Changes in Money Supply' in *Financial Statistics*.[123] This table showed quarterly changes in broad money (M3) as the summation of the government's borrowing requirement, less sales of government debt outside the banking sector, plus bank lending to the private sector, plus external transactions affecting money. This was the prototype of what subsequently became a presentation of changes in M3 in terms of its counterparts – domestic credit expansion (DCE) and externals etc.[124]

$$\Delta \, M_3 = DCE + \text{Externals}$$
$$DCE = PSBR - \text{public sector borrowing from the nbps}$$
$$+ \text{bank lending to nbps}$$
$$\text{Externals} = \Delta \text{ overseas £ deposits} + \Delta \text{ official fc reserves}$$
$$+ \Delta \text{ other external financings}$$

[120] *BEQB*, 20, no. 3 (Sept 1980), p. 281.
[121] G. B. Gorton, 'The history and economics of safe assets', *NBER Working Paper*, no. 22210 (April 2016), pp. 5–6.
[122] T. Balogh, *Studies in Financial Organization* (Cambridge: Cambridge University Press, 1947), pp. 148–53.
[123] Table 48, *Financial Statistics*, no. 50 (June 1966 et seq.).
[124] Tables 53–6, *Financial Statistics*, from November 1969; C. A. E. Goodhart, *Monetary Theory and Practice: The UK Experience* (London and Basingstoke: Macmillan, 1984), p. 124.

Where:

> PSBR = public sector borrowing requirement
> nbps = non-bank private sector
> fc = foreign currency

The counterparts' identity was true by definition, but the underlying model assumed that bank credit was determined by public and private sector demand, and that bank asset growth drove liability growth. In official circles, this seemed a reasonable description of what was going on in the 1960s, when the unfunded part of the public sector borrowing requirement (PSBR) determined bank lending to the public sector, and bank lending to the private sector was largely prescribed by quantitative controls. In effect, the government was in a position to control the domestic credit counterparts, and DCE was the main determinant of changes in M3. These measures went on to become published indicators of the government's intent to control money and credit: DCE ceilings being published in the late 1960s as part of the IMF package, and a published M3 objective from 1976.[125]

The idea that stability could be delivered by regulating credit growth did not sit comfortably with the view that working capital finance was inherently volatile and unpredictable. The Bank was persuaded of the need to free the clearing banks from the quantitative controls imposed on their lending during the 1960s and wanted to establish a different approach, leading to the revolution of 1971, known as Competition and Credit Control (CCC). These reforms did not simply restore the status quo ante the quantitative controls imposed in the 1960s, but initiated the dismantling of the clearing bank system, not to mention the Bank's 'no hands' approach to monetary control, using the credit counterparts. CCC and its various long-term consequences are pursued in Chapter 5.

---

[125] C. A. E. Goodhart and D. J. Needham, 'Why did Britain have broad money supply targets' (forthcoming).

5

Liability Management Redux

Before the money market revolution of 1971, the clearing bank regime had operated with few changes of substance since the 1890s. The clearers did not compete on rate for deposits, and rate competition on loans was limited. The clearers did not lend or borrow material sums directly with each other, and they did not rediscount acceptances into the market. The cartel operated by the Committee of London Clearing Bankers (CLCB) set common deposit and lending rates relative to Bank rate and, under the classical system, the Bank stabilised total bankers' balances (BBs) at a discount rate of its choosing. The clearers maintained significant holdings of gilts and money market instruments, including prime bank bills (PBBs): 70 per cent of their total assets in the 1950s, and still 40 per cent in the 1960s (Figures 5.1 and 5.2). The Bank's special relationship with the accepting houses and discount houses meant that these instruments remained undoubted credits that could always be traded. The clearers' advances were conservatively underwritten, being – for the most part – self-liquidating and supported by security over bankable assets. They did not provide long-term industrial finance, or mortgage loans for house purchase. They had some overseas business exposures, but these were limited. The clearers could be criticised for not doing more, but their narrow focus meant they served as secure custodians of the country's payment system, and flexible providers of working capital finance.[1]

During the 1960s, the clearers agreed to abide by quantitative controls, limiting the annual percentage increase in their lending, and qualitative

---

[1] E. T. Nevin and E. W. Davis, *The London Clearing Banks* (London: Elek, 1970), pp. 238–9; M. Collins and M. Baker, *Commercial Banks and Industrial Finance in England and Wales, 1860–1913* (Oxford: Oxford University Press, 2003), pp. 134–49.

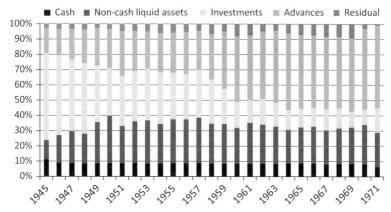

FIGURE 5.1 London clearing bank assets, 1945–1971.
Source: BOESA, no. 1 (1970), Table 9(1), no. 2 (1975), Table 8/2.

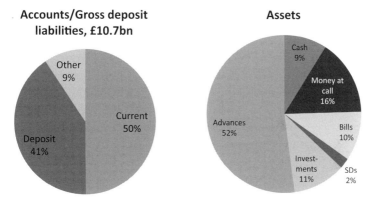

FIGURE 5.2 London clearing bank balance sheet, 10 December 1969.
Source: BOESA, no. 1 (1970), Table 9(1).

controls, directing lending to favoured borrowers, such as shipbuilders and exporters. The finance houses were subject to a parallel set of regulations, limiting the term of their instalment loans and hire purchase agreements. Credit restrictions were tightened significantly after the 1967 devaluation, as part of the government's attempts to improve the balance of trade and defend sterling. Britain's foreign currency reserves had to be bolstered by borrowing from the International Monetary Fund (IMF), and the government reluctantly agreed to publish ceilings on domestic credit expansion (DCE) in 1969.[2] Hitherto, the IMF had provided

---

[2] D. J. Needham, *UK Monetary Policy from Devaluation to Thatcher, 1967–82* (London: Palgrave Macmillan, 2014), pp. 27–8, 180.

stabilisation loans to developing countries, and these had been condi-
tional on the control of the central bank credit – their main source of
government finance. For the United Kingdom, the Treasury persuaded
the IMF that its conditionality would be better expressed in terms of a
ceiling on the growth of DCE – the domestic counterpart of M3 – since
the banking sector as a whole was the residual financier of government.[3]

The DCE ceilings were met – partly as a result of the draconian application of quantitative and qualitative controls – and the balance of trade
improved, allowing sterling to be stabilised at its new parity. The success
of the adjustment process, nevertheless, worried the clearers because it
was they who had faced the brunt of the policy, and they were in danger
of doing so again, whenever sterling came under pressure. As it happens,
the incoming Heath government was all too happy to let the DCE ceilings fall into abeyance in 1971, when the IMF's facilities were no longer
required, and this opened the door to a less restrictive credit policy.[4] For
its part, the Bank accepted the clearers' protestations, concluding that the
application of controls over the previous decade had led to distortions,
including the disintermediation of credit flows away from the clearers.[5]
The simple option would have been to abolish quantitative and qualitative controls, and revert to the traditional clearing bank model, but this
was not deemed to be expedient at the time. National Provincial and
London & Westminster had been allowed to merge in 1968, reducing the
big five High Street banks to four. In its early days, the Heath government
professed to be in favour of more competition, and potentially receptive to
complaints about the lack of competition in banking, including criticisms
of the CLCB's cartel. The Bank therefore presented its proposal for ending
direct controls on credit as part of an initiative to promote competition in
which the clearers agreed to disband their cartel. The proposals, known as
Competition and Credit Control (CCC), were published as a consultation
document in May 1971, and implemented in the following September.[6]

CCC proved to be a pyrrhic victory for those interested in more competition because the big four did not start to compete on rate for retail deposits,
or loans. Customers in search of better savings rates had to look to smaller

[3] W. M. Allen, memo dated 20/2/1968, Bank of England Archive, 5A175/1; C. A. E.
Goodhart, 'Financial innovation and monetary control', *Oxford Review of Economic
Policy*, 2, no. 4 (Winter 1986), p. 80; D. J. Needham (2014), pp. 25–9.
[4] F. H. Capie, *The Bank of England from the 1950s to 1979* (Cambridge: Cambridge
University Press, 2010), p. 649.
[5] F. H. Capie (2010), p. 427.
[6] 'Competition and credit control', consultative document issued on 14 May 1971 and
reprinted in *BEQB*, 11, no. 2 (June 1971), pp. 189–93.

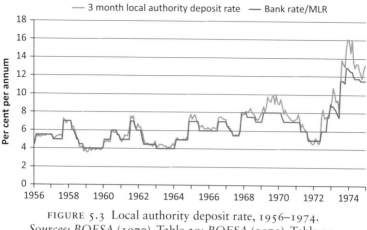

FIGURE 5.3 Local authority deposit rate, 1956–1974.
Sources: BOESA (1970), Table 29; *BOESA* (1975), Table 27.

building societies and local authority deposits (Figure 5.3). Abolition of the Building Societies Association (BSA) cartel might have opened up the prospect of larger building societies challenging the clearers to compete more aggressively for savings, but there was no official appetite for deregulating the mainstream building society sector. The BSA cartel helped to keep mortgage lending rates at sub-market levels, benefiting existing borrowers – an important electoral constituency. The abolition of the clearers' cartel did, however, provide cover for the clearers to discard longstanding inhibitions about competing on rate for wholesale funds. Some banks had already started to issue sterling certificates of deposit (£CDs) in the late 1960s, and CCC gave the clearers the green light to become more active in the interbank market, and they too started to issue £CDs (Figure 5.4).[7]

The US money-center banks had been tapping the New York money market for wholesale funds for a decade, and the clearers' international operations already had experience raising wholesale funds in London's Euromarkets.[8] CCC was a compromise, allowing the clearers' domestic operations to move away from the traditional model towards the euromarket model. The move from the 28 per cent liquidity ratio to the 12 ½ per cent reserve asset ratio (RAR) allowed the clearers to cut their traditional liquidity holdings, and they became more reliant on raising funds in the growing wholesale market among domestic banks. Direct interbank

[7] G. W. Taylor, 'New techniques in British banking: an examination of the sterling money markets and the principles of term lending', Gilbart Lecture on Banking (London: King's College London, 1973), pp. 29–30.
[8] C. A. E. G. Goodhart (Winter 1986), p. 81.

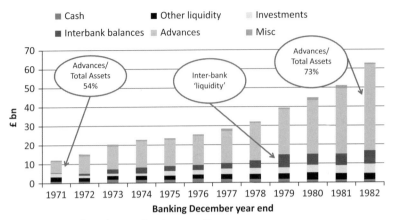

FIGURE 5.4 London clearing banks – sterling assets.
Sources: BOESA, no. 2 (1975), *BOESA* (1995); series break between 1974 and 1975.

transactions between clearers raised the possibility of bypassing the discount market, but the inclusion of secured money at call (MAC) in the RAR meant there were still incentives favouring the houses (until the ratio was abolished in 1981). In broad terms, the London money market adopted New York market practices, and the clearers became liability managers in respect of their domestic balance sheets.[9] This approach was followed by banks across the developed world with consequential declines in traditional liquid asset ratios.[10]

The style of balance sheet management that developed in New York in the 1960s was described by James Tobin and the Yale school as an exercise in portfolio optimisation in which banks, and other financial institutions (OFIs), adjusted their funding and lending in response to competitively determined interest rates.[11] Tobin argued that banks were not qualitatively

---

[9] N. H. Dimsdale and A. C. Hotson, *British Financial Crises since 1825* (2014), pp. 43–4; A. C. Hotson, 'The 1981 Budget and Its Impact on the Conduct of Economic Policy: Was It a Monetarist Revolution?' in D. J. Needham and A. C. Hotson (eds) *Expansionary Fiscal Contraction: The Thatcher Government's 1981 Budget in Perspective* (Cambridge: Cambridge University Press, 2014), pp. 137–41.

[10] M. Schularick and A. M. Taylor, 'Credit booms gone bust: monetary policy, leverage cycles, and financial crises, 1870–2008', *American Economic Review*, 102, no. 2 (2012), p. 1036.

[11] J. Gurley and E. S. Shaw, *Money in a Theory of Finance* (Washington DC: The Brookings Institution, 1960), pp. 247–99; J. Tobin, 'Commercial Banks as Creators of "Money"', Cowles Foundation Paper, no. 205, in D. Carson (ed.) *Banking and Monetary Studies* (Homewood, IL: Richard D. Irwin, 1963), pp. 408–10; J. Tobin and W. C. Brainard, 'Financial Intermediaries and the Effectiveness of Monetary Controls', *American*

different from OFIs, and that there was nothing particularly special about bank money – a view that chimed with the Radcliffian idea that liquidity was a continuum.[12] The portfolio-theoretic view of banking suggested that banks with sufficient capital should be free to make their own decisions about risk–reward trade-offs, rather than being hidebound by cartelised prices, lending norms, and demarcations between various institutional types. These restrictions were regarded as passé by the time of the CCC consultations, partly reflecting the influence of the portfolio view.

The clearers' core lending business remained the provision of working capital for businesses, but they also funded finance houses that provided equipment leases and consumer credit, including point-of-sale car loans, and other loans for hire purchase. Each of the big five clearers had acquired shareholding interests in the leading houses: Midland in Forward Trust, Barclays in Mercantile Credit, London & Westminster in Lombard Finance, National Provincial in North Central Finance, and Lloyds in Bowmaker.[13] The houses provided instalment credit, whereby the lender could resell the goods in the event of default, and this fitted with the traditional clearing bank remit of loans that were self-liquidating, and supported by security.[14] Equipment leases could finance machinery that generated cash flows to repay the loan, and consumer loans could be viewed as self-liquidating, if the borrower had a secure job with a regular salary. These loans were not risk-free, but they did offer a reasonable degree of maturity matching between loan repayments and cash receipts expected by the borrower.

In 1968, Barclays launched Barclaycard, Britain's first mass-market credit card, and the other clearers launched Access in 1972.[15] Credit card advances could be viewed as a downmarket form of overdraft with better margins and reasonably controllable risks. The clearers sought to differentiate their traditional branch banking services from those of their finance houses and credit card subsidiaries, but the rot set-in on the rule

Economic Review, 53, no. 2 (May 1963), pp. 383–9; Paul Krugman, 'The Conscience of a Liberal', *New York Times*, 24 August 2013.

[12] Radcliffe Committee, *Report of Committee on the Working of the Monetary System*, Cmnd. 827 (London: HMSO, 1959), chapter IV, paragraph 392; R. A. Werner, 'Can banks individually create money out of nothing? The theories and the empirical evidence', *International Review of Financial Analysis*, 36 (2014), pp. 9–10.

[13] Committee of London Clearing Bankers, *The London Clearing Banks, Evidence by the CLCB to the Committee to Review the Functioning of Financial Institutions* (London: Longman, 1978), Table 52, p. 271.

[14] Lord Crowther, *Report of the Committee on Consumer Credit* (2 vols, London: HMSO, March 1971), pp. 66–74.

[15] M. Ackrill and L. Hannah, *Barclays: The Business of Banking, 1690–1996* (Cambridge: Cambridge University Press, 2001), pp. 251–5.

that one clearer did not solicit business from a rival's customer. Lenders had to protect themselves against the claims of rival lenders, and this directed attention towards asset-based finance (i.e. collateralised loans) for businesses, rather than reliance being placed on the net worth of borrowers and their generalised credit standing.[16] Consumer credit relied on more elaborate credit referencing and credit monitoring, partly to check on borrowing from other lenders. It is not really true to say that collateral played a greater role than previously, but customers' multiple banking relationships meant that collateral had to be managed more explicitly.

Unfortunately, the clearers and a number of pension funds financed a fringe group of finance houses of lesser standing than those partially owned by the clearers.[17] This lower tier of finance houses included the likes of London and County and First National Finance Corporation (FNFC), both of which lent to commercial property developers, and Cedar Holdings, which offered second mortgages. These property financing businesses with grandiose names grew rapidly in the late 1960s and early 1970s, before the market crashed in 1973–5.[18] Some of these finance houses relied on short-term wholesale funding, which they periodically rolled over, and some retail funding, to finance longer-term loans, or projects such as property developments that took a number of years to come to fruition. The developers were not well capitalised, and their unfinished projects provided poor-quality security.[19] Without a lifeboat operation to save them, these finance houses would have quickly lost their funding with the onset of the property crash, putting them first in line for insolvency, followed by many of the developers they had financed.[20] In the event, the Bank orchestrated a lifeboat in which the clearers agreed to provide sufficient funding so that most of the houses were kept afloat, allowing them to realise their collateral over a number of years without fire sales. This meant that the developers could be bankrupted at the convenience of the houses, usually leaving unsecured creditors and shareholders with nothing. The Bank's view that the lifeboat would reduce the cost borne by the clearers – as opposed to everybody else – was probably vindicated.[21]

---

[16] W. Leaf, *Banking* (ed.) Ernest Sykes (3rd edn, 1935; reprinted 1937; 4th edn, London and New York: Oxford University Press, 1943), pp. 168–71.

[17] C. Gordon, *The Cedar Story: The Night the City Was Saved* (London: Sinclair-Stevenson, 1993), p. 58.

[18] C. Gordon (1993), pp. 26–7, 30–1, 40; F. H. Capie (2010), pp. 533–6.

[19] C. Gordon (1993), pp, 150, 152–3.

[20] C. Gordon (1993), pp. 193–203; F. H. Capie (2014), pp. 21–2.

[21] M. I. Reid, *The Secondary Banking Crisis, 1973–75: Its Causes and Course* (London: Macmillan, 1982), pp. 190–6.

Following the secondary banking crisis of 1973–5, the Bank subjected bank lending for commercial property development to greater scrutiny, but the old principle that banks and borrowers should avoid maturity transformation, née mismatching, fell on stony ground. The Bank attempted to implement prudential liquidity requirements, but it was unable to impede moves towards greater maturity transformation.[22] In 1980, the longstanding principle that the clearers should not lend on first mortgage for house purchase was countermanded as part of the Thatcher government's measures to promote home ownership and deregulate financial services. In time, the clearers' balance sheets came to be dominated by longer-term property-related lending, and short-term lending ceased to be the dominant part of their business.[23]

A key tenet of CCC was that money and credit growth should be regulated by price – that is to say, by interest rates – rather than quantitative controls. The idea that credit should be allocated on the basis of price, like any other resource, was commonplace in economic thinking, but this had not been the primary purpose of Bank rate policy in the past. In the nineteenth century, higher interest rates were sometimes seen as a means of dampening commodity speculation – by raising the carry cost of long positions – but working capital was not noted for being interest rate sensitive, particularly in the short run.[24] If higher interest rates were expected to persist, borrowers might seek to economise on their current assets, but this would be a secondary consequence of a policy directed at other ends. Bank rate would normally be deployed to defend the Bank's bullion reserves, when sterling came under pressure, or when the Bank decided to respond to market dislocation by acting as lender of last resort (LOLR). In the former case, higher sterling rates attracted foreign demand for London bills and bonds, which were paid for in bullion. As well as supporting sterling, the influx of funds could bolster the supply of credit. In the case of the LOLR, high rates deterred banks from shedding assets, unless they faced overwhelming liquidity problems. As Bagehot put it, higher rates would impose a 'heavy fine on [banks'] unreasonable timidity', helping to

[22] M. I. Reid (1982), p. 197.

[23] M. A. King, *The End of Alchemy: Money, Banking and the Future of the Global Economy* (London: Little, Brown, 2016), p. 255.

[24] R. S. Sayers, 'Bank Rate in Keynes's Century', Keynes Lecture, 1979, *Proceedings of the British Academy, LXV* (Oxford: Oxford University Press, 1981); A. B. Cramp, *Opinion on Bank Rate, 1822–60* (London, 1962); C. A. E. Goodhart and A. C. Hotson, 'The Forecasting and Control of Bank Lending' (1979) in C. A. E. Goodhart, *Monetary Theory and Practice: The UK Experience* (London: Macmillan, 1984), pp. 139–45.

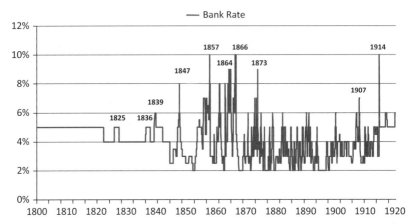

FIGURE 5.5 Bank rate, 1800 to 1920.
Source: Bank of England (Figure reproduced with kind permission of Oxford University Press, see page xii).

maintain the supply of credit, rather than choke off demand.[25] As a result, interruptions in credit supply and LOLR-lending were associated with a peak in interest rates – in contrast to the policy of cutting interest rates in response to the most recent credit crisis (Figure 5.5).

Under the CLCB cartel, higher interest rates resulted in wider margins for the clearers, both on funds arising from their non-interest-bearing (nib) current accounts, and on their own resources arising from paid-up shares. Before the First World War, the CLCB agreed that allowances (i.e. rates) paid on seven-day deposits should normally be capped at 5 per cent, allowing improved margins when rates rose sufficiently.[26] The fixed yield on the clearers' gilt-edged portfolios provided a partial match for these fixed-rate funds, but their overall margins still improved when interest rates rose in the 1920s. Conversely, the clearers faced margin compression when rates fell in the 1930s, damaging profitability.[27] They responded by setting a minimum lending rate of 5 per cent, for example, Bank rate plus 1 per cent with a minimum of 5 per cent.[28]

One of the advantages of lending to the finance houses – which became increasingly significant from the 1950s – was the houses' need for fixed-rate funding to match their instalment loans to customers. Most of their

[25] W. Bagehot, *Lombard Street, a Description of the Money Market* (London, 3rd edn, 1873), p. 197.
[26] J. W. Gilbart (ed.) A. S. Michie, *Gilbart on Banking: The History, Principles and Practice of Banking* (2 vols, London: George Bell, 1882), I, p. 323, fn.
[27] W. Leaf, 1935, 1943, pp. 99–100.
[28] W. Leaf, 1943, p. 177.

loans were at fixed rates of up to three years, although big-ticket items, such as aircraft leases, could be longer. The clearers provided medium-term fixed-rate funding that allowed the balance sheets of the finance houses to be broadly matched in terms of maturity and interest rate duration.[29] The clearers' longer duration lending – that is to say, their fixed-rate lending to finance houses – provided a degree of hedging against their fixed-rate (i.e. nib) liabilities, helping to stabilise their margins, notwithstanding the decline in their longer dated gilt holdings.[30] During the 1960s and 1970s, they successfully protected themselves against undue fluctuations in their margins, despite more variable interest rates, although there was still a residual, positive association between their margins and the level of interest rates.

After the cartel was abolished in 1971, the clearers could bid more, or less, aggressively for funds in wholesale markets, making their own decisions about acceptable spreads on new business.[31] Although the big four tended to move as a herd, they had the freedom to set their own agenda for margins, balance sheet growth, and credit quality. Each clearer set its own administered reference rate – base rate – for the pricing of administered rates on loans and deposits, but it should come as no surprise that base rates tended to follow Bank rate. Officials nevertheless attempted to downplay their role in the setting of interest rates, and Bank rate was renamed Minimum Lending Rate (MLR) with a view to it being set by a formula relative to Treasury bill (TB) rates.[32] This charade was started because the Heath government wanted to distance itself from interest rate setting, in furtherance of an attempt to secure agreement to an incomes policy. The TB formula was operated for five years, albeit with some official interference in the TB tender – pre-empting unwanted moves in MLR. By 1976, the Bank had had enough, and ended the pretence that the market set short-term interest rates. The traditional practice of signalling rate changes was reintroduced, resuscitating the classical system

---

[29] B. O. Bierwag, *Duration Analysis: Managing Interest Rate Risk* (Cambridge, MA: Ballinger, 1987), pp. 72–80; J. R. Hicks, *Value and Capital: An Inquiry into Some Fundamental Principles of Economic Theory* (Oxford: Clarendon Press, 1st edn, 1939; 2nd edn, 1946), p. 186.

[30] R. B. Platt, *Controlling Interest Rate Risk: New Techniques and Applications for Money Management* (New York: Wiley, 1986), pp. 44–5.

[31] Bank of England, *The Development and Operation of Monetary Policy 1960–1983* (Oxford: Clarendon Press, 1984), pp. 44; C. A. E. Goodhart, *Monetary Theory and Practice: The UK Experience* (London: Macmillan, 1984), p. 154; J. C. R. Dow and I. D. Saville, *A Critique of Monetary Policy: Theory and British Experience* (Oxford: Clarendon Press, 1st edn, 1988; 2nd edn with new preface, 1990) pp. 36–7.

[32] D. J. Needham, *UK Monetary Policy* (2014), p. 59.

(although it took until 2006 for Bank rate to be restored to the official lexicon).[33]

It is ironic that the CCC proposals promoted interest rates as a means of regulating domestic money and credit at the moment when the abolition of the cartel undermined the linkages between Bank rate, clearing bank margins, and the supply of credit. Bank officials convinced themselves that interest rate policy could still affect the growth of banks' balance sheets by influencing the public's willingness to hold deposits with them. The idea that the clearers' balance sheets were determined by customers' demand for deposits, rather than their demand for credit, ran counter to practitioners' experience, but officials were pleasantly surprised to find econometric evidence supporting a reasonably stable relationship between the public's demand for money, and a limited number of determinant variables – prices, real output and interest rates.[34] This work – initially undertaken for the United States, but subsequently extended to cover the United Kingdom – was summarised in an article entitled 'The Importance of Money', published in the *BEQB* in 1970, with the implication that interest rates could be used to stabilise money, and thence the wider economy.[35] The Bank article was a classic of its kind, combining an even-handed text with a deniable subtext for those in the know. It could be defended in Whitehall as being no more than a balanced exposition of the debate between monetarists and Keynesians, but a few comments were added at the end about new econometric evidence supporting the idea of a stable demand for money. The supporting evidence was included in appendices, although most of the empirical results were omitted when the article was republished in a much-cited book, sponsored by the Bank in 1984.[36] The new-fangled econometrics was not regarded as decisive by policymakers at the time, but it supported the idea – embedded in CCC – that interest rates could be used as a tool for managing domestic money and credit.[37]

[33] C. A. E. Goodhart, 'The Bank of England over the Last 35 Years', Bankhistorisches Archiv, Zeitschrift zur Bankengeschichte, Beiheft 43, Welche Aufgaben muß eine Zentralbank wahrnehmen? Historische Erfahrungen und europäische Perspektiven. 15. Wissenschaftliches Kolloquium am 7 November 2002 auf Einladung "Geld und Währung" (Stuttgart: Franz Steiner Verlag, 2004), p. 48.

[34] M. Friedman, 'Demand for money', *Journal of Political Economy*, 67, no. 4 (August 1959), pp. 327–51; D. Laidler and M. Parkin, 'Demand for money in the United Kingdom 1956–67: preliminary estimates', University of Essex Discussion Paper (unpublished).

[35] C. A. E. Goodhart and A. D. Crockett, 'The importance of money', *BEQB*, 10, no. 2 (June 1970), pp. 159–98.

[36] Bank of England (1984), pp. 14–30.

[37] D. J. Needham, *UK Monetary Policy* (2014), p. 33.

The willingness to use monetary and credit aggregates as indicators for setting interest rates persuaded the Bank to impose a mid-monthly reporting requirement on all the banks, in addition to their end-quarter reporting. The main clearers had self-reported on a monthly basis since the 1890s, but the Bank's standardised reporting requirements were intended to generate better quality data. It was hoped that more timely data for the sector as a whole would improve the quality of official decision making. Consistent mid-monthly reporting across the banking sector started in June 1971, and some historical data were collected back to April 1970.[38] Make-up day for reporting was set for the third Wednesday in the month, except December, which was the second Wednesday. Mid-monthly data were expected to be less distorted by end-month payments giving rise to a surge of transit items, and window dressing on half-yearly and year-end reporting dates. Not everyone in the Bank had been predisposed to publish monthly data for the monetary aggregates, believing that market practitioners – unlike officials – might be confused by erratic monthly movements, but it soon became clear that withholding the figures would be untenable, and plans were set in train for publishing monthly M3, its credit counterparts, and its components – in particular M1.[39]

The subsequent story of the stability of the UK demand for money can be summarised fairly simply. Initial optimism, based on data from the 1960s, was followed by doubts as more data from the early 1970s was added.[40] It was suggested that the breakdown of the broad money equations, particularly the M3/£M3 equation, might have resulted from disruption caused by the introduction of CCC.[41] It was hoped that this instability would be temporary, but the equations for £M3 continued to misbehave in the late 1970s.[42] It is surprising that the initial optimism about the stability of the demand for money was not tempered by the knowledge that the banks' balance sheets had grown in lockstep with nominal incomes in the

[38] Table and note in *BEQB*, 12, no. 1 (March 1972), p. 153.
[39] Bank of England, 'Changes in banking statistics', *BEQB*, 12, no. 1 (March 1972), p. 76–9.
[40] L. D. D. Price, 'The demand for money in the United Kingdom: a further investigation', *BEQB*, 12, no. 1 (March 1972), p. 43–55; C. A. E. Goodhart, 'The Conduct of Monetary Policy', *The Economic Journal*, 99 (June 1989), p. 314.
[41] G. Hacche, 'The demand for money in the United Kingdom: experience since 1971', *BEQB*, 14, no. 3 (September 1974), pp. 284–305; J. C. R. Dow and I. D. Saville (Oxford: Clarendon Press, 1988, 1990), p. 37.
[42] Richard T. Coghlan and Lesley M. Smith, 'A preliminary note on the demand for M3' (15 September 1977), HM Treasury Freedom of Information disclosure, 'Monetary policy in the late 1970s and in the 1981 Budget' (9 November 2006); J. S. Fforde, 'Setting monetary objectives', *BEQB*, 23, no. 2 (June 1983), p. 203.

1960s only as a result of quantitative controls, and that this linkage would not necessarily remain after their abolition. Narrow monetary aggregates fared slightly better; M1 was reasonably stable until the introduction of interest-bearing deposits on current accounts (ib sight deposits) in the late 1970s.[43] Ironically, the most robust equation related the demand for banknotes (the main component of broad M0) to consumer expenditure, where interest rates were found to have no significant impact. This was the one demand-for-money equation that realised operational success, forecasting note demand for the Bank's printing works in Debden, Essex.[44]

For the most part, traditional liquid assets were deemed to qualify for inclusion in the numerator of the reserve asset ratio (RAR): TBs, MAC, British government stocks (BGS) with one year or less to maturity, local authority bills eligible for rediscount at the Bank, and commercial bills eligible for rediscount at the Bank. Eligible commercial bills included PBBs, and were limited to 2 per cent of each bank's eligible liabilities (ELs), the latter being sterling deposits with an original maturity of up to two years, including net sterling interbank receipts.[45] The Bank could call for Special Deposits (SDs), which paid interest, but did not count as reserve assets. There was a presumption that SD calls could be used to push the banks and finance houses up against their RARs – 12 ½ per cent for the banks and 10 per cent for the finance houses – forcing them to moderate their balance sheet growth. In practice, strong credit demand encouraged the banks and finance houses to bid more aggressively for wholesale funds, some of which could be held as reserve assets to meet their RARs. The bidding up of wholesale market rates relative to the slower to adjust base-rate related lending, allowed some corporate treasury departments to borrow at base rate plus one percentage point, and acquire £CDs and place wholesale deposits at a slight premium. This form of arbitrage became known as round tripping, and exacerbated the expansion of banks' balance sheets.[46] The Bank argued that SD calls should not be regarded as a substitute for interest rate rises, but many academics remained in thrall to the prospect of curbing monetary growth using ratio controls.[47]

[43] R. T. Coghlan, 'A transactions demand for money', *BEQB*, 18, 1978, pp. 48–60; J. M. Trundle, 'The demand for M1 in the UK', Bank of England (1982), mimeo.

[44] Bank of England, 'Bank of England notes', *BEQB*, 18, no. 3 (September 1978), pp. 359–64, especially appendix, pp. 363–4.

[45] *BEQB*, 11, no. 4 (December, 1971), pp. 482–9.

[46] Bank of England (1984), p. 44.

[47] W. T. Newlyn and R. P. Bootle, *Theory of Money* (Oxford: Clarendon Press, 3rd edn, 1978, reprinted 1979); N. H. Dimsdale and A. C. Hotson (2014), pp. 43–4; F. H. Capie (2010), p. 502 refers to Brian Griffiths, Walter Newlyn and Michael Parkin.

By 1973 – two years after the launch of CCC – the Bank found itself unable to regulate money and credit, either by raising MLR, or by calling SDs. The Bank believed that further rises in MLR would eventually do the trick, but the Heath government was not willing to countenance an unprecedented rise in (nominal) interest rates. The abolition of the CLCB cartel had released the liability management genie from its bottle, and a counterrevolution to revive the traditional clearing bank model was not on the cards. Instead, the Bank cobbled together the Supplementary Special Deposits (SSD) scheme, universally known as the corset.[48] This was a device for reintroducing the much-derided quantitative controls, but without the embarrassment of doing so explicitly because the controls were applied to the liability side of banks' balance sheets. Banks whose sterling funding – defined as interest-bearing eligible liabilities (IBELS) – grew beyond pre-set percentages had to place progressively higher percentages of non-interest-bearing Supplementary Special Deposits (nib SSDs) with the Bank. Strictly speaking, nib SSDs imposed an increasing penalty on excessive lending, rather than excessive funding, because banks could deduct their net placing of funds in the interbank market from IBELs – in other words, on-lent interbank funds did not count for IBELs, but receiving interbank funds did. The SSD scheme was meant to be applied for short periods to tackle overheating in the credit market, but banks sought to anticipate its application by building up their IBELs during its suspension, and the scheme remained in force for most of the 1970s.[49]

The Bank's dalliance with monetarism – relying on a stable demand for money – had been short lived, but M3 and its counterparts remained part of the official forecasting system.[50] From March 1972, the Bank started to publish monthly M1 and M3 figures with seasonal adjustments, providing the market with a more timely reporting structure.[51] From December 1972, the Bank presented figures for M3 with reference to their credit counterparts in table 12 (3) of the *BEQB*.[52] The counterpart figures could be erratic, but there were 'offsetting movements' between them: an exceptionally high public sector borrowing requirement (PSBR) – reflecting increased net payments to the private sector – would tend to be partially

---

[48] C. A. E. Goodhart, 'Competition and credit control: some personal reflections', *Financial History Review*, 22, no. 2 (August 2015), p. 245.

[49] *BEQB*, 22, no. 1 (March 1982), p. 85.

[50] M. E. Hewitt, 'Financial forecasts in the United Kingdom', *BEQB*, 17, no. 2 (June 1977), pp. 188–95.

[51] Tables 12 (1) and 12 (2), 17, no. 1, *BEQB* (March 1972).

[52] Table 12 (3), 'Influences on money stock and domestic credit expansion', 17, no. 4 *BEQB* (December 1972), pp. 512–3, notes on p. 549.

offset by less private sector borrowing, and higher external inflows could be associated with lower bank lending. As a result, month-to-month changes in M3 tended to be less volatile than its counterpart series.[53] In press releases and informal briefings accompanying the figures, the Bank drew attention to special factors affecting the evolution of M3 and its counterparts, and each quarter the *BEQB* provided a more detailed assessment in the 'Monetary developments' section of the 'Economic commentary'.[54] Various technical refinements were adopted over the years, including a more sophisticated approach to seasonal adjustment.[55]

The regime for reporting the counterparts of money encouraged a number of stockbrokers to publish commentaries on the figures, making the monthly publication of table 12(3) an important part of the market's calendar. Greenwell's monthly review, prepared by its senior partner, Gordon Pepper, and his research colleagues, Robert Thomas and Geoffrey Wood, became the bellwether for the market, together with other influential commentators, included Alan Walters at Sebag's and Tim Congdon at Messel's.[56] Table 12(3) and the analysts' commentaries provided the basis for conversations round the market's luncheon tables on the prospects for the counterparts, and whether the authorities would respond promptly to adverse movements by raising MLR – or not. During the sterling crisis of 1976, the governor of the Bank, Gordon Richardson, persuaded the Labour Chancellor of the Exchequer, Denis Healey, to announce a guideline for the growth of M3, and after the crisis abated, the government continued to set monetary targets, expressed as growth ranges for the year ahead.[57] The target ranges were expressed in terms of £M3, rather than M3 – that is to say, M3 excluding the foreign currency deposits of UK residents, which were said to be irrelevant to the domestic economy. The change in definition was largely technical because exchange controls prevented most UK residents from holding foreign currency, the exceptions being the oil companies and

[53] Lesley M. Smith, note dated 8 June 1978, Bank of England Archive 5A175/10; *BEQB*, 17, no. 4 (December 1972), p. 513.

[54] A. C. Hotson, 'British Monetary Targets 1976 to 1987: A view from the fourth floor of the Bank of England', Special Paper 190, Financial Markets Group, London School of Economics and Political Science (7 March 2010), pp. 5, 12; *BEQB*, 19, no. 2 (June 1979), p. 123.

[55] 'Seasonal adjustment of monthly money statistics', *BEQB*, 18, no. 2 (June 1978), pp. 196–203.

[56] G. T. Pepper, *Inside Thatcher's Monetarist Revolution* (London: Palgrave Macmillan, 1998), p. 8.

[57] N. H. Dimsdale, 'British Monetary Policy since 1945', in N. F. R. Crafts and N. W. C. Woodward (eds) *The British Economy since 1945* (Oxford: Clarendon Press, 1991), pp. 126.

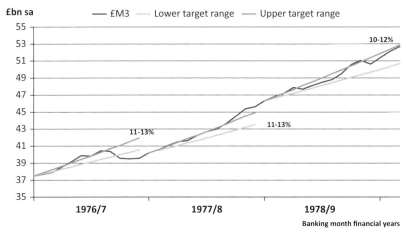

FIGURE 5.6 Labour government's £M3 target ranges.
Source: BEQB (March 1980), Table 11.1.

a few others who were allowed to do so. London-based banks were, of course, major players in the Euromarkets, taking foreign currency deposits from non-UK residents, but these were not included in M3, £M3, or any other measure of domestic money (Figure 5.6).[58]

The £M3 targets were not predicated on a stable demand for money – the Bank had already been badly bruised on that one – but a means of reassuring the market that the government would control its borrowing requirement – the PSBR – and raise interest rates promptly to fund its deficit, and (perhaps) limit bank lending. The unfunded public sector deficit of the early 1970s had been unprecedented, and was seen to be the main cause of rapid broad money growth (Figure 5.7). Reining in the unfunded public sector deficit was regarded by many market practitioners as a prerequisite for stability in the gilt and foreign exchange markets. In his memoirs, Healey explained that both he and his officials saw monetary targets as a pragmatic response to market problems that had not been addressed by the Keynesians, but this did not mean those involved had adopted Milton Friedman's monetarist principles:

My years at the Treasury had taught me that the neo-Keynesians were wrong in paying so little attention to the monetary dimension of economic policy, though both the Bank and Treasury had been working to undisclosed monetary targets

---

[58] M. D. K. W. Foot, 'Monetary Targets: Their Nature and Record in the Major Economies' in B. Griffiths and G. E. Wood (eds) *Monetary Targets* (London: Macmillan, 1981), p. 14; J. C. R. Dow and I. D. Saville (Oxford: Clarendon Press, 1988, 1990), Table 7.1, Monetary targets, 1976–1986, pp. 124–5.

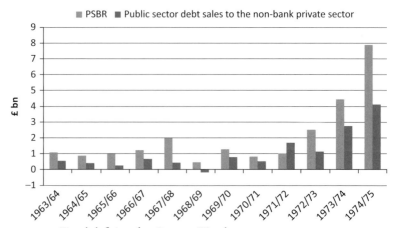

FIGURE 5.7 Fiscal deficits after Bretton Woods.
Source: BOESA, no. 2 (1975), Table 12/3 (Figure reproduced with kind permission of Cambridge University Press, see page xii).

since 1973. In 1976, before the IMF negotiations, I decided to publish these monetary targets, largely to placate the financial markets. But I never accepted Friedman's theories. Nor did I ever meet any private or central banker who took them seriously.[59]

The £M3 targets did affect the Labour government's policy responses to economic developments – its policy reaction function. In October 1976, the target was in danger of over-shooting, and Healey was able to secure Cabinet agreement to raise MLR to a peak level of 15 per cent, despite prime ministerial objections that had prevailed in the past (Figure 5.8).[60] The Treasury was able to impose greater budgetary control over spending departments for a couple of years, but the targets were not sufficient to prevent a spending spree in the run-up to the 1979 election. Perhaps the most demonstrable effect on policy was the decision in the autumn of 1977 to stick to the monetary target, and allow sterling to appreciate. An attempt to cap sterling would have required that MLR be kept low, and official intervention on the foreign exchanges. Both of these policies would have contributed to a monetary over-shoot, and – having put the target in place – the Labour government decided to keep it.[61] Strictly speaking, this monetary regime was not based on Friedman's prescriptions, but its Keynesian critics – and some of its friends – took it to be a form of monetarism. Even

[59] D. W. Healey, *The Time of My Life* (London: Michael Joseph, 1989), p. 491.
[60] D. W. Healey (1989), p. 430; A. C. Hotson (2010), p. 9.
[61] *BEQB*, 17, no. 3, September 1977, p. 300; A. C. Hotson (2010), p. 12; D. J. Needham, *UK Monetary Policy* (2014), pp. 113–8, 183.

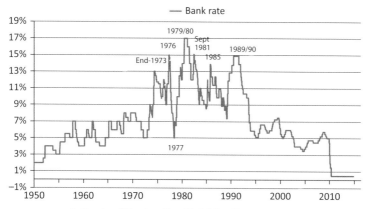

FIGURE 5.8 Bank of England's official lending rate, 1950 to 2013.
Source: Bank of England.

Richardson, one of its key proponents, concluded his Mais Lecture of 1978 by referring to it as an exercise in 'practical monetarism'.[62]

By the late 1970s, it was recognised that interest rates had a limited impact on private sector borrowing from the banks, particularly after the abolition of the CLCB cartel, but raising interest rates could help to sell more government debt to non-banks.[63] If the authorities raised interest rates to a point where the market thought rates could ease, investors – or perhaps speculators – could be induced to buy gilts with a view to a (short-term) capital gain (Figure 5.9). The raising of rates with a view to their subsequent decline became known as the Grand Old Duke of York, and was deployed to break logjams in gilt sales. Bank lending to the private sector was controlled by the SSD scheme, even though it was recognised that some disintermediation took place. The bill leak was an example of disintermediation whereby banks accepted commercial bills from corporate borrowers, instead of providing conventional loans, and resold the bills with the bank's guarantee outside the banking system. The system delivered reasonably accurate control – some would say cosmetic control – of reported £M3, with a safety valve allowing faster underlying (bill adjusted) broad monetary growth.[64] The bill leak was one of the factors that prompted the publication of wider

---

[62] G. W. H. Richardson, 'Reflections on the conduct of monetary policy', Mais Lecture, 9 February 1978, *BEQB*, 18, no. 1 (March 1978), p. 37.

[63] C. A. E. Goodhart and A. C. Hotson, 'The Forecasting and Control of Bank Lending' in C. A. E. Goodhart, *Monetary Theory and Practice: The UK Experience* (London, 1984), pp. 139–45.

[64] Bank of England, 'The role of the Bank of England in the money market', *BEQB*, 22, no. 1 (March 1982), pp. 86–94.

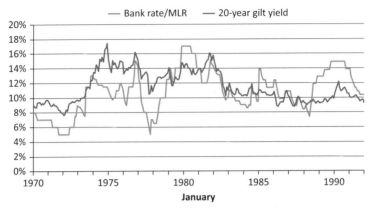

FIGURE 5.9 Risk and return of duration mismatch, 1970–1992.
Source: BEQB.

measures of liquidity – PSL1 and PSL2 – that included bills held outside the banking sector and other forms of near-money.[65]

It has to be said that university based academics found the counterparts approach bewildering.[66] Books on this peculiarly British approach to monetary policy were eventually published by some of those involved: the market practitioner Tim Congdon's in 1982; the senior Bank official Charles Goodhart's in 1984; and the gilts analyst Paul Temperton's in 1986.[67] Keynesians, steeped in demand management, criticised the emphasis on the PSBR, which everyone agreed was not a satisfactory measure of fiscal stance; Friedman was perplexed by the Brits' attempts to link monetary and fiscal policy. Disdain for the counterparts approach was one of the few points on which Keynesians and monetarists could agree.[68] It was surprising that the incoming Thatcher government professed to take Friedmanite monetarism seriously, but stuck with the previous government's leaky £M3 framework, using a monetary aggregate that palpably failed to exhibit a stable demand for money function.[69]

The downturn in the economy in the early years of the first Thatcher government led to an increased unfunded public sector deficit in 1980/81,

[65] *BEQB* (December 1982 and May 1987).
[66] N. Batini and E. Nelson, 'The UK's rocky road to stability', *FRB of St. Louis Working Paper Series* (March 2005), pp. 29–32.
[67] T. Congdon (1982); C. A. E. Goodhart (1984); P. V. Temperton (1986).
[68] J. C. R. Dow and I. D. Saville (Oxford: Clarendon Press, 1988, 1990), pp. 111–14.
[69] M. Friedman, 'Memoranda on monetary policy', *Treasury and Civil Service Committee*, HC 720-11 (London, 1980); N. H. Dimsdale, *Treasury and Civil Service Committee*, p. 186.

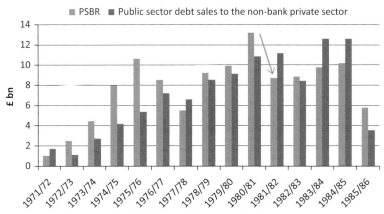

FIGURE 5.10 Financing the PSBR, 1971/72–1985/86.
Source: BEQB, Table 11.3 (Figure reproduced with kind permission of Cambridge University Press, see page xii).

and fears that it would not be contained – a repeat of the early 1970s. The essence of the 1981 Budget was the reining in of the PSBR, notwithstanding the recession. In addition, the government deliberately over-funded, selling more gilts to the non-bank private sector than required to finance its PSBR. This meant that the public sector's contribution to £M3 growth was largely negative in the years following the 1981 Budget, in stark contrast to the early 1970s (Figure 5.10).[70] This should have been sufficient for the government to meet the monetary targets set out in its Medium-Term Financial Strategy (MTFS), but these were massively over-shot as a result of the sustained expansion of bank lending to the private sector (Figure 5.11).[71]

Over-funding helped to reduce bank deposits, but the Bank had to accommodate consequential shortages in the money market by buying bills from the banks, allowing the banks to lower their assets in line with their lower liabilities. Treasury bill (TB) issuance was largely counterproductive because it created a shortage in the market that had to be offset by bill purchases. The stock of TBs outstanding was therefore allowed to dwindle away. The 'bill mountain' accumulating in the Banking Department of the Bank counted towards domestic bank credit, and led to a shortage of bills in the market. Lower bill yields opened up opportunities for bill arbitrage, a form of round tripping in which corporate treasurers borrowed using bank bills, and placed the funds in the interbank

[70] C. A. E. Goodhart (June 1989), pp. 327–8.
[71] A. C. Hotson, 1981 Budget (2014), p. 134.

% pa	Target period	1980/ 1981	1981/ 1982	1982/ 1983	1983/ 1984	1984/ 1985	1985/ 1986	1986/ 1987	1987/ 1988	1988/ 1989
Out-turn		19.4	12.8	11.2	9.4	11.9	16.9	19.0		
Targets announced										
March 1980	Feb 1980- April 1981	7 - 11	6 - 10	5 -9	4 - 8					
March 1981	Feb 1981- April 1983	-	6 - 10	5 - 9	4 - 8					
March 1982	Feb 1982- April 1983	-	-	8 - 12	7 - 11	6 - 10				
March 1983		-	-	-	7 - 11	6 - 10	5 -9			
March 1984		-	-	-	-	6 - 4	5 - 9	4 - 8	3 - 7	2 - 6
March 1985		-	-	-	-	-	5 - 9	4 - 8	3 - 7	2 - 6
March 1986		-	-	-	-	-	-	11 - 15	-	-

FIGURE 5.11 Medium-term financial strategy from the March 1980 budget. *Sources:* N. H. Dimsdale (1991), Table 4.7, p. 130; NIESR and OECD, Economic Outlook (Table reproduced with kind permission of Oxford University Press, see page xiii).

market. Bill arbitrage had the potential to inflate deposits, distorting the money figures, leaving the £M3 target even more difficult to interpret.[72] The combination of over-funding and the bill mountain led many, including successive chief economists at the Bank – Christopher Dow and John Flemming – to ask whether it was a useful way to proceed.[73]

One might wonder why the newly elected Conservative government did not give serious consideration to switching from £M3 to a target for M1, or nib M1. The downturn of the economy after the election led to an involuntary growth of inventories, increased corporate borrowing, and stronger £M3 growth. The Bank argued that, in this context, rapid growth of broad money did not reflect lax policy, but corporate distress. At a meeting in Downing Street, the governor, Gordon Richardson, used a characteristically patrician metaphor about his garden to emphasise the point: a garden thermometer – £M3 – might suggest it is warm outside, but if there is frost on the ground, one concludes that the thermometer is broken.[74] The governor's advice could have been used to de-emphasise

[72] Bank of England, 'A note on money market arbitrage', *BEQB*, 22, no. 2 (June 1982), pp. 207–8.
[73] J. S. Flemming's comments in P. Mizen (ed.) *Central Banking, Monetary Theory and Practice: Essays in Honour of Charles Goodhart*, 1 (Cheltenham: Edward Elgar, 2003), p. 126; J. C. R. Dow and I. D. Saville (Oxford: Clarendon Press, 1988, 1990), pp. 157–63.
[74] A. C. Hotson, 2010, p. 21; Lawson's Zurich speech, 'Thatcherism in practice', 14 January 1981, p. 5, includes an echo of the metaphor, 'a thermometer which gives a false reading … '.

the previous government's £M3 target, while retaining targets for its public sector counterparts, the PSBR and its funding. Given the government's willingness to demonstrate its serious intent to control the PSBR in a recession, it could have argued that it did not need to set a target for £M3 as a proxy for fiscal discipline.

It would have been difficult for the Thatcher government to abandon monetary targeting, but it could have presented an M1/nib M1 target as a worthy successor to £M3. A number of western governments, including the Heath government in Britain, had been criticised in the early 1970s for not raising nominal interest rates sufficiently in response to inflationary shocks. It was suggested that implicit interest rate targets could be destabilising, and a number of countries adopted narrow monetary targets as a means of guiding interest rate policy in an inflationary environment.[75] It is a moot point whether these targets were met with any exactitude, but M1 tended to be more controllable than broader aggregates – higher interest rates encouraging a shift out of nib sight deposits (part of M1) into ib term deposits (part of £M3) (Figure 5.12).[76] With or without monetary targets, national authorities started to raise interest rates more promptly, and by larger amounts than had hitherto been the case.[77] Paul Volcker adopted a more aggressive interest rate policy at the Fed from 1979, and it is credited with changing market perceptions about the authorities' willingness to use interest rates as a weapon against inflation.[78]

As it happens, the Bank had argued for the targeting of M1, as well as £M3, in November 1977.[79] The Bank's paper had accepted that the two aggregates could give conflicting signals, but suggested that dual targeting could assist the cause of an interpretational, medium-term approach. It is noteworthy that the Bank's chart on monetary objectives in the *BEQB* traditionally included M1 as a secondary indicator alongside M3/£M3, and the discussion of monetary targets in the June 1977 edition of the *BEQB* included a reference to the possibility of targeting more than one aggregate.[80]

[75] T. R. Saving, 'Monetary-policy targets and indicators', *Journal of Political Economy*, 75, no. 4, part 2 (August 1967), pp. 446–56; W. Poole, 'Optimal choice of monetary policy instruments in a simple stochastic macro model', *Quarterly Journal of Economics*, 84, no. 2 (May 1970), pp. 197–216.

[76] M. D. K. W. Foot, Monetary Targets (1981), pp. 29–35.

[77] Federal Reserve Bank of New York in P. Meek (ed.), 'Central bank views on monetary targeting', *Federal Reserve Bank New York* (May, 1982), pp. 32–41; E. Nelson (2000).

[78] J. B. Taylor (ed.) *Monetary Policy Rules* (Chicago: University of Chicago Press, 1999), pp. 13, 330–2.

[79] Bank of England paper, 'Monetary Targets, 1978–79' (16 November 1977), Bank of England Archive, 6A50/24; D. J. Needham, *UK Monetary Policy* (2014), p. 120.

[80] Bank of England, 'Economic commentary', *BEQB*, 17, no. 2 (June 1977), pp. 151–2.

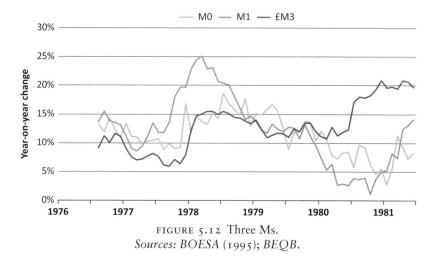

FIGURE 5.12 Three Ms.
Sources: BOESA (1995); BEQB.

At this stage, the Bank's forecasting equations for M1 were working well, in stark contrast to the wayward £M3 equations, and an emphasis on dual targets fitted with a longstanding view that switches between the two could be an indicator of economic prospects. Writing in the 1920s, Leaf had accepted that higher rates encouraged funds to flow from nib current accounts to ib deposit accounts, but he also suggested:

Even when deposit rates are low, business depression is usually accompanied by a rise in the ratio of deposit account balances to current accounts, and a sign of returning business activity can, in the opinion of many observers, be found in a reversal of this process.[81]

The Treasury's response to the Bank's internal paper of November 1977 was, however, strongly critical, Michael Bridgeman noting that 'one of the main attractions to the Governor of having M1 as a target [is] that it will give the Bank a much stronger say in interest rate policy.'[82] At the time, the Treasury's willingness to give up control over interest rates seemed to be as unlikely as the fall of the Berlin Wall.[83] Ministers of the Thatcher government were even more adamant that they should retain ultimate control over interest rates. The idea of delegating tactical

[81] W. Leaf (1943), p. 116.
[82] J. M. Bridgeman, 'Choice of target variable for 1978–79', 17 November 1977, HM Treasury Freedom of Information disclosure, 'Monetary policy in the late 1970s and in the 1981 Budget' (9 November 2006).
[83] J. M. Bridgeman, 'Monetary targets: rolling targets' (16 November 1977), HM Treasury Freedom of Information disclosure, 'Monetary policy in the late 1970s and in the 1981 Budget' (9 November 2006).

responsibility for adjusting interest rates to meet a target set by the government was regarded as inconceivable under British constitutional arrangements. The Bank was seen as the problem, rather than a potential solution. This had the curious consequence of ruling out M1 targeting.

The other candidate was monetary base control (MBC), which its proponents argued offered a more effective means of monetary management.[84] Before 1979, the monetary base had not been recognised as part of the lexicon of UK monetary aggregates, and a statistical exercise had to be undertaken to consider its definition, and compute consistent back series.[85] The monetary base – *aka* high-powered money, or base money – was meant to be a measure of the final settlement assets of the monetary system. These assets had changed over time – greater reliance being placed on bullion, foreign specie and current coins until the nineteenth century – and since then base money had largely been equated with central bank liabilities. For statistical purposes, the monetary base was defined as bankers' balances (BB), plus banks' till money, and notes and coin in circulation with the public – otherwise known as broad M0 (bM0). Bankers' balances (BB), a component of bM0, was otherwise known as narrow M0 (nM0).[86]

The classical system allowed the banks to economise on holdings of till money and BBs, and consequently cash held by the public comprised more than 90 per cent of bM0 (Figure 5.13). Public cash holdings were seasonal, peaking at Easter and on other Bank holidays, and were largely unresponsive to interest rate movements. In the 1980s, they grew slowly because advances in money transmission – credit cards, debit cards, and cash machines – allowed the public to economise on their holdings of cash.[87] The Bank accommodated seasonal fluctuations in demand, and made no attempt to manage the rate of growth of its monetary liabilities. The idea that bM0 should be targeted was regarded as risible, at least by Bank officials.[88]

The slow and predictable growth of bM0 nevertheless made it a politically attractive candidate to be targeted. When Alan Walters returned from the United States in January 1981 to work as Mrs Thatcher's economic adviser, he was quick to recognise that the economy was freezing over,

[84] Greenwell, 1979, 1980; H.M. Treasury and the Bank of England, *Green Paper on Monetary Control*, Cmnd 7858 (London, 1980).

[85] H.M. Treasury, *Economic Trends* (August, 1970), xi.

[86] Bank of England, 'The monetary base – a statistical note', *BEQB*, 21, no. 1 (March 1981), pp. 59–65.

[87] J. M. Trundle and P. V. Pemberton, 'Recent changes in the use of cash', *BEQB*, 22, no. 4 (December 1982), pp. 519–29.

[88] M. D. K. W. Foot, C. A. E. Goodhart and A. C. Hotson, 'Monetary base control', *BEQB*, 19, no. 2 (June 1979), pp. 149–59.

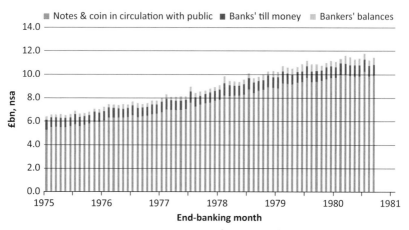

FIGURE 5.13 Components of monetary base, bMo.
Sources: BOESA (1995); BEQB.

and monetary policy was extremely tight, despite the rapid growth of £M3.[89] Searching for an aggregate that reflected the stance of policy, he commissioned Jürg Niehans to prepare a paper suggesting that bMo was a better indicator than £M3. The slow growth of bMo in the recession of 1979–80 was said to be indicative of the tightness of monetary policy.[90] Niehans's paper was not made public at the time but, after he became chancellor, Nigel Lawson did adopt bMo as an additional published indicator in 1984, alongside targets for broad money. MBC and the targeting of bMO followed a longstanding tradition that postulated a stable multiplier between base money and wider definitions of money, early exponents of which included Keynes and James Meade.[91] Their association with leading Keynesians did not debar MBC and the money multiplier from adoption as part of monetarist orthodoxy, alongside the professed stability of the relationship between money and prices – the long-run stability of the velocity of circulation of money. Academic interest in bMo as an indicator has therefore remained steadfast, at least in some quarters.[92]

[89] J. Hoskyns, *Just in Time: Inside the Thatcher Revolution* (London: Aurum, 2000), p. 256.
[90] J. Niehans, 'The appreciation of sterling: causes, effects, policies', Center for Research in Government, Policy and Business, Graduate School of Management, Rochester, NY(1981).
[91] J. M. Keynes, *Treatise on Money*, 1st edn 1930, reprinted in *The Collected Writings of John Maynard Keynes* (London and Basingstoke: Macmillan and Cambridge University Press, Royal Economic Society edn, 1971), VI, pp. 43–69; J. E. Meade, 'The amount of money and the banking system', *Economic Journal*, 44, no. 173 (March 1934), pp. 77–83.
[92] M. J. Oliver, 'The long road to 1981: British money supply targets from DCE to the MTFS' in D. J. Needham and A. C. Hotson (2014), p. 224; N. Batini and E. Nelson, 'The

Another variant of MBC was to target nM0, i.e. BBs, or a subset of BBs. In 1979, Volcker adopted a non-borrowed reserve (NBR) target as part of his more aggressive interest rate regime. NBRs were a component of banks' balances with the Fed, the US equivalent of BBs, and deviations from target gave rise to upward or downward pressures on money market rates within a band.[93] Milton Friedman argued that the UK authorities should do likewise, controlling the monetary base, and letting the market determine interest rates, rather than the other way round.[94] The UK government did not adopt nM0, or an NBR target, but a new money market regime was introduced in 1981, allowing short rates to fluctuate within a dealing band for bills. This was meant to be a first step on the way to MBC, and a step away from the longstanding classical system.[95] In the event, the US experiment with market-led rate setting was dropped after two years in favour of traditional procedures for signalling interest rate changes.[96] The NBR target had allowed Volcker to circumvent the cumbersome decision making process followed by the Federal Open Market Committee (FOMC), but once inflation was on a downward track, the traditional approach was deemed more appropriate.[97] The British authorities followed suit, reverting to the classical system in 1983, and finally giving up monetary targets in 1987.

Deregulation was part of the Thatcher government's neoliberal programme, but its ambitions in this regard were directed at Britain's nationalised industries in energy, telecoms and transport, rather than the banking sector. The implications of abolishing exchange controls were not fully appreciated at the time and, having set the ball rolling, it was accepted that the corset (SSD scheme) should likewise be abolished. This opened the door to an expansion of domestic bank intermediation, but did not necessarily mean the clearers would become mainstream providers of home finance.[98] The BSA's cartel kept politically sensitive

UK's Rocky Road to Stability', *FRB of St. Louis Working Paper Series* (March 2005), pp. 35–7.

[93] Federal Reserve Bank of New York (May and October 1982).

[94] M. Friedman, Memorandum submitted to the Treasury and Civil Service Committee, *Memoranda on Monetary Policy*, Session 1979–80 (London: HMSO, 17 July 1980), pp. 57–9; J. C. R. Dow and I. D. Saville (Oxford: Clarendon Press, 1988, 1990), pp. 142–3.

[95] C. A. E. Goodhart (2004), pp. 48–9.

[96] Bank for International Settlements, 'Changes in Money-Market Instruments and Procedures: Objectives and Implications' (Basle, March 1986), pp. 207–18.

[97] W. Greider, *Secrets of the Temple: How the Federal Reserve Runs the Country* (New York: Simon & Schuster, 1987), pp. 105–23.

[98] Bank of England, 'The supplementary special deposits scheme', *BEQB*, 22, no. 1 (March 1982), p. 74–85.

mortgage lending rates low relative to wholesale market rates, making it unattractive for wholesale funded institutions to enter the market. The societies operated on lower cost margins than the clearers, and could attract inflows of savings by offering fractionally better terms than the CLCB's lukewarm deposit rate. The societies dominated the short-term retail savings market because they offered selectively attractive rates, tax benefits for some, and saving with them was usually a precondition for a mortgage loan.[99] The clearers made no serious attempts to encroach on the savings flow of the societies, and government savings schemes – National Savings – were likewise managed not to take too much market share.[100]

Building societies operated in a looking-glass world when compared with modern retail banking. The BSA cartel limited competition on lending rates, and competition on savings rates was more apparent than real, allowing the sector to sustain a healthy gross margin between retail saving and lending rates. More ambitious societies competed against their rivals by extending their High Street coverage through branches and agencies, and by building brand and product awareness through regional TV advertising. Societies' balance sheets were driven by their ability to attract retail savings; their wholesale funding being limited by law and by the fact that mortgage lending rates were close to, and often below LIBOR, the wholesale market reference rate (Figure 5.14). There was therefore little scope for societies to undertake profitable mortgage lending by tapping wholesale markets. On the asset side of their balance sheets, societies earned more on their liquid assets (LIBOR-related rates), than on their mortgage lending (sub-LIBOR rates). For this reason, the societies' regulator, the Registrar of Friendly Societies (RFS), set a 30 per cent maximum for liquidity holdings as well as a 12 per cent minimum. A few societies maximised their profitability by holding close to the maximum level of liquidity allowed.[101] Conservative lending criteria and few sustained falls in house prices meant that loan quality remained high, and loan losses were miniscule. Scant regard was paid to the capital requirements of societies, and leverage ratios of 20 to 35 times were common. From time to time, smaller societies would encounter problems – usually weak management and occasionally fraud – and the larger societies would take it in turns to absorb

[99] M. H. Best and K. J. Humphries, 'The City and Industrial Decline' in B. Elbaum and W. Lazonick (eds) *The Decline of the British Economy* (Oxford: Clarendon, 1986), p. 236.

[100] E. T. Nevin and E. W. Davis (1970), pp. 242.

[101] A. C. Hotson, 1981 Budget (2014), pp. 137–41.

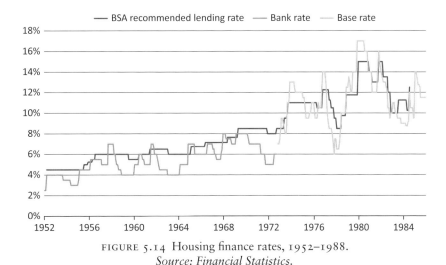

FIGURE 5.14 Housing finance rates, 1952–1988.
Source: Financial Statistics.

them.[102] It was understood that the building society sector would look after its own.

Building societies regulated their mortgage lending, depending on their inflow of retail savings. From time to time a shortfall of savings meant societies had to ration their mortgage lending, making creditworthy mortgage borrowers wait some months in a queue until they could be granted a loan.[103] One advantage of the system was that house price rises tended to be kept within certain bounds because excessive rises were choked off by mortgage rationing. When inflows were plentiful, societies lent more, but they did not start to compete on price – lowering margins – or accept lower quality borrowers. If societies experienced a surplus of inflows over their lending commitments, they would build up their (more profitable) liquidity and, if necessary, curb inflows by pricing their share accounts less competitively – ending special saving offers. In a curious way, the sector operated a monetarist system of control by adjusting lending rates in response to inflows (monetary growth), and by keeping lending in line with funding. Defenders of the system argued that mortgage lending flows were stabilised, and house price inflation was not exacerbated by aggressive lending.[104]

[102] I. F. Hay Davison and M. Stuart-Smith, *Grays Building Society*, Registry of Friendly Societies, Cmnd. 7557 (London: HMSO, 1979).

[103] Wilson, J. Harold, Baron Wilson of Rievaulx, *Committee to Review the Functioning of Financial Institutions*, Cmnd. 7937 (2 vols, London: HMSO, 28 June 1980), p. 112.

[104] M. Boddy, *The Building Societies* (London and Basingstoke: Macmillan, 1980), pp. 58–9.

The Thatcher government was strongly committed to wider home ownership, and took a dim view of the BSA's cartel and mortgage lending queues.[105] In 1980, it was agreed that the prohibition against clearing bank mortgage lending would end, allowing them to compete head to head with the building societies. This was arguably one of the most significant acts of deregulation of the UK financial sector in the post-war period. The BSA manoeuvred to allow societies to lend more, and to solve the queuing problem by raising the societies' lending rates relative to wholesale rates.[106] The tax rules were changed in 1983, allowing societies to pay interest gross on wholesale deposits, and the BSA cartel ceased to operate, although it was not formally abolished until November 1984.[107] The societies found themselves competing against newly formed specialist mortgage lenders who raised funds in the wholesale market.[108]

The BSA accepted faute de mieux the participation of others, including the clearing banks, in the mortgage market, but argued that they should not be subject to more restrictions than their competitors, the proverbial un-level playing field.[109] The BSA's lobbying proved to be successful and the government passed the Building Societies Act 1986, which empowered societies inter alia to raise up to 40 per cent of their funds from wholesale sources and to convert to banking status. The legislation and the ending of the cartel allowed the larger building societies to move from being deposit-led institutions, and become asset-led, like the banks (Figure 5.15). The sterling balance sheets of the leading societies were a sufficient match for the retail businesses of the clearing banks and, when the herd of major banks and building societies decided that growth of mortgage lending was a strategic priority, the home loan market expanded considerably. Societies found it relatively easy to expand by tapping wholesale markets, in part because they were perceived to be safe institutions, and partly because of a quirk: wholesale lenders were very senior creditors ranking ahead of not just the societies' capital and reserves, but also most of their retail savers who held share

---

[105] N. Lawson, *The View from No. 11: Memoirs of a Tory Radical* (London: Bantam Press, 1992), pp. 86–7.

[106] G. A. Davies, *Building Societies and Their Branches: A Regional Economic Survey* (London: Franey, 1981), p. 221.

[107] C. A. E. Goodhart (Winter 1986), p. 87; Bank of England, 'The development of the building societies sector in the 1980s', *BEQB*, 30, no. 4 (November 1990), pp. 503–4.

[108] Bank of England, *BEQB* (November 1990), p. 507.

[109] M. Boleat, *National Housing Finance Systems: A Comparative Study* (London: Croom Helm, 1985), p. 54–5.

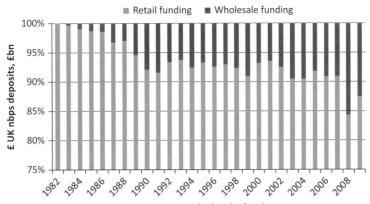

FIGURE 5.15 Building societies' wholesale funding, 1982–2009.
Source: Bank of England, *Monetary & Financial Statistics*, Table A2.2.1.

accounts (rather than deposits that ranked pari passu with other creditors).[110] Competition did not lead, at least initially, to a diminution of overall margins. Instead, a greater willingness to lend resulted in easier loan ratios, in particular higher loans relative to the values of underlying properties (LTVs) and higher repayments on loans relative to borrowers' income (income multiples).

The business models of the clearing banks and building societies gravitated towards each other. On the one hand, the clearers became more like building societies as mortgages became a significant part of their sterling loan books. On the other hand, societies became more like banks, and many of the larger ones demutualised and converted to banking status. An aspect of the larger societies becoming more like banks was their desire to offer a full range of retail banking products, including current accounts for making payments. The third largest society, Nationwide, started to pay interest on current accounts, challenging the clearing banks' longstanding practice of not paying interest on them. Other banks and societies followed suit, leading to a significant growth of ib sight deposits, a component of M1, and the breakdown of the M1 equations in the early 1980s.[111] The absence of a workable forecasting equation had not stopped the setting of targets in the past, but it did not help the candidature of M1, or nib M1.

[110] G. Speight, 'Building society behaviour and the mortgage-lending market in the interwar period: Risk-taking by mutual institutions and the interwar housebuilding boom', DPhil thesis, University of Oxford (2000), p. 15.

[111] J. M. Trundle and P. V. Pemberton, 'Recent changes in the use of cash', *BEQB*, 22, no. 4 (December 1982), pp. 519–29; J. M. Trundle, 'The demand for M1 in the UK' (Bank of England mimeo, 1982); A. C. Hotson (2010), p. 18.

Although the 1986 Act empowered building societies to demutualise and convert to banking status, it is a moot point whether deregulation of the mortgage market had already extinguished the last vestiges of mutuality in the building societies movement. The mutual ideal of saving regularly for a deposit and then borrowing from the same society to buy a house had already been brushed aside when societies started to lend to broker-introduced borrowers without the need for a regular saving record. As mutual institutions, societies were meant to balance the interests of their borrowers and savers when setting their interest rates. The BSA had taken over the mantle of rate setter, and the slowness with which it raised rates did reflect the interest of existing borrowers (if not savers and mortgage applicants). When the BSA ceased to set its recommended lending rate in the early 1980s, one of the last distinguishing features of the building society movement was lost. It is not very surprising that all but one of the larger societies subsequently decided to convert.

For the clearing banks, a key consequence of deregulation was the dramatic increase in the maturity mismatching of their balance sheets as they lent long on mortgages, and continued to borrow short in retail and wholesale markets. Traditionally, the societies had managed a similar maturity mismatch with the risk that short-term savings could be withdrawn, leaving a liquidity problem. However, the societies had not relied on wholesale funding, and their pool of retail savings was largely protected from competitors, both inside and outside the sector. Banks and building societies in the United Kingdom did manage to avoid the problem of duration mismatching – as distinct from maturity mismatching – a problem that necessitated bailouts for large numbers of US savings and loan associations (SLAs) in the 1980s.[112] SLAs typically offered mortgages with interest rates fixed for five years (long-duration assets). Their savings rates had been relatively sticky, but greater volatility of short-term interest rates since 1979 forced SLAs to raise their savings rates in line with market rates so as to maintain their funding (short-duration liabilities). Sharp rises in interest rates exposed a serious mismatch between their long duration assets and their short duration liabilities, leading to unprecedented losses.[113] In the United Kingdom, duration mismatching was not a problem because mortgage loans were normally provided with variable (adjustable) borrowing rates. Where fixed rates were offered,

[112] B. O. Bierwag, *Duration Analysis: Managing Interest Rate Risk* (Cambridge, MA: Ballinger, 1987), p. 192.
[113] L. L. Bryan, *Breaking Up the Bank: Rethinking an Industry under Siege* (Irwin, Homewood, 1988), p. 47.

duration matched funding was secured, often using interest rate swaps.[114] However, borrowers faced considerable interest rate uncertainty, and UK politicians came under electoral pressure to curb interest rate rises. There was talk of depoliticising interest rates by encouraging longer duration lending rates, but this market was slow to develop. This meant that ministers insisted on keeping political control over rates, and there was always a need to balance what was required for monetary control and the interests of home owners. The balancing act was particularly sensitive for the Thatcher government because of its espousal of home ownership, and its policy of selling council houses (social housing let by local authorities).

The unfettering of the clearers (and other banks) from the corset and the deregulation of the building societies unleashed a surge in domestic lending that was sustained through much of the 1980s. The shift in the trend of lending – as distinct from a one-off adjustment – was largely unexpected, and led to high levels of broad money growth. The persistent over-shooting of the MTFS targets left lots of political egg on face, but had the beneficial effect of facilitating economic growth. This had not been part of the government's monetarist plan, nor had it been predicted by official (Keynesian) forecasters. It meant that the government's fiscal restraint did not lead to a protracted recession – confounding the Keynesians – and inflation was curbed, despite rapid monetary growth – confounding the monetarists.

With the benefit of hindsight, one might ask why the government was not able to extricate itself more quickly from the political fallout from its doomed attempts to meet heroically low monetary targets.[115] Sir Ian Gilmour, a Conservative minister, joked that monetary policy had become 'the uncontrollable in pursuit of the indefinable', and the 1982 Budget did recast the MTFS in a more flexible format with a bewildering array of targets for a number of broad and narrow monetary aggregates.[116] In addition, a number of indicators (as distinct from targets) were mentioned, including the course of the exchange rate, apparent real interest rates, the state of certain asset markets, and the concurrent course of nominal GDP.[117] The government's policy was played out in two curiously

[114] S. K. Henderson and J. A. M. Price, *Currency and Interest Rate Swaps* (2nd edn, London: Butterworth, 1988), pp. 42–9.

[115] D. W. Healey (1989), p. 489.

[116] H. J. S. Young, *One of Us: A Biography of Margaret Thatcher* (London: Macmillan, 1989), p. 203; P. J. R. Riddell, *The Thatcher Government* (Oxford: Martin Robertson, 1983), p. 82; C. A. E. Goodhart (June 1989), p. 306.

[117] J. S. Fforde (June 1983), p. 200.

disconnected ways: at a political level it was held up as a totem of the Thatcher government's monetarist revolution, but at a technical level it was a means of allowing a non-monetarist policy to operate in monetarist clothing.[118] Would it have been better to come clean more quickly, and openly accept that deregulation required the adoption of financial targets other than broad money? Nominal GDP and the exchange rate were possibilities touted at the time.[119]

In his Zurich speech of January 1981, before the lynchpin Budget of that year, the then-junior Treasury minister, Nigel Lawson, advanced the argument that broad money tended to grow excessively while interest rates were high and inflation was being squeezed out of the system. He suggested that this would be a temporary phenomenon and that broad money growth would settle down over time.[120] Lawson and the inner circle of economic ministers ploughed on with the MTFS, and hoped the edifice could be made to work. This did not happen, severely testing the government's public enthusiasm for monetary targeting. In Lawson's first Budget as Chancellor in April 1984, he dropped the target for M1 and the then-broadest official definition of money, PSL2, which included building society accounts. These aggregates happened to be over-shooting, and it was at this point that he started to target bM0 with its track record for growing at a predictably slow rate.[121]

Mrs Thatcher's first Chancellor, Sir Geoffrey Howe, had accepted that interest rates should be adjusted in the light of exchange rate developments, notwithstanding the formalities of the monetary targets. This approach was maintained when Lawson became Chancellor, and sterling's weakness in the summer of 1984 and in the first quarter of 1985 led the government to raise Bank rate to 14 per cent and tighten fiscal policy. In the Budget of April 1985, Lawson announced that over-funding would cease, and be replaced by a policy of full funding. £M3 started to overshoot its target, but the authorities allowed Bank rate to decline in view of the strength of sterling and, in October 1985, the target for £M3 was suspended. Lawson tried to join the European exchange rate mechanism (ERM) during 1985, but this did not come to pass. In the Budget of

[118] G. T. Pepper, *Inside Thatcher's Monetarist Revolution* (London, 1998); W. J. G Keegan, *Mrs Thatcher's Economic Experiment* (London: Allen Lane, 1984), pp. 159–82, W. J. G. Keegan, *Mr. Lawson's Gamble* (London: Hodder and Stoughton, 1989), p. 60 and p. 67.
[119] R. Leigh-Pemberton 'Some aspects of UK monetary policy', *BEQB*, 24, no. 4 (December 1984), p. 475 and pp. 477–8.
[120] N. Lawson (14 January 1981), p. 6.
[121] N. H. Dimsdale (1991), pp. 133–4.

March 1986, a £M3 target of 11–15 per cent was set, but even this was over-shot by the banks expanding their mortgage lending. No target was set for broad money in the Budget of March 1987.[122]

By the end of its second term in 1987, there was no appetite within the Thatcher government to extend the MTFS, or formulate policy in terms of monetary targets. Mrs Thatcher was resistant to joining the ERM, but Lawson shadowed the deutsche mark for much of 1987 without making much of the policy to Mrs Thatcher. In 1988, the Treasury sought to promote a policy rule in which MLR was adjusted in response to changes in nominal income and the exchange rate. A formulaic policy rule proved to be too mechanical and had to be overridden after a short period. In his resignation speech, Lawson concluded that the Bank should be given greater autonomy for tactical decisions on interest rates, but it was clear that the prime minister would not countenance such a change.[123]

When it did finally arrive on the scene a decade later, inflation targeting proved to be highly successful, and it has to be asked why the authorities had bothered with an intermediate target for money in the 1970s and 1980s. Money supply might (or might not) be a useful indicator for forecasting inflation, but it was unlikely to be the only indicator.[124] As it happens, money proved to be a terrible indicator in the 1980s and targeting inflation directly would have provided a solution; there was no need to be too dogged about the monetary aggregates.[125] Sceptics of monetary targeting had made this point in the early 1980s to no avail.[126] Also, the advocacy of setting policy with reference to commodity prices went back a long way, not just to Wicksell in Sweden, but also to John Rooke, John Wheatley and Thomas Attwood in England at the end of the Napoleonic wars.[127] So why did the authorities remain wedded to monetary targets for so long? The answer seems to be that DCE ceilings in the late 1960s,

[122] N. H. Dimsdale (1991), pp. 136–7.

[123] C. A. E. Goodhart 'The Bank of England over the last 35 years', *Bankhistorisches Archiv*, Beih. 43, Welche Aufgaben muß eine Zentralbank wahrnehmen: historische Erfahrungen und europäische Perspektiven (Stuttgart: Franz Steiner Verlag, 2004), p. 44.

[124] M. D. Woodford, 'How important is money in the conduct of monetary policy', *Journal of Money, Credit and Banking*, vol. 40, no. 8 (December, 2008), pp. 1561–98.

[125] M. A King, 'No money, no inflation – the role of money in the economy', *BEQB*, 42, no. 2 (Summer 2002), pp. 162–77; P. M. W. Tucker, 'Managing the central bank's balance sheet: where monetary policy meets financial stability', *BEQB*, 44, no. 3 (Autumn 2004), pp. 359–82.

[126] F. T. Blackaby, 'Comments on Michael Foot's paper, Monetary Targets', in B. Griffiths and G. E. Wood (eds.), *Monetary Targets* (London, 1981), pp. 54–61.

[127] K. Wicksell, *Interest and Prices: A Study of the Causes Regulating Money*, English translation by R. F. Kahn (Jena: Gustav Fischer, 1898; London: Macmillan, 1936), p. 194;

the unpublished monetary guidelines of the early 1970s, and the published M3/£M3 targets of the late 1970s were indirect means of containing the PSBR via the counterparts identity.[128] The Thatcher Government took PSBR targeting seriously and did not need £M3 as a proxy for controlling the PSBR. It nevertheless kept a £M3 target as a self-denying ordinance in recognition of monetarist arguments.

The wider implications of deregulation on the credit cycle received limited attention, perhaps because there was no immediate crisis in domestic markets.[129] The Latin American debt crisis challenged the international banks – including UK ones – from 1982, but the problem was contained. The equity-market crash of 1987 was followed by a recession and some negative equity problems in the UK housing market in the early 1990s. This led to increased mortgage arrears and loan impairments in 1991, which were high compared to past experience, possibly suggesting an increase in pro-cyclical risk.[130] Bank profitability was hit, but this did not lead to sustained problems like those faced by the Japanese economy and its banks. The Asian and Russian banking crises of the 1990s and the bursting of the dot com bubble in 2000 presented problems, but not intractable ones for UK banks. It took the downturn of the US residential housing market from 2006, and the collapse of Lehman in 2008 for the international money market, including London's, to face paralysis. To understand why this shock proved fatal while other financial disturbances did not, it is useful to trace developments in London's money and credit markets since the reforms of 1979/80.

The flexibility of the bill market was put to the test in the early 1980s by the over-funding policy, and the consequential need for the Bank to alleviate shortages in the money market by buying substantial quantities of bills. As it happens, the market was quick to generate a sufficiency of bills, and there was no immediate need for the Bank to make major changes to its dealing practices.[131] In 1996, the Bank nevertheless decided to switch horses, and conduct its market operations by way of gilt repos rather than by dealing in bills. Instead of discounting bills at the Bank, market participants were allowed to sell gilt-edged stocks to the Bank for

J. Viner, *Studies in the Theory of International Trade* (New York and London: Harper, 1937), pp. 208–12.

[128] J. S. Fforde (June 1983), p. 200–8; B. Granville, *Remembering Inflation* (Princeton, NJ, and Oxford: Princeton University Press, 2013), chapters 2 and 4.

[129] C. A. E. Goodhart (June 1989), p. 501.

[130] C. Gordon (1993), p. 59, fn.

[131] A. L. Coleby, 'Bills of exchange: current issues in historical context', *BEQB* (December 1982), pp. 515–8.

cash, while simultaneously agreeing to repurchase them at a fixed price at a future date (a sale and repurchase agreement, or repo). The Bank was effectively providing loans collateralised with gilts.[132] The gilt repo system provided the Bank with an efficient mechanism for the conduct of its routine operations, and it proved to be resilient during the credit crunch of 2007–8.[133] Repo markets using other securities also prospered, but we shall see that many of these were found wanting in the crisis.

The securities market boom of the 1990s encouraged banks to move from strategies based on asset-led growth to ones based on the originate-underwrite-and-distribute model. Loans could be securitised so that the funding and credit risk could be borne by other parties, and traded as asset-backed securities (ABS). ABS could be repackaged as collateralised debt obligations (CDOs) whereby senior tranches of CDOs bore very little credit risk and junior ones carried disproportionate risk. Credit default swaps (CDS) could be used to repackage the risks further and create synthetic CDOs. There was scope to unbundle vertically integrated banking so that different parties could undertake its separate parts – origination, underwriting, funding (senior note-holders) and credit risk (junior note-holders). A number of leading US and European banks (mostly UK ones) ceded mortgage and other loans to off-balance-sheet special investment vehicles (SIVs), which issued ABS, which in turn were repackaged as CDOs and synthetic CDOs. ABS, and in particular residential mortgage-backed securities (RMBS), became an important new asset class traded in the money market. Senior tranche CDOs could be AAA-rated, ranking alongside the best rated sovereign and supranational credits.[134]

The markets for ABS and synthetic securities, including CDOs, appeared to be liquid and senior securitised debt became the successor to PBBs as the asset of choice for bank liquidity. Securitised debt of all kinds – not just gilts – was also used extensively as collateral for the repo funding of investment banks' proprietary trading businesses. The investment banks' prime brokerage units acted as intermediaries, allowing their investment clients – including hedge funds – to leverage their portfolios using repos.[135] Repo loans were arranged at a margin, or haircut below the value of collateral

[132] I. Plenderleith, 'Gilt repo – and beyond', *BEQB*, 36, no. 3 (August 1996), pp. 338–41; Bank of England, 'The first year of the gilt repo market', *BEQB*, 37, no. 2 (May 1997), pp. 187–97.
[133] P. M. W. Tucker (Autumn 2004), p. 377.
[134] N. H. Dimsdale and A. C. Hotson (2014), pp. 44–5.
[135] G. B. Gorton, 'Information, liquidity and the (ongoing) panic of 2007', *American Economic Review*, Papers & Proceedings, 99, no. 2 (May 2009), pp. 569–72.

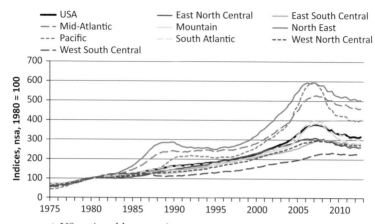

FIGURE 5.16 US regional house prices, 1975–2012.
Source: Federal Housing Finance Agency – all-transactions data, sales and appraisals
http://www.fhfa.gov/DataTools/Downloads/Pages/House-Price-Index.aspx

provided. The assets pledged as collateral had to be adjusted daily to allow for valuation changes, and for margin changes required by lenders. When the ABS markets were being promoted in the 1980s and 1990s, it was suggested that they would provide a means for the banking sector to cede risk to a wider pool of non-bank end investors. However, the appeal of ABS as a liquid asset, which could be used as collateral for repo funding, was so great that traditional banks and shadow banks became dominant holders, and less risk was shared with end investors.[136]

The path that led to the panic of 2008 started with a downturn in the US residential housing market in 2006, leading to falls in subprime RMBS values (Figure 5.16).[137] Subprime RMBS had been repackaged into CDOs and it was not necessarily clear which CDOs would be affected and by how much. Also, CDO structures relied on short-term funding, and were not self-liquidating. This meant that all CDO tranches of securitised debt, including supposedly low-risk ones, were exposed to refinancing risk – a key difference between this asset class and traditional liquid assets, notably PBBs.[138] The combination of refinancing risk, asset complexity and lack of transparency led repo lenders to play safe and reject certain asset types as collateral, and to insist on increased haircuts. Many of the assets were not

[136] Financial Services Authority, *The Turner Review: a regulatory response to the global banking crisis* (March 2009), pp. 14–16.
[137] G. B. Gorton, 'The Panic of 2007', FRB Kansas City, Jackson Hole Conference (25 August 2008).
[138] An important point made by Duncan Needham to the author.

actively traded and therefore collateral valuations relied on modelled prices (mark-to-model), which lenders subjected to greater scrutiny. A more discriminating repo market forced borrowers to value collateral more conservatively and apply larger haircuts. Borrowers were forced to realise long positions and sell assets. This in turn led to a vicious circle whereby lower asset prices reduced collateral values, and encouraged lenders to seek even larger haircuts, which in turn necessitated further forced sales.[139]

Prime brokerage made it possible for hedge funds and other investors to undertake bank-style maturity mismatching by using short-term repos to borrow, and relying on being able to roll them over so that they could fund longer-term investments. These leveraged investors were able to operate as shadow banks without the need for conventional bank loans. Prior to the summer of 2007 the scale of maturity mismatching in the repo market appears to have increased, but from the summer of 2007 repo lenders started to apply a more conservative approach. Rollovers stopped and large parts of the repo market shut down – there was no mechanism to protect collateral values.

The process whereby contagion shifted from the repo market to the interbank market is not exactly clear and it may never be established unequivocally. Some commercial banks were known to have some dependency on repo funding and there were rumours about commercial bank exposures to subprime RMBS. Some British banks had programmes for tapping wholesale funds swapped into sterling from US money market mutual funds. These funds were exposed to the repo market in the United States and faced customer withdrawals, and part of their response was to cut their lending to UK (and other) banks. Once it became clear that aggregate interbank funding was contracting, the market started to assess which banks would face funding difficulties and problems contracting their balance sheets.[140] In the United Kingdom, providers of wholesale funds backed away from Northern Rock and other converted building societies, and, following the collapse of Lehman Brothers in September 2008, the interbank market froze and all banks lost access to credit.[141]

There is a sense of déjà vu in the evolution of London's money and credit markets since 1971. Liability management has allowed wildly ambitious

[139] G. B. Gorton and A. Metrick, 'Securitised Banking and the Run on Repo', *Yale ICF Working Paper*, 09 – 14 (9 November 2010).
[140] M. A. King, *The End of Alchemy: Money, Banking and the Future of the Global Economy* (London: Little, Brown, 2016), p. 139.
[141] W. A. Allen, *International Liquidity and the Financial Crisis* (Cambridge and New York: Cambridge University Press, 2013), pp. 12–31.

bankers to go for growth – allowing them to become 'asset-driven' rather than 'liability-driven' – and many of them have come crashing down to earth, sometimes bringing the rest of the market with them.[142] Securitisation and repos have allowed lesser credits to rediscount paper into the mainstream money market, undermining its resilience in a crisis. The credit cycle has been disrupted by wayward asset values, and it has not been responsive to interest rate policy. These problems did not beset the market during London's century of stability, but they are reminiscent of difficulties encountered before the 1870s. Variable collateral values have been a particular problem of the post-1971 era and are considered further in Chapter 6.

---

[142] C. Matten, *Managing Bank Capital: Capital Allocation and Performance Measurement* (Chichester: Wiley, 1996), p. 56.

6

Bankers against Speculation

Our clearing bank authors – Gilbart, Sykes and Leaf – were greatly exercised by the need to finance 'legitimate trade', rather than 'speculative' undertakings.[1] Sykes suggested that the mid-Victorian crises were mainly caused by excessive speculation and price fluctuations (Figure 6.1):

The last of the series [of crises] occurred in 1875, and is generally ascribed to the reaction following the abnormally high prices of 1872 and 1873, and to the great amount of accommodation bills in existence.[2]

Sykes recognised that 'it is difficult to define speculation, because there is a speculative element in all modern business transactions', but suggested it could be characterised as 'that class of business enterprise which is prompted by the expectation of a rise or fall in prices, and which is often carried on with borrowed capital.'[3] Speculation was not objectionable in itself – stock market investments and private ventures provided the wellspring of Britain's capitalist development – but the use of bank credit for speculative undertakings was another matter altogether. Respectable bankers were meant to 'discriminate against speculative advances' where repayment depended on the favourable evolution of asset prices.[4] They could not look into borrowers'

---

[1] W. Leaf, *Banking* (London: Butterworth, 1st edn, 1926; 2nd edn, 1926; reprinted 1927, 1928, 1929, 1931) (ed.) E. Sykes (3rd edn, 1935; reprinted 1937; 4th edn, London and New York: Oxford University Press, 1943) p. 173; *Gilbart on Banking: The History, Principles and Practice of Banking* (ed.) A. S. Michie (2 vols, London: George Bells, 1882), I, pp. 241, 427.

[2] E. Sykes, *Banking and Currency* (London: Butterworth, 1st edn, 1905; 2nd edn, 1908; 3rd edn, 1911; 4th edn, 1918; 5th edn, 1923; 6th edn, 1925; 7th edn, 1932, 8th edn, 1937; 9th edn, 1947), p. 194.

[3] E. Sykes (1947), p. 197.

[4] W. Leaf (1943), p. 172.

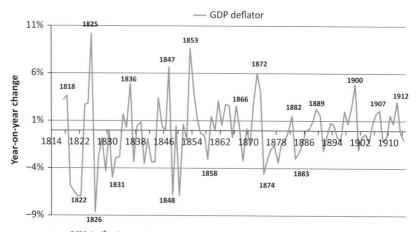

FIGURE 6.1 UK inflation, 1817–1914.
Sources: S. Hills et al. (2010); S.N. Broadberry et al. (2011) (Figure reproduced with kind permission of Oxford University Press, see page xii).

minds and ascertain the extent to which they were motivated by speculative considerations, but they could discern when the markets were gripped with speculative frenzies and provide a restraining influence.[5]

The main means of protecting the clearers against speculation was for them to stick to their mainstream business – the provision of working capital to established businesses and householders. Writing in the 1920s – during the high renaissance of the clearing bank era – Leaf suggested that 'the six months' or seasonal loan may be said to constitute the backbone of [their] business.'[6] Longer-term loans, such as mortgages, were the province of 'private investors who are prepared to lend through their solicitors or otherwise; and there are the insurance companies.'[7] Insurers had liabilities with predictable repayment dates spread over many years, and could therefore 'consider advances with a currency of several years.'[8] Leaf accepted that the clearers could legitimately provide bridging finance while a borrower negotiated a mortgage loan, debenture, or other capital raising, but warned that temporary loans were cheaper than long-term finance. This meant that branch managers must be confident that the borrower could secure permanent funding, and would not be tardy about doing so.[9] The

[5] E. Sykes (1947), p. 198.
[6] W. Leaf (1943), p. 165.
[7] W. Leaf (1943), p. 166.
[8] W. Leaf (1943), p. 166.
[9] Leaf (1943), p. 167; C. Gordon, *The Cedar Story: The Night the City Was Saved* (London: Sinclair-Stevenson, 1993), p. 57.

key was that borrowers could credibly repay the loan in the short term, and that assets could be realised in the event of a mishap. This meant managers should normally require security over bankable assets, although the clearers prided themselves on providing some loans based on the 'character and capacity' of the customer without the need for pledged assets.[10] In practice, unsecured loans would be agreed only for persons of property with unencumbered assets, such as a family farm, or business, or possibly an inheritance, particularly if it were an entailed estate. A legal undertaking not to pledge these assets to another party (negative pledge) would not be expected of the borrower, but there would be an informal undertaking to this effect (a de facto or tacit negative pledge).

Insisting that loans be short-term, self-liquidating, and supported by security over bankable assets did not put a complete stop to credit-fuelled speculation, but it helped to protect the lender from being an inadvertent participant in it. There were some exceptions to Leaf's rule against loans to speculators – nowadays known as leveraged investors. The clearers' loans to stock jobbers, via Stock Exchange money brokers (SEMBs), were used to finance their inventories of stocks and shares, and their stock borrowing. Money at call (MAC) placed with the discount houses funded the latter's bill portfolios.[11] Both stock jobbers and discount houses pledged their paper as security for their borrowing, including a margin requirement. The stock jobbers' security was liquid because their pledged assets were tradable on the London Stock Exchange (LSE), and the discount houses could always sell, or pledge, their bills to the Bank. The governance of these markets prevented them from pledging less liquid paper, in the manner of Gurney's prior to the 1866 crisis. In Leaf's time, the only disruption to the smooth running of these markets had been the closure of the LSE at the start of the First World War, a *force majeure* that required the term of the loans to be extended.[12] Similar problems arose in 1931 - after Leaf's death.

The clearers faced another area of risk that took the unexpected form of their investments in Consols. Bankers prized Consols as an undoubted asset that could be sold anonymously in a highly liquid secondary market. Long-term yields had fallen in the 1890s, but started to rise after the Boer War of 1899, and continued to do so in the run-up to the First World War (Figure 6.2). Banks had to provide against the declining market value of their Consol investments, and Yorkshire Penny Bank had to be rescued in

---

[10] Leaf (1943), p. 170.
[11] Leaf (1943), pp. 90–1.
[12] Leaf (1943), pp. 128–9.

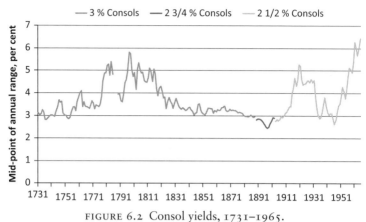

3 % Consols   — 2 3/4 % Consols   — 2 1/2 % Consols

FIGURE 6.2 Consol yields, 1731–1965.
Source: De Zoete & Gorton (July 1966). *See also* Neal (1990), pp. 242–257

1911 on account of these losses.[13] There was a tension between the unrivalled liquidity of Consols and the risk arising from the mismatch between banks' short-duration liabilities and their much longer duration Consols. The problem largely resolved itself in the interwar period when the government issued a surfeit of Treasury bills (TBs) and short- and medium-term British government stocks (BGS), as well as long ones – although the banks did have to provide for reduced BGS values, following the conversion of the 5 per cent War Loan in 1932.[14] When rising inflation led to catastrophic losses on long-dated BGS in the 1960s and 1970s, the clearers were not materially affected because they had already shortened the duration of their gilt portfolios. For the most part, it was private individuals and trusts that were left holding long-dated gilts with severely diminished values.

The risk of mismatches between the prices of banks' assets and liabilities was not a new one. In the 1790s, Thornton noted that the Bank's obligation to exchange its own banknotes for guineas could give rise to losses. If the market price of gold went to a premium over the mint price, the Bank was exposed to the possibility of supplying gold in the form of guineas at the mint price, and acquiring gold bullion at a 'losing price' (Figures 6.3 and 6.4).[15] The need to do this arose because the Bank was operating on a

[13] J. D. Turner, *Banking in Crisis: The Rise and Fall of British Banking Stability, 1800 to the Present* (Cambridge: Cambridge University Press, 2014b), pp. 157–9.

[14] W. Leaf (1943), p. 115; S. K. Howson, *Domestic Monetary Management in Britain, 1919–38* (Cambridge: Cambridge University Press, 1975), p. 144.

[15] H. Thornton, *An Enquiry into the Nature and Effects of the Paper Credit of Great Britain*, 1802 edn and Thornton's parliamentary speeches and evidence (ed.) F. A. von Hayek (London: Cass, 1939, reprinted 1962), p. 218.

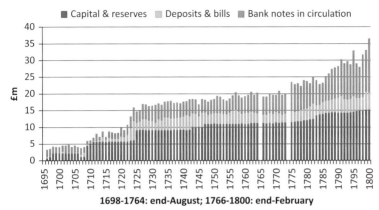

FIGURE 6.3 Bank of England liabilities during the eighteenth century. *Source: BEQB* (June 1967), Appendix cited on p. 159, Table A (notes issued less notes held by the Bank).

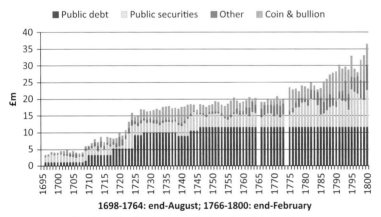

FIGURE 6.4 Bank of England assets during the eighteenth century. *Source: BEQB* (June 1967), Appendix cited on p. 159, Table A (notes issued less notes held by the Bank)

fractional reserve system whereby its banknote issuance was not fully backed by reserves of gold and silver in the form of bars and specie (Figure 6.5).

In the mid-nineteenth century, the Currency School was concerned that the Bank should bolster its liquidity and maintain public confidence by holding reserves that matched its banknote issuance more closely.[16] This reduced the basis risk of having to buy gold bars at a premium in

---

[16] J. Viner, *Studies in the Theory of International Trade* (New York and London: Harper, 1937), pp. 220–4.

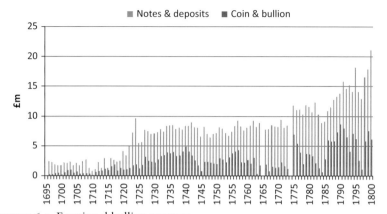

FIGURE 6.5 Fractional bullion reserves.
Source: BEQB (June 1967), Appendix cited on p. 159, Table A (notes issued less notes held by the Bank).

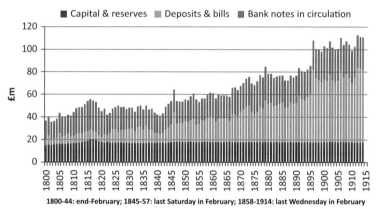

FIGURE 6.6 Bank of England liabilities during the nineteenth century.
Source: BEQB (June 1967), Appendix cited on p. 159, Table A (notes issued less notes held by the Bank).

a crisis, with a view to minting them into sovereigns, but holding more reserves left the Bank exposed to the risk of a declining bullion price – similar in effect to a declining Consols price (Figures 6.6 and 6.7). The Currency School appeared to be unconcerned about the Bank's basis risk on the downside, perhaps making the implicit assumption that the mint price provided a floor for the market price of gold. The halving of the silver price in the late nineteenth century could have left the Bank with losses, but the problem was contained because the Bank kept most of its reserves in gold, rather than silver (Figure 6.8). The clearers did start to

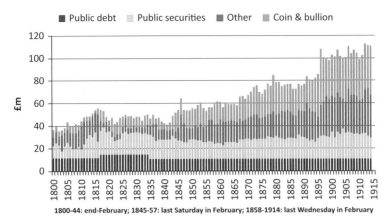

FIGURE 6.7 Bank of England assets during the nineteenth century.
Source: BEQB (June 1967), Appendix cited on p. 159, Table A (notes issued less notes held by the Bank).

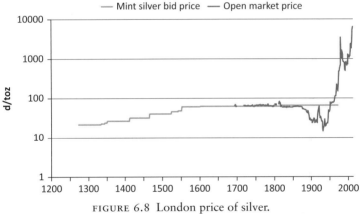

FIGURE 6.8 London price of silver.
Source: G. Clark and P. Lindert, UCD database (9 April 2006).

accumulate their own gold reserves in the first decade of the twentieth century, and tacitly assumed that the mint price would act as a floor.[17]

The clearers liked to present themselves as instinctively risk averse, but their capacity to take risk was limited because of their leverage. Earlier banking models had worked on the basis that the lender was better capitalised than the borrower: for example, Lombardian families of great wealth financed enterprising, but poorly capitalised merchants during the

[17] L. S. Pressnell, 'Gold reserves, banking reserves, and the Barings crisis of 1890' in C. R. Whittlesey and J. S. G. Wilson (eds) *Essays in Honour of R. S. Sayers* (Oxford: Clarendon Press, 1968), pp. 220–1.

Renaissance. Private bankers were entrusted with other people's assets precisely because of their great wealth and acceptance of unlimited liability. The first chartered bank in London – the Bank of England – was initially distrusted by some goldsmiths and private bankers because its shareholders enjoyed limited liability. It operated with a relatively modest leverage ratio of up to two times during the eighteenth century. In the nineteenth century, it rose steadily to five times, but the quality of its assets – mostly claims on the British government, bullion, and bills – allowed it to retain its status as an undoubted institution.

When joint-stock banking was allowed in England in the mid-nineteenth century, their shareholders still faced unlimited liability. John Turner has shown that 'the aggregate wealth of all shareholders greatly exceeded banks' public liabilities', suggesting that these banks still operated in the Lombardian tradition.[18] When an unlimited-liability bank failed, its liquidator was able to make calls on shareholders, and depositors were recompensed in full – a system of depositor protection that worked pretty well.[19] More banks adopted limited liability in the late nineteenth century – particularly after the City of Glasgow Bank (CGB) debacle of 1878 – but most of them issued partly paid shares, leaving shareholders liable for calls at the behest of banks' directors. Turner examined a sample of banks with limited liability and found that the average depositor was 100 per cent covered by (issued albeit partly paid) shareholder capital and reserves.[20] These banks were fractional reserve banks in terms of their liquid investments, but they were barely leveraged with regard to their issued share capital and reserves.

The Lombardian banking model was quietly discarded in the decade before the First World War when deposit-leverage ratios of the major banks rose to three times issued share capital and reserves, and ten times paid-up capital and reserves. The pressures of state funding during the war, and the effects of inflation led to a mushrooming of the clearers' balance sheet totals, without a commensurate increase in the nominal value of their share capital. This led to an erosion of the ratio of issued shares and reserves relative to deposits, and overall deposit-leverage ratios rose to seven times.[21] This unprecedented level of leverage meant the big five clearers were operating a very different business model to that of their precursors in the late nineteenth century. Their preoccupation with asset quality became more a matter of necessity than of choice.

[18] J. D. Turner (2014b), p. 114.
[19] J. D. Turner (2014b), p. 119.
[20] J. D. Turner (2014b), pp. 123–6.
[21] J. D. Turner (2014b), pp. 128–33, especially table 5.10.

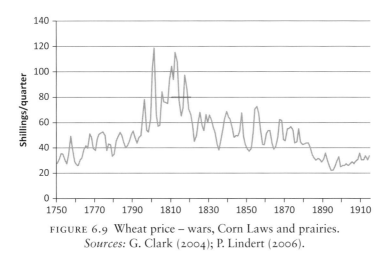

FIGURE 6.9 Wheat price – wars, Corn Laws and prairies.
Sources: G. Clark (2004); P. Lindert (2006).

The clearers' competitive strength rested on their ability to offer low-cost working capital to established firms. Surprisingly, the borrower had to be better capitalised than the lender, and the banks' loans had to have prior claims over other creditors, rather than ranking pari passu with everyone else. The seniority of the banks' claims, and the subordination of trade creditors and others, was achieved in law – and in practice – by each clearer being able to monitor cash flows, terminate its facilities at short notice, and realise security over bankable assets. In times of trouble, this could mean that the clearers got their money back at the expense of the poor old trade creditors, and shareholders were left with little or nothing. These arrangements nevertheless remained in the interests of shareholders of companies with large and variable working capital requirements. Using permanent capital instead of variable finance to meet working capital requirements tended to be inefficient and diluted companies' earnings per share.

The clearing bank authors accepted that sharp movements in commodity prices could adversely affect firms with large working capital requirements with potentially disruptive effects on the acceptance market, and credit markets generally. Gilbart and Sykes took the view that commodity price stabilisation was an important contributor to banks' asset quality. They had in mind the stabilisation of grain prices, following the opening up of the North American prairies (Figure 6.9), but prices of other key manufacturing inputs were also relatively stable – for example, steam coal prices, including anthracite (Figure 6.10).[22] Permanently lower grain prices did lead to agricultural decline in Britain, but the clearers

[22] *Gilbart on Banking: The History, Principles and Practice of Banking* (ed.) A. S. Michie (2 vols, London: George Bells, 1882), p. 427; E. Sykes (1947), pp. 193–8.

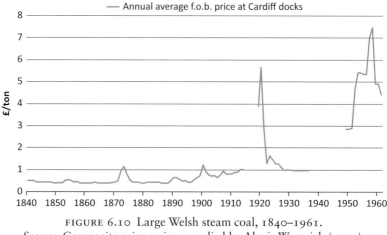

FIGURE 6.10 Large Welsh steam coal, 1840–1961.
Source: Composite price series complied by Alexis Wegerich (2014).

were exposed to the international grain trade and did not provide agricultural mortgages. Falling commodity prices in the interwar period did
adversely affect international lending, but the net effect on the British
economy was positive.[23]

Leaf argued that the clearers' national networks allowed them to be less
beholden to local interests, whereas country and district banks could be
more susceptible to connected lending, and pressures to support local lost
causes.[24] National networks were more difficult to control, but the clearers
were able to develop systems and controls for regulating their disparate
branches, and managers were expected to follow professional standards.
Links between professional status and social standing in branch localities
may have acted as a deterrent against fraud and malpractice, since discov-
ery would risk professional and social disgrace. In any event, the clearers
were successful at building reputations for impartiality and fair dealing.[25]
Respectable banking, nevertheless, had its limits, and it was accepted that
certain key business parameters – deposit rates and cash ratios – should be
stipulated formally, rather than being left to directors' consciences.

Leaf recognised that the clearers remained open to criticism for not
providing start-up finance, and permanent capital for industry. To the
extent that Germany's universal banks did this, Leaf pointed out that

[23] N. H. Dimsdale and N. Horsewood, 'The Financial Crisis of 1931 and the Impact of the
Great Depression on the British Economy' in N. H. Dimsdale and A. C. Hotson (eds)
British Financial Crises since 1825 (Oxford: Oxford University Press, 2014), p. 130.

[24] W. Leaf (1943), p. 171.

[25] W. Leaf (1943), pp. 234–5.

they protected their position by holding controlling interests in their client companies and participated in their governance through interlocking directorships. The clearers could not provide permanent capital and guidance on industrial restructuring without a similar system of control, and this was alien to Anglophone capitalism.[26] Montagu Norman, the Bank's governor for much of the interwar period, initiated a range of official initiatives to provide restructuring finance, but the impact of these schemes was limited.[27] Leaf argued that the clearers could maintain their current levels of credit provision without raising additional capital, provided they were not expected to behave as Germany's universal banks did, and provide long-term loans.[28] The British government had no desire to upset this particular applecart, and no serious attempt was made to develop the clearers' role as owners of industrial companies.

After the Second World War, the Treasury wanted to give industrial and commercial companies priority in the queue to raise capital, and resisted moves by the clearers to do so. Their balance sheets grew more rapidly than their capital base, and – as a consequence – the clearers' leverage ratios increased to a level in excess of 20 times.[29] In contrast, the accepting houses operated with leverage ratios of between 3 and 4 times, albeit with greater risk.[30] Receding pressures of wartime finance allowed the clearers to revert to their primary role as providers of working capital, and the relaxation of credit restraints in 1958 allowed an expansion of consumer credit.[31] The easing of restrictions proved to be temporary, and credit controls were re-imposed during the 1960s.[32]

The Bank recognised that the clearers' raison d'être was being thwarted, and their traditional business was being disintermediated to finance houses, accepting houses, discount houses, and trade creditors.

---

[26] W. Leaf (1943), pp. 158–64; M. H. Best and K. J. Humphries, 'The City and Industrial Decline', in B. Elbaum and W. Lazonick (eds) *The Decline of the British Economy* (Oxford: Clarendon, 1986), p. 224; M. Collins and M. Baker, *Commercial Banks and Industrial Finance in England and Wales, 1860–1913* (Oxford: Oxford University Press, 2003), pp. 200–2.

[27] M. H. Best and K. J. Humphries (1986), pp. 229–34; R. S. Sayers, *The Bank of England 1891–1944* (2 vols and appendix, Cambridge: Cambridge University Press, 1976), 1, pp. 314–30, 2, pp. 546–51.

[28] W. Leaf (1943), p. 112.

[29] J. D. Turner (2014b), pp. 130, 133, 134.

[30] J. S. Fforde, *The Bank of England and Public Policy 1941–1958* (Cambridge: Cambridge University Press, 1992), pp. 751–2.

[31] E. T. Nevin and E. W. Davis, *The London Clearing Banks* (London: Elek, 1970), p. 238.

[32] W. A. Allen, *Monetary Policy and Financial Repression in Britain, 1951–59* (Basingstoke: Palgrave Macmillan, 2014), pp. 147–50.

The launching of Competition and Credit Control (CCC) in 1971 was the Bank's attempt to free the clearers from direct controls, and allow them to rebuild their franchise with industrial and commercial companies, particularly SMEs.[33] This could not happen overnight and, in the meantime, the clearers used their balance sheet strength to lend to finance houses, and other secondary banks, that were funding, inter alia, property developers, and second mortgages. These forms of lending did not fall within traditional parameters, but the clearers could view them as interbank lending, or at least wholesale market lending to other financial institutions (OFIs). As we know, the finance houses were not sufficiently well capitalised to cope with the property crash of 1973–5, and the losses fell back on the clearers. Worse still, balance sheet controls were re-imposed in the form of the Supplementary Special Deposit (SSD) scheme.[34]

Britain's relative economic decline in the 1960s and 1970s rekindled interest in German and Japanese models of banking with their supposed emphasis on long-term industrial finance and corporate stewardship.[35] Those with knowledge of the clearers recognised their limitations in this sphere and advocated moves to promote larger merchant banks to fill the gap, but nothing came of this during the 1970s.[36] It was noticeable that ownership of industry was increasingly concentrated in the hands of a relatively small group of institutional investors, made up of leading life assurers, pension funds and fund managers. In view of this, there was some talk of investing institutions, rather than the banks, taking a more strategic role in the restructuring of British industry, but the Thatcher reforms of the 1980s moved in a different direction.[37]

The clearers therefore stuck to their knitting, and limited growth in domestic markets left international lending as the other main outlet. In the 1960s, euro-market loan syndications had been presented as high-quality credits that banks could match fund, avoiding the need to hold traditional liquid assets, and requiring limited capital backing. The relative stability of oil and other commodity prices since the Second World War provided a benign environment for this type of cross-border lending (Figure 6.11). The implications of less stable commodity prices – OPEC I in 1973 and OPEC II in 1979 – for international banking were not fully appreciated at the time, and the Euromarkets became a centre for

[33] Bank of England, *The Development and Operation of Monetary Policy 1960–1983* (Oxford: Clarendon Press, 1984), pp. 2, 8, 35, 38, 39–41.
[34] Bank of England (1984), pp. 42–4, 117–27.
[35] M. H. Best and K. J. Humphries (1986), pp. 224, 236–7.
[36] F. H. Capie, *The Bank of England from the 1950s to 1979* (Cambridge: Cambridge University Press, 2010), p. 440.
[37] F. H. Capie (2010), pp. 801–8.

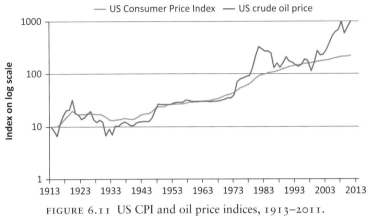

FIGURE 6.11 US CPI and oil price indices, 1913–2011.
Sources: US Department of Labor; US Energy Information Administration.

petro-recycling, financing countries with balance of payments deficits. The idea that commercial banks should play a role recycling global imbalances initially found official favour, but sovereign borrowers financed trade deficits by rolling over euro-market credits, exposing themselves to refinancing risk.[38] After Volcker raised dollar interest rates, they also started to face higher servicing costs on their floating-rate debt, leading to the onset of the Latin American debt crisis starting in 1982. Euro-credits had become a modern form of accommodation paper, falling well outside Leaf's conception of an appropriate clearing bank loan.

Throughout the 1960s and 1970s there was an unresolved conflict between the authorities' desire to regulate domestic credit – and/or broad money – and the modus operandi of the clearers as flexible providers of working capital. Credit controls did smooth the growth trajectory of the clearers' balance sheets during the 1960s, but excess demand for credit led to disintermediation. History repeated itself with the SSD scheme during the 1970s, and attempts to use interest rates to regulate short-term credit proved to be equally ineffectual, the banks having been allowed to liability manage. Changes in output tended to have a geared effect on working capital requirements, at least in the short term, and these effects were normally interest inelastic.[39] The involuntary stock building associated with the downturn in 1980–1 had to be funded and proved to be similarly insensitive to interest rates. The clearing bank authors would

[38] T. Balogh, 'Oil recycling: The need for a new lending facility?', *Lloyds Bank Review*, no. 137 (July 1980), p. 21.
[39] C. A. E. Goodhart and A. C. Hotson, 'The Forecasting and Control of Bank Lending' (1979) in C. A. E. Goodhart, *Monetary Theory and Practice: The UK Experience* (London: Macmillan, 1984), pp. 139–45.

have been amazed at attempts to regulate the financing counterpart of working capital, considering it to be the result of wider economic developments, rather than their cause.[40]

On the other hand, the clearing bank authors had taken it as read that credit institutions should not use short-term monies for long-term lending. Speculative advances to leveraged borrowers should also be circumscribed and, where this did take place, some sort of regulatory overlay was needed, as in the case of loans to stock jobbers and discount houses.[41] In the 1930s, some building societies broke all these rules, and more. Acting as liability managers, they competed on rate for short-term funds and provided long-term loans with high loan-to-value (LTV) ratios. They contributed to the recovery of the wider economy, but societies were exposed to the risk of falls in property values, and scares about the same, causing refinancing risk. All in all, they were budding prototypes of Northern Rock's business model, although the Second World War intervened before disaster struck.[42]

After the Second World War the sector was successfully stabilised by the introduction of a recommended lending rate, set by the Building Societies Association (BSA), which had the effect of limiting liability management.[43] Its lagged adjustment had the effect of stabilising saving inflows, and thence mortgage lending – an informal system of monetary targeting for the home finance sector. Monetarists might object that monetary control by way of a cartelised rate was not what Friedman had in mind, but actually Friedman argued that the usefulness of monetarism was an empirical matter, depending on the stability of the demand for money.[44] Equations estimated using US data for the 1950s and 1960s gave grounds for some optimism, but they depended on Regulation Q, which had the effect of cartelising the own rate on money, allowing a rise in market interest rates to have a contractionary effect on the demand for money. Friedmanite monetarism was founded on the banking model of its time, in which domestic banks were still operating largely without liability management.

Viewed in this light, the Thatcher government's monetary reforms of the early 1980s do seem curious, to say the least. A successful system of monetarist control of the home finance sector was discarded and, at the

---

[40] W. Leaf (1943), p. 161.
[41] W. Leaf (1943), p. 172.
[42] N. H. Dimsdale and N. Horsewood (2014), pp. 130–3; S. K. Howson (1975), pp. 108–16.
[43] M. Boddy, *The Building Societies* (London and Basingstoke: Macmillan, 1980), pp. 86–8; M. Boleat, *National Housing Finance Systems: A Comparative Study* (London: Croom Helm, 1985), pp. 51–2.
[44] M. Friedman, 'Demand for money', *Journal of Political Economy*, 67, no. 4 (August 1959), pp. 327–51.

same time, dire attempts were made to control the uncontrollable – a broad monetary aggregate traditionally associated with an erratic working capital cycle. The government needed the provision of home finance to grow more rapidly – to accommodate council house sales – and this could have been agreed. The BSA could have raised its recommended rate more aggressively, rather than allowing its rate setting function to lapse. The banks and others could have been allowed to enter the mortgage market, but only by way of separate subsidiaries – proprietary building societies – subject to a recommended rate set by a reconstituted BSA. Instead, the government allowed all comers – the banks, converted building societies and the remaining mutual building societies – to liability manage, thereby undermining the potency of the interest rate weapon, and opening the door to an explosive credit cycle.

The Basel Accords were applied internationally and were meant to mitigate the risks of an otherwise deregulated banking market. Basel II nevertheless accommodated the trend towards mortgage lending, allowing residential mortgage loans to be 50 per cent risk-weighted, compared to a 100 per cent weight for most other forms of commercial lending.[45] This meant that mortgage loan books could be leveraged 25 times, compared with 12 ½ times for commercial loan books, assuming a capital-to-risk assets ratio of 8 per cent (12 ½ times). The low loss experience on standard mortgage books nevertheless persuaded many that the 50 per cent risk weighting and leverage ratio of 25 times was unduly conservative, and banks responded by financing them off-balance sheet. Credit growth in developed economies tended to outstrip monetary growth, and excessive leverage is seen by many to be a bugbear of the post-1970s age.[46] Basel III has been implemented since the 2008 crisis, amid much talk about the need for lower leverage, but official plans fall far short of the 10 times multiple set by the clearers in the interwar period.

The 2007–8 crisis exposed at least two other fault lines in our financial system, the first of these being refinancing risk. The off-balance sheet vehicles used to finance banks' ceded assets relied on short-term finance, and were exposed to refinancing risk. When refinancing started to dry up in 2007, many ceding banks decided to finance their vehicles irrespective

[45] M. B. Gordy and E. A. Heitfield, 'Risk-based regulatory capital and Basel II', in A. N. Berger, P. Molyneux and J. O. S. Wilson, *The Oxford Handbook of Banking* (Oxford: Oxford University Press, 1st edn, 2010), pp. 357–76.
[46] M. Schularick and A. M. Taylor, 'Credit booms gone bust: monetary policy, leverage cycles, and financial crises, 1870–2008', *American Economic Review*, 102, no. 2 (2012) pp. 1036.

of whether they had a contractual obligation to do so. Ceding banks felt compelled to become lenders of last resort (LOLR) for their supposedly autonomous financing vehicles, and the authorities felt compelled to act as LOLR to the ceding banks. Off-balance sheet vehicles were not the problem per se; it was their mismatched funding.

The second fault line of our financial system is the terms on which mortgage loans are granted, and their effect on speculative behaviour. This is the elephant in the room that everyone ignores, and warrants further consideration. The traditional mortgage allowed landed families to raise funds with the option of regaining ownership of their mortgaged land. To give an example, an estate might yield rents from tenants of £5 per annum. The estate might be valued at 20 years' purchase, i.e. £5 per annum x 20 years = £100, a 5 per cent rental yield. The estate could be mortgaged to another party in exchange for cash of two-thirds its value, £100 x 2/3 = £67, giving the mortgagee (i.e. lender) an enhanced yield of £5/£67 = 7.5 per cent per annum. The mortgagor (i.e. borrower) would have the option to repurchase the estate for the value of the loan – £67 – after five years. If the value of the property was still £100, the mortgagor would enjoy an equity of redemption of £100 – £67 = £33, and it would be worthwhile repaying the loan, even if the estate had to be sold. If the estate's value fell below £67, there would be negative equity of redemption, and the mortgagor could decide not to exercise their option to redeem the mortgage.[47] The investment proposition offered to mortgagees was therefore the immediate prospect of an enhanced rental yield, and the possibility of being left with the asset if valuations fell.

Although modern mortgages give rise to similar incentives as ancient ones, the parties involved are in different financial circumstances. A modern mortgage allows a householder to acquire an equity interest in a property and avoid paying rent to someone else. The implicit rental yield on the property may, or may not, equate to the interest rate charged on the mortgage loan, but they tend to be similar under normal circumstances. With a relatively modest LTV of 80 per cent, the borrower is investing with five times leverage – the same as that enjoyed by the Bank in the late nineteenth century. If property prices collapse, borrowers may be able to walk away from the loan, even if the legal small print includes recourse to them personally. If property prices rise, homeowners enjoy the effect of

---

[47] A. Offer, *Property and Politics 1870–1914: Landownership, Law, Ideology and Urban Development in England* (Cambridge: Cambridge University Press, 1981), p. 137; E. H. Blake, 'Mortgages: Some notes on law and practice', *The Auctioneers' Institute of the United Kingdom* (London, 11 November 1908), p. 15.

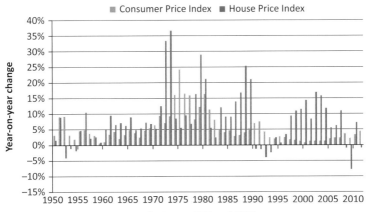

FIGURE 6.12 UK inflation – CPI and HPI, 1950–2011.
Source: Economic Trends.

five times leverage. On these terms, households have every incentive to get on the property ladder, precisely because they are being offered speculative advances of the kind deplored by the clearing bank authors.

This puts modern mortgage lenders in a curious position. They are not landowners with surplus funds seeking extra yield, and the possibility of enlarging their estates. They are highly leveraged intermediaries placing customers' deposits in what amounts to a real estate investment trust (REIT) with a portfolio of residential properties, plus a derivative overlay. The derivative cedes the upside potential of house prices in exchange for interest payments, but leaves the REIT exposed to falls in property prices. A credit structure following the canons of bill finance would look for a closer match between borrowers' residential assets and their mortgage debt, and between the assets and liabilities of lenders. One way of doing this would be for mortgage lenders to offer interest on deposits that tracks the house price index (HPI), and to lend on the same basis. Mortgage borrowers' indebtedness would be adjusted in line with the HPI plus a margin, less repayments. Owner–occupiers' equity would therefore comprise their own resources invested in a property, plus changes in the total value of the property relative to the HPI. Householders would not be able to speculate on house prices using borrowed funds (Figure 6.12).

The policy options regarding mortgage loans go far beyond the remit of this study, but it is possible to draw some general conclusions from historical experience. The simplest solution to recent problems would be to revert to the time honoured rule that mainstream lenders should stick to a maximum LTV of two-thirds – a borrower leverage ratio of two times.

Conservative LTVs have allowed lenders to face sharp fluctuations in the housing cycle – for example, the United States in the 1920s – without threatening the mainstream banking sector.[48] This approach has considerable appeal but seems to be politically unacceptable, particularly in Anglophone countries, where high levels of residential property ownership are seen to be a democratic imperative. Are we therefore beholden to the deregulated mortgage lending model we adopted in the 1980s with its high borrower and lender leverage, no restrictions on liability management, no collective management of inflows, and heroic levels of maturity transformation, née mismatching? Or can we find a way out of this dangerous place?

Chapter 7 is our concluding one, and we shall look for solutions by comparing London's classical system and its clearing bank model with the deregulated banking system that emerged after 1971. While there is no single way of avoiding crises, we can identify ways and means of living in a world with historically high levels of lender and borrower leverage.

---

[48] E. N. White, 'Lessons from the Great American Real Estate Boom and Bust of the 1920s' in E. N. White, K. Snowden and P. Fishback (eds), *Housing and Mortgage Markets in Historical Perspective* (Chicago: University of Chicago Press, 2014), pp. 115–58.

7

History and Policy

Banking is presented in modern texts as a form of intermediation in which short-term deposits are used to fund longer-term lending, where the former are nearly risk-free and the latter are riskier.[1] Banks are supposed to manage the resulting liquidity risk by pooling asynchronous payments across their balance sheets, and to use the interbank market to pool liquidity risk across the sector. Banks are expected to manage credit risk using tiered balance sheet structures in which depositors enjoy the benefit of being senior creditors, and loan losses are absorbed by shareholders and subordinated debt holders.[2] This is presented as normal banking practice, ignoring the fact that the clearing banks did not undertake maturity and credit transformations of great significance. Unlike the clearers, the building societies did undertake significant maturity transformations, but relied on cartelised rates to manage their liquidity. Either these uncomfortable facts are left unrecognised or it is suggested that these institutions were not fully developed banking intermediaries, and that deregulation allowed them to fulfil their proper roles.[3]

It is not obvious that the post-1971 banking model is a better one, and that reliance can be placed on liability management, and tiers of junior creditors taking first losses. The pre-1971 model delivered stability

---

[1] M. A. King, *The End of Alchemy: Money, Banking and the Future of the Global Economy* (London: Little, Brown, 2016), pp. 5, 8–9, 40, 59, 104, 187.

[2] X. Freixas and J-C. Rochet, *Microeconomics of Banking* (Cambridge, MA: MIT Press, 2nd edn, 2008), pp. 217–59; A. N. Berger, P. Molyneux and J. O. S. Wilson, *The Oxford Handbook of Banking* (Oxford: Oxford University Press, 2012), pp. 1, 21–2.

[3] X. Freixas and J-C. Rochet (2008), pp. 5–6.

by curbing liability management, and regulating liquidity. Its component parts can be summarised as follows:

1 The cartel, orchestrated by the Committee of London Clearing Bankers (CLCB), curbed liability management, making it difficult for individual clearers to gain market share by lending aggressively. As a result, the system was less prone to shocks affecting the supply of credit.

2 The clearers' mainstay was working capital finance, and the classical system allowed them to accommodate fluctuations in demand for this type of credit. The clearing bank authors were at pains to point out that their lending supported legitimate trade, rather than speculative undertakings.

3 Strictly speaking, businesses with large working capital requirements were exposed to basis risk if the market price of their current assets fell (relative to their current liabilities), but their facilities could be terminated at short notice, and their current assets could be liquidated. In other words, their loans were match funded against possible cash realisations and, in the event of a shortfall, the bank would typically have security over fixed assets as well.

4 At least one-third of the clearers' funds were invested in reserve assets, comprising British government stocks (BGS), Treasury bills (TBs), money at call (MAC), and prime bank bills (PBBs). The classical system ensured that these investments were easily converted into cash in the form of bankers' balances (BBs).

5 The market remained confident that the Bank would act as lender of last resort (LOLR) in the face of a run on the banks, and – partly for this reason – it was not called upon to provide unstinting support in the manner suggested by Bagehot. Instead, the Bank orchestrated a lifeboat for Baring's in 1890, and stood behind the accepting houses in 1914 and 1931.

6 Building societies accepted substantial maturity mismatching, suggesting that they faced more serious liquidity risks than the clearers, but they did not hold proportionately more liquid assets. Instead, the Building Societies Association (BSA) used its recommended lending rate to manage the pool of savings available to societies, and this proved to be an effective mechanism for regulating their liquidity and lending.

7 Stability in foreign exchange and commodity markets supported the resilience of the banking system. The fixed exchange rates of

the gold standard and Bretton Woods eras were helpful in this regard; likewise, the stability of grain prices in the first decade of the twentieth century and oil prices after the Second World War. Instability in commodity markets requires significant countervailing measures if banking stability is to be maintained.

The clearers operated with leverage ratios of around 10 times during the interwar period, rising to 20 times after the Second World War. This was strikingly high when compared with the joint-stock banks of the late nineteenth century. The clearers' resilience turned on the quality of their assets, rather than on their capital backing. The building societies operated on higher leverage ratios than the clearers – 20 to 30 times – but loan losses on residential mortgages were miniscule in the post-war era before deregulation. In short, the clearing banks and building societies had a low risk appetite and relied on the stability of asset counterpart values.

The focus on stabilising asset prices had a long provenance predating the clearing banks. The success of minted currencies and convertible notes depended on the stabilisation of bullion prices. The Bank of England held bullion reserves in the eighteenth and nineteenth centuries to support its note issuance, but this left it exposed to a potentially serious mismatch between the prices of its bullion assets and those of its sterling liabilities. Failure to stabilise the gold price could have weakened the Bank and undermined its standing in the market. The stability of commodity prices – for example, wheat prices in the first decade of the twentieth century – had important implications for the stability of the bill market, and the clearers' lending. Modern money is largely backed by real property, and we should not be surprised if instability in property prices disrupts our monetary system.[4] This raises the question of whether we need to find ways and means of stabilising property prices, or whether we should revert to a system where banks hold short-maturity assets that are easier to stabilise (Figure 7.1).

The other key theme of London's search for monetary stability has been the need to limit bankers' ability to fund actively. Restrictions on liability management were arguably one of the most important means of stabilising money and credit markets in the late nineteenth century. This option has

---

[4] E. E. Leamer, 'Housing is the business cycle', *NBER Working Paper Series*, no. 13428 (2007); A. Offer, 'Narrow Banking, Real Estate, and Financial Stability in the UK, c. 1870–2010', in N. H. Dimsdale and A. C. Hotson (eds) *British Financial Crises since 1825* (Oxford: Oxford University Press, 2014), p. 164.

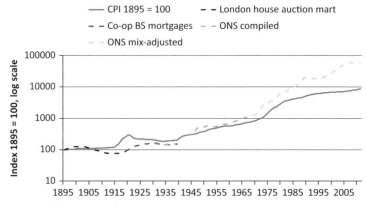

FIGURE 7.1 UK house and consumer prices, 1895–2011.
Sources: L. Samy, 'Indices of house prices and rent prices of residential property in London, 1895–1939', *University of Oxford Discussion Papers in Economic and Social History*, no. 134 (April 2015); Table 22, Historical HPI data, ONS (March 2012).

barely been discussed since the 2007–8 crises, notwithstanding its historical importance. Instead, macro-prudential regulation has been touted as a means of dampening credit-induced property bubbles. This is curious, because macro-prudential regulation – for example, restrictions on mortgages with loan-to-value (LTV) ratios above a specified threshold – is a euphemism for selective credit controls. Past experience suggests that permanent credit controls – like those of the 1960s – give rise to disintermediation, and temporary ones – such as the Supplementary Special Deposit (SSD) scheme – lead to anticipatory behaviour by the banks. Macro-prudential regulation seems destined to lead to both. From the 1890s until 1971, restrictions on liability management provided an effective tool for stabilising the system, but our neoliberal sensibilities are offended by talk of cartelised reference rates.[5]

The CLCB cartel did lead to disintermediation in favour of other financial institutions (OFIs) that were allowed to compete on rate for funds, notably the insurers in the 1920s, the building societies in the 1930s, and the finance houses and accepting houses after the Second World War. The competitive challenge presented by the building societies during the 1930s was recognised as being potentially destabilising, and the BSA's cartel was instigated after the war, curbing the scope for societies to liability manage. Like the clearers, the societies did suffer

5 J. Williamson, 'What Washington Means by Policy Reform', chapter 2 in J. Williamson (ed.) *Latin American Adjustment: How Much Has Happened?* (Washington, DC: Institute of International Economics, 1990).

some disintermediation; for example, mortgages were offered by finance houses using funds from pension schemes. There was some talk of bringing the finance houses into line with a cartel organised by the Finance Houses Association (FHA), but this did not come to pass.[6] Some disintermediation was tolerated, but not too much, and a balance was struck between banks and OFIs. In contrast, modern policymakers assume that liability management should prevail, *tout court*.

When the banks and building societies were being deregulated in the 1970s and 1980s, it was taken for granted that they could accept more risk, and manage it themselves, without the support of cartelised rates, and traditional forms of reserve asset. It is striking that the leverage ratio for mortgage books, implied by Basel II, was pretty well in line with the leverage ratio of building societies in the 1950s and 1960s.[7] The main change since that time was not the amount of capital supporting mortgage books, but the dismantling of (i) the interest rate weapon as a means of restraining the supply of mortgage credit and (ii) the BSA rate as a mechanism for protecting the liquidity of mismatched mortgage institutions. Instead, we place reliance on state deposit insurance and capital adequacy.

Following the 1980s deregulation, the banks and converted building societies have been able to accommodate the demand for mortgage credit in much the same way that the traditional clearers accommodated the demand for working capital. This has proved to be problematic because mortgagors are free to use the flexible supply of credit to speculate on the differential between changes in the value of their own homes, and mortgage interest rates (MIR). Rising property prices increase the value of collateral available to support loans, and income multiples tend to accommodate the availability of more security, rather than act as a binding constraint. This has allowed house price speculation to become a national pastime, turning the traditional predisposition against speculative advances on its head.

There are ways and means of curbing speculation, but this might require a restoration of prescribed terms for loans and deposits. To illustrate the point, one could envisage mortgage interest charges being accrued at a rate linked to the house price index (HPI) and mortgage loans being match funded using deposits paying an HPI-linked rate of interest.

[6] J. S. Fforde, *The Bank of England and Public Policy, 1941–1958* (Cambridge: Cambridge University Press, 1992), pp. 775–9.

[7] C. A. E. Goodhart, *The Basel Committee on Banking Supervision: A History of the Early Years, 1974–1977* (Cambridge: Cambridge University Press, 2011), p. 220; Y. Cassis, 'Do Financial Crises Lead to Policy Change?' in N. H. Dimsdale and A. C. Hotson (eds) *British Financial Crises since 1825* (Oxford: Oxford University Press, 2014), pp. 185–7.

This would mean that prospective homebuyers could save for a deposit, and earn an HPI-related rate of interest, providing a hedge against house price rises. Savings invested in homes would confer an equity interest in them, and this would rise as mortgage loans were paid off, but borrowed funds would not be provided in a form making it possible to speculate on the HPI–MIR differential. This would decouple the right to buy a home from the right to use borrowed funds to speculate on house prices.

This approach would have a number of implications for saving and borrowing: for example, buy-to-let mortgages would be HPI-linked – discouraging speculative investors – but pension savers would be allowed to invest in HPI-linked deposits and real property, including their own homes. This would mean householders could own equity in their homes directly, and through their pensions, but they could not leverage their returns on residential property. The imposition of prescribed terms for mortgage lending could give rise to disintermediation, but there are countermeasures that could be deployed to discourage it. For example, the Land Registry could follow rules whereby it would not register the interests of non-authorised lenders providing non-prescribed loans.

This is not to suggest there is only one way of tackling the problems we face, but the lack of historical perspective in policy circles is disconcerting. Typically, a monetary doctrine emerges, broadly in tune with contemporary principles and practice, and a sophisticated model is constructed to provide an ex post rationalisation for it. This is what Locke did with his inviolate silver standard; likewise, the Currency School's proposals for note issuance; and our current regime is justified with reference to the Diamond–Dybvig (DD) model of banking. Within their own terms of reference, these models are logically consistent, and constructs of great beauty, but that does not necessarily make them true. We have come full circle from Keynes's complaint that 'practical men who believe themselves to be quite exempt from any intellectual influence, are usually slaves to some defunct economist.'[8] Nowadays, our macroeconomic establishment uses complex models as a public relations device to defend current orthodoxies.[9]

---

[8] J. M. Keynes, *The General Theory of Employment Interest and Money*, 1st edn 1936, reprinted in *The Collected Writings of John Maynard Keynes* (London and Basingstoke: Macmillan and Cambridge University Press, Royal Economic Society edn, 1973), VII, p. 383.

[9] A. M. Sbordone, A. Tambalotti, K. Rao, K. Walsh, 'Policy analysis using DSGE models: An introduction', *FRBNY Economic Policy Review* (October 2010).

Instead of enslaving ourselves to the model du jour, we should consider historical experience using an eclectic range of models, and test them against the facts, including quantitative data. A historicist approach should seek to clarify past successes and failures without being sentimental about particular eras. As Forrest Capie suggests, drawing on a quotation attributed to Mark Twain, 'History never repeats itself but it rhymes.'[10] There is quite a lot of rhyming in the longue durée of monetary history, and it behoves us to formulate current policy with reference to historical experience. Having spent the last four decades deregulating our money and credit markets, we should start by asking ourselves whether we have retained the means of stabilising them. This author is not convinced.

---

[10] J. R. Colombo, 'A Said Poem', in *Neo Poems* (Vancouver, BC: Sono Nis Press, 1970), p. 46; F. H. Capie, 'British Financial Crises in the Nineteenth and Twentieth Centuries', in N. H. Dimsdale and A. C. Hotson (eds) *British Financial Crises since 1825* (Oxford: Oxford University Press, 2014), p. 22.

Appendix – English Mint Prices, 1158–1946
(Tables A.1 to A.7)

Tables prepared by A. C. Hotson and N. J. Mayhew as part of a project undertaken by the Winton Institute for Monetary History, May 2015.

TABLE A.1 *English Mint silver prices, 1158–1542 (part 1: 1158 to 1335)*

Indentures						Coinage		Prices			
						Face value of coin	English/foreign coin	Gross mint price	Mintage	Seigniorage	Total deductions =(B)+(C)
Start			End					(A)	(B)	(C)	(D)
Yr	Mo	Day	Yr	Mo	Day	d	'E' or 'F'	d/Tower lb			
1158	–	–	–	–	–	1	–	242	–	–	12.0
1180	–	–	–	–	–	1	–	242	6.00	6.00	12.0
1205	–	–	–	–	–	1	–	242	–	6.00	–
1234	–	–	–	–	–	1	–	242	–	–	–
1247	–	–	1250	–	–	1	E	242	10.00	6.00	16.0
1247	–	–	1250	–	–	1	F	242	6.00	6.00	12.0
1250	–	–	1278	–	–	1	–	242	6.00	6.00	12.0
1279	–	–	1280	Jan	–	1	E	243	10.00	9.00	19.0
1279	–	–	1280	Jan	–	1	F	243	8.00	9.00	17.0
1280	Jan	–	1280	May	–	1	E	245	7.00	14.00	21.0
1280	Jan	–	1280	May	–	1	F	245	5.50	13.50	19.0
1280	May	–	1280	Dec	–	1	E	245	7.00	14.00	21.0
1280	May	–	1280	Dec	–	1	F	245	5.50	14.00	19.5
1280	Dec	–	1281	Feb	–	1	E	245	6.50	14.50	21.0
1280	Dec	–	1281	Feb	–	1	F	245	5.50	14.00	19.5
1281	Feb	–	1283	Oct	–	1	E	243	6.50	9.50	16.0
1281	Feb	–	1283	Oct	–	1	F	243	5.50	9.00	14.5
1283	Oct	–	1285	May	–	1	E	243	6.50	10.00	16.5
1283	Oct	–	1285	May	–	1	F	243	5.50	9.00	14.5
1285	May	–	1286	Aug	–	1	E	243	6.00	10.00	16.0
1285	May	–	1286	Aug	–	1	F	243	5.50	9.00	14.5
1286	Aug	–	1287	Nov	–	1	E	243	5.50	10.50	16.0
1286	Aug	–	1287	Nov	–	1	F	243	5.50	9.00	14.5
1287	Nov	–	1290	Jul	–	1	E	243	5.25	10.75	16.0
1287	Nov	–	1290	Jul	–	1	F	243	5.25	9.25	14.5
1290	Jul	–	1309	Jun	–	1	E	243	5.50	10.50	16.0
1290	Jul	–	1309	Jun	–	1	F	243	5.50	6.00	11.5
1309	Jun	–	1311	Oct	–	1	E	243	5.25	10.75	16.0
1309	Jun	–	1311	Oct	–	1	F	243	5.25	6.25	11.5
1311	Oct	–	1335	May	–	1	E	243	5.50	10.50	16.0
1311	Oct	–	1335	May	–	1	F	243	5.50	6.00	11.5

Source: A. C. Hotson and N. J. Mayhew, 'English Mint silver and gold prices, 1158–1946', Winton Institute for Monetary History (May 2015)

| | (H) 1 Tower lb = | 5,400 grains | Tower dwt = 22.5 grains | | |
| | (I) 1 troy lb = | 5,760 grains | Troy dwt = 24 grains | | |

Net mint price =(A)–(D)	Fineness	Gross mint price =(A)/240	Net mint price =(E)/240	Deductions /GMP =(D)/(A)	Gross mint price =(F)*(I)/(H)	Net mint price =(G)*(I)/(H)
(E)		(F)	(G)			
	%	d/Tower dwt		%	d/troy dwt	
230.0	92.5%	1.0083	0.9583	5.0%	1.0756	1.0222
230.0	92.5%	1.0083	0.9583	5.0%	1.0756	1.0222
–	92.5%	1.0083	–	–	1.0756	–
–	92.5%	1.0083	–	–	1.0756	–
226.0	92.5%	1.0083	0.9417	6.6%	1.0756	1.0044
230.0	92.5%	1.0083	0.9583	5.0%	1.0756	1.0222
230.0	92.5%	1.0083	0.9583	5.0%	1.0756	1.0222
224.0	92.5%	1.0125	0.9333	7.8%	1.0800	0.9956
226.0	92.5%	1.0125	0.9417	7.0%	1.0800	1.0044
224.0	92.5%	1.0208	0.9333	8.6%	1.0889	0.9956
226.0	92.5%	1.0208	0.9417	7.8%	1.0889	1.0044
224.0	92.5%	1.0208	0.9333	8.6%	1.0889	0.9956
225.5	92.5%	1.0208	0.9396	8.0%	1.0889	1.0022
224.0	92.5%	1.0208	0.9333	8.6%	1.0889	0.9956
225.5	92.5%	1.0208	0.9396	8.0%	1.0889	1.0022
227.0	92.5%	1.0125	0.9458	6.6%	1.0800	1.0089
228.5	92.5%	1.0125	0.9521	6.0%	1.0800	1.0156
226.5	92.5%	1.0125	0.9438	6.8%	1.0800	1.0067
228.5	92.5%	1.0125	0.9521	6.0%	1.0800	1.0156
227.0	92.5%	1.0125	0.9458	6.6%	1.0800	1.0089
228.5	92.5%	1.0125	0.9521	6.0%	1.0800	1.0156
227.0	92.5%	1.0125	0.9458	6.6%	1.0800	1.0089
228.5	92.5%	1.0125	0.9521	6.0%	1.0800	1.0156
227.0	92.5%	1.0125	0.9458	6.6%	1.0800	1.0089
228.5	92.5%	1.0125	0.9521	6.0%	1.0800	1.0156
227.0	92.5%	1.0125	0.9458	6.6%	1.0800	1.0089
231.5	92.5%	1.0125	0.9646	4.7%	1.0800	1.0289
227.0	92.5%	1.0125	0.9458	6.6%	1.0800	1.0089
231.5	92.5%	1.0125	0.9646	4.7%	1.0800	1.0289
227.0	92.5%	1.0125	0.9458	6.6%	1.0800	1.0089
231.5	92.5%	1.0125	0.9646	4.7%	1.0800	1.0289

TABLE A.I *English Mint silver prices, 1158–1542 (part 2: 1335 to 1542)*

	Indentures					Coinage		Prices	
						Face value of coin	English/ foreign coin	Gross mint price	Mintage
	Start			End				(A)	(B)
Yr	Mo	Day	Yr	Mo	Day	d	'E' or 'F'	d/Tower lb	
1335	May	–	1343	Dec	–	0.5	E	266.4dwt	7.5
1335	May	–	1343	Dec	–	0.5	F	266.4dwt	7.5
1335	May	–	1343	Dec	–	0.25	E	266.4dwt	9.5
1335	May	–	1343	Dec	–	0.25	F	266.4dwt	9.5
1343	Dec	–	1344	Jan	–	1	–	270	9
1344	Jan	–	1344	Jul	–	1	–	270	9
1344	Jul	–	1345	Jun	–	1	–	266	8
1345	Jun	–	1346	Jul	–	1	–	268	
1346	Jul	–	1349	Jan	–	1	–	270	6.75
1349	Jan	–	1351	Jun	–	1	–	270	5.25
1351	Jun	–	1355	May	–	1	–	300	8
1355	May	–	1361	Mar	–	1	–	300	5
1361	Mar	–	1412	–	–	1	–	300	7
1412	–	–	1445	–	–	1	–	360	9
1445	–	–	1445	Dec	–	0.5, 0.25	–	396	7+10
1445	Dec	–	1446	Jun	–	05, 0.25	–	396	9+10
1446	Jun	–	1459	–	–	1	–	360	9
1459	–	–	1461	–	–	1	–	360	11
1461	–	–	1464	–	–	1	–	360	9
1464	–	–	1466	–	–	1	–	450	14
1466	–	–	1467	–	–	1	–	450	14
1467	–	–	1470	–	–	1	–	450	14
1470	–	–	1471	–	–	1	–	450	14
1471	–	–	1489	–	–	1	–	450	12
1489	–	–	1504	–	–	1	–	450	10
1504	–	–	1505	–	–	1	–	450	–
1505	–	–	ch	–	–	1	–	450	10
1522	May	31	1523	Oct	26	1	–	474	–
1523	Oct	26	1526	Nov	5	1	–	450	10
1526	Nov	5	1542	May	–	1	–	506.25	9.375

Source: A. C. Hotson and N. J. Mayhew (May 2015)

| | | | | (H) 1 Tower lb = | 5,400 grains | Tower dwt = 22.5 grains | | |
| | | | | (I) 1 troy lb = | 5,760 grains | Troy dwt = 24 grains | | |

Seigniorage	Total deductions =(B)+(C)	Net mint price =(A)−(D)	Fineness	Gross mint price =(A)/240	Net mint price =(E)/240	Deductions /GMP =(D)/(A)	Gross mint price =(F)*(I)/(H)	Net mint price =(G)*(I)/(H)
(C)	(D)	(E)		(F)	(G)			
			%	d/Tower dwt		%	d/troy dwt	
–	26.4dwt	252.0	83.3%	–	1.0500	–	–	1.1200
–	20.4dwt	258.0	83.3%	–	1.0750	–	–	1.1467
–	26.4dwt	254.0	83.3%	–	1.0583	–	–	1.1289
–	20.4dwt	260.0	83.3%	–	1.0833	–	–	1.1556
6	11.5dwt	258.5	92.5%	1.1250	1.0771	4.3%	1.2000	1.1489
–	16dwt	–	92.5%	1.1250	–	–	1.2000	–
6	14	252.0	92.5%	1.1083	1.0500	5.3%	1.1822	1.1200
6dwt = 6.7	–	254.0	92.5%	1.1167	1.0583	–	1.1911	1.1289
–	14dwt	–	92.5%	1.1250	–	–	1.2000	–
–	14dwt	–	92.5%	1.1250	–	–	1.2000	–
–	14dwt	–	92.5%	1.2500	–	–	1.3333	–
6.5625	11.6	288.0	92.5%	1.2500	1.2000	3.9%	1.3333	1.2800
3	10.0	290.0	92.5%	1.2500	1.2083	3.3%	1.3333	1.2889
3	12.0	348.0	92.5%	1.5000	1.4500	3.3%	1.6000	1.5467
7	24.0	372.0	92.5%	1.6500	1.5500	6.1%	1.7600	1.6533
7	26.0	370.0	92.5%	1.6500	1.5417	6.6%	1.7600	1.6444
3	12.0	348.0	92.5%	1.5000	1.4500	3.3%	1.6000	1.5467
3	14.0	346.0	92.5%	1.5000	1.4417	3.9%	1.6000	1.5378
3	12.0	348.0	92.5%	1.5000	1.4500	3.3%	1.6000	1.5467
40	54.0	396.0	92.5%	1.8750	1.6500	12.0%	2.0000	1.7600
24	38.0	412.0	92.5%	1.8750	1.7167	8.4%	2.0000	1.8311
18	32.0	418.0	92.5%	1.8750	1.7417	7.1%	2.0000	1.8578
10	24.0	426.0	92.5%	1.8750	1.7750	5.3%	2.0000	1.8933
6	18.0	432.0	92.5%	1.8750	1.8000	4.0%	2.0000	1.9200
2	12.0	438.0	92.5%	1.8750	1.8250	2.7%	2.0000	1.9467
–	–	38d/ozt	–	1.8750	–	–	2.0000	–
2	12.0	438.0	92.5%	1.8750	1.8250	2.7%	2.0000	1.9467
–	–	450.0	92.5%	1.9750	1.8750	2.5%	2.1067	2.0000
2	12.0	438.0	92.5%	1.8750	1.8250	2.7%	2.0000	1.9467
1.875	11.3	495.0	92.5%	2.1094	2.0625	2.2%	2.2500	2.2000

TABLE A.1 *English Mint silver prices, 1158–1542 (part 3)*

	References		
1158	C, p. 90	1335	A, p. 175; C, pp. 144–5, 700
1180	C, p. 102	1335	A, p. 175
1205	C, p. 98	1335	A, p. 175
1234	C, pp. 103–4	1335	A, p. 175
1247	A, p. 176	1343	A, p. 177; C, pp. 134–5
1247	A, p. 176	1344	A, p. 177; C, pp. 134–5
1250	A, p. 176	1344	A, p. 177; C, pp. 134–5
1279	A, p. 176; C, p. 134	1345	A, p. 177
1279	A, p. 176; C, p. 134	1346	A, p. 178
1280	A, p. 176b; C, p. 134	1349	A, p. 178
1280	A, p. 176b; C, p. 134	1351	A, p. 178
1280	A, p. 176b; C, p. 134	1355	A, p. 179; C, p. 134
1280	A, p. 176b; C, p. 134	1361	A, p. 179; C, pp. 134–5
1280	A, p. 176b; C, p. 134	1412	C, pp. 134–5
1280	A, p. 176b; C, p. 134	1445	A, p. 179; C, p. 176
1281	A, p. 176; C, p. 134	1445	A, p. 179; C, p. 176
1281	A, p. 176; C, p. 134	1446	C, pp. 134–5
1283	A, p. 176; C, p. 134	1459	A, p. 179; C, p. 196
1283	A, p. 176; C, p. 134	1461	A, p. 179; C, p. 196
1285	A, p. 176	1464	A, p. 179; C, p. 196
1285	A, p. 176	1466	A, p. 179; C, p. 196
1286	A, p. 176; C, pp. 134, 700	1467	A, p. 179; C, p. 196
1286	A, p. 176; C, pp. 134, 700	1470	A, p. 179; C, p. 196
1287	A, p. 176	1471	A, p. 179; C, p. 196
1287	A, p. 176	1489	A, p. 179; C, p. 196
1290	A, p. 176; C, pp. 134, 700	1504	A, p. 181
1290	A, p. 176; C, pp. 134, 700	1505	A, p. 179; C, p. 196
1309	A, p. 176; C, p. 700	1522	A, p. 181; CC, p. 70
1309	A, p. 176; C, p. 700	1523	A, p. 181; CC, p. 70
1311	A, p. 176	1526	C, p. 196
1311	A, p. 176		

Source: A. C. Hotson and N. J. Mayhew (May 2015)

TABLE A.2 *English Mint silver prices, 1542–1560 (pure silver)*
Calculations during the debasement period, from 1542 to 1560, were based on a lb troy of pure silver,
rather than on a lb of sterling silver.
Sterling silver equivalent values are set out in a separate table below.

Indentures			Prices – Pure Ag			Fineness	Deductions /GMP =(B)/(A)	Pure Ag	
			Gross mint price	Total deductions	Net mint price =(A)–(B)			Gross mint price =(A)/240	Net mint price =(C)/240
	Start		(A)	(B)	(C)			d/troy dwt	
Yr	Mo	Day		d/troy lb		%	%		
1526	Nov	–	584	–	570	92.50%	–	2.4333	2.3750
1542	May	–	759	183	576	75.83%	24.1%	3.1625	2.4000
1544	Jun	–	768	144	624	75.00%	18.8%	3.2000	2.6000
1545	Apr	–	1,152	480	672	50.00%	41.7%	4.8000	2.8000
1546	Apr	–	1,728	1,056	672	33.33%	61.1%	7.2000	2.8000
1547	Apr	5	1,728	960	768	33.33%	55.6%	7.2000	3.2000
1548	Oct	–	1,728	912	816	33.33%	52.8%	7.2000	3.4000
1549	Jan	–	1,728	–	–	66.66%	–	7.2000	–
1549	Oct	–	1,728	864	864	50.00%	50.0%	7.2000	3.6000
1550	Apr	–	1,728	696	1,032	50.00%	40.3%	7.2000	4.3000
1550	Aug	–	1,728	768	960	50.00%	44.4%	7.2000	4.0000
1551	Apr	–	3,456	2,016	1,440	25.00%	58.3%	14.4000	6.0000
1551	Oct	–	782	13	769	92.08%	1.7%	3.2583	3.2042
1553	Aug	–	785	19	766	91.66%	2.4%	3.2708	3.1917
1557	Aug	–	785	20	766	91.66%	2.5%	3.2708	3.1896
1560	Nov	–	778	19	759	92.50%	2.4%	3.2417	3.1625

References: C, pp. 233–5; S, p.65; C, p. 730
Source: A. C. Hotson and N. J. Mayhew (May 2015)

TABLE A.3 *English Mint silver prices, 1542–1560 (sterling silver alloy equivalent)*

Indentures			Prices – Ag sterling alloy			Fineness		References	Ag sterling alloy		
			Gross Mint price	Total deductions	Net Mint price =(A)–(B)				Deductions /GMP =(B)/(A)	Gross Mint price =(A)/240	Net Mint price =(C)/240
Start			(A)	(B)	(C)						
				d/troy lb						d/troy dwt	
Yr	Mo	Day				%			%		
1526	Nov	–	540	12	528	92.50%		A, pp. 181–2; [C, p. 720]	2.2%	2.25	2.2
1542	May	–	703	107	596	75.83%		C, p. 720	15.2%	2.93	2.5
1544	June	–	710	129	582	75.00%			18.1%	2.96	2.4
1545	Apr	–	1,066	444	622	50.00%			41.7%	4.44	2.6
1546	Apr	–	1,599	977	622	33.33%			61.1%	6.66	2.6
1547	Apr	5	1,599	888	710	33.33%			55.6%	6.66	3.0
1548	Oct	–	1,599	844	755	33.33%			52.8%	6.66	3.1
1549	Jan	–	1,599	–	–	66.66%			–	6.66	–
1549	Oct	–	1,598	799	799	50.00%		See Pure Ag section	50.0%	6.66	3.3
1550	Apr	–	1,598	733	866	50.00%			45.8%	6.66	3.6
1550	Aug	–	1,598	638	960	50.00%			39.9%	6.66	4.0
1551	Apr	–	3,197	1,865	1,332	25.00%			58.3%	13.32	5.6
1551	Oct	–	723	12	711	92.08%			1.7%	3.01	3.0
1553	Aug	–	726	18	709	91.66%			2.4%	3.03	3.0
1557	Aug	–	726	18	708	91.66%			2.5%	3.03	3.0
1560	Nov	–	720	18	702	92.50%		C, p. 732	2.5%	3.00	2.9

Source: A. C. Hotson and N. J. Mayhew (May 2015)

TABLE A.4 *English Mint silver prices, 1560–1946 (sterling silver alloy equivalent)*

Indentures			Prices – Ag sterling alloy					Fineness	References	Ag sterling alloy		
Start			Gross Mint price	Mintage	Seigniorage	Total deductions =(B)+(C)	Net Mint price =(A)–(D)			Deductions /GMP =(D)/(A)	Gross Mint price =(A)/240	Net Mint price =(E)/240
			(A)	(B)	(C)	(D)	(E)					
Yr	Mo	Day						%		%	d/troy dwt	
					d/troy lb							
1560	–	–	720	–	–	18	702	92.5%	C, p. 732	2.5%	3.0000	2.9250
1583	–	–	720	14	8	22	698	92.5%	F, p. 435; C, p. 736	3.1%	3.0000	2.9083
1601	–	–	744	14	10	24	720	92.5%	C, p. 737	3.2%	3.1000	3.0000
1604	–	–	744	14	16	30	714	92.5%	C, p. 738	4.0%	3.1000	2.9750
1623	–	–	744	14	10	24	720	92.5%	C, p. 741	3.2%	3.1000	3.0000
1666	–	–	744	–	–	0	744	92.5%	C, pp. 745–6	0.0%	3.1000	3.1000
1817	–	–	792	–	–	0	792	92.5%	C, pp. 757–8	0.0%	3.3000	3.3000
1920	–	–	–	–	–	–	–	50.0%	C, pp. 558–9	–	–	–
1946	–	–	–	–	–	–	–	cupro-nickel	C, pp. 582–3	–	–	–

Source: A. C. Hotson and N. J. Mayhew (May 2015)

TABLE A.5   *English Mint gold prices, 1257–1492 (part 1)*

Indentures

(c) Tower lb   5,400   gr

									Gross mint price =(a)*[(c)/(b)]				Mintage			Seigniorage			
									(A)				(B)			(C)			
Date from			Piece	Weight (b)	Face value (a)				d / Tower lb										
Year	Mnth	Day		grs	£	s	d	Total in d	Total in d	£	s	d	s	d	Total in d	£	s	d	Total in d
1257	Aug	–	penny	44.4	0	1	8	20	2,432	10	2	8.4	–	–	–	–	–	–	–
1343	Dec	4	florin	54.0	0	3	0	36	3,600	15	0	0	3	6	42	1	0	0	240
1344	Jul	9	noble	136.7	0	6	8	80	3,156	13	3	0	3	4	40		5	0	60
1345	Jun	23	noble	136.7	0	6	8	80	3,156	13	3	0	2	0	24		5	0	60
1346	Jul	28	noble etc.	128.6	0	6	8	80	3,360	14	0	0	1	8	20		10	0	120
1349	Jan	27	noble etc.	128.6	0	6	8	80	3,360	14	0	0	1	2	14		10	6	126
1351	Jun	20	noble etc.	120.0	0	6	8	80	3,600	15	0	0	2	0	24		7	3	87
1355	May	31	noble etc.	120.0	0	6	8	80	3,600	15	0	0	1	2	14		5	6	66
1361	Mar	5	noble etc.	120.0	0	6	8	80	3,600	15	0	0	1	8	20		3	4	40
1394	Oct	9	noble etc.	120.0	0	6	8	80	3,600	15	0	0	1	6	18		3	6	42
1409	–	–	noble etc.	112.5	0	6	8	80	3,840	16	0	0	2	0	24		4	8	56
1413	Apr	14	noble etc.	108.0	0	6	8	80	4,000	16	13	4	2	4	28		3	6	42
1422	Feb	13	noble etc.	108.0	0	6	8	80	4,000	16	13	4	1	6	18		3	6	42
1445	Dec	13	noble etc.	108.0	0	6	8	80	4,000	16	13	4	2	4	28		3	6	42
1464	Aug	13	noble etc.	108.0	0	8	4	100	5,000	20	16	8	2	4	28	2	7	8	572
1465	Mar	6	ryal etc.	120.0	0	10	0	120	5,400	22	10	0	2	4	28		18	6	222
1469	Mar	2	ryal etc.	120.0	0	10	0	120	5,400	22	10	0	2	6	30		12	0	144
1471	Mar	6	angel	80.0	0	6	8	80	5,400	22	10	0	2	6	30		8	0	96
1472	Feb	23	angel	80.0	0	6	8	80	5,400	22	10	0	2	6	30		5	0	60
1492	Nov	20	angel	80.0	0	6	8	80	5,400	22	10	0	1	10	22		0	8	8

Shading coded notes:
    Derived number in Challis with some fractional differences with gross mint price
    1409 indenture was probably not operative.
Source: A. C. Hotson and N. J. Mayhew (May 2015)

| | | | | | | | | Fine gold | 23ct | 3.5gr |
| | | | | | | | | Crown gold | 22ct | 0gr |

Total deductions =(B)+(C)				Net mint price =(A)–(D)				Gross mint price =(A)/240	Net mint price =(E)/240	Remedy	Fineness	
(D)				(E)				(F)	(G)			
								£ / Tower lb				
Total in d	£	s	d	Total in d	£	s	d	£	£	ct	ct	gr
–	–	–	–	–	–	–	–	10.1351	–	–	23	3.0
282	1	3	6	3,318	13	16	6	15.0000	13.8250	1/8	23	3.5
100	0	8	4	3,056	12	14	8	13.1500	12.7333	1/8	23	3.5
84	0	7	0	3,072	12	16	0	13.1500	12.8000	1/8	23	3.5
140	0	11	8	3,220	13	8	4	14.0000	13.4167	1/8	23	3.5
140	0	11	8	3,220	13	8	4	14.0000	13.4167	1/16	23	3.5
111	0	9	3	3,489	14	10	9	15.0000	14.5375	1/16	23	3.5
80	0	6	8	3,520	14	13	4	15.0000	14.6667	1/16	23	3.5
60	0	5	0	3,540	14	15	0	15.0000	14.7500	1/16	23	3.5
60	0	5	0	3,540	14	15	0	15.0000	14.7500	1/16	23	3.5
80	0	6	8	3,760	15	13	4	16.0000	15.6667	1/8	23	3.5
70	0	5	10	3,930	16	7	6	16.6667	16.3750	1/8	23	3.5
60	0	5	0	3,940	16	8	4	16.6667	16.4167	1/16	23	3.5
70	0	5	10	3,930	16	7	6	16.6667	16.3750	1/8	23	3.5
600	2	10	0	4,400	18	6	8	20.8333	18.3333	1/8	23	3.5
250	1	0	10	5,150	21	9	2	22.5000	21.4583	1/8	23	3.5
174	0	14	6	5,226	21	15	6	22.5000	21.7750	1/8	23	3.5
126	0	10	6	5,274	21	19	6	22.5000	21.9750	1/8	23	3.5
90	0	7	6	5,310	22	2	6	22.5000	22.1250	1/8	23	3.5
30	0	2	6	5,370	22	7	6	22.5000	22.3750	1/8	23	3.5

TABLE A.5 *English Mint gold prices, 1257–1492 (part 2)*

Date from			References
Year	Mnth	Day	
1257	Aug	–	W, I, pp. 78–9; A, p. 163
1343	Dec	4	C, pp. 163–5, 700–1; W, I, p. 9; A, p. 163
1344	Jul	9	C, p. 701; W, I, p. 9
1345	Jun	23	C, p. 701; W, I, p. 9
1346	Jul	28	C, p. 701; W, I, p. 9
1349	Jan	27	C, p. 702; W, I, p. 9
1351	Jun	20	C, p. 703; W, I, p. 9
1355	May	31	C, p. 704; W, I, p. 9
1361	Mar	5	C, p. 705; W, I, p. 9
1394	Oct	9	C, p. 707; W, I, p. 9
1409	–	–	C, p. 708; W, I, p. 34
1413	Apr	14	C, p. 708; W, I, p. 34
1422	Feb	13	C, pp. 708–9; W, I, p. 34
1445	Dec	13	C, p. 710; W, I, p. 34
1464	Aug	13	C, p. 712; W, I, p. 34
1465	Mar	6	C, p. 713; W, I, p. 34
1469	Mar	2	C, p. 713; W, I, p. 34
1471	Mar	6	C, p. 714; W, I, p. 34
1472	Feb	23	C, p. 714; W, I, p. 34
1492	Nov	20	C, p. 718; W, I, p. 34

Source: A. C. Hotson and N. J. Mayhew (May 2015)

			Indentures						Gross mint price =(a)*[(c)/(b)] (A)				Mintage (B)			Seigniorage (C)			
													(c) troy lb 5,760 gr						
Date from			Piece	Weight (b)	Face value (a)				d / troy lb										
Year	Mnth	Day		grs	£	s	d	Total in d	Total in d	£	s	d	s	d	Total in d	£	s	d	Total in d
1509	Aug	6	angel	80.0		6	8	80	5,760	24	0	0	1	10	22	–	–	8	8
1526	Aug	22	angel	80.0		7	4	88	6,336	26	8	0	1	10	22	–	–	8	8
1526	Nov	5	sovereign	240.0	1	2	6	270	6,480	27	0	0	1	10	22	–	–	8	8
1526	Nov	5	crown	57.3		5	0	60	6,030	25	2	6	1	10	22	–	–	8	8
1533	Apr	6	sovereign	240.0	1	2	6	270	6,480	27	0	0	2	1	25	–	–	8	8
1533	Apr	6	crown	57.3		5	0	60	6,030	25	2	6	2	4	28	–	–	8	8
1542	May	16	sovereign	200.0	1	0	0	240	6,912	28	16	0	3	4	40	1	–	8	248
1545	Mar	27	–	–	–	–	–	–	7,200	30	0	0	–	–	–	–	–	–	–
1546	Apr	1	–	–	–	–	–	–	7,200	30	0	0	–	–	–	–	–	–	–
1546	Oct	–	–	–	–	–	–	–	7,200	30	0	0	–	–	–	–	–	–	–
1547	Apr	5	sovereign	192.0	1	0	0	240	7,200	30	0	0	–	–	–	–	–	–	–
1548	Feb	16	sovereign	192.0	1	0	0	240	7,200	30	0	0	–	–	–	–	–	–	–
1549	Jan	24	sovereign	169.4	1	0	0	240	8,160	34	0	0	–	–	–	–	–	–	–
1550	Dec	18	sovereign	240.0	1	4	0	288	6,912	28	16	0	–	–	–	–	–	–	–
1551	Oct	5	sovereign	240.0	1	10	0	360	8,640	36	0	0	–	–	–	–	–	–	–
1551	Oct	5	sovereign	174.6	1	0	0	240	7,920	33	0	0	–	–	–	–	–	–	–
1553	Aug	20	sovereign	240.0	1	10	0	360	8,640	36	0	0	–	–	–	–	–	–	–
1558	Dec	31	sovereign	174.5	1	0	0	240	7,920	33	0	0	–	–	–	–	–	–	–
1560	Nov	8	sovereign	240.0	1	10	0	360	8,640	36	0	0	–	–	–	–	–	–	–
1572	Apr	19	angel	80.0		10	0	120	8,640	36	0	0	1	6	18	–	2	6	30
1578	Sep	15	angel	80.0		10	0	120	8,663	36	1	11	3	5	40.5	–	2	6	30
1583	Jan	30	angel	80.0		10	0	120	8,640	36	0	0	4	9	57	–	1	3	15
1593	Jun	10	sovereign	174.5	1	0	0	240	7,920	33	0	0	5	9	69	–	1	3	15
1601	Jul	29	angel	78.9		10	0	120	8,760	36	10	0	4	9	57	–	5	3	63
1601	Jul	29	sovereign	171.9	1	0	0	240	8,040	33	10	0	5	9	69	–	4	3	51
1604	Nov	11	unite	154.8	1	0	0	240	8,928	37	4	0	6	5	77	1	3	7	283
1605	Jul	16	angel	71.1		10	0	120	9,720	40	10	0	6	0	72	1	4	0	288
1611	Dec	14	angel	–	–	–	–	–	–	–	–	–	–	–	–	–	–	–	–
1611	Dec	14	unite	–	–	–	–	–	–	–	–	–	–	–	–	–	–	–	–

Shading coded notes:
    Derived number in Challis with some fractional differences with gross mint price
Source: A. C. Hotson and N. J. Mayhew (May 2015)

Fine gold 23ct 3.5gr

Crown gold 22ct 0gr

Total deductions =(B)+(C)				Net mint price =(A)–(D)				Gross mint price =(A)/240	Net mint price =(E)/240	Remedy	Fineness	
(D)				(E)				(F)	(G)			
								£ / troy lb				
Total in d	£	s	d	Total in d	£	s	d	£	£	ct	ct	gr
30.0	0	2	6.0	5,730	23	17	6	24.0000	23.8750	1/8ct	23	3.5
30.0	0	2	6.0	6,306	26	5	6	26.4000	26.2750	–	23	3.5
30.0	0	2	6.0	6,450	26	17	6	27.0000	26.8750	–	23	3.5
30.0	0	2	6.0	6,000	25	0	0	25.1250	25.0000	–	22	0
33.0	0	2	9.0	6,447	26	17	3	27.0000	26.8625	1/8ct	23	3.5
36.0	0	3	0.0	5,994	24	19	6	25.1250	24.9750	1/6ct	22	0
288.0	1	4	0.0	6,624	27	12	0	28.8000	27.6000	1/6ct	23	0
540.0	2	5	0.0	6,660	27	15	0	30.0000	27.7500	–	22	0
1,020.0	4	5	0.0	6,180	25	15	0	30.0000	25.7500	–	20	0
960.0	4	0	0.0	6,240	26	0	0	30.0000	26.0000	–	20	0
360.0	1	10	0.0	6,840	28	10	0	30.0000	28.5000	1/4ct	20	0
240.0	1	0	0.0	6,960	29	0	0	30.0000	29.0000	1/4ct	20	0
240.0	1	0	0.0	7,920	33	0	0	34.0000	33.0000	1/6ct	22	0
33.0	0	2	9.0	6,879	28	13	3	28.8000	28.6625	–	23	3.5
33.0	0	2	9.0	8,607	35	17	3	36.0000	35.8625	1/8ct	23	3.5
36.0	0	3	0.0	7,884	32	17	0	33.0000	32.8500	1/6ct	22	0
48.0	0	4	0.0	8,592	35	16	0	36.0000	35.8000	1/6ct	23	3.5
48.0	0	4	0.0	7,872	32	16	0	33.0000	32.8000	1/6ct	22	0
60.0	0	5	0.0	8,580	35	15	0	36.0000	35.7500	1/8ct	23	3.5
48.0	0	4	0.0	8,592	35	16	0	36.0000	35.8000	1/8ct	23	3.5
70.5	0	5	10.5	8,592	35	16	0	36.0938	35.8000	1/8ct	23	3.5
72.0	0	6	0.0	8,568	35	14	0	36.0000	35.7000	1/8ct	23	3.5
84.0	0	7	0.0	7,836	32	13	0	33.0000	32.6500	1/6ct	22	0
120.0	0	10	0.0	8,640	36	0	0	36.5000	36.0000	1/8ct	23	3.5
120.0	0	10	0.0	7,920	33	0	0	33.5000	33.0000	1/6ct	22	0
360.0	1	10	0.0	8,568	35	14	0	37.2000	35.7000	1/6ct	22	0
360.0	1	10	0.0	9,360	39	0	0	40.5000	39.0000	1/8ct	23	3.5
540.0	2	5	0.0	–	–	–	–	–	–	–	23	3.5
540.0	2	5	0.0	–	–	–	–	–	–	–	22	0

TABLE A.6 *English Mint gold prices, 1509–1817 (part 2: 1612 to 1817)*

Indentures

(c) troy lb   5,760 gr

				Face value (a)	Gross mint price =(a)*[(c)/(b)]	Mintage						Seigniorage			
					(A)	(B)						(C)			
Date from			Piece	Weight (b)			d / troy lb									
Year	Mnth	Day		grs	£	s	d	Total in d	Total in d	£	s	d	s	d	Total in d	£	s	d	Total in d
1612	May	18	angel	71.1		11	0	132	10,692	44	11	0	6	0	72	–	2	0	24
1612	May	18	unite	154.9	1	2	0	264	9,816	40	18	0	6	5	77	–	2	0	24
1618	Jan	16	–	–	–	–	–	–	–	–	–	–	6	0	72	–	–	–	–
1618	Jan	16	–	–	–	–	–	–	–	–	–	–	6	5	77	–	–	–	–
1619	Aug	20	–	–	–	–	–	–	–	–	–	–	6	0	72	–	–	–	–
1619	Aug	20	–	–	–	–	–	–	–	–	–	–	6	5	77	–	–	–	–
1623	Jul	17	angel	–		10	0	120	10,680	44	10	0	6	0	72	–	9	0	108
1623	Jul	17	unite	140.5	1	0	0	240	9,840	41	0	0	6	5	77	–	8	7	103
1626	Aug	14	unite	140.5	1	0	0	240	9,840	41	0	0	5	0	60	2	7	0	564
1626	Nov	8	angel	–		10	0	120	10,680	44	10	0	6	0	72	–	9	0	108
1626	Nov	8	unite	140.5	1	0	0	240	9,840	41	0	0	6	5	77	–	8	7	103
1649	Jul	27	angel	–		10	0	120	10,680	44	10	0	6	0	72	–	9	0	108
1649	Jul	27	unite	140.5	1	0	0	240	9,840	41	0	0	6	5	77	–	8	7	103
1660	Jul	20	unite	140.5	1	0	0	240	9,840	41	0	0	6	5	77	–	8	7	103
1661	–	–	unite	140.5	1	1	4	256	10,495	43	14	7	6	5	77	–	8	7	103
1663	Dec	24	guinea	129.4	1	0	0	240	10,680	44	10	0	6	5	77	–	8	7	103
1666	Dec	20	guinea	129.4	1	0	0	240	10,680	44	10	0	0	0	0	–	0	0	0
1670	Oct	8	guinea	129.4	1	0	0	240	10,680	44	10	0	0	0	0	–	0	0	0
1686	Jul	23	guinea	129.4	1	0	0	240	10,680	44	10	0	0	0	0	–	0	0	0
1689	Apr	2	guinea	129.4	1	0	0	240	10,680	44	10	0	0	0	0	–	0	0	0
1700	Dec	23	guinea	129.4	1	0	0	240	10,680	44	10	0	0	0	0	–	0	0	0
1703	Jan	14	guinea	129.4	1	0	0	240	10,680	44	10	0	0	0	0	–	0	0	0
1718	May	6	guinea	129.4	1	1	0	252	11,214	46	14	6	0	0	0	–	0	0	0
1732	Aug	23	guinea	129.4	1	1	0	252	11,214	46	14	6	0	0	0	–	0	0	0
1748	Feb	7	guinea	129.4	1	1	0	252	11,214	46	14	6	0	0	0	–	0	0	0
1770	Nov	28	guinea	129.4	1	1	0	252	11,214	46	14	6	0	0	0	–	0	0	0
1815	Aug	16	guinea	129.4	1	1	0	252	11,214	46	14	6	0	0	0	–	0	0	0
1817	Feb	6	sovereign	123.3	1	0	0	240	11,214	46	14	6	0	0	0	–	0	0	0

Shading coded notes:
    Derived number in Challis with some fractional differences with gross mint price
Source: A. C. Hotson and N. J. Mayhew (May 2015)

										Fine gold 23ct 3.5gr		
										Crown gold 22ct 0gr		

Total deductions =(B)+(C)				Net mint price =(A)−(D)				Gross mint price =(A)/240	Net mint price =(E)/240	Remedy	Fineness	
(D)				(E)				(F)	(G)			
								£ / troy lb				
Total in d	£	s	d	Total in d	£	s	d	£	£	ct	ct	gr
96.0	0	8	0.0	10,596	44	3	0	44.5500	44.1500	1/8ct	23	3.5
101.0	0	8	5.0	9,715	40	9	7	40.9000	40.4792	1/6ct	22	0
378.0	1	11	6.0	–	–	–	–	–	–	–	23	3.5
316.8	1	6	4.8	–	–	–	–	–	–	–	22	0
180.0	0	15	0.0	–	–	–	–	–	–	–	–	–
180.0	0	15	0.0	–	–	–	–	–	–	–	22	0
180.0	0	15	0.0	10,500	43	15	0	44.5000	43.7500	1/8ct	23	3.5
180.0	0	15	0.0	9,660	40	5	0	41.0000	40.2500	1/6ct	22	0
624.0	2	12	0.0	9,216	38	8	0	41.0000	38.4000	–	22	0
180.0	0	15	0.0	10,500	43	15	0	44.5000	43.7500	1/8ct	23	3.5
180.0	0	15	0.0	9,660	40	5	0	41.0000	40.2500	1/6ct	22	0
180.0	0	15	0.0	10,500	43	15	0	44.5000	43.7500	1/8ct	23	3.5
180.0	0	15	0.0	9,660	40	5	0	41.0000	40.2500	1/6ct	22	0
180.0	0	15	0.0	9,660	40	5	0	41.0000	40.2500	1/6ct	22	0
180.0	0	15	0.0	10,315	42	19	7	43.7295	42.9795	1/6ct	22	0
180.0	0	15	0.0	10,500	43	15	0	44.5000	43.7500	1/6ct	22	0
0.0	0	0	0.0	10,680	44	10	0	44.5000	44.5000	1/6ct	22	0
0.0	0	0	0.0	10,680	44	10	0	44.5000	44.5000	1/6ct	22	0
0.0	0	0	0.0	10,680	44	10	0	44.5000	44.5000	1/6ct	22	0
0.0	0	0	0.0	10,680	44	10	0	44.5000	44.5000	1/6ct	22	0
0.0	0	0	0.0	10,680	44	10	0	44.5000	44.5000	1/6ct	22	0
0.0	0	0	0.0	10,680	44	10	0	44.5000	44.5000	1/6ct	22	0
0.0	0	0	0.0	11,214	46	14	6	46.7250	46.7250	1/6ct	22	0
0.0	0	0	0.0	11,214	46	14	6	46.7250	46.7250	1/6ct	22	0
0.0	0	0	0.0	11,214	46	14	6	46.7250	46.7250	1/6ct	22	0
0.0	0	0	0.0	11,214	46	14	6	46.7250	46.7250	1/6ct	22	0
0.0	0	0	0.0	11,214	46	14	6	46.7250	46.7250	1/6ct	22	0
0.0	0	0	0.0	11,214	46	14	6	46.7250	46.7250	1/6ct	22	0

TABLE A.6 *English Mint gold prices, 1509–1817 (part 3)*

Year	Date from		References	Year	Date from		References
	Mnth	Day			Mnth	Day	
1509	Aug	6	C, p. 719; W, I, p. 50	1612	May	18	C, pp. 739–40
1526	Aug	22	C, p. 720; W, I, p. 50	1612	May	18	C, pp. 739–40
1526	Nov	5	C, p. 720; W, I, p. 50	1618	Jan	16	C, p. 740
1526	Nov	5	C, p. 720; W, I, p. 50	1618	Jan	16	C, p. 740
1533	Apr	6	C, p. 720; W, I, p. 50	1619	Aug	20	C, p. 741
1533	Apr	6	C, p. 720; W, I, p. 50	1619	Aug	20	C, p. 741
1542	May	16	C, p. 721; W, I, p. 50	1623	Jul	17	C, p. 741
1545	Mar	27	C, p. 721; W, I, p. 50	1623	Jul	17	C, p. 741
1546	Apr	1	C, p. 721; W, I, p. 50	1626	Aug	14	C, p. 742
1546	Oct	–	C, p. 722; W, I, p. 50; C (1967), pp. 460–3	1626	Nov	8	C, pp. 742–3
1547	Apr	5	C, p. 723; W, I, p. 50	1626	Nov	8	C, pp. 742–3
1548	Feb	16	C, pp. 724–5; W, I, p. 50	1649	Jul	27	C, p. 744
1549	Jan	24	C, pp. 725–6; W, I, p. 50	1649	Jul	27	C, p. 744
1550	Dec	18	C, p. 727; W, I, p. 50	1660	Jul	20	C, pp. 343–51, 745
1551	Oct	5	C, p. 727; W, I, p. 50	1661	–	–	F, p. 97
1551	Oct	5	C, p. 727; W, I, p. 50	1663	Dec	24	C, pp. 338, 343–51, 745; F, 97
1553	Aug	20	C, pp. 728–9; W, I, p. 50	1666	Dec	20	C, pp. 343–51, 745; F, p. 119
1558	Dec	31	C, p. 731; W, I, p. 50	1670	Oct	8	C, pp. 745–6
1560	Nov	8	C, p. 732; W, I, p. 50	1686	Jul	23	C, pp. 747–9

1572	Apr	19	C, p. 733; W, I, p. 50
1578	Sep	15	C, p. 734; W, I, p. 50
1583	Jan	30	C, p. 736; W, I, p. 50
1593	Jun	10	C, p. 736; W, I, p. 50
1601	Jul	29	C, p. 737; W, I, p. 50
1601	Jul	29	C, p. 737; W, I, p. 50
1604	Nov	11	C, p. 738; W, II, pp. 4–5
1605	Jul	16	C, p. 739; W, II, pp. 4–5
1611	Dec	14	C, p. 739
1611	Dec	14	C, p. 739
1689	Apr	2	C, pp. 747–9
1700	Dec	23	C, pp. 747–9
1703	Jan	14	C, pp. 747–9
1718	May	6	C, p. 750
1732	Aug	23	C, pp. 751–7
1748	Feb	7	C, pp. 751–7
1770	Nov	28	C, pp. 751–7
1815	Aug	16	C, pp. 751–7
1817	Feb	6	C, pp. 757–8

Source: A. C. Hotson and N. J. Mayhew (May 2015)

TABLE A.7 *Data Sources: Silver and Gold prices at the English Mint*

A	Allen, Martin, *Mints and Money in Medieval England* (Cambridge: Cambridge University Press, 2012)
C	Challis, Christopher E., ed., *A New History of the Royal Mint* (Cambridge: Cambridge University Press, 1992)
C (1967)	Challis, Christopher E., 'The debasement of the coinage, 1542–1551', *Economic History Review*, 20, no. 3 (December 1967), pp. 441–466
CC	Challis, Christopher E., *The Tudor Coinage* (Manchester: Manchester University Press, 1978)
F	Feavearyear, Albert E., ed. E. Victor Morgan, *The Pound Sterling: A History of English Money* (Oxford: Oxford University Press, 2nd edn, 1963)
G	Gould, John Dennis, *The Great Debasement: Currency and the Economy in Mid–Tudor England* (Oxford: Clarendon Press, 1970)
S	Spufford, Peter, 'Debasement of the Coinage and its Effects on Exchange Rates and the Economy: in England in the 1540s, and in the Burgundian–Habsburg Netherlands in the 1480s' in John H. Munro (ed.), *Money in the Pre–Industrial World: Bullion, Debasements and Coin Substitutes* (London: Pickering & Chatto, 2012)
W	Woodhead, Peter, *Herbert Schneider collection*, part I, *English gold coins and their imitations, 1257–1603*, part II, *English gold coins 1603 to the 20th Century*, in series: Sylloge of coins of the British Isles (London: Spink, 1996)

Source: A. C. Hotson and N. J. Mayhew (May 2015)

Glossary of Technical Terms

acceptance bill accepted by a bank, thus accepting the obligation to honour the bill on its due date

acceptance credit bill drvawn on and accepted by an accepting house or bank on behalf of a customer

acceptance house endorser and rediscounter of bills, precursor of accepting houses

acceptance market the heart of London's money market in the late nineteenth and early twentieth centuries where banks and other investors bought and sold accepted bank bills, in particular fine bank bills and prime bank bills (PBB)

accepting house acceptor of bills and rediscounter of them into the money market; successor to the acceptance houses and latterly a member of the Accepting Houses Committee (AHC)

acceptor drawee of a bill who becomes an acceptor upon signing it, thus accepting the obligation to honour the bill on its due date

accommodation time allowed to settle a debt, used in the eighteenth and nineteenth centuries to describe facilities and advances provided by banks

accommodation bill alternative term for accommodation paper, but using the term 'bill' to refer to paper that is not properly drawn can lead to confusion

accommodation paper documented instruction that is drawn and accepted in the manner of a bill, but does not meet the requirements of being properly drawn; for example, there may be no underlying consignment of goods. Also known as finance paper

advance bank loan to a customer

aliquot denomination of a coin that can be divided into another an integral number of times, e.g. 1 s, 6 d, 1 d, or £1, double crown (10 s), crown (5 s), half-crown (2 s 6 d)

allowances *see* deposit allowances

assignat French note issued by the Revolutionary government

avoirdupois pound (lb) measure of weight for dry goods other than bullion:

    (i) 1 avoirdupois pound (lb) = 16 ounces (oz)
    (ii) 14 lb = 1 stone
    (iii) 8 stone = 1 hundredweight
    (iv) 20 hundredweight = 1 ton = 2,240 lb

see also Tower pound (Tower lb) and troy pound (lbt)

balance sheet total total assets equal to total liabilities including share capital and reserves

bancassurance contraction of 'banque et assurances'; a business model combining banking and insurance, notably endowment mortgages in Britain; *see also* endowment mortgages, neo-clearers

Bank *see* Bank of England

bank bill bill endorsed by a bank, or acceptance house; *see also* fine bank bill, prime bank bill, trade bill

Bank note promissory note issued by the Bank of England; *cf.* banknote

Bank of England Governor and Company of the Bank of England – a plural noun, but the Bank accepted singular usage of the abbreviated form from 1978 (Capie, 2010, page xxi)

Bank rate Bank of England's minimum lending rate, known as Minimum Lending Rate (MLR) from October 1972, superseded by dealing rate bands in August 1981 and repo rates from May 1997. The term 'Bank rate' was restored in August 2006

bankable asset saleable asset that is readily accepted by banks as security for a loan; it should be relatively easy to sell at a reasonably predictable price in the event of a default

bankers' balances (BBs) UK banks' deposits with the Bank of England

Banking School opponents of statutory reserve requirement for the Bank of England's note issuance; *cf.* Currency School

banknote generic term for a promissory note issued by a bank, for example, a Bank of England note, or a country bank note; *see also* convertible banknote; *cf.* Bank note

barter, or countertrade exchange of good A for good B without the intermediation of a currency, or means of exchange

Basel I, II, and III Accords prepared by Basel Committee on Banking Supervision (BCBS); the committee started its work in 1975 and Basel I was adopted in 1988, and implemented in 1992; discussions on Basel II started in 1998 and it was agreed in 2004; Basel III was agreed in 2010–11

Basel Accords recommendations for the regulation of banks prepared by the Basel Committee on Banking Supervision (BCBS) at the Bank for International Settlements (BIS) in Basel; the name of the BCBS initially used the Anglophone 'Basle', but it was changed to 'Basel' in deference to local opinion in 1998 (Goodhart, 2011, p, 7)

base money *see* monetary base

base rate administered reference rate set by each clearing bank after the abolition of the Committee of London Clearing Bankers (CLCB) cartel in 1971; the rates charged on advances were set at a margin above base rate, and the rate paid on deposits was set at a margin below base rate; a clearing bank's base rate would normally be aligned with MLR, but divergences could arise

basis point one-hundredth of 1 per cent, mainly used for expressing differences of interest rates

basis risk risk associated with:

   (i) divergence of the collateral value of a coin from its nominal value
  (ii) divergence of the nominal value of paper money from the value of its asset backing
 (iii) imperfect hedging – the non-convergence of the spot and futures prices of an asset
 (iv) mismatch between the yield on an asset and its funding cost, for example, base-rate related loan and London interbank offered rate (LIBOR) related funding, *aka* spread risk
  (v) market value of a firm's current assets relative to its current liabilities

bearer paper negotiable instrument payable to whoever has possession of it, for example:

  (i) promissory note
 (ii) bill owned by its holder by virtue of endorsement in blank, or simply by delivery without written assignment

Big Bang reforms introduced in the New York securities market in the mid-1970s and then in London in 1986–7

bill   form of negotiable short-term instrument; *see* bank bill, bill of exchange, dollar bill, commercial bill, local authority bill, paper credit, Treasury bill (TB)

bill arbitrage   low risk trade undertaken by corporate treasurers who borrowed using acceptance credits, and placed the funds at a profit in the interbank market; *see also* round tripping

bill broker   agent for discounting bills, otherwise known as a discount broker

bill discounting   *see* discounting

bill leak   bills accepted by banks and sold to non-banks; these bills did not count towards £M3, but were included in Private Sector Liquidity 1 (PSL 1)

bill mountain   accumulation of bills in the Banking Department of the Bank resulting from over-funding and the need to accommodate consequential money market shortages; *see also* over-funding

bill of exchange   *see* commercial bill; terms used interchangeably

bill of lading   document of title for a consignment of goods, signed by shipper upon receipt of goods and presented by consignee at their destination; bills of lading were often held by banks providing acceptances, and they could be assigned by endorsement

bill on London   bill accepted or endorsed by an institution based in London

bond   debt instrument normally with a maturity of more than one or two years with periodic interest payments and repayment of principal at maturity

book   abbreviation for accounts book; used as an abbreviation for a bank's lending book, or a jobber's holdings of securities

brassage   fees covering mint masters' time and expenses; from the French, *droit de brassage*, right to mint coins; *cf.* mintage, seigniorage (Munro, 2012, pp. 3–4)

bridge, or bridging finance   temporary loan in anticipation of long-term finance, or permanent capital raising

Britannia silver   11 ozt 10 dwt of silver per 1 lbt of metal, a millesimal fineness of 958; *see also* sterling silver

British government stock (BGS)   long-term security issued by the British government and listed on the London Stock Exchange; see *also* Consols, gilts, War Loan

broker   intermediary acting as agent on behalf of a principal; *see also* stockbroker; *cf.* dealer

broker–dealer   dual capacity firm combining functions of stockbroker and stock jobber

builder certificate of deposit (CD)   short-term negotiable instrument issued by a building society

Building Societies Association (BSA)   trade body of British building societies; *cf.* BSC

Building Societies Commission (BSC)   statutory body that took over responsibility for regulating building societies from the Registrar of Friendly Societies (RFS) in 1986; BSC incorporated into Financial Services Authority (FSA) in 2001; *cf.* BSA

building society   friendly society offering residential mortgages to its members; abbreviated to 'society' when the context is clear; known as 'builders' in the money market, e.g. builder CDs; *see also* friendly societies

bullion   precious metal, notably gold and silver, available for minting; bullion could be in bars, but the Bank often classified foreign specie available for minting as bullion

bushel   measure of weight for dry goods, notably the Winchester bushel:

  (i) 2 gallons = 1 peck, 4 pecks = 1 bushel, 8 bushels = 1 quarter
  (ii) equivalent to 35.2 litres

The imperial bushel introduced in 1824 was slightly larger

call down or cry down a coin   lower the denomination of a coin in circulation, usually before a recoinage; *cf.* cry up or call up a coin, raising the coin

call money   money available without notice; *see also* callable deposit, money at call (MAC), sight deposit

callable deposit   immediately withdrawable deposit; *see also* call money, money at call (MAC), sight deposit

cap   trading mechanism setting a maximum price; *cf.* floor or collar

capital adequacy   capital relative to risk weighted assets and other exposures; *see also* leverage ratio

capital and reserves   issued share capital and accumulated reserves arising from retained earnings

carat   metallic fineness expressed in parts of 24; a carat is subdivided into 4 grains; *see also* fine gold, Crown or standard gold, Britannia and sterling silver

cash   final settlement asset – historically, current coins, joined by Bank of England banknotes in the eighteenth century; also, bankers' balances at the Bank (BBs) – the banks' final settlement asset from the 1850s; *see also* Mo, nMo, bMo

cash ratio, or cash-deposit ratio   a commonly cited balance sheet ratio for banks, comprising till money and BBs as a proportion of deposit balances; formalised at 8 per cent for the clearers after the Second World War and replaced by the 30 per cent liquidity ratio in 1951, reduced to 28 per cent in 1963; 1 ½ per cent cash ratio – ratio of bankers' balances (BBs) to eligible liabilities (ELs) – was introduced in 1981 after the reserve asset ratio (RAR) was abolished

certificate of deposit (CD)   negotiable instrument issued by a bank or building society with an original maturity of up to two years

chattel   personal property that is moveable, such as furniture and cattle, or an interest in land that is less than freehold, such as a lease

cheque   order to a bank to pay a specified sum from the drawer's current account; US: check; *see also* draft

clausing   statement on the face of a bill giving details of the consignment of goods in respect of which the bill is drawn

clearer, clearing bank   clearing banks in London were originally members of the London Bankers' Clearing House (LBCH), and latterly members of the Committee of London Clearing Bankers (CLCB), subsequently the Committee of London and Scottish Bankers (CLSB) (Sayers, 1976, p. 552)

clearing   the process of calculating amounts due to and from each bank, confirming these amounts, and checking that funds are available; *cf.* settlement (B. Norman et al., June 2011, p. 5, fn. 1)

clearing bank authors   editors and authors of a genre of books on banking practice in London during the nineteenth and twentieth centuries; those cited in this study include J. W. Gilbart, G. Rae, A. S. Mitchie, E. Sykes and W. Leaf

clearing house   establishment allowing member banks to exchange cheques, drafts and bills among themselves and settle the net amounts due in cash

coin   stamped metal piece used as currency; *see* current coin and specie

collar   *see* floor

collateral   asset pledged as security for the repayment of a debt, to be forfeited in the event of a default; *see also* quasi-collateralisation

collateral value   market value of pledged or underlying asset; *see also* intrinsic value

commercial bill   an unconditional order in writing, prepared and signed by a drawer, addressed to a drawee; upon signing, the drawee becomes the acceptor of the bill; the acceptor agrees to pay a sum of money for a specified consignment of goods to a payee, or to the order of the payee, at a fixed or determinable date.

Competition and Credit Control (CCC)   proposals published by the Bank of England in May 1971

connected lending   loans to parties related to a bank, e.g. family or business associates, or shareholders of the bank

Consols   contraction of consolidated annuities, undated British government stock first issued in the eighteenth century, the issuer having an option to repay at par; *see also* British government stock (BGS), gilts, War Loan

contingent capital   various forms:

  (i) a contingent claim on shareholders to subscribe for uncalled shares, when required to do so by the bank's directors, up to a pro rata maximum of their existing shareholding
  (ii) *see* reserve liability
  (iii) debt that converts into equity when certain triggers are met
  (iv) *see* hybrid capital

conversion   term used in Building Societies Act 1986 to refer to the demutualisation of a building society; the transfer of its engagements, i.e. its business, to a proprietary company with shareholding members; *see also* demutualisation

convertibility   right to exchange a credit instrument for another asset, for example, a banknote for current coin at par; sometimes used confusingly to refer to the exchangeability of an instrument at any market price

convertible banknote   note issued by a bank which is redeemable at par in current coins; *see also* banknote

conveyancer   agent for changing the ownership of property from one party to another

corset   colloquial name for the Supplementary Special Deposits (SSD) scheme coined by Gilbert Wood at the Bank (Capie, 2010, p. 659, fn. 61)

council houses   British social housing let by local authorities

counterparts of money   the assets and non-monetary liabilities that make up the rest of the balance sheet of monetary institutions; a change in the banking sector's monetary liabilities equals the change in its assets, less the change in its non-monetary liabilities

counterparty limits   preset maxima set by lenders on their exposures to individual names, e.g. a limit on a lender's holding of bills accepted by a particular accepting house, or bank

countertrade   cross border trade without currency; *see* barter

country banks   banks based outside London; *also* district banks

credit   the term is used variously to describe:

(i)   entry by a bank to a customer's account recording a sum received; *cf.* debit
(ii)   loan instrument, or agreement to defer settlement of a debt
(iii)   abbreviation for paper credit

Crown gold   Crown or standard gold with a fineness of 22 carats (c), a millesimal fineness of 916

crying up or calling up a coin   *see* raising the coin; *cf.* call down a coin

currency   multiple usage:

(i)   accepted means of payment, e.g. notes and coin; *see also* foreign currency (fc)
(ii)   term to maturity of a bill, advance, or other asset

Currency School   proponents of statutory control of Bank of England's issuance of notes requiring automatic reserve backing; proposals reflected in the 1844 Act; *cf.* Banking School

current or drawing account   bank account against which cheques can be drawn for immediate payment; *US usage*: demand deposit or checking account; *see also* sight deposit

current assets   assets realisable within a year, for example, accounts receivable, stocks, work in progress (WIP); *cf.* fixed assets

current coin   minted coins of the realm providing legal tender for settling debts; *see also* specie

current liabilities   obligations payable within a year, for example, accounts payable, and short-term funding

dealer   intermediary acting as principal, US usage adopted in the UK as part of Stock Exchange reforms of 1986; *see also* stock jobber, *cf.* broker

debasement   used variously to describe:

  (i)   reduced fineness of coins of given nominal value, sometimes used to refer to reduced weight as well; *cf.* devaluation, raising the coin, or
  (ii) the loss of value (i.e. purchasing power) of fiat currencies; *see also* inflation

debenture   document executed in favour of a creditor including:

  (i)   a covenant to make a schedule of payments, e.g. on a bond
  (ii)   a grant of security over certain assets by way of fixed and floating charges
  (iii) creditor rights to appoint an administrator to run the company and realise assets in the event of default

US usage: a debenture bond is an unsecured debt instrument

debit   entry by a bank to a customer's account recording a sum paid out; *cf.* credit

default   failure to fulfil an obligation, in particular the terms of a loan agreement

deflation   *see* inflation

Δ   delta, operand denoting change of a variable, e.g. Δ DD

demand deposit or checking account   *US usage*: deposit available without notice, account against which checks can be drawn; *see also* sight deposit, current account

demutualisation   transfer of the business of a mutual society to a proprietary company with shareholding members; *see also* conversion

demurrage   depending on context:

  (i)   costs associated with the storage of bullion
  (ii) charge incurred for the delayed loading or unloading of a ship

denomination   alternative term for the face value of a coin, banknote or stamp; *see also* face value, nominal value, tender value

deposit   until the 1970s, bank accounts requiring notice of withdrawal were called deposit accounts, for example, seven-day deposit accounts; in contrast, cheques could be drawn against current accounts and funds withdrawn without notice; US usage distinguishes between demand deposits and time deposits; the Bank refers to sight deposits and term deposits; *cf.* share account, wholesale deposit

deposit allowances   nineteenth-century term for interest rate paid on seven-day deposits and money at call (MAC); set at a margin below Bank rate; *see also* deposit rate

deposit bank   banks, including clearers, that relied on deposits for funding, in contrast to accepting houses that relied on rediscounting; discount houses were funded with money at call (MAC), but would not normally be described as deposit banks

deposit rate   term for interest rate paid on seven-day and other term deposits; set at a margin below Bank rate; *see also* deposit allowance

devaluation   the value of a currency may be reduced in a variety of ways:

   (i) reducing the weight of coins of given nominal value

   (ii) the same result can be achieved by raising the denomination of coins of given weight; *see also* raising the coin

   (iii) the term is sometimes used to refer to coins of reduced fineness as well; *see also* debasement

   (iv) reduced value of paper currency relative to others

discount broker   agent for discounting bills, otherwise known as a bill broker; *see also* money broker

discount house   bill intermediary acting as principal; latterly a member of the London Discount Market Association (LDMA)

Discount Office   part of Bank of England, absorbed into Chief Cashier's Office in 1974 (Reid, 1982, p. 195)

discount rate   annualised yield paid on a discounted bill

discounting   act of buying or selling a bill before its maturity; *see also* commercial bill

disintermediation   the redirection of financial flows away from their usual intermediaries; *see also* reintermediation

dollar bill   potentially confusing term for legal tender notes issued by the US Treasury since 1862

doubloon   Spanish gold coin

draft   written order to pay a specified sum; *see also* bill of exchange, cheque

drawee   person to whom bill is addressed by a drawer

drawer   person who issues and signs a written instruction to pay a specified sum of money

ducat   originally a Venetian gold coin; subsequently a similar one was minted by the Dutch

duration   average life of a security (Bierwag, 1987, pp. 57–8); Hicks used the term 'average period' (Hicks, 1946, p. 186); a measure of a bond's interest rate sensitivity based on the (present-value weighted) average term of its interest and principal repayments; *cf.* maturity

duration mismatch or duration gap   Various usages;

   (i)   balance sheet exposure to interest rate changes

   (ii) difference between the duration of an institution's assets and its liabilities; *cf.* maturity mismatch

eligible liabilities (ELs)   sterling resources available to a bank:

   (i)   sterling deposits, with an original maturity of up to two years, from UK and overseas non-bank residents; plus

   (ii) sterling interbank deposits of any term, from the UK banking sector, net of claims; plus

  (iii) issued sterling CDs of any term, net of sterling CD holdings; plus

  (iv) banks' net deposit liabilities in sterling to its overseas offices; plus

   (v) banks' net liability in currencies other than sterling

encumbered assets   mortgage or other claim on property or other assets; *see also* negative pledge

endorsee   person to whom a bill or cheque is assigned by endorsement; *also* Latinate indorsee

endorser   payee or subsequent owner who assigns a bill or cheque by signing it on the back in favour of an endorsee, or to bearer; *also* Latinate indorser

endowment mortgage   interest only mortgage with a single repayment of principal at maturity; the borrower also pays regular premiums to an endowment policy designed to repay the principal outstanding at the end of the mortgage term, or on the borrower's death, if earlier; *see also* endowment policy

endowment policy   life insurance policy that pays an accumulated sum at maturity, or a specified sum on the insured's death, if earlier; premiums can either be paid as a single sum, or more usually by regular premiums over the life of the policy

entailed estate   property held in a trust restricting its sale or inheritance to certain persons, often requiring that it pass to succeeding generations of a family

equity of redemption   mortgagor's right to repay the loan and regain title to the property at any time subject to a notice period

Euromarket   starting in the late 1950s, lending funded with non-UK resident deposits, mostly in US dollars, placed with London-based banks

exchange controls   restrictions on residents of a particular jurisdiction from holding foreign currencies, foreign securities, and offshore bank accounts

Exchequer bill   debt instrument issued by the Exchequer, a precursor to the Treasury bill (TB)

face value   prescribed value of a coin, banknote or stamp, which may be inscribed on its face; *see also* denomination, nominal value, tender value

facility   abbreviation of loan facility, an agreement allowing a bank customer to draw down a loan which may be of a fixed, or varying amount up to a limit; *see* overdraft

factor   provider of commodity finance, for example, a corn factor; *see also* invoice discounter

Fed   abbreviation for the Federal Reserve; used variously to describe the market operations of the Federal Reserve Bank (FRB) of New York, the decisions of the Federal Open Market Committee (FOMC), and the Federal Reserve Board

finance house   lending institution without the status of being a bank, many of which joined the Finance Houses Association (FHA); the Bank used the term in preference to secondary bank, or fringe bank

finance paper, or finance bill   interchangeable terms for accommodation paper

financial repression   credit policies and capital controls designed to reduce the cost of borrowing for governments and other favoured parties at the expense of savers

fine bank bill   bill drawn on and accepted by a London bank, or accepting house of undoubted standing, but not endorsed by a discount house (Gillett Brothers, 1964, p. 19); *see also* bank bill, prime bank bill, trade bill

fine gold   gold with a fineness of 23 c 3.5 gr, a millesimal fineness of 995

fineness   proportion of pure metal; *see* fine and standard gold; sterling and Britannia silver

first mortgage   mortgage secured on property with no prior claimant to the security; *see also* second mortgage

fixed assets   assets purchased for long-term use, such as land, buildings and equipment; *cf.* current assets

fixed capital   *see* permanent capital

floor or collar   trading mechanism setting a minimum price

force majeure   unforeseeable circumstance that prevents the fulfilment of a contract

foreclosure   taking possession of a mortgaged property when the mortgagor defaults on the loan

foreign bill   commercial bill with either a drawer, or a payee, or both based outside Britain; it can still be a bill on London if it is accepted in London

foreign currency (fc)   medium of exchange issued by another jurisdiction

freehold   permanent right to tenure of an estate in land; historically, all land belonged to the Crown

friendly societies   mutual institutions owned by customers qualifying as members; includes building societies and industrial benevolent insurance societies; *see also* Registrar of Friendly Societies (RFS)

fringe bank   *see* finance house

geared investment   *see* leveraged investment

gilts   contraction of 'gilt-edged stocks', a vernacular term for British government stock (BGS); *see also* BGS, Consols, War Loan

gold points   rates of foreign exchange likely to cause movements of gold among countries adhering to the gold standard

grain   24 gr = 1 troy dwt, 20 dwt = 1 ozt, 12 ozt = 1 troy pound (lbt); 22 ½ gr = 1 Tower dwt

guinea   English coin minted from 1663 until 1799; 129.4 grains of standard fineness, 22 carat (c), gold mined in West Africa

haircut   various usages:

  (i) debt reduction, for example, debt forgiveness in a restructuring
  (ii) deduction applied to the value of collateral when determining the amount required to secure a loan, for example, a loan structured as a repo; *cf.* margin requirement

high-powered money   *see* monetary base

High Street banks   usually a reference to the big five (and subsequently the big four) London clearing banks with branches in High Streets across the country; *see also* clearer

hire purchase (HP)   agreement providing for the rental of consumer goods or business machinery owned by a finance company; the user would normally have a contractual right to take ownership of the asset once all payments have been made; *US usage*: rent to own; *see also* lease

house   potentially confusing usage:

    (i) abbreviation for a discount house, issuing house, accepting house, or even finance house, depending on the context

   (ii) issuing and accepting houses were component parts of merchant banks and these were also referred to as houses

hybrid capital   various forms:

    (i) subordinated bank debt

   (ii) bank debt convertible into equity if certain triggers are met; *see also* contingent capital

income multiple   ratio of mortgage debt to gross income; *see also* loan-to-value (LTV) ratio

indenture   *see* mint indenture

inflation, deflation   rate of change of prices; lower inflation means a decline in the rate of increase of prices, but a continued rise in the price level; *see also* debasement

industrial benevolent insurance societies   *see* friendly societies

inland bill   commercial bill with a drawer and payer based in Britain; *see also* bill, acceptance credit

instrument   negotiable paper, referred to as a credit or debt instrument, being both an asset of a lender and a liability of a borrower; *see also* paper credit

insurers   abbreviation for insurance companies, including life assurance offices; general insurers providing property, casualty and other types of non-life liability cover; and composite insurers providing both life and non-life cover

interest-bearing eligible liabilities (IBELS)   eligible liabilities (ELs) excluding non-interest-bearing deposits; *see also* ELs

intrinsic value   market value of a coin's metal; *see also* collateral value

invoice discounter   provider of finance for accounts receivable, with or without recourse to the creditor in the event of default by the debtor; *see also* factor

issued shares or capital   paid-up and uncalled shares issued by a joint-stock company; *see* paid-up shares or capital

jobber   abbreviation of stock jobber; *see also* stock jobber, dealer

joint-stock bank   banking company whose stock is jointly owned by its shareholders

lease contractual agreement allowing a lessee to use a tangible or intangible asset for a period, after which the asset reverts to its owner, the lessor, or it can be acquired by the lessee; the lessee pays rent to the lessor; *see also* HP agreement

legal tender coins or banknotes that creditors are required to accept at their face/nominal value in payment of a debt

lessee the user of an asset in a leasing transaction; *see also* lease

lessor the owner of an asset in a leasing transaction; *see also* lease

letter of credit documentary evidence of an acceptance credit, or other type of loan, or guarantee

leverage ratio multiple of total assets (or deposits) to issued (paid-up and uncalled) share capital and accumulated reserves; *see also* capital adequacy

leveraged (or geared) investment assets partly financed with borrowing, increasing investors' risk and expected return

liability management competitive bidding on rate for deposits, allowing a bank to manage its funding, and potentially enabling it to pursue a more aggressive lending programme

lien right to take possession of another person's property until a debt is discharged

liquid reserves *see* reserves, part (i)

liquidity ratio formalised in 1951; initially requiring the clearing banks to hold at least 30 per cent of their deposits in liquid assets, reduced to 28 per cent in 1963; liquid assets were defined as money at call (MAC), eligible paper, bankers' balances (BB) and till money

local authority bill paper issued by a local authority, mostly in the 1930s

local authority loan, or deposit term deposit taken by a local authority

Louis d'Or French gold coin; *see also* pistole

make-up day designated days for the preparation of financial statements, including balance sheets, for internal use or for public reports; for example, half-yearly reports on 30th June and 31st December; the main banks published monthly returns from 1891; all banks were required to submit mid-monthly reports to the Bank from 1971; make-up day was on the third Wednesday of the month, and the second Wednesday in December

macro-prudential regulation selective credit controls, for example, quantitative limits on mortgage lending above a specified loan-to-value (LTV) ratio

margin   variously defined as:

(i) percentage point difference between a lending rate and its funding rate; *see also* spread

(ii) total interest received, less total interest paid – net interest income (NII) – plus, in some cases, other income received, as a proportion of total assets

margin requirement   contractual term requiring that the market value of pledged assets be maintained at a specified margin above the quantum of funds borrowed; *cf.* haircut

match fund   loan or other asset funded with a liability having the same term to maturity

maturity   abbreviation of term to maturity. Term to repayment of principal; see also currency, tenor, usance; *cf.* duration

maturity mismatch   a balance sheet that typically comprised assets with a longer term to maturity than its liabilities, although the mismatch could be the other way; *see also* mismatch risk, maturity transformation

maturity, original or residual   original, or residual term until repayment is due; *cf.* duration

maturity transformation   means the same as maturity mismatch but sounds positive; *see also* maturity mismatch

merchant bank   adviser to sovereign and corporate issuers of securities, underwriter of securities and acceptor of bills; the leading houses were members of the Accepting Houses Committee (AHC) and Issuing Houses Committee (IHC)

metallist coins   specie or pieces exchanged at their intrinsic, or collateral value; also known as valorist coins (D. Fox, 2013, p. 140); *cf.* nominalist coins

millesimal   parts per thousand

Mint   Royal English Mint, London Mint

mint condition coin   unworn coin of similar condition to one delivered from the Mint

mint indenture   contract between the Crown and moneyers working at the Mint, specifying the terms on which current coins should be minted: nominal value, weight, fineness, brassage (mint masters' fees) and seigniorage

mint price   nominal value of coins offered by the Mint against delivery of bullion of unit weight and fineness; terms set by the Mint indenture

mint ratio   ratio of mint prices of gold and silver

mintage   various usages:

(i) deductions stipulated in the Mint indenture to cover brassage (mint masters' fees) and seigniorage

(ii) also used more generally to mean the minting of coins, or the number of pieces minted

mismatch risk   difference between the value of an asset and its funding, for example, a currency or commodity holding financed with sterling debt; *see also* maturity mismatch, maturity transformation

moidore   Portuguese gold coin

monetary aggregates   monetary liabilities of banks; *see* definitions of money, nM0, bM0, M1, M2, £M3, M3, M4, PSL 1, PSL 2 (in List of Abbreviations)

monetary base   *aka* high-powered money, base money; final settlement asset of the monetary system, comprising currency (notes and coin) and banks' cash reserves (bankers' balances and till money); *see* nM0, bM0.

money brokers   modern discount brokers, acting as agents in the inter-bank and wholesale markets, facilitating trades in foreign exchange and money market instruments; *cf.* Stock Exchange money brokers (SEMBs)

money-center banks   New York clearing banks

money market instruments   negotiable instruments traded on London's money market with same-day settlement, including bills of exchange, Treasury bills (TBs), and certificates of deposit (CDs)

moral hazard   lack of incentive to guard against risk when a party is protected against its consequences, for example, by insurance

mortgage   transfer of interest in real property to a lender, on condition the interest will be returned to the owner when the terms of the mortgage have been satisfied; *see also* endowment mortgage, first and second mortgage

mortgage loan   loan secured by a mortgage on real property

mortgagee   lender in a mortgage transaction; *see also* mortgage

mortgagor   borrower in a mortgage transaction; *see also* mortgage

mutual   building society or insurance company owned by its saving and/or borrowing members, and sharing some or all of its profits among them

negative pledge   agreement to leave certain assets unencumbered, and not to pledge them to other parties; *see also* unencumbered assets

neo-clearers successors to the clearing banks after the abolition of the CLCB in 1985, and the absorption of the CLSB in the British Bankers' Association (BBA) in 1991; the neo-clearers adopted bancassurance strategies centred on endowment mortgages; *see also* bancassurance, endowment mortgage

net assets accounting value of total assets less liabilities other than share capital and reserves

net current assets assets realisable within a year minus liabilities repayable within a year; *see also* current assets, current liabilities, working capital

nominal value value of a coin specified in the Mint's indenture; a coin's nominal value would normally be the same as its face value/proclaimed value; *see also* denomination, face value, Mint indenture, tender value

nominalist coins coins exchanged by tale at their nominal, or face value; *cf.* metallist coins

note abbreviation of promissory note; *see also* paper credit

numéraire commodity of given weight and fineness with an ascribed unit value, providing a measure of value for other goods

obligator party committed to make a payment

option a right, but not an obligation, to purchase an asset at an agreed exercise price on date(s) in the future

option, in the money option with an exercise price below the current market price of the asset

overdraft current account with a borrowing facility offering variable drawdown to a pre-agreed limit

over-funding selling more public sector debt to the non-bank private sector than the size of the PSBR; *see also* bill mountain

over-the-counter (OTC) trading direct exchanges between institutions rather than trading through a centralised exchange; *cf.* stock exchange

overtrading engaging in more business than can be safely financed, for example, financing fixed assets with short-term borrowing

paid-up shares or capital shares issued by joint-stock banks in the late nineteenth century could be partly paid-up and partly uncalled, i.e. partly paid; in many cases, banks' articles gave directors certain rights to call on shareholders to subscribe for issued but uncalled shares at their nominal value

paper or paper credit negotiable short-term instrument encompassing bills of exchange of all types, Treasury bills (TBs), certificates of deposit (CDs), and promissory notes; *see also* money market instruments

par value nominal or face value of a coin or security, as distinct from its market value

pari passu ranking of loans or creditors claims that rank equally in bankruptcy proceedings; *cf.* subordinated lender, senior creditor

passable guinea following the order in -council of 12 April 1776, a guinea piece was deemed passable at 21 s if it were no more or less than 1 ½ grains of its prescribed weight of 129.4 grains (0.26958 ozt) of standard fineness gold

payee party with a contractual right to receive a payment

payer party with a contractual obligation to make a payment

pension funds institutional investors sponsored by the nationalised industries and private companies to manage funds to pay employees' pensions on their retirement

permanent or fixed capital long-term finance including share capital, accumulated reserves arising from retained earnings, and debenture stocks

piece coin of specified value; from the French, *une pièce de monnaie*, a coin; *see also* pillar piece of eight

pillar piece of eight silver coin, also known as a Spanish dollar, equivalent to eight reals

pistole French name for a Spanish gold coin, the double escudo; the term was also used for other gold coins of about the same value, for example, the Louis d'Or

pledged asset asset given as security against the fulfilment of a loan or other contract

policy reaction function adjustment of government policy instruments in response to economic developments, for example, Bank rate changes in response to deviations of inflation from an inflation target

pound sterling unit of account: £ 1 = 20 s = 240 d, where £ = libra, lira, livre, pound sterling; s = soldus, sol, shilling; d = denier, old penny

pound weight *see* avoirdupois pound, Tower pound and troy pound; *see also* bushel

proclaimed value value of coin specified by royal proclamation and later by statute; *see also* face value, tender value

prime bank bill (PBB) two-name paper accepted by an accepting house and endorsed by a discount house; *see also* fine bank bill

prime brokerage services offered by investment banks and securities firms to hedge funds and others allowing them to borrow securities to cover short positions, and finance long positions using repos

promissory note written promise to pay a sum of money in a specified period for value received

public sector borrowing requirement (PSBR) central and local government disbursements less tax receipts (primary deficit), plus redemptions of public sector debt

qualitative controls controls prioritising certain types of lending provided by the clearers; *see also* quantitative controls

quantitative controls credit controls limiting the rate of growth of the clearers' lending during the 1960s; *see also* qualitative controls

quasi-collateralisation claims or loans supported by assets without being legally secured on them; *see also* clausing, negative pledge

quick liabilities short-term claims with limited or no required notice of withdrawal, e.g. deposits and banknotes

quick ratio reserves as a proportion of quick liabilities; *see also* quick liabilities, reserve ratio

raising or crying up the coin raising the denomination of current coins; *cf.* call down or cry down

real bills properly drawn bills rather than accommodation paper

real estate previously US usage with the same meaning as real property, but now used internationally

real property land and immovable property attached to land; *cf.* chattels; see also real estate

recoinage periodic renewal of the coinage, requiring an exchange of old coins for newly minted ones, after which the old coins would cease to be current

rediscount resale of a bill by a bank, accepting house, or discount house; *see also* accepting house

Regulation Q Regulation Q of the Glass-Steagall Act 1933 put limits on the payment of interest on deposits; it was phased out by March 1986 (Gilbert, 1986)

reintermediation the redirection of financial flows back to their customary intermediaries; *see also* disintermediation

repo sale and repurchase agreement

reserves refers to:

> (i) assets held by banks to settle payments, or liquid assets that can easily be converted to a settlement asset, e.g. bankers' balances (BBs)

(ii) accumulated retained profits, part of shareholders' funds – a liability

reserve assets defined types of liquid asset counted in the numerator of the reserve asset ratio (RAR) comprising:

(i) bankers' balances (BBs) – not Special Deposits (SDs), or Supplementary Special Deposits (SSDs);
(ii) British government and Northern Ireland TBs;
(iii) secured money at call (MAC) with LDMA institutions;
(iv) British government stocks (BGS) with a residual maturity of less than one year;
(v) local authority bills eligible for rediscount at the Bank;
(vi) commercial bills eligible for rediscount at the Bank, i.e. eligible bank bills, up to a maximum of 2 per cent of eligible liabilities (ELs)

reserve asset ratio (RAR) banks were required to hold at least 12 ½ per cent of their ELs in reserve assets from September 1971, and finance houses were required to hold 10 per cent; the RAR for banks was reduced to 10 per cent in January 1981, temporarily reduced to 8 per cent for most of March and April 1981, and abolished in August 1981

reserve liability contingent claim on shareholders to subscribe for uncalled shares in the event of insolvency (rather than at the directors' discretion); *see also* contingent capital

reserve ratio reserves as a proportion of total assets, or deposits; *see also* quick ratio, reserve asset ratio (RAR)

retail deposit current accounts and savings accounts with relatively small balances that offer either no interest or an administered deposit rate related to a bank's base rate; *cf.* wholesale deposit

round tripping a form of arbitrage in which corporate treasurers borrowed at a base-rate related rate and on-lent the funds at a profit in the interbank market, also known as the merry-go-round; *see also* bill arbitrage

secondary bank *see* finance house

second mortgage loan with claim on property that is ranked after that of a first mortgage

securities certificate attesting credit, the ownership of shares and bonds

seigniorage Crown's profit from minting; *cf.* mintage, brassage

senior creditor   party with claim that ranks above other creditors in the event of a liquidation; *cf.* pari passu creditor, subordinated creditor

settlement   transfer of funds extinguishing an obligation; *cf.* clearing

shadow bank   institution undertaking maturity transformation in the manner of a bank, but not regulated like one; the term is said to have been first used by Paul McCulley of Pimco at Jackson Hole in 2007; it has become an overused term, referring loosely to less regulated financial intermediaries.

share account   funds placed with a building society conferring membership rights; share account holders rank below other creditors of the society, including depositors; *cf.* deposit

shutter   modern euphemism for closing or liquidating a fund; *cf.* shuttings

shuttings   closure of government stock transfer books while preparing dividend warrants on Consols; *cf.* shutter

sight, payment on   immediate payment, or on presentation of a bill or other demand for payment

sight deposit   account with funds available for use without notice; *US usage*: demand deposit; see also money at call (MAC)

societies   abbreviation of building societies, or friendly societies; *see also* building societies, friendly societies

sovereign   British coin minted from 1817 until 1919 with a face value of one pound sterling, comprising 123.27447 grains of standard gold

spot   transaction for immediate delivery and cash settlement, i.e. on the spot

spread   basis point (bp) difference between (running) yield on specified assets, and their cost of funding, as a proportion of total assets; *see also* margin

Special Deposits (SD)   introduced in 1958 and first called in 1960; a percentage of gross advances to be held on deposit with the Bank and not counting towards the liquidity ratio

specie   used broadly to describe all coins minted with precious metal, but often used to refer to foreign specie circulating within the country as distinct from current coins of the realm

speculation   investment in shares or property in the hope of gain, but with the risk of loss

spread risk   possibility of a reduced spread between loan rates and their funding cost; *see also* basis risk

Square Mile informal name for the City of London, and a metonym for its financial services sector (Chambers, 2014, p. 255)

standard (or Crown) gold gold of 22 carats and millesimal fineness of 916; *see* Crown gold

sterling abbreviation of pound sterling; *see* pound sterling; *cf.* sterling silver

sterling silver standard of fineness for silver, 11 ozt 2 dwt of fine silver per 1 lbt of metal including alloy, equivalent to 5,328 gr per 5,760 gr of metal, a millesimal fineness of 925; *see also* Britannia silver, pound sterling, carat

stockbroker intermediary acting as agent for buying and selling securities

stock exchange formal market for trading securities, e.g. London Stock Exchange; *cf.* over-the-counter (OTC) trading

Stock Exchange money broker (SEMB) arranged loans from the clearing banks to stock jobbers, secured against the latter's securities; cf. money brokers

stock jobber market maker in securities acting as principal; *see also* dealer

stock and trade finance short-term loans to finance stocks, i.e. inventories, and short-term trading debts; *see also* working capital finance

stocks used variously to mean:

  (i) goods awaiting manufacture or sale, otherwise known as inventories (*US usage*)
 (ii) certificates of share capital issued by a company called stocks or shares
(iii) British government stocks (BGS) and long-term debt issued by companies called gilt-edged stocks and loan stocks, respectively

subordinated creditor, or lender party with claims that ranks below those of others in the event of a liquidation; *cf.* pari passu creditor, senior creditor

subprime classification of borrowers with a poor or limited credit history

Supplementary Special Deposit (SSD) scheme mechanism, colloquially known as the corset, for controlling the balance sheet growth of the banks; it determined the quantity of non-interest-bearing Supplementary Special Deposits (nib SSDs) each bank had to place at the Bank depending on the rate of growth of its interest-bearing eligible liabilities (IBELs) above a preset threshold

swap an exchange of liabilities between two borrowers, for example, a fixed interest rate loan for a variable rate loan, or an exchange of currency liabilities

syndicated loans, or credits loans arranged by lead bank(s) and distributed to a wider group of banks

tale tendering of coins by number, rather than by weight, for the settlement of debts; *see also* nominalist coins

tender value exchange value of a coin for settling a debt; it could be prescribed by royal proclamation, or set by statute, or it could be allowed to vary depending on the intrinsic value of the coin; *see also* denomination, face value, legal tender, nominal value

tenor term to payment of a bill; *see also* currency, maturity, usance

term yield curve fitted curve of the yield on money market instruments against their residual term to maturity (usually up to one or two years); *see also* yield curve

till money notes and coins held in banks' branches and at head office; *see also* vault cash

ton long or imperial ton; under the avoirdupois system of measurement 14 lb = 1 stone, 8 stone = 1 hundredweight, 20 hundredweight = 1 ton = 2,240 lb

1 short ton = 2000 lb. 1 long ton = 1.016 metric tonnes
see also avoirdupois pound

Tower pound (Tower lb) Tower pound used exclusively at the Tower of London Mint until replaced by the troy pound in 1526; 5,400 troy gr = 1 Tower libra/pound weight; *cf.* avoirdupois pound; troy pound

tracker fund investment fund that aims to follow the value of a stock market index

trade bill/paper bill not accepted or endorsed by a bank; *see also* bill, bank bill

transit items cheques and other bank payments in the course of collection through the clearing system, known as the float

Treasury HM Treasury commissioners, and latterly HM Treasury

Treasury bill (TB) negotiable instrument issued by the British and Northern Ireland governments with an original maturity of up to one year

troy pound (lbt) troy pound, 5,760 gr = 240 dwt = 12 ozt = 1 troy libra/pound weight; troy units of weight were adopted by the Mint in 1526; *cf.* avoirdupois pound, Tower pound

uncalled shares or capital issued shares that are not paid-up; *see* paid-up shares or capital

underwrite   undertake to provide credit, or to place shares

unencumbered asset   property without a mortgage or other claim on it; *see also* negative pledge

unite   gold coin first issued in 1604, after the accession of James I, and named after the union of Scotland and England; it was supplanted by the guinea in 1663

universal bank   banking group combining commercial and investment banking activities; these banks could take controlling interests in key clients and agree to interlocking directorships

usance   term to payment of (foreign) bill of exchange; *see also* currency, maturity, tenor

valorist coins   *see* metallist coins

vault cash   cash (in this case notes and coin) held in banks' branches and at head office (*US usage*); *see also* till money

walk clerk   bank messenger who presents drafts, bills and cheques to other banks for collection

War Loan   undated British government stock issued to finance government expenditure during the First World War; *see also* British government stock, Consols, gilts

wholesale deposits, or funds   large deposits and certificates of deposit (CDs) that bear a market rate of interest, rather than an administered deposit rate related to a bank's base rate; *cf.* retail deposit

window dressing   transactions designed to manage a bank's balance sheet on a make-up/reporting day to present it in a favourable light, for example, with a higher cash ratio than was usually the case

working capital   resources used by a business for its day-to-day trading operations; net current assets (NCA) is an accounting term for a firm's net working capital; *see also* current assets, current liabilities

working capital finance   short-term borrowing used to finance a firm's working capital, e.g. stocks and accounts receivable; *see also* stock and trade finance

years' purchase   reciprocal of yield, for example, a 5 per cent per annum rental yield is $100/5 = 20$ years' purchase

yield curve   fitted curve of the yield on fixed-interest securities against their residual term to maturity (usually from one or two years to irredeemable); *see also* term yield curve

Bibliography

I MANUSCRIPT AND ARCHIVAL SOURCES

Special Collections, Senate House Library, University of London

Goldsmiths' Library of Economic Literature

http://senatehouselibrary.ac.uk/our-collections/historic-collections/.

Castaing, John, The Course of the Exchange, and other things, London, 1698, recto of oblong quarter sheet published on Tuesday and Fridays:

- John Castaing from 1698.
- John Castaing and Edward Jackson from 1725.
- Edward Jackson from 1730.
- George Shergold 1733.
- Peter Smithson from 1764.
- No known from 1780.
- Edward, and later James Wetenhall from 3 Nov 1786.

Catalogue of the Goldsmiths' Library of Economic Literature, volume III, Athlone Press, 1982, p. 56; Microfilm prepared by University of London Photographic Department, order number 4152 dated 23 May 1955, using originals from Stock Exchange library, Bank of England Archive and British Library:

- Reel GS15/1, 1698–1719.
- Reel GS15/2, 1720–1730.
- Reel GS15/3, 1731–1741.
- Reel GS15/4, 1742–1759.
- Reel GS15/5, 1760–1783.
- Reel GS15/6, 1784–1798.
- Reel GS15/7, 1799–1810.
- Reel GS15/8, 1811–1817.
- Reel GS15/9, 1817–1821.

- Reel 3567, 1822–1825.
- Reel 3568, 1826–1834.

Hard Copy

- 1811–1817.
- 1817–1868.

Guildhall Library, London

Holdings of Castaing's Course of Exchange.
Originals in closed access store 1458–1460:

- 1698–1720, 1727, 1732, 1734, 1736–9.
- 1742–1889, duplicates for 1825–27.

Microfilm for 1890–1901, 6 reels nos. 2299–2304.

British Library

Holdings of Castaing's Course of Exchange: 1/1/1720 to 30/12/1755, 6/2/1750, 4/1/1791 to 13/12/1791.

Freke, John, Freke's Prices of Stocks &c., London, 14/3/1718, 15/4/1718 [British Library, 713.h.2,3].

Freke, John, 'The prices of the several stocks, annuities, and other publick securities, &c. with the course of exchange.' From Wednesday 26 March 1714 to Friday 25 March 1715, [London] sold by the author, [1714–15]. The Making of The Modern World, Web (9 December 2011).

Bank of England Archive

www.bankofengland.co.uk/CalmView/.

2A 109/1 – Castaign's gold and silver, bar and coin prices recorded in folio, annual averages from 1718 to 1758, twice weekly, 1759 to 1855.

2A 109/2 – Gold bar prices, Bank Rate, exchanges in Paris, Berlin, Vienna, New York, daily, Jan 1908–May 1915.

2A 109/3 – Gold bar prices, Bank Rate, exchanges in Paris, Italy, Amsterdam, Madrid, Petrograd, daily, 1915–August 1923.

2A 109/4 – Gold bar prices, Bank Rate, exchanges in Paris, Milan, Amsterdam, Madrid, New York, Berlin, daily, September 1923–September 1931.

2A 109/5 – Daily exchange, Gold and silver bar prices, Bank rate, daily, October 1931–December 1962; exchanges in Paris, Milan, Amsterdam, Madrid, New York, Berlin, daily, October 1931–February 1932.

2A 109/6 – Bar gold and silver, daily, January 1963–May 1973.

Bullion Ledgers, 1770–1809: M2/52 & 53, AB 259/1&2.

II STATISTICAL PUBLICATIONS AND DATABASES

Statistical Publications

Bank of England, *Annual Report*.
Bank of England, *Financial Stability Report*.

Bank of England, *Monetary & Financial Statistics*.
Bank of England Quarterly Bulletin.
www.bankofengland.co.uk/archive/Pages/digitalcontent/historicpubs/quarterly
    bulletins.aspx.
www.bankofengland.co.uk/publications/Pages/quarterlybulletin/default.aspx.
Bank of England Statistical Abstract (BOESA), no. 1 (1970); no. 2 (1975);
    parts 1 and 2 (1992); parts 1 and 2 (1993); parts 1 and 2 (1994); parts 1
    and 2 (1995).
Economic Trends, London: HMSO.
Financial Statistics, London: HMSO.

Databases

Allen, Robert C., price indices.
www.nuffield.ox.ac.uk/users/allen.
Allen, Robert C., and Richard W. Unger.
www.gcpdb.info/howto.html.
Bank of England.
www.bankofengland.co.uk/research/Pages/onebank/datasets.aspx#4.
Clark, Gregory and Peter Lindert UCD database.
http://gpih.ucdavis.edu/Datafilelist.htm.
Clark, Gregory and Peter Lindert (2006), Institute of International Social History,
    Price data, Global Price and Income History Group.
http://gpih.ucdavis.edu/#.
UK Data Service.
www.ukdataservice.ac.uk/.

III PRINTED SOURCES, WORKING PAPERS AND UNPUBLISHED THESES

Accominotti, Olivier, 'London merchant banks, the central European panic and
    the sterling crisis of 1931', *Journal of Economic History*, 72, no. 1 (March
    2012), pp. 1–43.
    'Global Banking and the International Transmission of the 1931 Financial Crisis'
    (London School of Economics, CEPR, and Banque de France, January 2016).
Ackrill, Margaret, and Leslie Hannah, *Barclays: The Business of Banking, 1690–
    1996* (Cambridge: Cambridge University Press, 2001).
Admati, Anat R., and Martin F. Hellwig, *The Bankers' New Clothes: What Is
    Wrong with Banking and What to Do about It* (Princeton, NJ, and Woodstock,
    England: Princeton University Press, 2013).
Acres, Wilfred Marston, *The Bank of England from Within, 1694–1900* (2 vols,
    London: Oxford University Press, 1931).
Ahamed, Liaquat, *Lords of Finance: 1929, the Great Depression, and the Bankers
    Who Broke the World* (London: Heinemann, 2009).
Allen, Martin, *Mints and Money in Medieval England* (Cambridge: Cambridge
    University Press, 2012).
Allen, Martin, and D'Maris Coffman (eds) *Money, Prices and Wages: Essays in Honour
    of Professor Nicholas Mayhew* (Basingstoke: Palgrave Macmillan, 2015).

Allen, William A., *Inflation Targeting: The British Experience* (London: Centre for Central Banking Studies, 1999).

'Liquidity regulation and its consequences', *Central Banking*, XXI, no. 4 (2010), pp. 33–7.

'Quantitative monetary policy and government debt management in Britain since 1919', *Oxford Review of Economic Policy*, 28, no. 4 (2012), pp. 804–36.

International Liquidity and the Financial Crisis (Cambridge and New York: Cambridge University Press, 2013).

Monetary Policy and Financial Repression in Britain, 1951–59 (Basingstoke: Palgrave Macmillan, 2014).

'Asset choice in British central banking history, the myth of the safe asset, and bank regulation', *Journal of Banking and Financial Economics*, 2, no. 4 (2 June 2015), pp. 5–18.

'International banking as it happened: A review of "The Lion Wakes – a modern history of HSBC" by Richard Roberts and David Kynaston' (9 September 2015) http://papers.ssrn.com/sol3/papers.cfm?abstract_id=2670006.

Antipa, Pamfili, 'How fiscal policy affects the price level: Britain's first experience with paper money', *Banque de France Working Paper*, no. 525 (November 2014).

Artis, Michael J., and Mervyn Lewis, *Monetary Control in the United Kingdom* (Oxford: Philip Allan, 1981).

Asgill, John, and Nicholas Barbon, *An Account of the Land-Bank* (London: T. Milborn, 1695).

Ashton, T. S., *Economic Fluctuations in England, 1700–1800* (Oxford: Clarendon Press, 1959).

Ashton, T. S., and R. S. Sayers, *Papers in English Monetary History* (Oxford: Clarendon Press, 1953).

Ashworth, Herbert, *The Building Society Story* (London: Franey, 1980).

Atack, Jeremy, and Larry D. Neal (eds) *The Origins and Development of Financial Markets and Institutions: From the Seventeenth Century to the Present* (Cambridge: Cambridge University Press, 2009).

Atkin, John, *The Foreign Exchange Market of London: Development since 1900* (London and New York: Routledge, 2005).

Attali, Jacques, *A Man of Influence: Sir Siegmund Warburg 1902–82* (London: Weidenfeld & Nicolson, 1986).

Augar, Philip, *The Death of Gentlemanly Capitalism: The Rise and Fall of London's Investment Banks* (London: Penguin, 2000).

Bagehot, Walter, *The English Constitution* (London, 1867; Longmans, 1915; Fontana, 1963).

Lombard Street, a Description of the Money Market (London: Henry S. King, 3rd edn 1873; 14th edn 1915; New York: Wiley, reprinted 1999).

Ball, Prof R. Jim, *Report of the Committee on Policy Optimisation*, Cmnd. 7148 (London: HMSO, 1978).

Balogh, Thomas, *Studies in Financial Organization* (Cambridge: Cambridge University Press, 1947).

'Oil recycling: The need for a new lending facility?' *Lloyds Bank Review*, no. 137 (July 1980), pp. 16–29.

Bank for International Settlements, 'Changes in Money-Market Instruments and Procedures: Objectives and Implications' (Basle, March 1986).

Bank of England, 'Commercial bills', *BEQB*, 2, no. 4 (December 1961), pp. 26–31. www.bankofengland.co.uk/archive/Pages/digitalcontent/historicpubs/quarterlybulletins.aspx.

'The management of money day-by-day', *BEQB*, 3, no. 1 (March 1963), pp. 15–21.

'Bank of England liabilities and assets: 1696 onwards', *BEQB*, 7, no. 2 (Appendix 'Bank of England liabilities and assets: 1696 to 1966') (June 1967), p. 160. www.bankofengland.co.uk/research/Pages/onebank/datasets.aspx#5.

'The London discount market: Some historical notes', *BEQB*, 7, no. 2 (June 1969), pp. 144–56.

'The UK banking sector 1952–67', *BEQB*, 9, no. 2 (June 1969), pp. 176–200.

'The euro-currency business of banks in London', *BEQB*, 10, no. 1 (March 1970), pp. 31–49.

'Monetary management in the United Kingdom', *BEQB*, 11, no. 1 (March 1971), pp. 37–47.

'Competition and credit control: Text of a consultative document issued on 28th May 1971', *BEQB*, 11, no. 2 (June 1971), pp. 189–93.

'Key issues in monetary and credit policy', *BEQB*, 11, no. 2 (June 1971), pp. 195–210.

'Changes in banking statistics', *BEQB*, 12, no. 1 (March 1972), p. 76–9.

'National balance sheets: A new analytical tool', *BEQB*, 12, no. 4 (December 1972), pp. 496–508.

'New banking statistics', *BEQB*, 15, no. 2 (June 1975), pp. 162–5.

'DCE and the money supply – a statistical note', *BEQB*, 17, no. 1 (March 1977), p. 39.

United Kingdom Flow of Fund Accounts: 1963–1978 (May 1978).

'Bank of England notes', *BEQB*, 18, no. 3 (September 1978), pp. 359–64.

'Monetary base – a statistical note', *BEQB*, 21, no. 1 (March 1981).

'The role of the Bank of England in the money market', *BEQB*, 22, no. 1 (March 1982).

'The supplementary special deposits scheme', *BEQB*, 22, no. 1 (March 1982), pp. 74–85.

'A note on money market arbitrage', *BEQB*, 22, no. 2 (June 1982), pp. 207–8.

'Composition of monetary and liquidity aggregates, and associated statistics', *BEQB*, 22, no. 4 (December 1982), pp. 530–7.

The Development and Operation of Monetary Policy 1960–1983 (Oxford: Clarendon Press, 1984).

'Measures of broad money', *BEQB*, 27, no. 2 (May 1987), pp. 212–9.

'The role of brokers in the London money markets', *BEQB*, 37, no. 2 (May 1990), pp. 221–7.

'The development of the building societies sector in the 1980s', *BEQB*, 30, no. 4 (November 1990), pp. 503–10.

'The first year of the gilt repo market', *BEQB*, 37, no. 2 (May 1997), pp. 187–97.

The Bank of England's Sterling Monetary Framework (Red Book) (updated November 2014) www.bankofengland.co.uk/markets/Documents/money/publications/redbook.pdf.

Bank of England, and Financial Services Authority, 'The Bank of England, Prudential Regulation Authority: Our approach to banking supervision' (May 2011).

The Bankers' Magazine, Journal of the Money Market (49 vols, London: Richard Groombridge, 1844–1889).

Baring, Sir Francis, *Observations on the Establishment of the Bank of England* (London, 1797).

Batini, Nicholetta, and Edward Nelson, 'The UK's rocky road to stability', *FRB of St. Louis Working Paper Series* (March 2005).

Beach, W. E., *British International Gold Movements and Banking Policy, 1881–1913* (Cambridge, MA: Harvard University Press, 1935).

Bellman, Sir C. Harold, *The Building Society Movement* (London: Methuen, 1927).

Bierwag, Gerald O., *Duration Analysis: Managing Interest Rate Risk* (Cambridge, MA: Ballinger, 1987).

Berger, Allen N., Philip Molyneux, and John O. S. Wilson, *The Oxford Handbook of Banking* (Oxford: Oxford University Press, 1st edn 2010, paperback edn 2012, 2nd edn 2015).

Bernanke, Ben S., Thomas Laubach, Frederic S. Mishkin, and Adam Posen, *Inflation Targeting: Lessons from the International Experience* (Princeton, NJ, and Oxford: Princeton University Press, 1999).

Best, Michael H., and K. Jane Humphries, 'The City and industrial decline' in Bernard Elbaum and William Lazonick (eds) *The Decline of the British Economy* (Oxford: Clarendon, 1986), pp. 223–39.

Bignon, Vincent, Marc Flandreau, and Stefano Ugolini, 'Bagehot for beginners: The making of lender-of-last-resort operations in the mid-nineteenth century', *Economic History Review*, 65, no. 2 (May 2012), pp. 580–608.

Billings, Mark, and Forrest H. Capie, 'Capital in British Banking 1920–70', *Business History*, 49 (2007), pp. 139–62.

Blackaby, Frank, 'Comments on Michael Foot's paper, Monetary Targets', in B. Griffiths and G. E. Wood (eds) *Monetary Targets* (London: Macmillan, 1981), pp. 54–61.

Blake, Edwin Holmes, 'Mortgages: Some notes on law and practice', *The Auctioneers' Institute of the United Kingdom* (London, 11 November 1908), pp. 13–43.

Blanchard, Olivier J., David H. Romer, A. Michael Spence, and Joseph E. Stiglitz, *In the Wake of the Crisis* (Cambridge, MA, and London: MIT Press with the International Monetary Fund, 2012).

Bloomfield, Arthur I., *Monetary Policy under the International Gold Standard, 1880–1914* (New York: FRB of New York, 1959).

Boddy, Martin, *The Building Societies* (London and Basingstoke: Macmillan, 1980).

Boleat, Mark, *National Housing Finance Systems: A Comparative Study* (London: Croom Helm, 1985).

Boll, Mark, *The Building Society Industry* (London: Allen & Unwin, 1982).

Bordo, Michael D., 'The lender of last resort: Alternative views and historical experience', *FRB Richmond Economic Review*, 76, no. 1 (January/February 1990), pp. 18–29.

Bosanquet, Charles, *Practical Observations on the Report of the Bullion Committee* (London: J. M. Richardson, 1810).

Bowen, H. V., 'The Bank of England during the Long Eighteenth Century, 1694–1820', in Richard Roberts and David Kynaston (eds) *The Bank of England: Money, Power and Influence, 1694–1994* (Oxford: Clarendon Press, 1995).

Boyer-Xambeu, Marie-Thérèse, Ghislain Deleplace, and Lucien Gillard, 'Régimes monétaires, points d'or et "serpent bimétallique" de 1770 à 1870', *Revue Économique*, 45, no. 5 (1994), pp. 1139–74.

Brittan, Samuel, *The Treasury under the Tories 1951–1964* (London: Martin Secker & Warburg and Harmondsworth: Penguin, 1964).

Steering the Economy: The Role of the Treasury (London: Martin Secker & Warburg, 1968; Harmondsworth: Penguin, 1971).

Britton, Andrew J., *The Trade Cycle in Britain 1959–1982* (Cambridge: Cambridge University Press, 1986).

Macroeconomic Policy in Britain 1974–1987 (Cambridge: Cambridge University Press, 1991).

Broadberry, S. N., B. M. Campbell, A. Klein, M. Overton, and B. van Leeuwen, 'British economic growth, 1270–1870: An output-based approach', Department of Economic History, London School of Economics (18 December 2011) www.google.co.uk/#q=Broadberry%2C+S.N.%2C+B.M.+Campbell%2C+A.+Klein%2C+M.+Overton%2C+B.+van+Leeuwen%2C+%E2%80%98British+economic+growth%2C+1700–1870:+an+output-based+approach%E2%80%99%2C+Department+of+Economic+History%2C+London+School+of+Economics+(18th+December+2011).

Bryan, Lowell L., *Breaking Up the Bank: Rethinking an Industry under Siege* (Homewood, IL: Irwin, 1988).

Bulow, Jeremy, Jacob Goldfield, and Paul Klemperer, 'Market-based capital regulation', *Vox* (29 August 2013) www.voxeu.org/article/market-based-bank-capital-regulation.

Burk, Kathleen, *Morgan Grenfell 1838–1988: The Biography of a Merchant Bank* (Oxford: Oxford University Press, 1989).

Burnett, John, *A Social History of Housing, 1815–1970* (London: Methuen, 1st edn 1978, 2nd edn 1986).

Calicó, X., *Numismática Española: Catálogo general con precious de las monedas espaānolas acuñadas desde los Reyes Católicos hasta Juan Carlos I: 1474–2001* (Barcelona: Aureo & Calicó, 2008).

Calomiris, Charles W., and Charles M. Kahn, 'The role of demandable debt in structuring optimal banking arrangements', *American Economic Review*, 81, no. 3 (June 1991), pp. 497–513.

Calomiris, Charles W., and Stephen H. Haber, *Fragile by Design: The Political Origins of Banking Crises and Scarce Credit* (Princeton, NJ, and Oxford: Princeton University Press, 2014).

Capie, Forrest H., 'Banking in Europe in the nineteenth century: The role of the central bank' in Richard E. Sylla, Richard H. Tilly, Gabriel Tortella (eds) *The State, the Financial System and Economic Modernization* (Cambridge: Cambridge University Press, 1999).

'The emergence of the Bank of England as a mature central bank' in Donald Winch and Patrick K. O'Brien (eds) *The Political Economy of British Historical Experience, 1688–1914* (Oxford: Oxford University Press, 2002).

The Bank of England from the 1950s to 1979 (New York: Cambridge University Press, 2010).

'British financial crises in the nineteenth and twentieth centuries' in Nicholas H. Dimsdale and Anthony C. Hotson (eds) *British Financial Crises since 1825* (Oxford: Oxford University Press, 2014), pp. 9–23.

Capie, Forrest H., and Alan Webber, *A Monetary History of the United Kingdom, 1870–1982.* Vol. I: *Data, Sources, Methods* (London: Allen & Unwin, 1985; London: Routledge, 1995, 2008).

Capie, Forrest H., and Michael Collins, 'Have the banks failed British industry? An historical survey of bank/industry relations in Britain, 1870–1990', *Institute of Economic Affairs* (1992).

Capie, Forrest H., and Geoffrey E. Wood, 'Central banks and inflation: An historical perspective', *Central Banking*, 2, nos 2 & 3 (Summer 1991 & Winter 1991/2).

Banking Theory, 1870–1930 (7 vols, London: Routledge, 1999).

Money over Two Centuries (Oxford: Oxford University Press, 2012).

Capie, Forrest H., and Mark Billings, 'Evidence on competition in English commercial banking 1920–70', *Financial History Review*, 11 (2004), pp. 69–103.

Carey, Daniel, 'John Locke, money, and credit', in Daniel Carey and Christopher J, Finlay (eds) *The Empire of Credit: The Financial Revolution in Britain, Ireland and America, 1688–1815* (Dublin and Portland, Oregon: Irish Academic Press, 2011).

Carlin, Wendy, and David W. Soskice, *Macroeconomics: Institutions, Instability and the Financial System* (Oxford: Oxford University Press, 2015).

Castaing, John, Edward Jackson, George Shergold, and Peter Smithson, *The Course of the Exchange, and Other Things* (London, January 1698 to October 1786), *see* section I of bibliography.

Cassel, Karl Gustav, *The Nature and Necessity of Interest* (London, 1903).

Money and Foreign Exchange after 1914 (London: Constable, 1922).

Cassis, Youssef, 'The emergence of a new financial institution: Investment trusts in Britain, 1870–1939' in J. J. van Helten and Y. Cassis, *Capitalism in a Mature Economy: Financial Institutions, Capital Exports and British Industry, 1870–1939* (Aldershot: Edward Elgar, 1990).

Finance and Financiers in European History 1880–1960 (Cambridge: Cambridge University Press, 1992).

'Do financial crises lead to policy change?' in Nicholas Dimsdale and Anthony Hotson (eds) *British Financial Crises since 1825* (Oxford: Oxford University Press, 2014), pp. 174–89.

Casson, Mark and Nigar Hashimzade (eds) *Large Databases in Economic History: Research Methods and Case Studies* (Abingdon: Routledge, 2013).

Casson, Mark and Catherine Casson, 'Modelling the medieval economy: Money, prices and income in England, 1263–1520' in M. Allen and D'M. Coffman (eds) *Money, Prices and Wages: Essays in Honour of Professor Nicholas Mayhew* (Basingstoke: Palgrave Macmillan, 2015).

Chadha, Jagit S., and Nicholas H. Dimsdale, 'A long view of real rates', *Oxford Review of Economic Policy*, 15, no. 2 (Summer 1999), pp. 17–45.

Chadha, Jagit S., and Sean Holly, *Interest Rates, Prices and Liquidity: Lessons from the Financial Crisis* (Cambridge: Cambridge University Press, 2011).

Challis, Christopher E., 'The debasement of the coinage, 1542–1551', *Economic History Review*, 20, no. 3 (December 1967), pp. 441–66.

The Tudor Coinage (Manchester: Manchester University Press, 1978).

(ed.), *A New History of the Royal Mint* (Cambridge: Cambridge University Press, 1992).

Chambers, David, 'The City and the corporate economy since 1870' in Sir Roderick C. Floud, K. Jane Humphries, and Paul Johnson (eds) *The Cambridge Economic History of Modern Britain*. Vol. II: *1870 to the Present* (Cambridge: Cambridge University Press, 2014), pp. 255–78.

Checkland, S.G., *Scottish Banking: A History, 1695–1973* (Glasgow: Collins, 1975).

Chernow, Ron, *The Warburgs: A Family Saga* (London: Chatto & Windus, 1993).

Cipolla, Carlo Maria, *Money, Prices and Civilisation in the Mediterranean World, Fifth to Seventeenth Centuries* (Princeton, NJ: Princeton University Press, 1956).

Clancy, Kevin, 'The recoinage and exchange of 1816–17' (University of Leeds PhD thesis, 1999).

Clapham, Sir John, *The Bank of England: A History*, I: 1694–1797; II: 1797–1914 (Cambridge: Cambridge University Press, 1st edn 1944, reprinted 1958, 1966, 1970, 2008).

Clarida, R. G. J., J. Gali, and M. Gertler, 'The science of monetary policy: A new Keynesian perspective', *Journal of Economic Literature*, 37, no. 4 (December 1999), pp. 1661–1707.

Clark, Gregory, 'The price history of English agriculture, 1209–1914' in Alexander J. Field (ed.), *Research in Economic History*, 22 (Amsterdam, 2004).

'The macroeconomic aggregates for England, 1209–2008', UC Davis, Economics WP 09-19 (revised 2009).

Cleary, E. J., *The Building Society Movement* (London: Elek, 1965).

Cleveland, Harold van B., and Thomas F. Huertas, *Citibank, 1812–1970*, Harvard Business History Studies (Cambridge, MA, and London: Harvard University Press, 1985).

Clews, Roger, Chris Salmon, and Olaf Weeken, 'The Bank's money market framework', *BEQB*, 60, no. 4 (2010, Q4), pp. 293–4.

Cobham, David, *The Making of Monetary Policy in the UK, 1975–2000* (Chichester: Wiley, 2003).

Coffman, D'Maris, *Excise Taxation and the Origins of Public Debt* (Basingstoke: Palgrave Macmillan, 2013).

Coffman, D'Maris, Adrian Leonard, and Larry D. Neal, *Questioning Credible Commitment: New Perspectives on the Rise of Financial Capitalism* (Cambridge: Cambridge University Press, 2013).

Coghlan, Richard T., 'A transactions demand for money', *BEQB*, 18, no. 1 (March 1978), pp. 48–60.

  Money, Credit and the Economy (London: Allen & Unwin, 1981; Abingdon: Routledge, 2011).

Cole, A. C., 'Notes on the London money market', *Journal of the Institute of Bankers*, XXV, Part III (March 1904), pp. 133–46.

Coleby, A. L., 'Bills of exchange: current issues in historical context', *BEQB* (December 1982), pp. 514–518.

  'The Bank's operational procedures for meeting monetary objectives', *BEQB* (June 1983), pp. 209–215.

Collins, Michael, *Money and Banking in the UK: A History* (London: Croom Helm, 1988; London: Routledge, reprinted 1990).

Collins, Michael, and Mae Baker, *Commercial Banks and Industrial Finance in England and Wales, 1860–1913* (Oxford: Oxford University Press, 2003).

Colombo, John Robert, 'A said poem', in *Neo Poems* (Vancouver, Canada: Sono Nis Press, 1970), p. 46.

Committee of London Clearing Bankers, *The London Clearing Banks, Evidence by the CLCB to the Committee to Review the Functioning of Financial Institutions* (London: Longman, 1978).

Congdon, Tim G., *Monetary Control in Britain* (London and Basingstoke: Macmillan, 1982).

Connor, R. D., *The Weights and Measures of England* (London: HMSO, 1989).

Cottrell, Philip L., *Industrial Finance 1830–1914: The Finance and Organization of English Manufacturing Industry* (London and New York: Methuen, 1980).

  'The domestic commercial banks in the City of London, 1870–1939' in Y. Cassis (ed.), *Finance and Financiers in European History 1880–1960* (Cambridge: Cambridge University Press, 1992).

Craig, Alan K., *Spanish Colonial Silver Coins in the Florida Collection* (Gainesville: University of Florida, 2000).

Craig, Sir John H. M., *Newton at the Mint* (Cambridge: Cambridge University Press, 1946).

  The Mint: A History of the London Mint from AD 287 to 1948 (Cambridge: Cambridge University Press, 1953).

Cramp, A. B., *Opinion on Bank Rate, 1822–60* (London, 1962).

Crowther, Geoffrey, Baron Crowther of Headingley, *Report of the Committee on Consumer Credit* (2 vols, London: HMSO, March 1971).

Cunliffe Report, *First Interim Report of the Committee on Currency and the Foreign Exchanges after the War*, Cmnd 9182 (1918).

Currie, David, 'Macroeconomic policy design and control theory – a failed partnership?', *Economic Journal*, 95 (June 1985), pp. 285–306.

Curzio, Alberto Quadrio, and Roberto Scazzieri, 'Historical stylisations and monetary theory', in R. Scazzieri, A. K. Sen, and S. Zamagni (ed.), *Markets,*

Money and Capital (Cambridge: Cambridge University Press, 2008), pp. 185–203.

Dale, Richard, *The Regulation of International Banking* (Cambridge: Woodhead-Faulkner, 1984).

Dalton, J., *The Banker's Clerk* (London, 1843).

Darling, Alastair, *Back from the Brink: 1,000 Days at Number 11* (London: Atlantic Books, 2011).

Daunton, Martin J., *House and Home in the Victorian City: Working-Class Housing 1850–1914* (London: Edward Arnold, 1983).

Davies, Aled, 'The evolution of British monetary targets, 1968–79', University of Oxford Discussion Papers in Economic and Social History, No. 104 (October 2012) www.nuff.ox.ac.uk/economics/history/Paper104/davies104.pdf.

Davies, Glyn A., *Building Societies and Their Branches: A Regional Economic Survey* (London: Franey, 1981).

History of Money from Ancient Times to the Present Day (Cardiff: University of Wales Press, 1994, revised edn 1996, 3rd edn 2002).

Davis, Lance E., and Robert E. Gallman, *Evolving Financial Markets and International Capital Flows: Britain, the Americas, and Australia, 1865–1914* (Cambridge and New York: Cambridge University Press, 2001).

Davison, I. F. Hay, and M. Stuart-Smith, *Grays Building Society*, Registry of Friendly Societies, Cmnd. 7557 (London: HMSO, 1979).

del Mar, Alexander, *History of Monetary Systems* (London: Effingham Wilson, 1895).

Denham, Andrew, and Mark Garnett, 'The nature and impact of think tanks in contemporary Britain', *Contemporary British History*, 10, no.1 (1996), pp. 43–61, 50.

'Influence without responsibility? Think tanks in Britain', *Parliamentary Affairs*, 52, no. 1 (1999), pp. 46–57.

Denzel, Markus A., *Handbook of World Exchange Rates, 1590–1914* (Farnham: Ashgate, 2010).

Desan, Christine, *Making Money: Coin, Currency, and the Coming of Capitalism* (Oxford: Oxford University Press, 2014).

Deutsche Bundesbank, 'The longer-term trend and control of the money stock', *Monthly Report*, 37, no. 1 (January 1985), pp. 13–26.

'The Deutsche Bundesbank: Its monetary policy instruments and functions', Special series, 7 (1987).

de Zoete & Gorton, 'Changes in Bank rate since 1694 and movements in long-term interest rates since 1731: A study over two centuries' (July 1966).

Diamond, Douglas W., 'Financial intermediation and delegated monitoring', *Review of Economic Studies*, 51 (July 1984), pp. 393–414.

'Banks and liquidity creation: A simple exposition of the Diamond-Dybvig model', *FRB of Richmond Economic Quarterly*, 93, no. 2 (Spring, 2007), pp. 189–200.

Diamond, Douglas W., and Philip H. Dybvig, 'Bank runs, deposit insurance, and liquidity', *Journal of Political Economy*, 91, no. 3 (1983), pp. 401–19; reprinted in *FRB of Minneapolis Quarterly Review*, 24, no. 1 (Winter 2000), pp. 14–23.

Diamond, Douglas W., and Raghuram Rajan, 'Liquidity risk, liquidity creation and financial fragility: A theory of banking', *Journal of Political Economy*, 109, no. 2 (April 2001), pp. 287–327.

Diaper, Stefanie Jane, 'The history of Kleinwort, Sons & Co. in merchant banking' (University of Nottingham PhD thesis, 1983).

'Merchant banking in the inter-war period: The case of Kleinwort, Sons & Co.', *Business History*, 26, no. 4 (1986), pp. 56–76.

Dickson, P. G. M., *The Financial Revolution in England: A Study in the Development of Public Credit, 1688–1756* (London: Macmillan, 1967).

Dimsdale, Nicholas H., 'British monetary policy and the exchange rate 1920–38', *Oxford Economic Papers, Supplement*, 33 (July 1981); reprinted in W. A. Eltis and P. J. N. Sinclair (ed.), *The Money Supply and the Exchange Rate* (Oxford: Clarendon Press, 1981).

'The Treasury and Civil Service Committee and the British monetarist experiment', in Mauro Baranzini (ed.), *Advances in Economic Theory* (Oxford: Blackwell, 1982), p. 183–206.

'Money, interest and cycles in Britain since 1830', *Greek Economic Review*, 12, Supplement (1990), pp. 153–96.

'British monetary policy since 1945', in N. F. R. Crafts and N. W.C. Woodward (eds) *The British Economy since 1945* (Oxford: Clarendon Press, 1991).

Dimsdale, Nicholas H., and Nicholas Horsewood, 'The financial crisis of 1931 and the impact of the Great Depression on the British economy' in N. H. Dimsdale and A. C. Hotson (eds) *British Financial Crises since 1825* (Oxford: Oxford University Press, 2014), pp. 116–38.

Dimsdale, Nicholas H., and Anthony C. Hotson, 'Financial crises and economic activity in the UK since 1825' in N. H. Dimsdale and A. C. Hotson (eds) *British Financial Crises since 1825* (Oxford: Oxford University Press, 2014), pp. 24–57.

British Financial Crises since 1825 (Oxford: Oxford University Press, 2014).

'Monetary trends in the UK since 1870' in M. Allen and D'M. Coffman (eds) *Money, Prices and Wages: Essays in Honour of Professor Nicholas Mayhew* (Basingstoke: Palgrave Macmillan, 2015), pp. 228–49.

Dow, J. Christopher R., *The Management of the British Economy, 1945–60*, NIESR (Cambridge: Cambridge University Press, 1964, 1970).

Dow, J. Christopher R., and Iain D. Saville, *A Critique of Monetary Policy: theory and British Experience* (Oxford: Clarendon Press, 1st edn 1988, 2nd edition with new preface, 1990, paperback 2001).

Dow, J. Christopher R., Christopher T. Taylor, and Graham Hacche (eds) *Inside the Bank of England: memoirs of Christopher Dow, Chief Economist 1973–84*, with a foreward by Sir Kit McMahon (Basingstoke: Palgrave Macmillan, 2013).

Dyer, G. P., and P. P. Gaspar, 'Reform, the New Technology and Tower Hill, 1700–1966', in C. E. Challis (ed.), *A New History of the Royal Mint* (Cambridge: Cambridge University Press, 1992), pp. 398–606.

Edwards, Jeremy, and Sheilagh Ogilvie, 'Universal banks and German industrialization: A reappraisal', *Economic History Review*, 49, no. 3 (August, 1996), pp. 427–46.

Eichengreen, Barry, *Golden Fetters: The Gold Standard and the Great Depression, 1919–39* (New York and Oxford: Oxford University Press, 1992, 1996, 2003).
  Globalizing Capital, a History of the Monetary System (Princeton, NJ, and Oxford: Princeton University Press, 1996; 2nd edn 2008).
  Hall of Mirrors: The Great Depression, the Great Recession, and the Uses – and Misuses – of History (New York: Oxford University Press, 2015).
Eichengreen, Barry, and Marc Flandreau, 'The Federal Reserve, the Bank of England, and the rise of the dollar as an international currency, 1914–1939', *Open Economies Review*, 23 (2012), pp 57–87.
Einzig, Paul, *The History of Foreign Exchange* (New York: Macmillan, 1962, 1970).
Elliott, Geoffrey, *The Mystery of Overend and Gurney: A Financial Scandal in Victorian London* (London: Methuen, 2006).
Ellis, Aytoun, *Heir of Adventure: The Story of Brown Shipley & Co., Merchant Bankers, 1810–1960* (London: Brown Shiple, 1960).
Eltis, Walter A., and Peter J. N. Sinclair (eds) *The Money Supply and the Exchange Rate* (Oxford: Clarendon Press, 1981).
Evelyn, John, *The Diary of John Evelyn*, ed E. S. de Beer (6 vols, Oxford: Clarendon Press, 1955).
Fallon, Ivan, *Black Horse Ride: The Inside Story of Lloyds and the Banking Crisis* (Robson Press, 2015).
Fay, Stephen, *Portrait of an Old Lady: Turmoil at the Bank of England* (London: Viking, 1987; Penguin edn 1988).
Feavearyear, Sir Albert E., *The Pound Sterling: A History of English Money* (Oxford: Oxford University Press, 1931).
  The Pound Sterling: A History of English Money (ed.), E. Victor Morgan (Oxford: Oxford University Press, 2nd edn 1963).
Federal Deposit Insurance Corporation, *History of the 80s*: Vol. I: *An Examination of the Banking Crises of the 1980s and Early 1990s* (FDIC, 1997).
Federal Reserve Bank of New York, *Tri-Party Repo Infrastructure Reform, a White Paper Prepared by the FRB New York* (17 May 2010) www.newyorkfed.org/prc.
Federal Reserve Bank of New York, and Paul Meek (ed.), 'Central bank views on monetary targeting', *FRB New York* (May 1982).
  'US monetary policy and financial markets', *FRB New York* (October 1982).
Ferguson, Niall, *The World's Banker: The History of the House of Rothschild* (London: Weidenfeld & Nicolson, 1998).
  The Ascent of Money: A Financial History of the World (London: Penguin, 2009).
Fetter, Frank W., *Development of British Monetary Orthodoxy 1797–1875* (Cambridge, MA: Harvard University Press, 1965, reprinted Fairfield, NJ: A. M. Kelly, 1978).
Fforde, John S., 'Setting monetary objectives', *BEQB*, 23, no. 2 (June 1983); reprinted in *The Development and Operation of Monetary Policy 1960–1983: A Selection of Material from the Quarterly Bulletin of the Bank of England* (Oxford: Clarendon Press, 1984).
  The Bank of England and Public Policy 1941–1958 (Cambridge: Cambridge University Press, 1992).

Financial Services Authority, *The Turner Review: A Regulatory Response to the Global Banking Crisis* (March 2009).

'A regulatory response to the global banking crisis: Systemically important banks and assessing the cumulative impact', Turner Review Conference Discussion Paper 09/4 (October 2009) www.fsa.gov.uk/pages/Library/Policy/Policy/2009/09_16.shtml.

Financial Stability Board, 'Global shadow banking monitoring report 2015' (12 November 2015) www.fsb.org/.

Fisher, Irving, *The Purchasing Power of Money* (New York: Macmillan, 1911, revised edns 1922 and 1931).

Stabilizing the Dollar: A Plan to Stabilize the General Price Level without Fixing Individual Prices (New York: Macmillan, 1920).

Flandreau, Marc, and Stefano Ugolini, 'The Crisis of 1866', in N. H. Dimsdale and A. C. Hotson (eds) *British Financial Crises since 1825* (Oxford: Oxford University Press, 2014), pp. 76–93.

Flemming, John S., *Inflation* (Oxford: Oxford University Press, 1976).

Fletcher, Gordon A., *Discount Houses in London: Principles, Operations and Change* (London and Basingstoke: Macmillan, 1976).

Foot, Michael D. K. W., 'Monetary targets: Their nature and record in the major economies' in B. Griffiths and G. E. Wood (eds) *Monetary Targets* (Macmillan, London, 1981), pp. 13–46; see Blackaby for comments on Michael Foot's chapter, pp. 54–61.

Foot, Michael D. K. W., Charles A. E. Goodhart and Anthony C. Hotson, 'Monetary base control', *BEQB*, 19, no. 2 (June 1979), pp. 149–59; reprinted without appendix in Bank of England (1984), pp. 129–136.

Forbes, William, *A Methodical Treatise Concerning Bills of Exchange* (Edinburgh, 1718).

Fox, David, 'The case of mixt monies', *Cambridge Law Journal*, 70, no. 1 (March 2011), pp. 144–74.

'The structures of monetary nominalism in the pre-modern common law', *Journal of Legal History*, 34, no. 2 (2013), pp. 139–71.

Freixas, Xavier, and Jean-Charles Rochet, *Microeconomics of Banking* (Cambridge, MA, and London: MIT Press, 1st edn 1997, 2nd edn 2008).

Friedman, Milton, 'A monetary and fiscal framework for economic stability', *American Economic Review*, 38, 3 (June 1948), pp. 245–64.

'Demand for money', *Journal of Political Economy*, 67, no. 4 (August 1959), pp. 327–51.

'Should there be an independent monetary authority?' in Leland B Yeager (ed.), *In Search of a Monetary Constitution* (Cambridge, MA: Harvard University Press, 1962).

'The role of monetary policy', *American Economic Review*, 58, no. 1 (March 1968), pp. 1–17.

'Inflation and Unemployment: The New Dimension of Politics', Institute of Economic Affairs, Occasional Paper 51 (May 1977).

Memorandum submitted to the Treasury and Civil Service Committee, *Memoranda on Monetary Policy*, Session 1979–80 (London: HMSO, 17 July 1980).

Money Mischief: Episodes in Monetary History (New York: Harcourt Brace Jovanovich, 1992).

Friedman, Milton, and Anna Schwartz, *A Monetary History of the United States, 1867–1960* (Princeton, NJ: Princeton University Press, 1963).

Gali, J., and M. Gertler, 'Inflation dynamics: A structural econometric analysis', *Journal of Monetary Economics*, 44, no. 2 (October 1999), pp. 195–222.

'Macroeconomic modelling for monetary policy evaluation', *Journal of Economic Perspectives*, 21, no. 4 (Fall 2007), pp. 25–45.

Giannini, Curzio, *The Age of Central Banks* (Cheltenham: Edward Elgar, 2011).

Gilbart, James William, *A Practical Treatise on Banking* (London, 1st edn 1827, 3rd edn 1834, 5th edn 1849, 6th edn 1856).

The Logic of Banking (London, 1859).

The History and Principles of Banking: The Laws of Currency etc., IV (8 vols, London, 1866).

The Principles and Practice of Banking, 1873 edn reprinted in Forrest Capie and Geoffrey E. Wood (eds) *Banking Theory, 1870–1930*, 1 (7 vols, London: Routledge, 1999).

(ed.), A. S. Michie, *Gilbart on Banking: The History, Principles and Practice of Banking* (2 vols, London: George Bell, 1882).

(ed.), Ernest Sykes, *The History, Principles and Practice of Banking* (2 vols, London: George Bell, 1907, 1922).

Gilbert, R. Alton, 'Requiem for Regulation Q: What it did and why it passed away', *FRB of St. Louis*, 68, no. 2 (February 1986), pp. 22–37.

Gillett Brothers, *The Bill on London* (London: Chapman Hall, 1964).

Glassman, Debra, and Angela Redish, 'Currency depreciation in early modern England and France', *Explorations in Economic History*, 25, no. 1 (1988), pp. 75–97.

Goodhart, Charles A. E., *The New York Money Market and the Finance of Trade, 1900–1913* (Cambridge, MA: Harvard University Press, 1969).

The Business of Banking, 1891–1914 (London: Weidenfeld & Nicolson, 1972; Aldershot: Gower, 1986).

Money, Information and Uncertainty (London and Basingstoke: Macmillan, 1st edn 1975, 2nd revised edn 1989).

Monetary Theory and Practice: The UK Experience (London and Basingstoke: Macmillan, 1984).

'Financial innovation and monetary control', *Oxford Review of Economic Policy*, 2, no. 4 (Winter 1986).

The Evolution of Central Banks (Cambridge, MA: MIT Press, 1988).

'The conduct of monetary policy', *Economic Journal*, 99 (June 1989), pp. 293–346.

'Two concepts of money: Implications for the analysis of optimal currency areas', *European Journal of Political Economy*, 14 (1998), pp. 407–32.

'Myths about the lender of last resort', Financial Markets Group, London School of Economics, Special paper no. 120 (1999).

'What weight should be given to asset prices in the measurement of inflation?', *Economic Journal*, 111, 472 (June 2001).

'The Bank of England over the last 35 years' in *Bankhistorisches Archiv, Zeitschrift zur Bankengeschichte*, Beiheft 43, *Welche Aufgaben muß eine Zentralbank wahrnehmen? Historische Erfahrungen und europäische Perspektiven*. 15. Wissenschaftliches Kolloquium am 7 November 2002 auf Einladung der Stiftung 'Geld und Währung' (Stuttgart: Franz Steiner Verlag, 2004), pp. 29–54.

John Flemming, 1941–2003: A Biography (Windsor: Wilton 65, 2007).

'The continuing muddles of monetary theory: A steadfast refusal to face facts', *Economica*, 76, Supplement 1 (October 2009), pp. 821–30.

The Regulatory Response to the Financial Crisis (Cheltenham and Northampton, MA: Edward Elgar, 2010).

The Basel Committee on Banking Supervision: A History of the Early Years, 1974–1977 (Cambridge: Cambridge University Press, 2011).

'Competition and credit control: Some personal reflections', *Financial History Review*, 22, no. 2 (August 2015), pp. 235–46.

Goodhart, Charles A. E., and Andrew D. Crockett, 'The importance of money', *BEQB*, 10, no. 2 (June 1970), pp. 159–98.

Goodhart, Charles A. E., and Paul V. Temperton, 'The UK exchange rate, 1979–81: A test of the overshooting hypothesis' (Oxford Money Study Group, 1982).

Goodhart, Charles A. E., and Anthony C. Hotson, 'The forecasting and control of bank lending' (1979) in C. A. E. Goodhart, *Monetary Theory and Practice: The UK Experience* (London: Macmillan, 1984), pp. 139–45.

Goodhart, Charles A. E., and Boris Hofmann, *House Prices and Macroeconomy: Implications for Banking and Price Stability* (Oxford and New York: Oxford University Press, 2007).

Goodhart, Charles A. E., and Dimitrios P. Tsomocos, *Financial Stability in Practice: Towards an Uncertain Future* (Cheltenham: Edward Elgar, 2012).

Gordon, Charles, *The Cedar Story: The Night the City Was Saved* (London: Sinclair-Stevenson, 1993).

Gordy, Michael B., and Erik A. Heitfield, 'Risk-based regulatory capital and Basel II', in Allen N. Berger, Philip Molyneux, and John O. S. Wilson, *The Oxford Handbook of Banking* (Oxford: Oxford University Press, 1st edn 2010), pp. 357–76.

Gorton, Gary B., 'The Panic of 2007', *FRB Kansas City*, Jackson Hole Conference (25 August 2008).

'Information, liquidity and the (ongoing) Panic of 2007', *American Economic Review*, Papers & Proceedings, 99, no. 2 (May 2009).

Slapped by the Invisible Hand: The Panic of 2007 (Oxford: Oxford University Press, 2009).

'The history and economics of safe assets', *NBER Working Paper*, no. 22210 (April 2016).

Gorton, Gary B., and Andrew Metrick, 'Securitised banking and the run on repo', *Yale ICF Working Paper*, 09–14 (9 November 2010).

Goschen, George Joachim, first viscount, *The Theory of the Foreign Exchanges* (London, 1861).

Essays and Addresses on Economic Questions (London: Edward Arnold, 1905).

Gould, John Dennis, *The Great Debasement: Currency and the Economy in Mid-Tudor England* (Oxford: Clarendon Press, 1970).

Graeber, David, *Debt: The First 5,000 Years* (New York: Melville House, 2011).

Granville, Brigitte, *Remembering Inflation* (Princeton, NJ, and Oxford: Princeton University Press, 2013).

Green, Edwin, *Debtors to Their Profession: A History of the Institute of Bankers 1879–1979* (Abingdon: Routledge, 1979).

   The Making of a Modern Banking Group: A History of the Midland Bank since 1900 (privately printed, 1979).

Greenwell & Co., W. 'A monetary base for the UK: A practical proposal', supplementary bulletin (2 July 1979).

Greenwell Associates, W., 'Monetary base control', *Special Monetary Bulletin* (21 April 1980), p. 3.

Greenwood, John, 'US corporate and household balance sheet update based on flow of funds data for 2010 Q2' (Invesco, 5 October 2010).

   'UK: Can shadow banking help explain booms & busts?' (Invesco, 19 July, 2013).

Gregory, Theodor E., Select *Statutes, Documents and Reports Relating to British Banking, 1832–1928* (2 vols, London: Oxford University Press, 1929).

Gregory, Theodor E., and A. Henderson, *The Westminster Bank through a Century* (2 vols London: Westminster Bank, 1936).

Greider, William, *Secrets of the Temple: How the Federal Reserve Runs the Country* (New York: Simon & Schuster, 1987).

Griffiths, Brian, baron Griffiths of Fforestfach, *Competition in Banking*, Hobart Papers, no. 51 (London: Institute of Economic Affairs, 1970).

   'The determination of the Treasury bill tender rate', *Economica*, New series, 38, no. 150 (1970), pp. 180–91.

   'How the Bank has mismanaged monetary policy', *The Banker*, 126, no. 610 (1976), pp. 1411–9.

   'The reform of monetary control in the United Kingdom', *Annual Monetary Review*, no.1, City University Centre for Banking and International Finance, London (October 1979), pp. 28–41.

   et al., 'Monetary control ... critique of Cmd 7858', City Banking and International Finance (1980).

Griffiths, Brian, and Geoffrey E. Wood, *Monetary Targets* (London: Macmillan, 1981).

   Monetarism in the United Kingdom (London: Macmillan, 1984).

Gurley, John, and E. S. Shaw, *Money in a Theory of Finance* (Washington DC: The Brookings Institution, 1960).

Hacche, Graham, 'The demand for money in the United Kingdom: Experience since 1971', *BEQB*, 14, no. 3 (September 1974).

   Review article of 'The Bank of England: 1950s to 1979' by Forrest Capie (New York: Cambridge University Press, 2010)' *Economica*, 80 (April 2013), pp. 372–8.

Hacche, Graham, and John Townend, 'Exchange rates and monetary policy: Modelling sterling's effective exchange rate, 1972–80', in W. A. Eltis and P. J. N. Sinclair (eds) *The Money Supply and the Exchange Rate* (Oxford: Clarendon Press, 1981).

Hahn, L. Albert, *Volkswirtschaftliche Theorie des Bankkredits* (Tübingen: J. C. B. Mohr, 1st edn 1920, 2nd edn 1924, 3rd edn 1930).

 Economic Theory of Bank Credit (ed.), Clemens Matt, translation of 1920 edn and second part of 1930 edn, introduction by Harald Hagemann (Oxford: Oxford University Press, 2015).

Hambros Bank, *Hambros Bank Ltd., London: 1839–1939* (London, 1939).

Hamilton, Earl J., *American Treasure and the Price Revolution in Spain, 1501–1650* (Cambridge, MA: Harvard University Press, 1934; New York: Octagon, 1970).

Hamilton, James D., *Time Series Analysis* (Princeton, NJ: Princeton University Press, 1994).

Hankey, Thomson, *The Principles of Banking, Its Utility and Economy* (London, 1st edn 1867, 4th edn 1887, reprinted by Elibron Classics, 2006).

Hannaford, Charles F., *Cheques: Their Origin and Development, and How They Are Handled by an English Bank* (London, Pitman, 1923).

Hansen, Alvin H., *Full Recovery or Stagnation?* (London: Adam and Charles Black, 1938).

 Monetary Theory and Fiscal Policy (New York: McGraw-Hill, 1949).

 A Guide to Keynes (New York: McGraw-Hill, 1953).

 Business Cycles and National Income (London: Allen and Unwin, 1964; London and New York: Routledge, 2003).

Harvey, Paul D. A., 'The English inflation of 1180–1220', *Past & Present*, 61 (November 1973), pp. 3–30.

Healey, Denis W., baron Healey of Riddlesden, *The Time of My Life* (London: Michael Joseph, 1989).

Henderson, Schuyler K., and John A. M. Price, *Currency and Interest Rate Swaps* (London: Butterworth, 2nd edn 1988).

Hendry, David F., 'Predictive failure and econometric modelling in macroeconomics: The transactions demand for money', in Paul Ormerod (ed.), *Economic Modelling: Current Issues and Problems in Macroeconomic Modelling in the UK and the US* (London: Heinemann, 1980).

Hendry, David F., and Neil R. Ericsson, 'Assertion without empirical basis: An econometric appraisal of *monetary trends in … the United Kingdom* by Milton Friedman and Anna Schwartz', Bank of England Panel of Academic Consultants, 22 (October 1983).

Hewitt, Michael E., 'Financial forecasts in the United Kingdom', *BEQB*, 17, no. 2 (June 1977) pp. 188–95.

Hicks, Sir John R., 'Mr Keynes and the "classics": A suggested interpretation', *Econometrica*, 5, no. 2 (April 1937), pp. 147–59.

 Value and Capital: An Inquiry into Some Fundamental Principles of Economic Theory (Oxford: Clarendon Press, 1st edn 1939, 2nd edn 1946).

Hill, Christopher, *The Century of Revolution, 1603–1714* (London: Thomas Nelson, 1961).

Hills, Sally, Ryland Thomas, Nicholas H. Dimsdale, 'The UK recession in context – what do three centuries of data tell us?', *BEQB*, 60, no. 4 (2010 Q4)

www.bankofengland.co.uk/publications/quarterlybulletin/threecenturies
ofdata.xls.

Hixson, William, F., foreword by John H. Hotson, *A Matter of Interest: Reexamining
Money, Debt and Real Economic Growth* (New York and London: Praeger,
1991).

*Triumph of the Bankers: Money and Banking in the Eighteenth and Nineteenth
Centuries* (Westport, CT, and London: Praeger, 1993).

Hodgson, Leonard C., *Building Societies: Their Origins, Methods and Principles*
(London: John Long, 1929).

Holdsworth, Sir William S., *A History of English Law* (eds) A. L. Goodhart and
H. G. Hanbury (London: Methuen, 1956, reprinted 2003).

Holgate, H. C. F., 'Loans, overdrafts and deposits', *Bankers' Magazine* (November
1938), pp. 739–43.

Holmes, Anthony R., and Edwin Green, *Midland: 150 Years of Banking Business*
(London: Batsford, 1986).

Holtrop, Marius W., 'Method of monetary analysis used by De Nederlandische
Bank', *IMF Staff Papers*, 5, no. (3) (1957), pp. 303–316.

'Memorandum of evidence submitted by the president of the Netherlands Bank,
5th November 1958', in *Principal Memoranda of Evidence Submitted to the
Committee on the Working of the Monetary System, Volume 1* (London: HMSO,
1960), pp. 260–268.

Horsefield, J. Keith, *British Monetary Experiments, 1650–1710* (Cambridge,
MA: Harvard University Press, 1960: London: Bell, 1960).

Hoskyns, John, *Just in Time: Inside the Thatcher Revolution* (London: Aurum,
2000).

Hotson, Anthony C., 'British monetary targets 1976 to 1987: A view from the
fourth floor of the Bank of England', Special Paper 190, Financial Markets
Group, London School of Economics and Political Science, *ISSN 1359-
9151-190* (7 March 2010) www2.lse.ac.uk/fmg/workingPapers/specialPa-
pers/2010.aspx.

'Currency stabilisation and asset-price anchors: An examination of medieval
monetary practices with some implications for modern policy', *VOX* (23
April 2013) http://voxeu.org/article/medieval-monetary-practices.

'The 1981 Budget and its impact on the conduct of economic policy: Was
it a monetarist revolution?' in D. J. Needham and A. C. Hotson (eds)
*Expansionary Fiscal Contraction: The Thatcher Government's 1981 Budget
in Perspective* (Cambridge: Cambridge University Press, 2014), pp. 123–47.

review of Duncan Needham's book, *UK monetary policy from devaluation
to Thatcher, 1976–82, Economic History Review*, 68, no. 2 (May 2015),
pp. 743–5.

Hotson, Anthony C., and Terence C. Mills, 'London's market for bullion and spe-
cie in the eighteenth century: The roles of the London Mint and the Bank of
England in the stabilization of prices' in M. Allen and D'M. Coffman (eds)
Money, Prices and Wages: Essays in Honour of Professor Nicholas Mayhew
(Basingstoke: Palgrave Macmillan, 2015), pp. 211–27.

Hotson, Anthony C., and Nicholas J. Mayhew, 'English Mint silver and gold
prices, 1158–1946', Winton Institute for Monetary History (May 2015).

Houghton, John, *A Collection, for Improvement of Husbandry and Trade*, London, Nos. 1–582, 1692–1703 (Farnborough: Gregg International, reprint, 1969).

House of Commons, Treasury and Civil Service Committee, *Memoranda on Monetary Policy*, Session 1979–80 (London: HMSO, 17 July 1980).

Monetary Policy, Session 1980–81 (3 vols, London: HMSO, 24 February 1981).

enquiries March 1980, questionnaire 24th April 1980, *Report on Medium-Term Financial Strategy* (February 1981).

Howe, Sir R. E. Geoffrey, baron Howe of Aberavon, *Conflict of Loyalty* (London: Macmillan, 1994).

Howarth, F. R., *The Banks in the Clearing House* (London, 1905).

Our Banking Clearing System and Clearing Houses (London, 1st edn 1884, 4th edn 1907).

Howson, Susan K., *Domestic Monetary Management in Britain, 1919–38* (Cambridge: Cambridge University Press, 1975).

Sterling's Managed Float: The Operations of the Exchange Equalisation Account, 1932–39 (Princeton, NJ: Princeton University Press, 1980).

British Monetary Policy, 1945–51 (Oxford: Clarendon Press, 1993).

'Money and monetary policy since 1945' in Sir Roderick C. Floud and Paul Johnson (eds) *The Cambridge Economic History of Modern Britain, Volume 3* (Cambridge: Cambridge University Press, 2004), pp. 134–66.

Huber, Joseph, 'Modern money theory and the new currency theory', *Real-World Economics Review*, 66 (13 January 2014), pp. 38–57 www.paecon.net/PAEReview/issue66/Huber66.pdf.

Hume, David, 'Of money' (1752) in *Essays: Moral, Political, and Literary* (Edinburgh: Cadell, Donaldson and Creech, 1777) (ed.), Eugene F. Miller (Indianapolis, IN: Liberty Fund, revised edn 1987), pt. II, essay III, I.

Hume, Joseph, *Thoughts on the New Coinage: With Reflections on Money and Coins, and a New System of Coins and Weights, on a Simple and Uniform Principle* (London: J. J. Stockdale, 1816).

Humphrey, Thomas M., 'Lender of last resort: The concept in history', *FRB Richmond Economic Review*, 75, no. 2 (March/April 1989), pp. 8–16.

Hurn, Stanley, *Syndicated Loans: A Handbook for Banker and Borrower* (New York and London: Woodhead-Faulkner, 1990).

Hutchison, John, *The Practice of Banking: Embracing the Cases at Law and in Equity Bearing upon All Branches of the Subject* (4 vols, London: Effingham Wilson, 1881–1891).

Jackson, Andrew, and Ben Dyson, *Modernising Money: Why Our Monetary System Is Broken and How It Can Be Fixed* (London: Positive Money, 2012).

Jackson, C., and M. Sim, 'Recent developments in the sterling overnight money market', *BEQB*, 53, no. 3 (2013), pp. 223–32.

Jackson, Patricia, 'Deposit protection and bank failures in the United Kingdom', *Bank of England Financial Stability Review* (Autumn 1996), pp. 38–43 www.bankofengland.co.uk/archive/Documents/historicpubs/fsr/1996/fsrfull9610.pdf.

Jastram, Roy W., *Silver, the Restless Metal* (John Wiley, 1981).

The Golden Constant: The English and American Experience, 1560–2007 (Cheltenham: Edward Elgar, 2009).

Jevons, W. Stanley, *Money and the Mechanism of Exchange* (London, 1872; London: Henry S. King, 1875; London: Kegan Paul, Trench, Trübner, 9th edn 1890).

Jobst, Clemens, and Kilian Rieder, 'Principles, circumstances and constraints: The Nationalbank as lender of last resort 1816–1931', *Monetary Policy and the Economy* (Oesterreichische Nationalbank, Q3-Q4 2016), pp. 140–62 www .oenb.at/dam/jcr:ce383d85-91a4-4b23-b176-d47eaf91f3a7/mop_2016_q3_ in_focus_07_Jobst_Rieder.pdf.

Johnson, Harry G. (ed.), *Readings in British Monetary Economics* (Oxford: Clarendon Press, 1972).

Johnston, R. B., *The Economics of the Euro-Market: History, Theory and Policy* (London and Basingstoke: Macmillan, 1983).

Jones, D. W., *War and Economy in the Age of William III and Marlborough* (Oxford, 1988).

Jones, Edgar, *Accountancy and the British Economy, 1840–1980: The Evolution of Ernst and Whinney* (London: Batsford, 1981).

Joplin, Thomas, *An Essay on the General Principles and Present Practice of Banking in England and Scotland* (Newcastle upon Tyne: Edward Walker, 3rd edn 1822).

Jordà, Òscar, Moritz Schularick and Alan M. Taylor, 'The great mortgaging: Housing finance, crises, and business cycles', *FRB of San Francisco Working Paper Series*, no. 2014–23 (September 2014); *NBER Working Paper*, no. 20501 (September 2014); *Economic Policy*, CEPR, 31, no. 85 (2016), pp. 107–52.

Jordà, Òscar, 'Betting the house', *NBER Working Paper*, no. 20771 (December 2014); *Journal of International Economics*, 96, Supplement 1 (July 2015), pp. S2–S18.

Joslin, D. M. 'London private bankers, 1720–1785', *Economic History Review*, 7, no. 2 (1954), pp. 167–86.

Kay, John, 'Narrow banking: The reform of banking regulation' (December 2009) www.johnkay.com/wp-content/uploads/2009/12/JK-Narrow-Banking.pdf.
Other People's Money: Masters of the Universe or Servants of the People? (London: Profile, 2015).

Keegan, William J. G., *Mrs Thatcher's Economic Experiment* (London: Allen Lane, 1984).
Mr. Lawson's Gamble (London: Hodder and Stoughton, 1989).

Kelly, E. M., *Spanish Dollars and Silver Tokens: An Account of the Issues of the Bank of England 1797–1816* (London: Spink & Son, 1976).

Kerridge, E., *Trade and Banking in Early Modern England* (Manchester: Manchester University Press, 1988).

Keynes, John Maynard, baron Keynes of Tilton, *Indian Currency and Finance*, 1st edn 1913, reprinted in *The Collected Writings of John Maynard Keynes*, Vol. I (London and Basingstoke: Macmillan and Cambridge University Press, Royal Economic Society edn 1971).

A Tract on Monetary Reform, 1st edn 1923, reprinted in *The Collected Writings of John Maynard Keynes*, Vol. IV (London and Basingstoke: Macmillan and Cambridge University Press, Royal Economic Society edn 1971).

Treatise on Money, 1st edn 1930, reprinted in *The Collected Writings of John Maynard Keynes*, Vols V and VI (London and Basingstoke: Macmillan and Cambridge University Press, Royal Economic Society edn 1971).

The General Theory of Employment Interest and Money, 1st edn 1936, reprinted in *The Collected Writings of John Maynard Keynes*, Vol. VII (London and Basingstoke: Macmillan and Cambridge University Press, Royal Economic Society, edn 1973).

Kindleberger, Charles P., *Manias, Panics and Crashes: A History of Financial Crises* (London: Macmillan, 1978).

A Financial History of Western Europe (London: Allen & Unwin, 1984; New York and Oxford: Oxford University Press, 2nd edn 1993; Abingdon: Routledge, reprint of 1st edn 2006).

Kindleberger, Charles P., and Richard Z. Aliber, *Manias, Panics and Crashes: A History of Financial Crises* (Basingstoke: Palgrave Macmillan, 2011).

King, Mervyn A., baron King of Lothbury, 'No money, no inflation – the role of money in the economy', *BEQB*, 42, no. 2 (Summer 2002), pp. 162–77.

'Monetary policy: Practice ahead of theory', Mais Lecture, *BEQB*, 45, no. 2 (Summer 2005), pp. 226–36.

'Twenty years of inflation targeting', Stamp Memorial Lecture, London School of Economics (9 October 2012) www.bankofengland.co.uk/publications/pages/speeches/default.aspx.

The End of Alchemy: Money, Banking and the Future of the Global Economy (London: Little, Brown, 2016).

King, Wilfred T. C., *History of the London Discount Market* (London: Cass, 1936; Abingdon: Routledge, 2006).

Kotlikoff, Laurence J., *Jimmy Stewart Is Dead: Ending the World's Ongoing Financial Plague with Limited Purpose Banking* (Hoboken, NJ: John Wiley & Sons, 2010).

Krugman, Paul R., 'Who was Milton Friedman?' *Journal of Monetary Economics*, 55, no. 4 (May 2008), pp. 835–56.

'Response to Nelson and Schwartz', *Journal of Monetary Economics*, 55, no. 4 (May 2008), pp. 857–60.

'Economics in the crisis' in his column 'The Conscience of a Liberal', *New York Times* (5 March 2012) http://krugman.blogs.nytimes.com/2012/03/05/economics-in-the-crisis/.

Kunz, Diane B., *The Battle for Britain's Gold Standard in 1931* (London: Croom Helm, 1987).

Kuttner, Robert, 'Agreeing to disagree: Robert Kuttner speaks with Milton Friedman', *American Prospect* (5 January 2006).

Kydland, Finn E., and Edward C. Prescott, 'Rules rather than discretion: The inconsistency of optimal plans', *Journal of Political Economy* (1977), pp. 473–91.

Kynaston, David, *The City of London* (4 vols, London: Chatto & Windus, 2001).

Laidler, David, and Michael Parkin, 'Demand for money in the United Kingdom 1956–67: Preliminary estimates', *University of Essex Discussion Paper* (unpublished).

Law Commission, *Fiduciary Duties of Financial Intermediaries*, Law Comm no. 350 (2014).

Lawson, Nigel, baron Lawson of Blaby, 'Thatcherism in Practice: A Progress Report', Speech to the Zurich Society of Economists, H.M. Treasury Press Release (14 January 1981) www.margaretthatcher.org/archive/displaydocument .asp?docid=109506.

 The View from No. 11: Memoirs of a Tory Radical (London: Bantam Press, 1992).

Leaf, Walter, *Banking* (London: Butterworth, 1st edn September 1926, 2nd edn November 1926, reprinted 1927, 1928, 1929, 1931).

 Banking (ed.), Ernest Sykes (3rd edn 1935, reprinted 1937, 4th edn London and New York: Oxford University Press, 1943).

 Banking (1943), reprinted in F. H. Capie and G. E. Wood (eds) *Banking Theory, 1870–1930*, 7 (7 vols, London: Routledge, 1999).

Leamer, Edward E., 'Let's take the con out of econometrics', *American Economic Review*, 73, no. 1 (1983), pp. 31–43.

 'Housing is the business cycle', *NBER Working Paper Series*, no. 13428 (2007).

Leigh-Pemberton, Robert (Robin), baron Kingsdown, 'Some aspects of UK monetary policy', *BEQB*, 24, no. 4 (December 1984), pp. 474–81.

Leijonhufvud, Axel, *On Keynesian Economics and the Economics of Keynes* (Oxford: Oxford University Press, 1968).

Leonard, Adrian, 'Trouble indemnity', History & Policy paper, Cambridge (2012).

Lewis, J. Parry, *Building Cycles and Britain's Growth* (London: Macmillan, 1965).

Li, Ming-Hsun, *The Great Recoinage of 1696 to 1699* (London: Weidenfeld & Nicolson, 1963).

Liikanen, Erkki A., *High-Level Expert Group on Reforming the Structure of the EU Banking Sector, Final Report* (Brussels, 2 October 2012).

Lindahl, Erik, *Studies in the Theory of Money and Capital* (London, 1939).

Liverpool, Sir Charles Jenkinson, first earl of, *A Treatise on the Coins of the Realm: In a Letter to the King* (Oxford: Oxford University Press for Cadell & Davies, 1805; Bank of England edn 1880).

Llewellyn, David T., G. E. J. Dennis, M. J. B. Hall and J. G. Nellis, *The Framework of UK Monetary Policy* (London, 1982).

Locke, John, *Some Considerations of the Consequences of the lowering of Interest, and raising the value of Money...* (1692, 2nd edn 1696).

 Short Observations on a printed paper, entitled For encouraging the coining of Silver money in England, and after for keeping it here (1695, 2nd edn 1696).

 Further Considerations Concerning Raising the Value of Money (1695, 2nd edn 1695, corrected 3rd edn 1696).

 Locke on Money (ed.), Patrick H. Kelly (2 vols, Oxford: Oxford University Press, 1991).

 'Repairing the coin' in Ming-Hsun Li, *The Great Recoinage of 1696 to 1699* (London: Weidenfeld & Nicolson, 1963), Appendix IV, pp. 224–36.

London, Simon, 'Lunch with the FT: Milton Friedman', *Financial Times* (7 June 2003).

Lowndes, William, *A Report Containing an Essay for the Amendment of the Silver Coins* (London: Charles Bill, 1695).

Lucas, Robert E., 'Econometric policy evaluation – a critique', in Karl Brunner and Allan Meltzer, eds, *The Phillips Curve and Labor Markets*. vol. 1: *Carnegie-Rochester Conference on Public Policy, a supplementary series to the Journal of Monetary Economics* (Amsterdam: Elsevier, January 1976), pp. 19–46.

 'Interest rates and currency prices in a two-country world', *Journal of Monetary Economics*, 10, no. 3 (1982), pp. 335–60.

Machet, Robert, *An Enquiry into the Effects Produced on the National Currency and Rates of Exchange…* (London: Baldwin, 1st edn 1810, 3rd edn 1811).

Macaulay, Frederick R., *Some Theoretical Problems Suggested by: The Movements of Interest Rates, Bond Yields and Stock Prices in the United States since 1856* (NBER, 33, 1938; London: Risk Books, 1999).

MacDonald, James, *A Free Nation Deep in Debt: The Financial Roots of Democracy* (New York: Farrar, Straus and Giroux, 2003; Princeton, NJ, and Oxford: Princeton University Press, 2006).

MacLeod, Henry Dunning, *The Theory and Practice of Banking* (2 vols, London: Longman, 1st edn 1855, 2nd edn 1866, 3rd edn 1875, 4th edn 1883–6, 5th edn 1892).

Macmillan Committee, *Committee on Finance and Industry*, Cmd 3897 (London: HMSO, 1931).

Marius, John, *Advice Concerning Bills of Exchange* (1651).

Marshall, Alfred, *Money Credit and Commerce* (London: Macmillan, 1923).

Martin, Felix, *Money: The Unauthorised Biography* (London: Bodley Head, Random House, 2013).

Matten, Chris, *Managing Bank Capital: Capital Allocation and Performance Measurement* (Chichester: Wiley, 1996).

Matthews, Philip W., *Handbook to the London Bankers' Clearing House* (London: Eden Fisher, 1st edn 1910, 2nd edn 1912).

 The Bankers' Clearing House (London: Pitman, 1921).

Mayhew, Nicholas J., 'From Regional to Central Minting, 1158–1464' in C. E. Challis (ed.), *New History of the Royal Mint* (Cambridge: Cambridge University Press, 1992), pp. 83–178.

 Sterling: The Rise and Fall of a Currency (London: Allen Lane, 1999).

 Sterling: The History of a Currency (New York: Wiley, 2000; London: Penguin, 2000).

 'Silver in England 1660–1800: Coinage outputs and bullion exports from the records of the London Tower Mint and the London Company of Goldsmiths', in J. H. A. Munro (ed.), *Money in the Pre-Industrial World: Bullion, Debasements and Coin Substitutes* (London: Pickering & Chatto, 2012), pp. 97–110.

 'Prices in England, 1170–1750', *Past & Present*, no. 219 (May 2013).

 'The quantity theory of money in historical perspective', in M. Casson and N. Hashimzade (eds) *Large Databases in Economic History: Research Methods and Case Studies* (Abingdon: Routledge, 2013), pp. 62–96.

McCulley, Paul, and Jonathan Fuerbringer, *Your Financial Edge: How to Take the Curves in Shifting Financial Markets and Keep Your Portfolio on Track* (Hoboken, NJ: Wiley, 2007).

McCulloch, John R., 'On fluctuations in the supply and value of money', *Edinburgh Review*, no. 86 (1826).

(ed.), *A Select Collection of Scarce and Valuable Tracts on Money* (London, 1856).

McCusker, John J., *Money and Exchange in Europe and America, 1600–1775: A Handbook* (Chapel Hill, NC: University of North Carolina Press, 1978; London: Macmillan, 1978).

European Bills of Entry and Marine Lists: Early Commercial Publications and the Origins of the Business Press (Cambridge, MA.: Harvard University Library, 1985).

McCusker, John J., and Cora Gravesteijn, *The Beginnings of Commercial and Financial Journalism: The Commodity Price Currents, Exchange Rate Currents, and Money Currents of Early Modern Europe* (Amsterdam: NEHA, 1991).

McLeay, Michael, Amar Radia and Ryland Thomas, 'Money creation in the modern economy', *BEQB* (2014 Q1), pp. 14–27.

Meade, James E., 'The amount of money and the banking system', *Economic Journal*, 44, no. 173 (March 1934), pp. 77–83.

Mehrling, Perry, *The New Lombard Street: How the Fed Became a Dealer of Last Resort* (Princeton, NJ: Princeton University Press, 2011).

Melton, Frank T., *Sir Robert Clayton and the Origins of English Deposit Banking, 1658–1685* (Cambridge: Cambridge University Press, 1986).

Menger, C., 'On the origin of money', *Economic Journal*, 2, no. 3 (1892), pp. 239–55.

Menzel, Sewall, *Cobs, Pieces of Eight and Treasure Coins: The Early Spanish-American Mints and Their Coinages, 1536–1773* (New York: American Numismatic Society, 2004).

Mian, Atif, and Amir Sufi, *House of Debt: How They (and You) Caused the Great Recession, and How We Can Prevent It from Happening Again* (Chicago and London: University of Chicago Press, 2014).

Michie, Ranald C., *The London Stock Exchange: A History* (Oxford: Oxford University Press, 1999).

'The City of London as a global financial centre, 1880–1939: Finance, foreign exchange, and the First World War' in P. L. Cottrell, E. Lange, and U. Olsson (eds) *Centres and Peripheries in Banking* (Aldershot: Ashgate, 2007).

British Banking: Continuity and Change from 1694 to the Present (Oxford: Oxford University Press, 2016).

Miles, David, Jing Yang and Gilberto Marcheggiano, 'Optimal Bank Capital', External MPC Unit, Discussion Paper, 31 (January 2011).

Mill, John Stuart, *Principles of Political Economy, with Some of Their Applications to Social Philosophy* (2 vols, London: J. W. Parker, 1848).

Mills, Terence C., and Raphael N. Markellos, *The Econometric Modelling of Financial Times Series* (Cambridge: Cambridge University Press, 2008).

Minsky, Hyman P., *Stabilizing an Unstable Economy* (New Haven, CT: Yale University Press, 1986; New York: Macmillan, 2008).

Mizen, Paul (ed.), *Central Banking, Monetary Theory and Practice: Essays in Honour of Charles Goodhart*, 1 (Cheltenham: Edward Elgar, 2003).

Monetary History, Exchange Rates and Financial Markets, 2 (Cheltenham: Edward Elgar, 2003).

Moore, Charles, *Margaret Thatcher: The Authorized Biography*, 1 (London: Allen Lane, 2013).

Moore, Paul, and Mike Haworth, *Crash Bank Wallop: The Memoirs of the HBOS Whistleblower* (London: New Wilberforce Media, 2015).

Moran, Michael, *The Politics of Banking: The Strange Case of Competition and Credit Control* (London: Macmillan, 1st edn 1984, 2nd edn 1986).

Morgan, Kenneth O., *Britain since 1945: The People's Peace* (Oxford and New York: Oxford University Press, 1st edn 1991, 3rd edn 2001).

Morris, Robert, '*Banking and Currency* by Ernest Sykes', *Journal of Political Economy*, 14, no. 2 (February, 1906), pp. 124–6.

Munro, John H. A. (ed.), *Money in the Pre-Industrial World: Bullion, Debasements and Coin Substitutes* (London: Pickering & Chatto, 2012).

Murphy, Anne L., *The Origins of English Financial Markets* (Cambridge: Cambridge University Press, 2009).

'The financial revolution and its consequences' in Sir Roderick C. Floud, K. Jane Humphries and Paul Johnson (eds) *The Cambridge Economic History of Modern Britain*. Vol. I: *1700–1870* (Cambridge: Cambridge University Press, 2014), pp. 321–43.

Neal, Larry D., 'The rise of a financial press: London and Amsterdam, 1681–1810', *Business History*, 30, no. 2 (April 1988), pp. 163–78.

The Rise of Financial Capitalism: International Capital Markets in the Age of Reason (Cambridge: Cambridge University Press, 1990).

'A tale of two revolutions, international capital flows, 1789–1819', *Bulletin of Economic Research*, 43, no. 1 (1990), pp. 307–37.

'The finance of business during the industrial revolution' in Sir Roderick C. Floud and Donald McCloskey (eds) *The Cambridge Economic History of Modern Britain*. Vol. I: *1700–1860* (Cambridge: Cambridge University Press, 1st edn 1981, 2nd edn 1994), pp. 151–81.

'The financial crisis of 1825 and the restructuring of the British financial system', *Federal Reserve Bank of St. Louis Review*, 80 (1998), pp. 53–76.

'The monetary and financial architecture of Europe from 1648 to 1815', *Financial History Review*, 7, no. 2 (October, 2000), pp. 117–40.

Neal, Larry D., and Stephen Quinn, 'Networks of information, markets, and institutions in the rise of London as a financial centre, 1660–1720', *Financial History Review*, 8, no. 1 (April 2001), pp. 7–26.

Neal, Larry D., and Eugene N. White, 'The Glass-Steagall Act in historical perspective', *Quarterly Review of Economics and Finance*, 52 (2012), pp. 104–13.

Neal, Larry D., and Lance E. Davis, 'The evolution and the structure and performance of the London Stock Exchange in the first global financial market, 1812–1914', *European Review of Economic History*, 10, no. 3 (December 2016), pp. 279–300.

Needham, Duncan J., 'Britain's money supply experiment, 1971–73', *University of Cambridge Working Papers in Economic and Social History*, 10 (September 2012).

UK Monetary Policy from Devaluation to Thatcher, 1967–82 (Basingstoke: Palgrave Macmillan, 2014).

'The 1981 budget: "A Dunkirk, not an Alamein"' in D. J. Needham and A. C. Hotson (eds) *Expansionary Fiscal Contraction: The Thatcher Government's 1981 Budget in Perspective* (Cambridge: Cambridge University Press, 2014), pp. 148–80.

Needham, Duncan J., and Anthony C. Hotson (eds) *Expansionary Fiscal Contraction: The Thatcher Government's 1981 Budget in Perspective* (Cambridge: Cambridge University Press, 2014).

Nelson, Edward, 'UK monetary policy 1972–97: A guide using Taylor rules', *Bank of England Working Paper*, no. 120 (2000).

Nevin, Edward T., and E. W. Davis, *The London Clearing Banks* (London: Elek, 1970).

Newlyn, Walter T., *Theory of Money* (Oxford: Clarendon Press, 1st edn 1962, 2nd edn 1971), see also Newlyn and Bootle (1978, 1979).

'The supply of money and its control', *Economic Journal*, 74, no. 214 (June 1964).

Newlyn, Walter T., and R. P. Bootle, *Theory of Money* (Oxford: Clarendon Press, 3rd edn 1978, reprinted 1979), see also Newlyn (1962, 1971).

Newton, Sir Isaac, 'Concerning the Amend't of English Coyns', GL.MS.62, ff. 34–6, 1695 in Ming-Hsun Li, *The Great Recoinage of 1696 to 1699* (London: Weidenfeld & Nicolson, 1963), appendix III, pp. 217–23.

'Memorial concerning the proportion of gold and silver in value' (London, 1701).

Niehans, Jürg, *The Theory of Money* (Baltimore: Johns Hopkins University Press, 1978).

'The appreciation of sterling: Causes, effects, policies', Center for Research in Government, Policy and Business, Graduate School of Management, Rochester, NY (February 1981).

Nightingale, Pamela, 'The evolution of weight-standards and the creation of new monetary and commercial links in northern Europe from the tenth century to the twelfth century', *Economic History Review*, 38, no. 2 (May 1985), pp. 192–209.

'Monetary contraction and mercantile credit in later medieval England', *Economic History Review*, 43, no. 4 (November 1990), pp. 560–75.

'English medieval weight-standards revisited', *British Numismatic Journal*, 78 (2008).

Nishimura, Shizuya, *The Decline of Inland Bills of Exchange in the London Money Market, 1865–1913* (London: Cambridge University Press, 1971).

Nogués-Marco, Pilar, 'Competing bimetallic ratios', *Journal of Economic History* (0022-0507), 73 (2), 2013, p. 445.

Norman, Ben, Rachel Shaw, and George Speight, 'The history of interbank settlement arrangements: Exploring central banks' role in the payment system', *Bank of England Working Paper*, No. 412 (June 2011).

Offer, Avner, *Property and Politics 1870–1914: Landownership, Law, Ideology and Urban Development in England* (Cambridge: Cambridge University Press, 1981).

'From "buy to let" to rent control: 1870–1920', presented at Winton Institute Colloquium, University of Oxford (November 2010).

'Narrow banking, real estate, and financial stability in the UK, c. 1870–2010', in N. H. Dimsdale and A. C. Hotson (eds) *British Financial Crises since 1825* (Oxford: Oxford University Press, 2014), pp. 158–73.

Officer, Lawrence H., *Between the Dollar-Sterling Gold Points: Exchange Rates, Parity, and Market Behaviour* (Cambridge: Cambridge University Press, 1996).

Ogden, Tessa, 'An analysis of Bank of England discount and advance behaviour, 1870–1914', in J. Foreman-Peck (ed.), *New Perspectives in the Late-Victorian Economy: Essays in Quantitative Economic History 1860–1914* (Cambridge: Cambridge University Press, 1991), pp. 305–43.

Oliver, Michael, 'A response to Denham and Garnett's "the nature and impact of think tanks in contemporary Britain"', *Contemporary British History*, 10, no. 2 (1996), pp. 80–6.

Palgrave, Sir Robert H. Inglis, *Bank Rate and the Money Market* (London: John Murray, 1903).

Parliamentary Papers 1810–11, 69: Abstract of Account of the Prices Paid by the Bank of England for Gold and Silver Bullion in each year from 1697 to the 28th February 1811 (15 March 1811).

Patinkin, Don, *Money, Interest and Prices: An Integration of Monetary and Value Theory* (Evanston, IL: Row, Peterson, 1956; New York: Harper & Row, 2nd edn 1965; Cambridge, MA: MIT Press, abridged edn 1989).

Paulson, Hank, *On The Brink* (New York: Headline, 2010).

Persaud, Avinash, *Reinventing Financial Regulation: A Blueprint for Overcoming Systemic Risk* (New York: Apress, 2015).

Pepper, Gordon T., *Inside Thatcher's Monetarist Revolution* (Basingstoke: Palgrave Macmillan, 1998).

Phillips, Alban W., 'The relation between unemployment and the rate of change of money wage rates in the United Kingdom, 1861–1957', *Economica*, 25, 100 (November 1958), pp. 283–99.

Phillips, Chester A., *Bank Credit: A Study of the Principles and Factors Underlying Advances Made by Banks to Borrowers* (New York: Macmillan, 1920).

Phillips, Chester A., Thomas F. McManus, and Richard W. Nelson, *Banking and the Business Cycle: A Study of the Great Depression in the United States* (New York: Macmillan, 1937).

Platt, Robert B., *Controlling Interest Rate Risk: New Techniques and Applications for Money Management* (New York: Wiley, 1986).

Plenderleith, Ian, 'Gilt repo – and beyond', *BEQB*, 36, no. 3 (August 1996), pp. 338–41.

Pohl, Manfred, and Sabine Freitag, *Handbook on the History of European Banks* (Aldershot: Edward Elgar, 1994).

Polack, Jacques J., and Victor Argy, 'Credit policy and balance of payments', *Staff Papers*, 16, International Monetary Fund (1971), pp. 1–24.

Poole, William, 'Optimal choice of monetary policy instruments in a simple stochastic macro model', *Quarterly Journal of Economics*, 84, no. 2 (May 1970), pp. 197–216.

Postel-Vinay, Natacha, 'Debt dilution in 1920's America: Lighting the fuse of a mortgage crisis', *EHES Working Papers in Economic History*, no. 53 (March 2014).

'What caused Chicago bank failures in the Great Depression? A look at the 1920s', *Department of Economics, University of Warwick* (October 2014).

Powell, Ellis Thomas, *Evolution of the Money Market 1385–1915* (London: Cass, 3rd edn 1966).

Pressnell, Leslie S., *Country Banking in the Industrial Revolution* (Oxford: Oxford University Press, 1956).

'Gold reserves, banking reserves, and the Barings crisis of 1890' in C. R. Whittlesey and J. S. G. Wilson (eds) *Essays in Honour of R. S. Sayers* (Oxford: Clarendon Press, 1968).

'Cartels and competition in British banking: A background study', *Banca Nazionale del Lavoro Quarterly Review*, 95 (1970), pp. 373–405.

Price, F. G. Hilton, *A Handbook of London Bankers* (London: Chatto & Windus, 1876; New York: B. Franklin, 1970).

Price, Lionel D. D., 'The demand for money in the United Kingdom: A further investigation', *BEQB*, 12, no. 1 (March 1972), pp. 43–55.

Price, Seymour J., *Building Societies: Their Origin and History* (London: Franey, 1958).

Quinn, Stephen, 'Tallies or reserves? Sir Francis Child's balance between capital reserves and extending credit to the Crown, 1685–1695', *Business and Economic History*, 23, no. 1 (Fall 1994), pp. 39–51.

'Gold, silver and the Glorious Revolution: Arbitrage between bills of exchange and bullion', *Economic History Review*, XLIX, 3 (August 1996), pp. 473–90.

'Goldsmith-banking: Mutual acceptance and interbank clearing in Restoration London', *Explorations in Economic History*, 34 (1997).

'Money, finance and capital markets' in Sir Roderick C. Floud and Paul Johnson (eds) *The Cambridge Economic History of Modern Britain*. Volume 1: *Industrialisation, 1700–1860* (Cambridge: Cambridge University Press, 2004), pp. 147–74.

Quinn, Stephen, and William Roberds, 'Responding to a shadow banking crisis: The lessons of 1763' *FRB of Atlanta Working Paper Series*, 2012–8 (June 2012).

Radcliffe Committee, *Committee on the Working of the Monetary System*, Cmnd. 827 (London: HMSO, August 1959).

Rae, George, *The Country Banker: His Clients, Cares, and Work* (London: John Murray, 1st edn 1885, 1894, 5th edn 1902, 6th edn 1918, 1924, 7th edition revised by Ernest Sykes 1930, 1976; London: Routledge, 1999).

The Country Banker: His Clients, Cares, and Work, 1885 edn reprinted in F. H. Capie and G. E. Wood (eds) *Banking Theory, 1870–1930*, 3 (7 vols, London: Routledge, 1999).

Rajan, Raghuram G., *Fault Lines: How Hidden Fractures Still Threaten the World Economy* (Princeton, NJ, and Oxford: Princeton University Press, 2010).

Redish, Angela, 'The evolution of the gold standard in England', *Journal of Economic History*, 50, no. 4 (December 1990), pp. 789–806.

Bimetallism: An Economic and Historical Analysis (Cambridge: Cambridge University Press, 2000).

Redish, Angela, and Warren E. Weber, 'A model of commodity money with minting and melting', *Federal Reserve Bank of Minneapolis Research Department Staff Report 460* (July 2011).

Reid, Margaret I., *The Secondary Banking Crisis, 1973–75: Its Causes and Course* (London: Macmillan, 1982; London: Hindsight Books, 2003).

Reinhart, Carmen M., and Kenneth Rogoff, *This Time Is Different: Eight Centuries of Financial Folly* (Princeton, NJ, and Oxford: Princeton University Press, 2009).

Reinhart, Carmen M., Jacob Kirkegaard and M. Balen Sbrancia, 'Financial repression redux', *Peterson Institute for International Economics* (June 2011).

Ricardo, David, *Proposals for an Economical and Secure Currency* (London: John Murray, 2nd edn, 1816).

'Bullion essays' in Piero Sraffa and M. H. Dobb (eds) *The Works and Correspondence of David Ricardo, Pamphlets and Papers 1809–11* (11 vols, Cambridge: Cambridge University Press, 1951–73).

Richards, Richard D., *The Early History of Banking in England* (London: P. S. King & Son, 1929, reprinted 1965).

'The first fifty years of the Bank of England' in J. G. van Dillen, *History of the Principal Public Banks* (Hague, 1934), pp. 201–72.

Richardson, Gordon W. H., baron Richardson of Duntisbourne, 'Reflections on the conduct of monetary policy', Mais Lecture, 9 February 1978, *BEQB*, 18, no. 1 (March 1978), pp. 31–7.

Riddell, Peter J. R., *The Thatcher Government* (Oxford: Martin Robertson, 1983).

Roberts, Richard, *Schroders: Merchants and Bankers* (Basingstoke: Macmillan, 1992).

Saving the City: The Great Financial Crisis of 1914 (Oxford: Oxford University Press, 2013).

'"How we saved the City": The management of the financial crisis of 1914' in Nicholas H. Dimsdale and Anthony C. Hotson (eds) *British Financial Crises since 1825* (Oxford: Oxford University Press, 2014), pp. 94–115.

Roberts, Richard, and David Kynaston (eds) *The Bank of England: Money, Power and Influence, 1694–1994* (Oxford: Clarendon Press, 1995).

The Lion Wakes: A Modern History of HSBC (London: Profile Books, 2015).

Rogers, David, *The Big Four British Banks: Organisation, Strategy and Future* (Basingstoke: Macmillan, 1999).

Rolnick, Arthur J., François R. Velde, and Warren E. Weber, 'An essay on medieval monetary history', *Journal of Economic History*, 56, No. 4 (December, 1996), pp. 789–808.

Royal Commission, *Inquiry into the Recent Changes in the Relative Values of the Precious Metals*, First Report (London, 1887), Second Report, Final Report, Appendix to Final Report (London, 1888).

Ryan-Collins, Josh, Tony Greenham, Richard Werner, and Andrew Jackson, *Where Does Money Come From? A Guide to the UK Monetary and Banking System* (New Economics Foundation, 2011).

Saleuddin, Rasheed, *Regulating Securitized Products: A Post Crisis Guide* (Basingstoke: Palgrave Macmillan, 2015).

Samuelson, Paul A., *Economics: An Introductory Analysis* (New York: McGraw-Hill, 1st edn 1948; New York and London: McGraw-Hill, 2nd edn 1951).

'An exact consumption-loan model of interest with or without the social contrivance of money', *Journal of Political Economy*, 66, no. 6 (December 1958), pp. 467–82.

'Credo of a lucky textbook author', *Journal Economic Perspectives*, 11, 2 (Spring 1997), pp. 153–60.

Samuelson, Paul A., and Robert M. Solow, 'Problem of achieving and maintaining a stable price level: Analytical aspects of anti-inflation policy', *American Economic Review*, Papers and Proceedings, 50, no. 2 (May 1960), pp. 177–94.

Samy, Antoninus, *The Building Society Promise: Access, Risk, and Efficiency 1880–1939* (Oxford, Oxford University Press, 2016).

Samy, Luke G. (Br. Antoninus), 'The building society promise: The accessibility, risk and efficiency of building societies in England, c 1880–1939' (University of Oxford DPhil thesis, Trinity Term 2010).

'The paradox of success: The effect of growth, competition and managerial self-interest on building society risk-taking and market structure, c. 1880–1939', *University of Oxford Discussion Papers in Economic and Social History*, no. 86 (January 2011).

'Extending home ownership before the First World War: The case of the Co-operative Permanent Building Society, 1884–1913', *Economic History Review*, 65, 1 (2012), pp. 168–93.

'Indices of house prices and rent prices of residential property in London, 1895–1939', *University of Oxford Discussion Papers in Economic and Social History*, no. 134 (April 2015).

Sargent, Thomas J., and Bruce D. Smith, 'Coinage, debasements, and Gresham's Laws', *Economic Theory*, 10, no. 2 (1997), pp. 197–226.

Sargent, Thomas J., and Francois R. Velde, *The Big Problem of Small Change* (Princeton, NJ, and Oxford: Princeton University Press, 2002).

Saving, Thomas R., 'Monetary-policy targets and indicators', *Journal of Political Economy*, 75, no. 4, part 2 (August 1967), pp. 446–56.

Sayers, Richard S., *Bank of England Operations 1890–1914* (London: P. S. King, 1936).

Modern Banking (Oxford: Clarendon Press, 1st edn 1938, 2nd edn 1947, 3rd edn 1951, 4th edn 1958, 5th edn 1960, 6th edn 1964, 7th edn 1967).

Lloyds Bank in the History of English Banking (Oxford: Clarendon Press, 1957).

Central Banking after Bagehot (Oxford: Clarendon Press, 1957).

The Bank of England 1891–1944 (2 vols and appendix, Cambridge: Cambridge University Press, 1976).

'Bank rate in Keynes's century', Keynes Lecture, 1979, *Proceedings of the British Academy*, LXV (Oxford: Oxford University Press, 1981).

Sbordone, Argia M., Andrea Tambalotti, Krishna Rao, and Kieran Walsh, 'Policy analysis using DSGE models: An introduction', *FRBNY Economic Policy Review* (October 2010).

Scammell, W. M., *The London Discount Market* (London: Elek Books, 1968).

Scazzieri, R, A. K. Sen, and S. Zamagni, *Markets, Money and Capital* (Cambridge: Cambridge University Press, 2008).

Schenk, Catherine R., *The Decline of Sterling: Managing the Retreat of an International Currency, 1945–1992* (Cambridge and New York: Cambridge University Press, 2010).
  'Sterling and monetary policy, 1870–2010' in Sir Roderick C. Floud, K. Jane Humphries and Paul Johnson (eds) *The Cambridge Economic History of Modern Britain*. Vol. I: *1700–1870* (Cambridge: Cambridge University Press, 2014), pp. 448–75.
Schubert, E., 'Arbitrage in the foreign exchange markets of London and Amsterdam during the eighteenth century', *Explorations in Economic History*, 26 (1989), pp. I-20.
Schularick, Moritz, and Alan M. Taylor, 'Credit booms gone bust: Monetary policy, leverage cycles, and financial crises, 1870–2008', *American Economic Review*, 102, no. 2 (2012) pp. 1029–61.
Schumpeter, Joseph A., *History of Economic Analysis* (London: Allen & Unwin, 1954; New York: Oxford University Press, 1954).
Schuster, Sir Felix, 'Our gold reserves', *Journal of the Institute of Bankers*, XXVIII, Part I (January 1907), pp. 1–22.
Schwartz, Anna J., 'Real and pseudo financial crises' in F. Capie and G. E. Wood (eds) *Financial Crises and the World Banking System* (London: Macmillan, 1986), pp. 11–31, and in A. J. Schwartz (ed.), *Money in Historical Perspective* (Chicago: University of Chicago Press, 1987), pp. 271–88.
Scratchley, Arthur, *Treatise on Benefit Building Societies and Life Assurance Societies: With Suggestions for the Formation of Local Enterprise Encouragement Companies* (2 vols, London, 1867).
Shaw, William Arthur (ed.), *Select Tracts and Documents Illustrative of English Monetary History 1626–1730* (London, 1896, London: G. Hardy, 1935, reprinted 2009).
  The History of the Currency, 1252–1894 (London: Clement Wilson, 1896; New York: B. Franklin, 2nd edn 1967).
Shaw, William Arthur, and Alfred Wigglesworth, *The Principles of Currency, Credit and Exchange* (London: Pitman, 1934).
Sheppard, David K., *The Growth and Role of UK Financial Institutions, 1880–1962* (London: Methuen, 1971; London: Routledge, 2006).
Shin, Hiroki, 'Paper Money: The nation, and the suspension of cash payments in 1797', *Historical Journal*, 58, no. 2 (2015), pp. 415–42.
Shin, Hyun Song, 'Reflections on Northern Rock: The bank run that heralded the global financial crisis', *Journal of Economic Perspectives*, 23, no. 1 (Winter 2009), pp. 101–19.
  Risk and Liquidity (Oxford: Oxford University Press, 2010).
Shubik, Martin, *Money and Financial Institutions: A Game Theoretic Approach* (Cheltenham: E. Elgar, 1999).
  Theory of Money and Financial Institutions (Cambridge, MA, and London: MIT Press, 1999).
Smith, Adam, *An Inquiry into the Nature and Causes of the Wealth of Nations* (ed.), J. R. McCulloch (Edinburgh, 1776; Edinburgh: Adam Black, 1828).
  An Inquiry into the Nature and Causes of the Wealth of Nations (eds) R. H. Campbell, A. S. Skinner, and W. B. Todd (2 vols, Oxford: Clarendon, 1976).

An Inquiry into the Nature and Causes of the Wealth of Nations (ed.), Kathryn Sutherland (Oxford: Oxford University Press, 1993).

Smith, Matthew, *Thomas Tooke and the Monetary Thought of Classical Economics* (London and New York: Routledge, 2011).

Speight, George, 'Building society behaviour and the mortgage-lending market in the interwar period: Risk-taking by mutual institutions and the interwar housebuilding boom' (University of Oxford DPhil thesis, 2000).

Spufford, Peter, *Handbook of Medieval Exchange* (London and Woodbridge, Suffolk: Royal Historical Society, 1986).

Money and Its Use in Medieval Europe (Cambridge: Cambridge University Press, 1988).

'Debasement of the coinage and its effects on exchange rates and the economy: In England in the 1540s, and in the Burgundian–Habsburg Netherlands in the 1480s' in J. H. A. Munro (ed.), *Money in the Pre-Industrial World: Bullion, Debasements and Coin Substitutes* (London: Pickering & Chatto, 2012), pp. 63–85.

Stead, Francis R., *Bankers' Advances* (London: Pitman, 1919).

Steuart, Sir James, *An Inquiry into the Principles of Political Oeconomy* (eds), Andrew S. Skinner, Noboru Kobayashi and Hiroshi Mizuta (2 vols, London, 1st edn 1767, 2nd edn 1805; 4 vols, London: Pickering & Chatto, 1998).

Principles of Banks and Banking of Money, As Coin and Paper: With the Consequences of Any Excessive Issue on the National Currency, Course of Exchange, Price of Provisions, Commodities and Fixed Incomes (London: J. Davis, 1810).

Stiglitz, Joseph E., 'The efficiency of market prices in long-run allocations in the oil industry', *Studies in Energy Tax Policy*, Stanford Institute for Mathematical Studies in the Social Sciences, Reprint no. 210 (1975).

The Roaring Nineties: Seeds of Destruction (New York: W. W. Norton; London: Allen Lane, 2003).

Stiglitz, Joseph E., and John Driffill, *Economics* (New York: W. W. Norton, 2000).

Stock, James, and Mark Watson, 'Has the business cycle changed and why?' *NBER Working Paper*, no. 9127 (2002).

Sykes, Ernest, *Banking and Currency* (London: Butterworth, 1st edn 1905, 2nd edn 1908, 3rd edn 1911, 4th edn 1918, 5th edn 1923, 6th edn 1925, 7th edn 1932, 8th edn 1937, 9th edn 1947).

Sykes, Joseph, *The Amalgamation Movement in English Banking, 1825–1924* (London: King, 1926).

Tarshis, Lorie, *The Elements of Economics: An Introduction to the Theory of Price and Employment* (Boston: Houghton Mifflin, 1947).

Taylor, Geoffrey W., 'New techniques in British banking: An examination of the sterling money markets and the principles of term lending', in *Gilbart Lecture on Banking* (London: King's College London, 1973).

Taylor, John B., 'Discretion versus policy rules in practice', *Carnegie-Rochester Conference Series on Public Policy*, 39 (1993), pp. 195–214.

(ed.), *Monetary Policy Rules* (Chicago: University of Chicago Press, 1999).

'The financial crisis and the policy responses: An empirical analysis of what went wrong', *NBER Working Paper*, no. 14631 (January 2009).

Taylor, Russell, *Going for Broke: How Banking Mismanagement in the Eighties Lost Billions* (New York: Simon & Schuster, 1993).

Temin, Peter, and Hans-Joachim Voth, *Prometheus Shackled: Goldsmith Banks and England's Financial Revolution after 1700* (New York and Oxford: Oxford University Press, 2013).

Temperton, Paul V., *A Guide to UK Monetary Policy* (Basingstoke: Macmillan, 1986).

Theil, H., *Economic Forecasts and Policy* (Amsterdam: North Holland, 1961).

Tholstrup, Jens, 'The Nordic banking crises of the late 1980s and early 1990s: Why did Denmark avoid a systemic crisis?' (University of Oxford MSc thesis, September 2013).

Thornton, Henry, *An Enquiry into the Nature and Effects of the Paper Credit of Great Britain* (London: J. Hatchard, 1802).

(ed.), F. A. von Hayek, *An Enquiry into the Nature and Effects of the Paper Credit of Great Britain*, 1802 edn and Thornton's parliamentary speeches and evidence (London: Cass, 1939, reprinted 1962) http://oll.libertyfund.org/titles/2041.

'Evidence given before the Committee of Secrecy of the House of Commons appointed to enquire into the outstanding demands of the Bank of England', March and April 1797, in Henry Thornton, *An Enquiry into the Nature and Effects of the Paper Credit of Great Britain* (ed.), F. A. von Hayek (London: Cass, 1939, reprinted 1962), pp. 277–312.

'Two speeches of Henry Thornton', May 1811, in Henry Thornton, *An Enquiry into the Nature and Effects of the Paper Credit of Great Britain* (ed.), F. A. von Hayek (London: Cass, 1939, reprinted 1962), pp. 323–61.

An Enquiry into the Nature and Effects of the Paper Credit of Great Britain (Philadelphia: James Humphreys, 1807, reprinted by Kessinger, 2008).

Tobin, James, 'Commercial banks as creators of "money"', Cowles Foundation Paper, no. 205, in Deane Carson (ed.), *Banking and Monetary Studies* (Homewood, Ill: Richard D. Irwin, 1963), pp. 408–19.

'The monetary interpretation of history', *American Economic Review*, 55, no. 3 (June 1965).

Tobin, James, and William C. Brainard, 'Financial intermediaries and the effectiveness of monetary controls', *American Economic Review*, 53, no. 2 (May 1963), pp. 383–400.

Tooke, Thomas, *Considerations on the State of the Currency* (London: J. Murray, 1826).

Treasury Committee, 'Report of the Committee on Bank Amalgamations, 1918'; *see also*, T. E. Gregory, *Select Statutes, Documents and Reports Relating to British Banking*, 1832–1928 (2 vols, London: Oxford University Press, 1929), p. 327.

Treasury, H. M., 'A note on definitions of money supply', *Economic Trends* (August 1970), xi.

'Monetary policy in the late 1970s and in the 1981 Budget' (released 9 November 2006) www.hm-treasury.gov.uk/foi_money7081_2006.htm.

Treasury, H. M., and Bank of England, Green Paper on *Monetary Control*, Cmnd. 7858 (London: HMSO, March 1980).

Tritton, J. H., 'The short loan fund of the London Money Market', *Journal of the Institute of Bankers*, XXIII, Part III (March 1902), pp. 95–107.

Trundle, John M., 'The demand for M1 in the UK' (Bank of England mimeo, 1982).

Trundle, John M., and Paul V. Pemberton, 'Recent changes in the use of cash', *BEQB*, 22, no. 4 (December 1982), pp. 519–29.

Tucker, Sir Paul M. W, 'Managing the central bank's balance sheet: Where monetary policy meets financial stability', *BEQB*, 44, no. 3 (Autumn 2004), pp. 359–82.

Truptil, Roger J., *British Banks and the London Money Market* (London: J. Cape, 1936).

Turner, J. Adair, baron Turner of Ecchinswell, *Economics after the Crisis: Objectives and Means* (Cambridge, MA, and London: MIT Press, 2012).

　Between Debt and the Devil: Money, Credit and Fixing Global Finance (Princeton, NJ, and Oxford: Princeton University Press, 2016).

Turner, John D., 'Holding shareholders to account: British banking stability and contingent capital' in N. H. Dimsdale and A. C. Hotson (eds) *British Financial Crises since 1825* (Oxford: Oxford University Press, 2014a), pp. 139–57.

　Banking in Crisis: The Rise and Fall of British Banking Stability, 1800 to the Present (Cambridge: Cambridge University Press, 2014b).

Usher, A. P., 'The origin of the bill of exchange', *Journal of Political Economy*, 22, no. 6 (June 1914), pp. 566–76.

van Dillen, Johannes G. (ed.), *History of the Principal Public Banks* (The Hague: M. Nijhoff, 1934; London: Frank Cass, 2nd impression 1964).

van Helten, Jean Jacques, and Youssef Cassis, *Capitalism in a Mature Economy: Financial Institutions, Capital Exports and British Industry, 1870–1939* (Aldershot: Edward Elgar, 1990).

Vickers, Douglas, *Studies in the Theory of Money 1690–1776* (New York: Augustus M. Kelley, 1968).

Vickers, Sir John, Interim *Report: Consultation on Reform Options*, Independent Commission on Banking (12 April 2011).

　Final Report of the Independent Commission on Banking (12 September 2011).

Vilar, Pierre, *A History of Gold and Money, 1450 to 1920*, tr. Judith White (Barcelona, 1960; London, 1967).

Viner, Jacob, *Studies in the Theory of International Trade* (New York and London: Harper, 1937).

von Mises, Ludwig H. E., *Theory of Money and Credit* (London: Jonathan Cape, 1953).

Wadsworth, John E., *The Banks and the Monetary System in the UK, 1959–1971: A Banking View of Developments from the Radcliffe Report to the Monetary Reforms of 1971* (London: Methuen, 1973).

Walker, Sir David A., *A review of corporate governance in UK banks and other financial industry entities: Final recommendations* (26 November 2009).

Wallis, Kenneth F., 'Econometric implications of the rational expectations hypothesis', *Econometrica*, 48, 1 (January 1980), pp. 49–72.

Walsh, Carl E., *Monetary Theory and Policy* (Cambridge, MA: MIT Press, 3rd edn 2010).

Walters, Sir Alan A., *Britain's Economic Renaissance: Margaret Thatcher's Reforms, 1979–1984* (New York and Oxford: Oxford University Press, 1986).

Wass, Sir Douglas W. G., *Decline to Fall: The Making of British Macro-Economic Policy and the 1976 IMF Crisis* (Oxford: Oxford University Press, 2008).

Werner, Richard A., 'Can banks individually create money out of nothing? The theories and the empirical evidence', *International Review of Financial Analysis*, 36 (2014), pp. 1–19.

'How do banks create money, and why can other firms not do the same? An explanation for the coexistence of lending and deposit-taking, *International Review of Financial Analysis*, 36 (2014), pp. 71–7.

'A lost century in economics: Three theories of banking and the conclusive evidence, *International Review of Financial Analysis* (2015).

Wetenhall, Edward, and James Wetenhall, *The Course of the Exchange* (London, 3 November 1786).

White, Eugene N., 'Lessons from the great American real estate boom and bust of the 1920s' in E. N. White, K. Snowden, and P. Fishback (eds) *Housing and Mortgage Markets in Historical Perspective* (Chicago: University of Chicago Press, 2014), pp. 115–58.

'How to prevent a banking panic: The Barings Crisis of 1890', 175 Years of *The Economist*, Conference on Economics and the Media, London (September 2015).

White, Eugene N., Kenneth Snowden, and Price Fishback (eds) *Housing and Mortgage Markets in Historical Perspective* (Chicago: University of Chicago Press, 2014).

White, Lawrence H., *Free Banking in Britain: Theory, Experience, and Debate, 1800–1845* (Cambridge: Cambridge University Press, 1984; London: Institute of Economic Affairs, revised edn 1995).

The Theory of Monetary Institutions (Malden, MA, and Oxford: Blackwell, 1999).

Whittlesey, C. R., and J. S. G. Wilson (eds) *Essays in Honour of R. S. Sayers* (Oxford: Clarendon Press, 1968).

Wicksell, Knut, *Interest and Prices: A Study of the Causes Regulating Money*, English translation by R. F. Kahn (Jena: Gustav Fischer, 1898; London: Macmillan, 1936).

Williamson, John, 'What Washington means by policy reform', chapter 2 in J. Williamson (ed.), *Latin American Adjustment: How Much Has Happened?* (Washington DC: Institute of International Economics, 1990) www.iie.com/publications/papers/paper.cfm?researchid=486.

Wilson, J. Harold, baron Wilson of Rievaulx, *Committee to Review the Functioning of Financial Institutions*, Cmnd. 7937 (2 vols, London: HMSO, 28 June 1980).

Winch, Donald, and Patrick K. O'Brien, *The Political Economy of British Historical Experience, 1688–1914* (Oxford: Oxford University Press, 2002).

Winton, J. R., *Lloyds Bank 1918–1969* (Oxford: Oxford University Press, 1982).

Withers, Hartley, *The Meaning of Money* (London: Smith Elder, 2nd edn 1909).

The English Banking System (Washington, DC: Government Printing Office, 1910).

Bankers and Credit (London: Nash and Grayson, 1924).

Wolf, Martin, *The Shifts and the Shocks: What We've Learned – and Have Still to Learn – from the Financial Crisis* (London: Allen Lane, 2014).

Wood, Geoffrey E., Terence C. Mills and Nicholas F. Crafts (eds) *Monetary and Banking History: Essays in Honour of Forrest Capie* (Abingdon: Routledge, 2011).

Wood, J. Elmer, *English Theories of Central Bank Control, 1819–1858* (Cambridge, MA: Harvard University Press, 1939).

Woodford, Michael D., *Interest and Prices: Foundations of a Theory of Monetary Policy* (Princeton, NJ: Princeton University Press, 2003).

'How important is money in the conduct of monetary policy?' *Journal of Money Credit and Banking*, 40, no. 8 (December 2008).

Woodhead, Peter, *Herbert Schneider collection, part I, English gold coins and their imitations, 1257–1603* in *Sylloge of Coins of the British Isles*, 47 (London: Spink, 1996).

Herbert Schneider collection, part II, English gold coins 1603 to the 20th Century in *Sylloge of Coins of the British Isles*, 57 (London: Spink, 2002).

Wormell, Jeremy, *The Gilt-Edged Market* (London: Allen & Unwin, 1985).

National Debt in Britain, 1850–1930 (London: Routledge, 1999).

The Management of the National Debt of the United Kingdom, 1900–1932 (London: Routledge, 2000).

Wray, L. Randall (ed.), 'Credit and state theories of money: The contributions of A. Mitchell Innes', CFEPS (2004).

Wray, L. Randall, and Mathew Forstater, *Money, Financial Instability and Stabilization Policy* (Cheltenham: Edward Elgar, 2006).

Yergin, Daniel, *The Prize: The Epic Quest for Oil, Money, and Power* (New York and London: Simon & Schuster, 1991).

The Quest: Energy Security, and the Remaking of the Modern World (London: Allen Lane, 2011).

Young, Hugo J. S., *One of Us: A Biography of Margaret Thatcher* (London: Macmillan, 1989).

Ziegler, Dieter, *Central Bank, Peripheral Industry: The Bank of England in the Provinces, 1826–1913*, translated by Eileen Martin (Leicester: Leicester University Press, 1990).

Ziegler, Philip, *The Sixth Great Power: Barings, 1762–1929* (London: Collins, 1988).

Zweig, Phillip L., *Wriston: Walter Wriston, Citibank, and the Rise and Fall of American Financial Supremacy* (New York: Crown, 1995).

Index